VARIETY AT NIGHT

IS

GOOD FOR YOU

For Jenny Blake

'There's a big future in nostalgia'

— Wyn Calvin

A journey round
92 London Variety Theatres

VARIETY AT NIGHT
IS GOOD FOR YOU

Inspired by
J.O. Blake

Compiled & illustrated by
Nicholas Charlesworth

With contributions from many other theatre enthusiasts

Foreword by John Earl   Edited by David F. Cheshire

The Badger Press
Westbury, Wiltshire

First published in Great Britain in 2015 by

THE BADGER PRESS

The imprint of

R.N.R. Charlesworth

39 Clay Close

Dilton Marsh

Westbury, Wiltshire

BA13 4DU

ISBN 978 0 9526076 6 3

Typeset in Baskerville and Myriad Pro by
Marlinzo Services, Frome, Somerset

Printed and bound by CPI Group (UK) Ltd, Croydon CR0 4YY

Contents

List of Halls

West End:
The Adelphi, The Alhambra, The Empire, Fielding's Music Hall, Gatti's (Arches), Holborn Empire, Leicester Square Theatre, London Casino, London Coliseum, London Hippodrome, London Palladium, London Pavilion, Lyceum Music Hall, The Middlesex, The Oxford, The Palace, The Prince of Wales, The Stoll, The Trocadero, The Tivoli, Victoria Palace, The Windmill.

North of the Thames:
The Bedford, Bow Palace, The Britannia, Camden Hippodrome, Canning Town Imperial, Chelsea Palace, Chiswick Empire, Collins' Music Hall, Crouch End Hippodrome, Ealing Hippodrome, East Ham Palace, Edmonton Empire, The Euston, Finsbury Park Empire, The Foresters', Golders Green Hippodrome, The Granville, Hackney Empire, Hammersmith Palace, Harrow Coliseum, Holloway Empire, Hoxton Varieties, Ilford Hippodrome, Islington Empire, Islington Palace, Kilburn Empire, The Kingston Empire, The London Shoreditch, McDonald's Music Hall, The Metropolitan, The Paragon/Mile End Empire, Poplar Hippodrome, The Queen's Poplar, Richmond Hippodrome, Royal Cambridge, Sadler's Wells Music Hall, Shepherds Bush Empire, The Shoreditch Olympia, Stoke Newington Alexandra, Stratford Empire, Stratford Royal Palace, Tottenham Palace, Walthamstow Palace, Willesden Hippodrome, Wilton's Music Hall, Wood Green Empire.

South of the Thames:
Balham Hippodrome, Battersea Palace, The Star Bermondsey, Brixton Empress, Brixton Hippodrome, Camberwell Empire, Camberwell Palace, The Canterbury Music Hall, Clapham Grand, Croydon Empire, Croydon Grand, Croydon Hippodrome, Gatti's-in-the-Road, Greenwich Hippodrome, Lewisham Hippodrome, New Cross Empire, Peckham Hippodrome, Penge Empire, Putney Hippodrome, Rotherhithe Hippodrome, South London Palace, The Surrey Music Hall, Woolwich Empire, Woolwich Hippodrome.

Foreword

I first met Nick Charlesworth at Hoxton Hall in 1963 when we co-operated on architectural display panels in an exhibition by the then newly-founded British Music Hall Society. The sheer numbers attending both the exhibition and the brilliant evening show (with Ada Reeve as star of honour) was evidence of a remarkable renewal of interest in the art of music hall but, up to that time, it has to be said that hardly any serious attention had been given to the buildings that housed the entertainment.

The infant Society's battle, that year, to save Wilton's Music Hall, was a great historic milestone in that respect. But I think the modest display that Nick and I contributed at Hoxton helped. It doesn't sound much now – a contemporary plan, lent by the LCC, of Collins's in pre-Variety days, with supper tables and chairs; a 1860s map of music hall locations, engravings, photographs and sketches of halls of every period – but looking back, I think ours was a bit of a first, too.

I remember being amazed that someone as young as Nick (well, he looked young to me in 1963!) could be so dedicated and knowledgeable about a subject that excited me, but hardly anyone else that I knew. We are all now familiar with the work he was just then setting out on. This book is the culmination of more than fifty years of producing delightfully drawn images of theatres and music halls.

There is always a danger with a book that has 'Variety' or 'Music Hall' in the title that it will be assumed to be yet another minor variation on the book that publishers always want and writers regularly provide, a potted history ranging from the Cyder Cellars and 'Sam Hall' to the Holborn Empire and Max Miller, loaded with pictures and anecdotes. This sort of thing is harmless enough in itself and can be worth the money as light entertainment, but I, for one have had enough of hearing the same old stories about the improper verses that Marie Lloyd is reputed to have sung. Oh no, she didn't!

The other danger is that old buffers like me will go on and on for page after page about the dear dead days of the halls and bemoan the fact that there are no great artistes, like... Well, you write the list. I happen to believe that it is not all in the past. We are living now through a golden age of entertainers.

But make no mistake. This is a different kind of book. Yes, there are past memories here, but they are in the highest class of oral history, the needle-sharp memories of the late J O Blake.

This book is yet another first and in one important respect, it is a long needed reference work. London Variety houses in the 1930s are portrayed here, not as a chance collection of what happens to be traceable in the way of photographs or drawings of widely varying quality, but as the clear vision of one man. Where buildings have ceased to exist – alas, the majority – Nick has re-created them from a variety of reliable sources and has presented them in his pleasing and consistent style, so that comparisons can safely be made.

This is a book that will spend far more time in the hand than on the shelf. I find it hard to believe that it has never been attempted before.

Well it has now!

John Earl

Introduction

I suppose Bournemouth Pavilion and New Royal Theatres were my introduction to live theatre, with Dorothy Ward and The Tom Katz Saxophone Six the earliest stars I can remember from those pantomime days of the 1940s. The latter were made up as black saxophonists in a production of *Robinson Crusoe* at The New Royal – a theatre still standing in Albert Road, Bournemouth. The town was the nearest entertainment centre to our farm near Wimborne, in Dorset.

'Dancing at The Bedford'

A move to Sussex in 1952 led to shows at several other theatres, among them Southsea King's, Worthing Connaught, Portsmouth Theatre Royal, Brighton Theatre Royal and Brighton Grand. However, the building that really fired my teenage imagination was the amazing one in the town's Middle Street, Brighton Hippodrome. As a family we went to pantomime there most years and as I became more independent I took myself off to numerous Variety shows there. The long, low exterior of the theatre gave little idea of the wonderful interior to follow. Before the show and during the interval I spent a lot time appreciating the sweep of the single circle with its closely-spaced orange light bulbs and the vast overall tent-like dome of this former circus building; the plaster figures and pair of fish over the quite low proscenium arch fascinated me. Then there were the two large boxes with their onion domes... Who designed this building, I wondered? It was a few years before I heard of Frank Matcham through a book on London by Pevsner.

The Brighton Hippodrome was always packed when I attended; it was the ideal place to see Richard Hearne, Eve Boswell, The Temperance Seven, Tony Hancock, The Skylons, Frankie Vaughan, Dick Emery, Dora Bryan, Jimmy Edwards, Dickie Henderson, Tommy Cooper, The Nitwits, Anne Shelton, Dick Haymes and many others strutting their stuff. And let us not forget Sidney Sharpe, the youngest MD on the Moss' Empires circuit when he was appointed in the 1930s. Variety theatre orchestras were always superb; the spot fell on the conductor's bald patch, he tapped his baton and away we went. I had caught the bug! I missed Max Miller here unfortunately, and one hopes that the controversy over the future of this wonderful showplace can be resolved, so that Brighton can once again have a home for big musical shows. While still at school I had read of the threatened loss of London's St. James's Theatre. In due course pictures of its demolition appeared in the press. I was inspired to do a large oil painting of the scene (which won an art prize at Canford School that year). Fortunately, a family visit to London enabled me to make a hurried detour to King Street to view the hallowed frontage of the cream-painted building before it left the scene. In the event, the replacement building has also been demolished.

MUSIC HALL

FINSBURY PARK EMPIRE (CAN 2248). Daily at 6 and 8.15 p.m. Fri.: THE AIR FORCE, with ERNIE LOTINGA, THE TWO STORRS, ROY MITCHELL, MILO, etc. Mon.: IT'S IN THE BAG, with MURRAY & MOONEY, JACKLEY & CLIFFORD, BERT & BROWNBILL & Co.

NEW CROSS EMPIRE (TID 3891). Daily at 5.45 & 8 p.m. Fri.: IT'S IN THE BAG, with MURRAY & MOONEY, JACKLEY & CLIFFORD, BERT BROWNBILL, etc. Mon.: NO ORCHIDS FOR MISS BLANDISH, adapted from the famous novel by James Hadley Chase.

CHELSEA PALACE, King's Road (FLA 9618). 6 & 8. Fri.: Big Bill Campbell's Rocky Mountain Rhythm. Mon.: The Squire's Party, with Morris and Cowley; Johnson Clarke; Hal Swain and his Swing Sisters, with Guest Artists. **CHISWICK EMPIRE** (CHI 0505). 6.25 & 8.30. Fri.: Novelty Box, with Koringa, Alfredo's Band, Australian Air Aces, etc. Mon.: Stephane Grappelly and his Swingtette; Renee Houston and Donald Stewart; Leon Cortez and Doreen Harris, etc. **EMPRESS, BRIXTON** (BRI 2201). 6 & 8.15. Fri.: Henry Hall's Orch., The Diamondos, etc. Mon.: Let's Be Gay, with Janise Hart, 4 Pagola's, etc. **HACKNEY EMPIRE** (AMH 4451). 6.25 & 8.30. Fri.: L for Laughter, revue, with Jack Simpson & his Sextette. Mon.: Younkman & his Band; Billy Danvers; Nellie Wallace, etc. **METROPOLITAN**, Edgware Rd. (AMB 2478). 6 & 8. Fri.: Herschel Henlere, Len Young, Leon Cortez; Musical Elliotts, etc. Mon.: Hal Swain & his Swing Sisters; Talbot O'Farrell; Ernest Shannon; Dolinoffs and Raya Sisters; Gladys Sewell, etc. **SHEPHERD'S BUSH EMPIRE** (SHE 4531). 6.25 & 8.30. Fri.: Venus Comes to Town, with Gaston & Andre. Mon.: Jack Simpson & his Sextet; Suzette Tarri; Tom Gamble & Co., etc. **WOOD GREEN EMPIRE** (BOW 4801). 6.25 & 8.30. Fri.: No Limit to Fun, with Naughton & Gold. Mon.: South American Way, with Arthur Askey, Buck & Chic, etc. Also Variety and Revues each week at **QUEEN'S**, Poplar (EAS 2385). **COLLIN'S**, Islington (CAN 3251) **WOOLWICH EMP.** (WOO 0156). **BEDFORD**, Camden T. (EUS 3860). **LEWISHAM HIP.** (HIT 1166). **EAST HAM PAL.** (GRA 0282). **ILFORD HIP.** (ILF 0043), 6 & 8. **ALEXANDRA**, Stoke Newington (CLI 1156), 6.15 & 8.15. **KINGSTON EMP.** (KIN 3131), 5.30 & 7.45. **KILBURN EMP.** (MAI 6566), 6.15 & 8.15. **CROYDON EMP.** (CRO 1941), 5.45 & 7.50. **GOLDER'S GREEN HIPP.** (SPE 0022), 6 & 8.15. **STREATHAM HILL** (TUL 3331), 6 & 8.15. **WALTHAMSTOW PAL.** (LAR 3040).

The London Halls open in 1943

At the same time, The Stoll Theatre and The Gaiety Theatre were needlessly being destroyed in Central London. In fact, all over the city beautiful theatres were being torn down – apparently without any appreciation of their magical qualities, or much thought being given to their possible future use. It was a terrible time.

If this was the position of legitimate theatres, then the situation of Variety theatres was even worse. On arrival in London as a printing student in September, 1958, I became determined to record as many as I could of these old theatres. The London Palladium and Victoria Palace were still doing good business with Variety and The Crazy Gang respectively, but in the suburbs only Chiswick Empire, The Metropolitan and Finsbury Park Empire were still open for business. I learned that only a month or so earlier Collins' Music Hall in Islington had closed through fire damage and that Woolwich Empire had closed down in the March of that year. The previous year had seen the loss of Brixton Empress and Chelsea Palace. With the thought that at the end of the Second World War there had still been nearly two dozen Variety theatres in London, there was clearly no time to lose.

Bus and Underground trips on our free Wednesday afternoons from college quickly became the norm for me, armed with a battered camera and a copy of the ABC map of London. Often the housebreakers were already in possession when I arrived on the scene, so that I witnessed the destruction of Lewisham Hippodrome, Woolwich Empire, Poplar Queen's, The Euston, The Islington Empire and Collins', Croydon Grand, Hammersmith King's and New Cross Broadway. When The Holborn Empire came down I acquired the large illuminated metal letters from the front of the building. Later, I was present when Chiswick Empire and The Metropolitan bit the dust. Fortunately, with the demolition of The Granville at Walham Green in 1971, the situation changed, but too late to save many a fine Variety theatre. But that is another story.

'Change and decay in all around I see!'

From the motley selection of photographs I had taken, a series of line-drawings was produced which I later printed as postcards. People even bought the cards from time to time, and I soon realised that there were others who liked old theatre buildings too. I was beginning to wonder whether I was a little eccentric – my family certainly thought so.

Some of my drawings even found their way into publications, such as *Amateur Stage* and *The Stage* newspaper. I became a founder member of The British Music Hall Society in September, 1963 after Ray Mackender and Gerald Glover hit on the idea of starting such a Society while walking home following the last night of The Metropolitan in Edgware Road. The editor of the Society's magazine, J.O. Blake, became a good friend, using my illustrations to accompany articles that he was using in *The Call Boy*. J.O. edited the magazine for over 20 years which is now in the capable hands of Geoff Bowden. The Society's historian, Bert Ross, and J.O. were fountains of knowledge on music hall and variety. J.O. was enthusiastic when I suggested that we might prepare a little book of drawings of Variety theatres throughout London. Colin Sorensen was encouraging as well, so we made a start in 1995. J.O. wrote a caption to each drawing, but as these were so interesting I asked him to expand them to paragraphs or even longer. He had attended many of the halls himself over the years, so his experiences were quite fascinating, although his knowledge was not so good of some of the outlying halls. I did my own research on these as time allowed in a busy work schedule and have been extremely fortunate in having contributions from many other theatre buffs. Some have also loaned original material, or copies of it, for possible inclusion and I have tried to list them all in the Acknowledgements. Special thanks must go to Gerald Smith, who has a great theatre collection; to Graeme Cruickshank, now resident in New Zealand; and to Brian O'Gorman, whose family is a large part of the Variety story. Martin Phillips has provided a constant stream of memorabilia, much of which we have used.

When J.O. Blake suddenly died in 1996, I continued to put the book together myself. Suddenly 20 years had flown by, and then semi-retirement made more time available to complete the task, of which the last year has been spent giving all the drawings an aqua-tint for more depth.

WYNDHAM'S. Tem 3028. 7 Th, Sat, 2.30. Edith Evans, Felix Aylmer, Frank Pettingell in Daphne Laureola. A new comedy by James Bridie. No perfs Dec 22 to 24.
TICKETS FOR ALL THEATRES at Keith Prowse, 159 New Bond-st. W.1. Branches Reg 6000. You Wt Bt Sts. We have them.

VARIETY THEATRES

BRIXTON EMPRESS. Bri 2201. 6.30, 8.45. CASEY'S COURT. Original Crazy Show.
BRIXTON EMP. Dec 26, 2.30, 6.30, 8.45. GOLDILOCKS & THE 3 LIVE BEARS.
CHELSEA PALACE. Fla 9618 6.30 & 8.40. IVY BENSON & Band, Evelyn Taylor.
CHISWICK EMP. (Chi 7651.) Com Dec 24th, 6.45. Subs twice dly, 2.30 & 6.45. Prince Littler's "JACK AND THE BEANSTALK."
CROYDON EMP. Cro 1941. 6.25 & 8.40. Opening Box Day. " Babes in the Wood."
FINSBURY PARK EMPIRE. Can 2248. Com Dec 22 & 23 at 7.15. Dec 24, 5 & 8. Magnificent Pantomime " CINDERELLA."
GOLDERS GREEN. Dec 24th. 7.0. Box. Day onwards 2.30 & 7.0. BABES IN THE WOOD. Eddie Gray, Jean Adrienne.
HACKNEY EMP. Amh 4451. 6.30 & 8.40. "Jane," Jasper Maskelyne,. H. Henlere
KINGSTON EMP. (Kin 3131.) Dec 26 & Dly 2.30 & 7. " Dick Whittington." B. Hale.
LEWISHAM HIPP. Xmas Panto " Aladdin." Grand Gala. Opening Xmas Eve, 7 p.m.
METROPOLITAN. Amb 2478. 6.30 & 8.45. Felix Mendelssohn & Hawaiian Serenadrs.
NEW CROSS EMP. 6.30 & 8.35. Jan Ralfini & Orch; also Quest for Talent.
SHEP. BUSH EMP. Dec 26, 2.30, 6.25, 8.40. R. Riding Hd. B. Reid & D. Squires
WOOD GREEN EMP. (Bow 4801.) Dec 26. DICK WHITTINGTON. 2.15, 6.15. 8.30.

CINEMAS (WEST END)

ACADEMY. Ger 2981. IT CONCERNS US ALL (U). 1.54, 4.24, 6.54. 9.24. STORY OF A RING (U) 1.0. 3.30, 6.0, 8.30.
ASTORIA. LITTLE WOMEN (Tech) (U). Progs com.: 12.40, 2.40, 5.15, and 7.55.

Some of the London Halls open in 1949

As many theatre enthusiasts have come to regret, the views of interiors of some lost theatres have proved very difficult to find, although sometimes they do turn up unexpectedly. Such a one is that of Croydon Empire, later the Eros Cinema, in North End. An ever-vigilant Gerald Smith discovered an indistinct photograph of its interior which he forwarded to me and there was sufficient detail for a drawing to be made of the quite elaborate Sprague interior. I have sought a photograph of this interior since 1959 when I first viewed the closed theatre on a fine summer's day. Where are the interiors of Balham Hippodrome, Walthamstow Palace or The South London Palace in its later form, I wonder?

The Final Decline of the London Halls: 1955, 1958, 1959, 1962

I must pay thanks to my editor, the late David Cheshire, who knowledge was invaluable and to John Earl, who has kindly written the Foreword, as well as up-dating me on various facts. Details of individual houses can certainly be found in all sorts of libraries and collections, but I have tried to bring together most of the London Variety theatres still in use or still standing during the 1930s and 1940s – even if in use as cinemas. I have not included many of the early halls, such as The Coal Hole,

The Cyder Cellars, or some of the early halls of the East End, which had already vanished. Many of these early halls have been covered elsewhere. I have included The Oxford which was such an important hall – although it was demolished in 1926. It is estimated that London lost about thirty-five Variety theatres in the decades after WW2. This does not include those lost to bombing or legitimate theatres also destroyed.

I hope the reader will find the book interesting and forgive me the time it has taken to assemble. Let us visit, cherish and keep our remaining stock of live theatres: we have some of the best in the world.

Nicholas Charlesworth

Acknowledgements

To my wife Wendy, for her computer skills and wonderful forbearance throughout the nineteen years of preparation

To David F Cheshire, who patiently kept the project on the rails, edited the text, filled in details of The Players' Theatre and Gatti's and supported the book with his usual enthusiasm

To John Earl for checking chapters and kindly writing the Foreword

To Martin Cooper of Marlinzo Services for design and pagination

To our printers, CPI Antony Rowe Ltd. of Chippenham, Wiltshire

Special thanks to Ted Bottle, Graeme Cruickshank, Maurice Friedman, Claire Jones, Brian O'Gorman, Martin Phillips and Gerald Smith for help which was well beyond the call of duty

I am also extremely grateful to the following that have helped me by loaning material, providing extra information and giving me much encouragement:

Leslie Aitchison	John Coleman	Ken Graham
John Alexander	David Conway	Rex Graham
Peter Arculus	Michael Coren	Wendy Hall
Ellis Ashton	Arthur Crabtree	Terry Hallett
Mr & Mrs R Bacon	John Cuningham	Bryan Hammond
Robert Barltrop	Jeff Darlow	Rae Hammond
John Benstead	Mrs Anne Davenport	Terry Hardy
Peter Bexon	John De Courcy	George Harris
Dr David Booth	Colin Devereaux	Paula Hayden
W. Bourne	Ken Dodd	Rod Hills
Geoff Bowden	Tony Douglass	George Hoare
John Bradbury	David Drummond	Iain Jee
Dr Melvyn Brookes	John Endacott	Peter King
Des Caffrey	Allen Eyles	Terry Kirtland
Wyn Calvin	Tony Fairclough	Lew Lane
John Carter	Keith Farbridge	Brian Lead
Roy Chambers	Norman Fenner	Terry Lomas
Alfred Chapman	B Finch	Geoff Lord
Duggie Chapman	Nigel Finch	Tony Mabbutt
Peter Chapman	Anne FitzSimons	Cameron Matheson
Peter Charlton	Bob Fox	Barbara McAndrews
Philip Chevron	John Frapwell	Geoff Mellor
Gail Leslie Clarkson	A.R. Ginn	Maurice Michel
Clyde Clayton	Alan Glencross	Simon Moss
John Cliff	Gerald Glover	Donald Mudie

Valantyne Napier
Suzanne Neath
Michael Newman
Robin Noscoe
Mike Ostler
Dick Playle
Tom Plummer
John Pope
P. Bryan Prosper
Geoff Quible
Roy Rivers
Ken Roe
Bert Ross
Don Ross
D J Rutter
Philip B Ryan
Keith Skone
Wendy & Jim Smith
Colin Sorensen
Alan Southwood
Colin Spencer

M. Stanton
Stan Stennett
Jack Strutt
Ken Sutcliffe
Colin Sutherland
Howard Swinson
John Taylor
The Beverley Sisters
Michael Thomas
Eddie Trigg
Max Tyler
John Wade
Cliff White
John S Wilkinson
Dr David Wilmore
Bob Williamson
Barry Wolsey
Peter Wood
Chris Woodward
Bermondsey Public Library
Borough of Hackney Archives

Cinema Theatre Association
Encore
Getty Images
GLC Architects' Department
Greater London Photographic Library
Lewisham Central Library
London Metropolitan Archives
Mander & Mitchenson Theatre Collection
National Monuments Record
Stratford Library (Local Studies)
The British Music Hall Society
The Era
The Museum of London
The Performer
The Stage
The Theatres Trust
University of Bristol Theatre Collection
Victoria & Albert Museum

THE WEST END HALLS

Adelphi Theatre

The Strand

The Adelphi Theatre: exterior (as rebuilt in 1930), with the old frontage of Adelphi Restaurant on the right

There have been several buildings on the Adelphi site, starting in 1806 with the Sanspareil which was built for Jane, the daughter of businessman John Scott. The young lady wrote and appeared successfully in her own shows until 1819, when her father sold the enlarged theatre to T. Willis Jones and J.T.G. Rodwell, who was a playwright. At this point the theatre changed its name to the one we know today and was generally very successful over the years. Only very briefly did it change its name again, in 1901 to The Century, following extensive alterations. In fact, the Adelphi building has had many changes, rebuilds, alterations and enlargements – in 1813, 1840, 1858, 1887 and 1900, and most recently in 1930. This rebuild was to the designs of Ernest Schaufelberg, but there are fragments of older buildings embedded in the new, particularly backstage and in the basement. In Maiden Lane at the rear of the theatre is the decorative Royal Entrance of 1868–69.

However, it is the decade from 1950 to 1960 that interests Variety fans: a decade that one book has dismissed as not being "worthy of the theatrical history books"! Jack Hylton, the former bandleader who had become a producer, ran Variety shows at the Adelphi for most of the 1950s.

London's West End was a bustling show business scene when in the autumn of 1954 my friend Brian O'Gorman was on leave from the army and looking for entertainment. He chose to attend *The Talk of the Town* at the Adelphi and – unbeknown to him – experienced a final flourish of the Variety era before television worked its influence. He could, of course, have gone to The Palladium, Victoria Palace, London Hippodrome, Prince of Wales or any one of over a dozen suburban halls to enjoy a lively Variety show. Today, of course, Variety and even Revue are sadly missing from the West End. The exhortation – "Let's go to a show" often meant a Variety show or Variety-Revue.

At the time Brian enjoyed the show its three stars were Vera Lynn, Jimmy Edwards and Tony Hancock, but the whole show was good and enjoyable, had good production values and included entertaining specialities, such as The Trio Bassi, a Risley act.

Vera Lynn, still flourishing at the age of 97 at the time of writing, showed star quality with much more than just the ability to sing a song. She made a great impression on the young Brian with her calm and assured personality.

The Royal Entrance in Maiden Lane

Jimmy Edwards, who had top billing, was not worth it, in Brian's opinion. He tried too hard with his rather obvious Schoolmaster act – better done earlier by Will Hay. The act was raucous, overstated, and lacking in sympathy. Edwards' musical interlude did not display a great deal of polished stagecraft, or even good timing. A few blasts on the trombone were no substitute. He was booked on the basis of his success in the radio show *Take it from Here*, showing that radio performers do not always translate well to the live stage. Edwards, like Tommy Handley, Dick Bentley, Bill Kerr, Richard Murdoch and Kenneth Horne, was better on the air. It might be mentioned that a spin-off from the radio show, called *Take it from Us*, had opened at the Adelphi in October, 1950. Jimmy Edwards was practically resident in the West End at this period, as he was also in *London Laughs*, with Tony Hancock and Joan Turner (Jill Day later took this spot).

The Schaufelberg interior of 1930

Tony Hancock, on the other hand, scored well in the show that Brian saw. There had been a lot of press coverage about his supposed weakness, or uncertainty in the face of a live London audience. Hancock's performance in a sketch as a lighthouse keeper, drenched in seawater every time the outside door was opened, is still remembered with delight. He put over his solo act with conviction and success. He was confident enough to have his white socks showing below his peg-top trousers, in keeping with the uncertain, distinct persona of his act. He lived down the assertions that he was merely imitating Sid Field.

Later, of course, Hancock made a huge name for himself with Sid James on television, although it was said that he did not relish live shows. I saw him on a Moss' Empires tour and again in Australia just before he died, but not really varying his act.

In February, 1954 Jack Hylton and George & Alfred Black presented Al Read in a Variety-Revue named after one of Read's catchphrases, *You'll Be Lucky*. It gave the star three good spots, as well as featuring songstress Shani Wallis. Great support came from Lauri Lupino Lane and George Truzzi in several offerings. Particularly remembered is their sketch as Mayfair Decorators, with plenty of wallpaper paste to hand. The John Tiller Girls in *A Tournament of Glamour* pleased many a tired businessman, while The Trio Hugony provided a Continental speciality. Others to appear in Variety-Revue at the Adelphi under Jack Hylton included Tommy Trinder, Arthur Askey, Tommy Cooper and a young Shirley Bassey.

Jack Hylton's tenure eventually ended, but before musicals took over completely Beatrice Lillie as *Auntie Mame* enjoyed a two-year run at the Adelphi from 1958, while *Charlie Girl*, starring Anna Neagle, ran for six years. Van Johnson with his Seventy-Six Trombones in *The Music Man* did well and there were revivals of such shows as *Me and My Girl* (with Emma Thompson and Robert Lindsay) and *Oklahoma!* More recently, *The King and I* and *Chicago* have had big successes here.

The theatre has been refurbished to its 1930s splendour, its restored and un-cluttered art deco exterior gracing The Strand once more. The 1878 building to its right, by Spencer Chadwick and formerly The Adelphi Restaurant, is still there, but in use for other purposes. It gives an idea of what the earlier Adelphi Theatre looked like.

Tony Hancock in pensive mood

Alhambra Theatre of Varieties

Leicester Square

The Alhambra: Leicester Square frontage (now rebuilt as The Odeon Cinema) with 'Mr Tower of London' billed

On 18 March, 1854 a handsome building in the 'Moorish' style opened in Leicester Square as The Royal Panopticon of Science and Art. It failed and in 1858 was taken over by E.T. Smith for entertainments. When circus was presented it enjoyed the patronage of Queen Victoria and two years later a stage was built so that it could become a music hall. Among the acts that appeared in 1861 were Leotard and Blondin.

Later in 1861 William Wild jnr. took over, and then in 1864 Frederick Strange spent £25,000 on improvements and declared his intention to make the theatre an establishment 'dedicated to the Lyric and Terpsichorean arts'. It did, but it also acquired a Bohemian notoriety and in 1870 the renewal of its licence was opposed because of the Can-Can performed by Wiry Sal. During the Franco-Prussian War a contest of voices took place between partisan sections of the audience. The theatre was again closed until Strange obtained a licence from the Lord Chamberlain; meanwhile the tables on the ground floor had been replaced by theatre seats. Strange left in 1872 and had several successors including Charles Morton and William Holland, who presented the comic operas of Offenbach until, on 7 December, 1882, the theatre was destroyed by fire.

Charing Cross Road frontage

The Alhambra reopened in 1883 with G.R. Sims' opera *The Golden Ring*. There were 1,800 seats in the stalls and three lyre-shaped balconies, plus the promenades. A music and dancing licence was at last granted in 1884, and henceforth Variety and two spectacular ballets was the fare provided. In 1892 Hollingshead presented *Aladdin* as a ballet featuring a glass curtain of 75,000 facets held together by 25 miles of wire. But it was an ominous sign when, in 1896–8, films were made on the theatre's roof and shown in the hall below.

Interior showing the original proscenium (later covered over)

The theatre was honoured by nearly a score of royal visits in 1897, Jubilee Year, and in the same year the Charing Cross Road entrance was built, in a similar Moorish style to the 40-years old original entrance. Ballet continued to attract, but spectacular musical and acrobatic acts became more common. By 1919 another partial re-construction took place under Frank Matcham. By this time ballet, at both the Alhambra and Empire, had declined owing to the rivalry of the Russian ballet and when Oswald Stoll acquired the theatre in 1916 the policy continued. *The Bing Boys Are Here* with George Robey, Violet Loraine and Alfred Lester began a series of long runs.

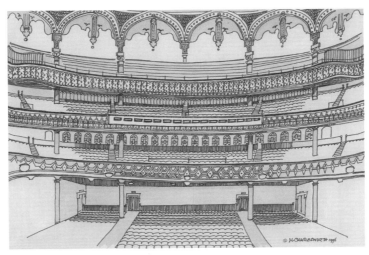

Interior from the stage, showing circles

The Diaghilev Ballet gave seasons in 1919 and 1921, interspersed by more revues with George Robey. In 1922, following another overhaul, Variety was presented three times daily. There were some excellent bills – one was headed by Jack Hylton's Band, Layton & Johnstone and Little Tich – and *Mr. Tower of London* introduced Gracie Fields to the metropolis. The Royal Variety Performances were given here in 1925 and 1926, but weekly Variety was presented only spasmodically; more often the bills read 'Super Talkies & Variety'. *Waltzes from Vienna* ran for 607 performances and there were more ballet seasons and revivals before *Tulip Time* chalked up 427 performances.

Auditorium of The Odeon Cinema which replaced the theatre in November, 1937

Jack Taylor's *The Show That Jack Built*, which I had to stand in the gallery slips to see, had a strong cast – Randolph Sutton, Jimmy James, Frank Randle and Mexano's Accordion Band – but had a short run and Dante's magic spectacle *Sim Sala-Bim* closed the theatre on 1 September, 1936. Theatre scenes in *Men Are Not Gods* were filmed at the Alhambra on Sunday, 8 October of that year immediately before the building was closed for demolition.

The Alhambra was demolished during 1936–7, giving place to the Odeon Cinema, which Viscount Wimborne described in the House of Lords as 'a black monstrosity', the building of which he did not think would have been sanctioned in any other European capital. The cinema opened on 2 November, 1937 and remains one of the few undivided cinema buildings in the West End of London, complete with its Compton theatre organ. Sadly, the interior was ruined during the modernisation of 1967, when the wonderful leaping figures on the side walls (by Raymond Britton Riviere) were plastered over. The etched glass doors also disappeared at this time. As John Earl has said, 'the story might serve as a horrible warning to all who believe that anything old needs to be brought into the present day'. The situation has been partially retrieved as the leaping figures have since been re-created; the Odeon continues to be the flagship of the circuit and often hosts film premieres.

Theatre logo from a programme

The Empire Theatre of Varieties

Leicester Square

The Empire Theatre: old exterior of 1884 (the first to carry this name) with Carl Hertz billed

The Empire was built on the northern side of Leicester Square, on the site formerly occupied by Leicester House (in Georgian times a royal residence) and Saville House. The site had subsequently been occupied by museums, panoramas, tableaux vivants, etc. until in 1860 the Eldorado Music Hall was built. This had a short life, being destroyed by fire. The site remained vacant until The Empire (the first theatre of this name) was built in 1884.

Designed by Thomas Verity with J. & A.E. Bull, it was immediately acclaimed the outstanding building of the period. The Grand Tier or Dress Circle was on the same level as the vestibule and was surrounded by private boxes and the famous promenade, 8ft 6in wide, which enabled 300 people to stroll and make assignations the while. The emblazoned sign, surmounted by the Royal Crown, attracted vast crowds.

At the opening on 17 April, 1884 the attraction was a musical spectacle, *Chilperic*, adapted from the French and with a ballet of fifty. Its three months run was followed by various pantomime burlesques, comic operas and a stage version of *Round the World in 80 Days*. Then Daniel Nicols, the founder and proprietor of the theatre, envisaged it as a music hall and formed a new Board of Directors including Augustus Harris, George Edwardes with Harry J. Hitchens retained as Managing Director. Katti Lanner was Ballet Mistress and M. Herve Musical Director. Its reopening was on 22 December, 1887.

The re-opening programme, once nightly with a Saturday matinee, at prices ranging from 6d to 5s was headed by two ballets, both long running, plus Variety including Charles Godfrey, Leo Stormont, The Two Macs, Belonini, Walter Munroe, La Petite Almoros, and two chanteuses. In the following weeks stars included Ada Lundberg, Alice Leamar, 3 Sisters Jonghmans, Sisters Bilton, Brothers Griffiths, Jenny Hill and Bessie Bonehill. In 1888 a new comedian made his debut at this house: the immortal Dan Leno.

'The Press Ballet' at the Empire in the 1890s, as drawn by Sam Sibbitt

In subsequent weeks Marie Loftus, Paul Cinquevalli, Paul Martinetti & his Pantomimists, Chirgwin, Jolly John Nash, and two famous acrobatic troupes, The Craggs and The Leopolds appeared. On 4 July, 1888 the Empire had its first Royal Command Performance in the presence of the Shah of Persia and our own Prince & Princess of Wales (later Edward VII and Queen Alexandra). A feature of the programme was the ballet *Cleopatra*, which ran for nine months. The Empire had now gained a reputation for ballet surpassing that of the Alhambra.

Charles Coborn, R.G. Knowles, Gus Elen and Marie Lloyd all appeared here in the '90s. The bills, each containing two ballets, were expensive, but the theatre was paying a dividend of 20%. On 7 November, 1897 Adeline Genée made her debut in the ballet *Monte Christo* and reigned supreme for twelve years. Russia's Lydia Kyasht and Britain's Phyllis Bedells succeeded her.

With its cosmopolitan audience The Empire relied on many 'Dumb' acts, notable ones being the Schaeffer Troupe, the world's highest paid acrobatic team, Loïe Fuller with her fire dance and the Bagessens, with their crockery smashing routine. Illusionists included Charles Morritt, Howard Thurston, Carl Hertz and David Devant, and there were such novel specialities as Hymack, the

Chameleon Comedian, and Vasco, the Mad Musician, whose son was later to go into theatre management.

Original interior of The Empire, 1884

The Empire's regular succession of comedians included, besides those already mentioned, Arthur Roberts, Ernest Shand, George Mozart, Albert Chevalier, Wilkie Bard and Little Tich, and ladies who never failed to shine were Ada Reeve, Evie Greene and Gertie Gitana. Straight Variety sometimes gave place to an aggregation like Pellisier's *Follies*, *The March Hares* and *The Will o' the Wisps*. Seasons of matinees were given by John Phillip Sousa and Johann Strauss and their respective Bands.

The new century saw such musical acts as Olga, Elgar & Eli Hudson, Jessie Broughton & Denis Creedon, Haydn Wood & Dorothy Court (*Roses of Picardy*) and the great tenor Sims Reeves. In 1915 Charles B. Cochran took over as manager for eighteen months, and it was he who initiated the booking of Horatio Bottomley, MP for thirty-minute displays of patriotic oratory.

Remaining exterior, a vestige of the old building in Leicester Street

As early as 1894 the Empire promenade (and the gay ladies of the night congregating there) had attracted the attention of Mrs. Ormiston Chant and her League of Purity. George Edwardes, then managing director, had compromised by erecting a trellis to screen the offending area; next night this obstruction was vandalised by some young bloods led by the redoubtable Winston Churchill. The promenade continued to attract spasmodic attention throughout the Edwardian era, but it was not until 1916 that the Bishop of London suggested that it constituted a temptation to troops on leave and Alfred Butt, then managing director, succumbed to the pressure and closed it.

The Empire was always the place for celebration on Boat Race nights and Rugby Internationals, but disturbances were frequent. The hall was favoured by numerous Royal visits.

Exterior of the new cinema, 1928

In 1896 *Lumiére's Moving Pictures* were first shown in London, but it was not until 1905 that the theatre's policy changed to include Revues, which became more frequent as Variety and Ballet dwindled. Under Alfred Butt musicals were very successful, *The Lilac Domino* notching up 747 performances from 1918, followed by *Irene* and *The Rebel Maid*. Later, no consistent policy was followed and in 1925 it was announced that the movie moguls had bought the theatre. There was a revival of *Henry VIII* with Sybil Thorndike and Lewis Casson; third serving man was played by Laurence Olivier. The Empire's last live production was *Lady Be Good* with Fred and Adele Astaire making their last appearance on stage together; the last performance on 22 January, 1927 was attended by the Prince of Wales (later better known as the Duke of Windsor).

There had been seasons of Variety and films between musical shows, but films were now to take over completely, as The Empire was demolished for a huge new cinema, opening in 1928 and seating 3,226 people – the biggest auditorium in the West End. Strangely, a fragment of Verity's Empire Theatre survived as a staff entrance and can still be seen in Leicester Street.

Rebuilt interior as cinema, c.1928

The forerunners of MGM acquired The Empire and the American Thomas W. Lamb was the architect of their new theatre, working in conjunction with Frank Matcham & Co. in London, still a good old firm, although Matcham himself had died in 1920. There was a proscenium on the east, rather than on the north as in the old building and this was put to use from 1949 to 1952 when Ciné-variety was presented by Nat Karson, from New York's Radio City Music Hall.

The live segments of the show ran for just under an hour, four times daily. Artistes such as 'Monsewer' Eddie Gray and Max Wall appeared, as well as The Empire Girls, Singers, Ballet and The Empire Concert Orchestra, conducted by George Melachrino; 12,500 customers saw the shows on Boxing Day, 1949. Each stage show had to run for four weeks to recover its costs, but not all films ran that long, meaning that regular film patrons had to risk seeing the same live show twice. In the end the live shows ceased, with the wide screen becoming the new attraction, until the huge theatre closed in 1961 to be completely remodelled. I explored the mass of steelwork in the gutted auditorium while the rebuilding was going on. Every scrap of the sumptuous High Renaissance decoration had been destroyed.

A very comfortable new cinema designed by George Coles opened in the former circle and I remember wondering whether I should really have been there – so luxurious were the seats and carpets! Downstairs a dance hall was constructed in the old stalls area. The newest Empire opened on 19 June, 1962. Eleven years later MGM sold the theatre to other interests. In 1989 the fine façade of the 1928 building was again opened to view, as part of a £2 million refurbishment scheme.

Cinema logo in the 1930s

EMPIRE THEATRE
OF VARIETIES,
LEICESTER SQUARE.

THE MOST BEAUTIFUL AND LUXURIOUS THEATRE IN THE WORLD.

Two Magnificent Ballets

PRODUCED BY

MR. AUGUSTUS HARRIS,

AND THE

BEST VARIETY ENTERTAINMENT

IN LONDON.

OPEN ALL THE YEAR ROUND

AT

EIGHT O'CLOCK EVERY EVENING.

Business communications to be addressed to Mr H. J. HITCHINS.

Fielding's Music Hall

The Prince Charles Theatre

Leicester Place, off Leicester Square

Fielding's Music Hall at The Prince Charles Theatre, 1964 with Cicely Courtneidge and Co. billed

The British Music Hall Society was formed in September, 1963 and membership grew rapidly, embracing enthusiasts keen on the gramophone records, the sheet music covers, the costumes, the buildings and "But of course" (to use dear old Horace Mashford's phrase) the artistes themselves.

Suddenly Music Hall was news, with newspapers and magazines running articles on the subject and interviews with our chairman – the much loved and much missed Ray Mackender. So it was particularly pleasing when a Variety season was presented at the Comedy Theatre in January, 1964. Dan Farson's *Nights at the Comedy*, provided spots for Marie Lloyd Jnr., Jimmy James, Mrs. Shufflewick, Queenie Watts, Kim Cordell, Jimmy Tarbuck and many others.

The next attempt to bring small-scale Variety back to the West End took place on the north side of Leicester Square, in Leicester Place to be exact. The Palladium and The Talk of the Town were, of course, still doing great business in their different ways with big – mainly American – recording and film stars. Leicester Place has a long history – including some interesting connections with popular entertainment, principally at Leicester House, one of the biggest residences in London and home of the Earls of Leicester. In 1672 John Evelyn dined there and was amazed by the post-prandial turn put on by one Richardson 'the famous Fire-Eater, who before us devoured Brimstone on glowing coales'. Later various members of the Royal Family lived there and Prince Frederick (father of George III) died in the grounds after reputedly being struck on the Adam's apple while playing cricket in 1751. Part of the House was taken over by Ashton Lever in 1774 to show his extraordinary collection of curiosities to a paying public while members of his Toxophilite [i.e. archery] Society operated in the grounds – it must be hoped more safely than the cricketers.

The Seventh Earl died heavily in debt and the House and grounds were auctioned in 1791. The site was then redeveloped with Lisle Street occupying the part formerly covered by the House and Leicester Place the grounds. Specialist entertainment soon sprang up with Robert Barker opening his famous Panorama in 1793 there. It closed in 1865, but the shell of the building still exists, containing now the Church of the Notre Dame. Charles Dibdin moved the interior of his Sans Souci Theatre from the Strand to an adjacent building in 1796. He operated it successfully for ten years or so, staging entertainments featuring his famous nautical songs, none of which would have been out of place in the early music hall. The Sans Souci was demolished in 1898 and offices were erected on the site.

These went like so many other buildings in the area during the Blitz, but it was not until 1958 that development of a new office block (designed by Carl Fisher Associates) commenced. Somewhat surprisingly, a small 358-seater theatre was incorporated and during construction it was announced that Harold Fielding had taken a long lease on it. Dame Flora Robson unveiled a foundation stone on 18 September, 1961 and just over a year later, on Boxing Day, 1962, Fielding put on his first show there. It was a nice friendly little theatre, but it was not welcomed by architectural critics. Peter Rawsthorne was especially scathing in *The Observer*: "Considering what a new theatre, even a microscopic one, *could* be in these enlightened times, the Prince Charles is probably the meanest and prissiest little building that I have ever seen in my life. Inside it looks like a television mock-up of a *demi-mondaine's* boudoir". And that was the politest part of his article! Most unfortunately, Fielding chose to open not with an original show, but a transfer. *Clap Hands*, an 'intimate' Canadian revue moved there, following a brief but successful run at the Lyric, Hammersmith. It did poor business at the Prince Charles and thereafter the new theatre struggled and – a bad sign – was in frequent use as a cinema. In 1964 Fielding decided to change course (possibly as the result of all the publicity the B.M.H.S. had got for Variety) and reopened as Fielding's Music Hall on 27 February. Our delight was well summarised in an announcement in the April, 1964 issue of *The Call Boy*.

The alterations, including the enlargement of the bar, were planned by Walter Marmorek, and to appeal to modern audiences, the show was presented as a Music Hall Revue, but gave scope for genuine Variety acts. Other production numbers were attractively staged and some ran on from one edition of the show to the next while individual acts changed regularly – depending on the artistes' other commitments. With Harold Fielding's numerous contacts many of the very top names of the day were involved. William Chappell did his usual brilliant job as director – his running orders were as ever spot-on; Loudon Sainthill produced some really amazing costume designs; Burt Rhodes advised on the music; while the lighting was in the inventive hands of the up-and-coming Richard Pilbrow.

I went to two of the shows and was entranced. It was good to see again in the West End such veterans as Billy Russell, Cicely Courtneidge (in a potted pantomime, *The Fairy Queen of the Enchanted Forest*) and Jimmy Edwards with his boisterous plumbing. Younger artistes were not left out, as comedians Hope & Keen ('Jokers Wild') scored in two spots and Marcia Owen was memorably 'Madame Ragtime' – her supporting girls including Aimi Macdonald. Joyce Grant was a riot in *Who'll Have Me?* Given by permission of The Players' Theatre, this was such a hit that it was held over for the next edition of the show. Fielding cast many of my favourites, including the balancers Duo Russmar (Rusty Sellars and Margaret) and cod strongmen Duo De Mille.

The enlarged bar was very atmospheric. Open from 5.30pm to 11pm, one could enjoy great sausage and mash while listening to Paul Horner at the piano above the chatter of some very happy theatregoers! Among the company at Fielding's were Julian Chagrin and George Ogilvie, with their hilarious representation of *Wimbledon, 1907*. Later that year they appeared in their own show, *Chaganog* at the Adelphi Theatre in the Strand. On another visit I was fortunate enough to see that great actor-manager Sir Donald Wolfit in that very dramatic monologue, *The Death of Bill Sykes* from *Oliver Twist*. He gave a truly barnstorming performance and seemed quite at home in a music hall – after all, one of his greatest successes was at the Bedford, Camden Town in 1949 where he and his company achieved 128 consecutive performances of Shakespeare, to over seventy per cent capacity.

It was a pity that the enterprise did not continue and now that the London Palladium seems to have gone entirely over to musicals, Variety is sorely missed in central London. Many of us BHMS members feel that one of the smaller West End theatres could be devoted to this type of show. The Apollo in Shaftesbury Avenue certainly has the right sort of auditorium. Such a show-place for mainstream light entertainment would surely be a magnet.

When Fielding's Music Hall had run its course, the Prince Charles Theatre went over to films full-time in June, 1965. Radical reconstruction of the auditorium took place three years later, when the stalls were lowered into the 'Gaiety Bar', with a circle inserted above. Since then ownership has changed several times, but the theatre has been mostly operated as a repertory cinema – showing a whole range of films, old and new, with varying degrees of success.

With acknowledgements to 'West End Cinemas' by Allen Eyles for film details.

Duo Russmar, 'A well-balanced pair'

Billy Russell, 'On behalf of the working classes'

Gatti's-under-the-Arches

Hungerford Market, The Strand

which became

The Players' Theatre Club

173–4, Hungerford Arches, Villiers Street, Strand

(A summary of an article by D.F. Cheshire)

Gatti's-under-the-Arches: exterior in Villiers Street, Strand

In the late nineteenth century the Gatti family was one of the busiest in the small world of London caterers. Carlo Gatti was the first of the Swiss-Italian family to arrive in London and in 1847 he tried his luck in town by building up a chain of stalls and two years later joined Battista Bollo in running a café in Leather Lane. The pair opened a chocolate and, later, ice-cream factory and showed their chocolate-making machine at the Great Exhibition.

Carlo's move to open spaces at Hungerford Market was defeated by a big fire there in 1854, but luckily he was fully insured. Fortune was with him again when he and his brother Giovanni were obliged to leave their shops in the Market when the South Eastern Railway bought them out for £7,750 (in today's money that would be £400,000), in order to build Charing Cross Station. By now they had managed to obtain a music licence for the shops there. Carlo invested the proceeds in the import of ice from Norway, the principal source of his family's wealth in the future. Having lost their Market café, the brothers opened a café-restaurant in Westminster Bridge Road in 1862; this led to the opening of Gatti's Palace of Varieties there, first licensed in 1865.

(To follow this part of the story, please turn to the chapter on Gatti's-in-the-Road on page 459)

Exterior while The Forum Cinema

The history of the Players' Theatre on this site began literally 'underneath the arches' of the new Charing Cross Station and it has been suggested that the two units that Carlo Gatti leased in 1866 were part of the original supports for the Hungerford Market. He firstly obtained a licence to enlarge the existing billiard saloon and then added a skating rink and a gymnasium. Then he improved the restaurant and opened the music hall. Carlo installed his vastly experienced daughter Rosa as proprietor over the river at Gatti's-in-the-Road. It was then an easy transfer at Charing Cross when she took over on her father's death in 1878.

In the meantime, the music hall there was successful and was popularly known as Gatti's-under-the-Arches. The terms 'Palace of Varieties' and 'Music Hall' were inter-changeable by this time, as shown by press-cuttings advertising the two halls.

Newspaper advertisement in 1901

G. & L. Carozza, the husbands of Rosa and her sister Augustine, were now running the Charing Cross hall and doing well with some attractive programmes. For example, during the week of 7 January, 1901 they offered the following: Three Brothers Horn & Co., Alethea, Pat Rafferty, Florrie Robina, Frank Coyne, Lottie Lennox, Signor & Madame Borelli, Harry Bedford, The Two Graces, Florrie Challis, George E Payne, Doris Vere and Dan Pedley.

But the opening of the nearby London Coliseum in 1904 was a disaster for them. With the new theatre's initial offering of four houses (approximately 10,000 people a day), the Carozzas decided that the game was up and closed their hall.

Interior while The Forum Cinema

It was five years before the premises re-opened as the West End's only boxing hall, with films shown when there were no matches on. Boxing was phased out when the newly-named Arena became a full-time cinema; it changed its name to the Villiers Cinema in 1918 and again to the Forum Cinema after a £30,000 conversion ten years later. When WW2 broke out the arches became an Auxiliary Fire Services depot and later an ENSA store. The space was cleared when the war ended.

Now the Players' Theatre Club arrived on the scene. Two young actors, Peter Ridgeway and Leonard Sachs, had in 1936 taken over the lease of an existing club theatre on the top floor of 43, King Street in Covent Garden. They discovered that the building had once housed an hotel, 'Evans', late Joy's' – once the most popular song-and-supper room in London. They had originally planned to present new plays at the club, but Ridgeway enlisted Harold Scott's help and their first Victorian music hall entertainment was presented on 6 December, 1937, with Leonard Sachs taking the chair in a part for which he will be forever remembered.

Exterior of Evans's Music and Supper Rooms, late Joy's

When war broke out in 1939 the club was not affected by the closure of theatres order, but moved to the Arts Theatre as a precaution – then back to the Evans' basement when bombing started in 1940. They were forced out to Albemarle Street at one point, when their basement became an air-raid shelter. On his return from war service in 1945 Leonard Sachs grabbed the lease of the Villiers Street arch, which had been left in a dreadful state. Club staff and members worked round the clock to bring the arch back to life as a music hall, although much larger than the club's previous rooms. The new Players' opened on St. Valentine's Day in 1946 and soon established itself as one of *the* places to go for a night out.

The Players' was regularly packed and a remarkable London Welsh team, consisting of Ivor Novello, Emlyn Williams and Dylan Thomas, was often there. Alfred Hitchcock always dropped by then he was in town. Sachs had busy acting commitments, so having got things off the ground, handed over control to Don Gemmell, Reginald Woolley and Gervaise Farjeon. Throughout the greater part of its life, most programmes at the Players' have consisted of the re-creation of songs and song scenas identified with Victorian music hall, but a large percentage of the artistes have been drawn from the legitimate theatre and from musical comedy. In the early days these included Ian Carmichael, Alec Clunes, Robert Eddison, Archie Harradine, Patricia Hayes, Vida Hope, Bernard Miles, Joan Sterndale Bennett, Fred Stone, Eleanor Summerfield, Leonard Sachs and Peter Ustinov. Edric Connor made his London debut there, while recently Bernard Cribbins, Clive Dunn, Hattie Jacques, Bill Owen and Prunella Scales came to the fore.

A 'traditional' pantomime was presented each year and sometimes the company launched into musicals, such as the astonishingly long-running *The Boy Friend*, which opened in April, 1953. However, it was the Variety format that I really enjoyed and I always looked forward to seeing Sheila Burnette, Catherine McCord, John Rutland, Josephine Gordon, Michael Kirk, Jim McManus, Nicholas Tudor and Jenny Wren. The Chairman's gavel was wielded in their own ways by Alan Curtis, Michael Kilgarriff, Dominic le Foe and Johnny Denis – the latter being one-time Chairman of The British Music Society.

Interior while The Players' Music Hall

With everything looking rosy, and with regular television shows and even overseas tours, the future looked assured. Leonard Sachs' chairmanship of *The Good Old Days* was truly international. Then, suddenly, it all ground to a halt in 1987, when a development company secured the rights to build on top of Charing Cross Station. This meant that the Arches would be needed for the sinking of massive new pillars, so with little notice the Players' had to close.

The developers were as co-operative and as generous as they could be, paying the cost of the Club's using the Duchess Theatre in the interim, as well as re-designing a new theatre for their eventual return to the Arches. The old atmosphere was quickly re-established at the Duchess, with late opening hours for the bars and restaurant. Business was fairly good, although inevitably quite a few members drifted away. However, the return to the Arches, albeit not on exactly the same site, was not to be so happy. Myriad rules and regulations – especially fire precautions – which had been ignored in the Villiers Street arch, now had to be observed. The entrance had been shunted off Villiers Street itself into Craven Passage, so it was not easy to attract passers-by. While the Players' was a members-only club, an independent wine bar for use by anyone opened up nearby in genuine cellars. Worse – a fashionably glamorous nightclub opened up just opposite the theatre entrance!

What with the increased running costs of the new building, which opened in 1990, sharply fallen membership and the imposition of a large fee by the developers, the club's finances started to prove highly problematic. Leonard Sachs eventually handed over the direction to others. Really dark clouds appeared on the horizon in 1992 and an appeal to raise £200,000 quickly was launched. Ten percent of this figure was raised by two Very Special Evenings chaired by Barry Cryer and Christopher Wren. The star-studded companies included Millicent Martin, Gordon Peters, Marti Webb, Peter John, Lisa Hull, Jim McManus, Rosie Ashe, Pat Lancaster and the 'Family le Foe'. Closing the club on Tuesday and Wednesday evenings proved cost-effective, but in spite of all this, the overall situation continued to be desperate.

It is to be hoped that audiences do improve quickly and that over a hundred years' history of popular entertainment 'under-the-arches' does not have to cease.

Tom Tinsley, Chairman at Gatti's-under-the-Arches

Leonard Sachs, The Immortal Chairman

Holborn Empire

242–5, High Holborn

Interior as Weston's Music Hall

Holborn Empire stood at the western end of High Holborn, and bounded on one side by a narrow thoroughfare called Little Turnstile. The latter had, in days of yore, existed to prevent cattle straying into Lincoln's Inn Fields. At its top stood the Six Cans & Punch Bowl, a tavern where, in the early 19th Century, harmonic meetings were held. The adjoining premises, which had been a Nonconformist chapel and later a National School, were acquired by a licensed victualler named Henry Weston who, inspired by the example of Charles Morton south of the river, converted them into a music hall. On 16 November, 1857, the elegant Weston's Music Hall opened.

The hall was 103ft long, 40ft high and 35ft wide, with a gallery projecting six feet from the side walls. It was divided longitudinally into ten highly decorated compartments, and was lighted by five magnificent chandeliers. There was a supper room at gallery level and great attention was given to ventilation.

Musical arrangements were in the hands of Mr. John Caulfield 'late of The Canterbury' whose orchestra opened the proceedings with the National Anthem followed by appropriate patriotic toasts. Henry Weston replied to one and was applauded to the echo. Mr. Alderman Wire then proposed a toast to the chairman himself, Mr. Huggins. He commented on the magnificence of the building devoted to the amusement of the public, which had cost Henry Weston between £8,000 and £9,000.

Weston and his son sold out to John Samuel Sweasey and William Holland in 1866 for £16,000. By 1868 the name had changed to the Royal Music Hall, the proprietor now being W.T. Purkiss, with Sam Adams as his manager. The hall was completely rebuilt in 1887 to designs by Lander & Bedells. *The Era* commented that the handsome new hall compared favourably with any in the metropolis, and was another instance that the taste for music hall was spreading in spite of the grandmotherly restrictions that hedged round the caterers. A spacious balcony overhung the stalls, elegantly upholstered in blue velvet, which sloped down to the orchestra, and the essential difference in the new and larger building was the increased size of the stage, which now had every facility for producing spectacular ballets, as exemplified in the opening attraction *Civilization*, which featured a real waterfall.

The Holborn Empire: exterior of The Royal, which was retained when the interior was rebuilt as the Empire

Serio and comic singers made up the bulk of the entertainment. They included Tom Bass, with humorous songs and patter, Sam Torr in his Salvation Army skit and G.H. Macdermott, the actor-vocalist later of *Jingo* fame. The Sisters Williams sang prettily, while dancing in different styles was contributed by Katie Seymour, Lottie Collins and the Sisters St. Felix. Mr & Mrs Watson sang a Tyrolean melody, Topsy Venn sang as she had done at the old Strand fifteen years before and the Sisters Collins offered duets. Two sketches of different types completed. The chairman was W.F. Fair of '*Tommy, make room for your uncle*' fame.

Throughout much of its life the hall had its particular favourites, who played long engagements or re-appeared regularly. In 1892 the hall, now re-named the Royal Theatre of Varieties, passed out of the hands of Purkiss and re-opened with Arthur Swanborough as manager. A new act-drop depicted the Thames at Richmond, the arched roof over the proscenium was painted with goddesses and cupids, and the boxes were pushed back to give greater visibility to balcony seat holders.

The re-opening bill included three outstanding serios: Ada Reeve, Florrie Robina and Billie Barlow. The coon studies of Eugene Stratton were balanced by the essentially English songs of Charles Bignell, Jolly John Nash and George Leyton. Florrie Gallimore was another who sang of the Tyrol. The burlesque team Brown, Newland & Le Clerq contrasted with the practical fooling of the M'Naughtons. Duettists Newman & Latimer and The Jackleys ('Society Marvels') were vocal doubles in contrast to two dumb acts, Ardel & West and trapezist Mdlle. Adelina. Marie Collins and Pearl Penrose were both serio-comics, and Virto played clarinet, cornet and saxophone. So many acts were present for this celebratory performance, which ran until after midnight, that Dan Leno had time for only one verse and Albert Chevalier for none at all.

In 1896 the Royal again came up for sale and was knocked down to Mr. John Brill, one of the vendors, at £40,500. In accordance with the contract of sale the frontage was rebuilt in 1897 to the designs of Ernest Runtz, assuming the dignified appearance with which we were familiar during the first half of the twentieth century.

In 1905 The Royal was bought by Walter Gibbons, who was in the process of building up a chain of theatres that would soon include the London Palladium. The handsome frontage remained but the body of the hall was completely rebuilt at a cost of £30,000. The new building was on three levels, for which purpose it was lowered to basement level, and to accommodate twice-nightly performances additional entrances and staircases were provided, with additional exits in Little Turnstile. Designed by Frank Matcham; after the style of most Moss and Stoll theatres its name was changed to the Holborn Empire. The source books give the theatre's capacity as 2,000, but those of us who attended it know that this is an exaggeration.

Exterior of The Holborn Empire with Max Miller billed

The new theatre opened in late January, 1906, having been closed since June, many frequenters of the old Royal helping to make up the crowded first-night audiences. They were able to admire the beauty of the marble-pillared proscenium while James Sale led the orchestra before giving place to Silent Tait, the 'speechless' magician; a sentimental sketch *Satan* concerning the rescue of a settler's wife by a faithful gorilla; Arthur Breton heading a romantic absurdity *A Trip to the Isle of Man*; The Two Bees (Harry & Flora Blake) giving impersonations of leading politicians and actors; Hill & Hull in a ventriloquial scena, and Lee & Kingston offering knockabout drollery; The Four Australian Lady Meister Singers singing *The Lost Chord*, J.W. Rickaby including 'Silk Hat Tony' with his wonderful comic songs, Frazer & Haley, Zaro & Arno and finally, of course, the Bioscope.

Walter Gibbons had launched the Holborn Empire, and was successfully running it in conjunction with his other London Theatres of Varieties, when he embarked on his most ambitious project, the London Palladium. The new theatre opened in 1910, but it soon became obvious that he had overreached himself, and in 1912 he relinquished control of the LTV circuit to Charles Gulliver.

New interior when reconstructed by Frank Matcham from The Royal

During the Gulliver regime what was probably the most dramatic event in the hall's history took place. On 4 August, 1914 – the day war broke out – an artiste named Maud Tiffany played the first and second houses, and then left the theatre, presumably to go home. She was never seen again. Her theatrical basket and props were left in her dressing room, and were stored at the theatre until its closure.

Charles Gulliver was by training an accountant, but he was quick to learn all about showmanship. Under his management the Holborn Empire maintained a policy of weekly Variety, and probably booked every star of significance in the business. But even Gulliver felt the pinch when the advent of the Talkies caused hall after hall to close. The LTV circuit sold out, the London Palladium and the Holborn Empire alone passing into the hands of the newly-formed General Theatres Corporation, whose managing director George Black and his assistant Val Parnell declared their intention to continue to run them as music halls.

George Black ran the GTC in conjunction with Moss' Empires from September, 1928. At the Palladium he instituted his long-running Crazy Shows which, alternating with Variety seasons, kept the box office humming throughout the 30's. But at Holborn he kept strictly to weekly-change Variety right up to the war. For fifty-two weeks of the year a different programme was offered each week, with performances at 6.30 and 9.00pm and prices from 1s to 3s 8d. There were eleven acts on the bill, unless the top was a band, and when a touring revue was booked it was usually boosted with additional acts.

Gracie Fields was the one star who consistently occupied top-of-the-bill during the 30's. Half way through the decade she was joined by Max Miller, with whose name the Holborn was to be forever identified thereafter. George Robey, now a veteran, and such contemporaries as Billy Bennett, Will Fyffe, Talbot O'Farrell and Randolph Sutton, shared top frequently. I can remember Stanley Holloway strolling onto the stage and contemptuously turning the microphone aside. George Clarke, the last of the dude comedians, was a regular visitor, as were Dick Henderson and Clarkson Rose. Those who had recently reached the top line included Ted Ray and Max Wall, while the USA gave us two outstanding comics in Will Mahoney and Vic Oliver.

Auditorium of the Matcham theatre which replaced the old Royal in 1906

America also sent over such singers as Belle Baker, Molly Picon, Harry Richman, The Street Singer and Sophie Tucker. The American influence was further seen in the countless British bands – those of Jack Hylton and Harry Roy, and Nat Gonella's Georgians being particular favourites at Holborn. Their singers – Les Allen, Elsie Carlisle & Sam Browne and Phyllis Robins – often became stars in their own right.

Flanagan & Allen were undisputed bill-toppers, and other popular doubles were Caryll & Mundy, Clapham & Dwyer, The Two Leslies, Max & Harry Nesbitt, Wright & Marion and Tommy Trinder. Doubles specialising in songs at the piano were Norman Long and the Western Bros. Newly arrived from concert party and radio was Arthur Askey.

Musical acts that appeared repeatedly included Larry Adler, Teddy Brown, Hutch, Turner Layton and Moreton & Kaye. Of dancing acts the Ganjou Bros. & Juanita were pre-eminent, and among impressionists the two sexes were represented by Florence Desmond and Afrique respectively. By the 30's comedy sketches were rare, but two aggregations maintaining the tradition were Duggie Wakefield & Co. and Joe Young in *Buying a Theatre*.

Good specialities always received their due need of applause at Holborn, good examples being Maurice Colleano & Co., The Diamond Brothers, Joe Jackson, The Four Jokers, Kafka, Stanley & Mae and, most famous of all, Wilson, Keppel & Betty. Few specialities topped bills, but there was an exception – the astonishingly accomplished Nicholas Brothers.

The occasion I best remember at the Holborn Empire was 1936, the night of the abdication of Edward VIII. At the end of the performance the MD, Syd Kaplan, raised his baton as was his wont. The audience was wondering what would be played. The band struck up '*Land of Hope and Glory*' and received a massive round of applause.

Soon after the outbreak of WW2 George Black presented Max Miller in a long-running revue, *Haw, Haw*, which was so successful that it was followed by a similar production, *Apple Sauce*. During the latter's run, on the night of 11–12 May, 1941 a Nazi bomb destroyed the theatre, fortunately after the audience had left the building. Bud Flanagan made the comment, 'Another German act brings the house down!' As the scenery and props had survived behind the iron, *Apple Sauce* was salvaged and continued its run at The London Palladium. Until 1951 it was hoped that the historic theatre would be rebuilt, but the authorities were more interested in social engineering and withheld permission. Ultimately, Moss' Empires lost heart and the Empire was demolished to make room for another office block.

Although the theatre's fame rests on its being one of the half-dozen longest surviving music halls, it had another claim to recognition. From 1922 to 1938 it was the London home – for matinees only – of the patriotic play, *Where the Rainbow Ends*.

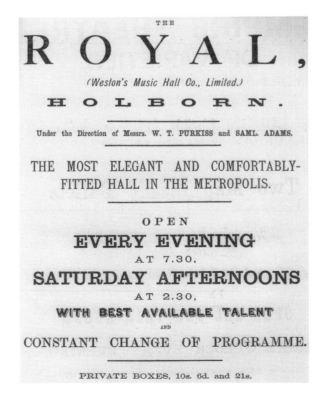

THE

R O Y A L,

(Weston's Music Hall Co., Limited.)

H O L B O R N.

Under the Direction of Messrs. W. T. PURKISS and SAML. ADAMS.

THE MOST ELEGANT AND COMFORTABLY-FITTED HALL IN THE METROPOLIS.

OPEN

EVERY EVENING

AT 7.30,

SATURDAY AFTERNOONS

AT 2.30,

WITH BEST AVAILABLE TALENT

AND

CONSTANT CHANGE OF PROGRAMME.

PRIVATE BOXES, 10s. 6d. and 21s.

Leicester Square Theatre

39–41, Leicester Square and St. Martin's Street

Leicester Square Theatre: exterior with Max & Harry Nesbitt and Co. billed

In 1892 plans were prepared by G.H. Greatback for another Variety theatre on Leicester Square, which would have rivalled the nearby Alhambra, and Empire – then at their height of popularity – but it was never built.

It was not until 1930 that a theatre, originally named The Buchanan Theatre, was actually built on the south side of the square. The consistently unlucky Walter Gibbons had gone into partnership with the popular musical comedy actor and dancer, Jack Buchanan, to purchase the site in 1928 – reputedly at the cost of £250,000. They engaged Andrew Mather to design a large theatre, intended for musical comedy productions. (Mather had designed the Capitol Cinema – later the Gaumont – in the Haymarket for Gibbons in 1925 and he later redesigned the Brixton Empress for Gibbons' Syndicate Varieties Ltd. in 1931). The builders of the new theatre were Gee Walker & Slater Ltd. and Jack Buchanan lived in a suitably elegant style in a flat at the top of the building until it was damaged by a German bomb in 1940.

Failure to acquire buildings at the rear meant that a full-size stage could not be accommodated, so the auditorium was redesigned while the theatre was under construction. It was consequently necessary to change its policy to Variety and films. On 19 December, 1930 the 1,760-seater theatre opened with Warner Bros.' film *Viennese Nights*, supported by a stage show. Walter Gibbons went bankrupt and the house went to Radio-Keith Orpheum (R.K.O.) as its major British showcase. It reopened as RKO Leicester Square in June 1931 after alterations planned by film and stage designer Edward Carrick – the son of the famous Edward Gordon Craig. Harry Roy appeared there in between films, calling the band he assembled for the occasion The R.K.Olians; Harry led on the clarinet and alto-sax.

But within a month R.K.O. pulled out and sold the theatre to County Cinemas under whose management it was known as The Olympic – with yet more alterations. This time they were by Alister Macdonald – the distinguished cinema-architect son of Prime Minister Ramsay Macdonald. However, it failed again and by August had become a Variety house once more, and for about a year it did pretty well with some strongish bills.

For example, in December, 1932 Max & Harry Nesbitt; Betty Fields (sister of Gracie); Wilson, Keppel & Betty; Du Calion; and Freddie Forbes headed an attractive bill. They were supported by Dekkar & Pan; Allen & Lavoie; Jean Florian; Earle Proctor; and Kittie Prince, with J.W. Jackson's Massed Dancing Chorus of no less than 80! The music was provided by Percival Mackey and his Band. In addition, Syd Roy was featured with the 'Lyricals'. Syd was the elder brother of Harry and equally well known at that time and when Harry Roy moved across the Square to the Café Anglais early in 1933 Syd took over the R.K.Olians.

Syd's instrument was the piano, but there is some doubt as to whether he played with the band – he certainly did not play on the R.K.Olians recordings of the time, as these featured the pianos of Cyril Kaye and Tony Fones. Syd carried on until late 1933, when the theatre's policy changed from live orchestra to theatre organ. A 2/10 Wurlitzer organ and a revolving stage were installed when the theatre was reconfigured as a Ciné-variety house. It is interesting to note that the biggest hit for Harry Roy came several years later in 1949 with his own composition *Leicester Square Rag*.

Interior showing stage and boxes

The Performer reviewed the bill of 27 March, 1933, of which four of the ten acts were held over from the previous week – Don Azpiazu and his Cuban Ensemble even repeating the same routine. Dezso Retter (comedy wrestler) and Fred Sanborn (comedy musician) were among the others retained. Eily Gerald headed The J.W. Jackson Girls, who 'put in good work'. Larry Kemble had 'the laughs flowing freely' with his cycle act, George Betton 'offered rich stories' – and a 'Chinese' song, while Shires &

Rai did 'splendidly with futuristic dances in changes of colourful costumes' – one of them made by the clever paper-tearer Harry Moore. Florence Sumner, with Yola De Fraine in her 'Rumba Rhythm' scene, and Tracy & Vinette completed the bill. Olly Aston and his Band and Will Ewen's Orchestra officiated from the pit alternately.

The two bands were still engaged at the theatre a month later for the show seen for a week in April, 1933. That great rhythm pianist, Billy Mayerl, was the attraction and seemed happy to play at the No. Two's as well as at luxury houses such as The Leicester Square Theatre – he was at Collins' in Islington in July, 1928. He also published his own piano tutor for others wishing to adopt his style. A smaller supporting bill of seven artistes included Iovka Hadji; Duncan Gray; George Jackley; Vardel Bros.; Lena Chisholm & Bill Hill; Nice, Florio & Lubow; and Kittie Prince. It was clear that the Variety business in the West End was not too good, despite the fact that the other halls in the Square were otherwise occupied. The Empire had been rebuilt as a super cinema and The Alhambra was in its final years, running an occasional hit film like *Atlantic* in 1934, while staging musical comedies such as *A Kiss in Spring*. It closed in 1936 and the Square's last live theatre, Daly's, in the following year. Both were rebuilt as cinemas.

In June, 1933 Jack Buchanan regained control and immediately leased it to United Artists. They re-opened it with Buchanan's own picture, *That's a Good Girl*. Following a closure for yet more redecoration in 1937, the theatre was expected to reopen as a Variety house again. However, the demand was clearly for films and Buchanan joined forces with a company headed by J. Arthur Rank. Thus the theatre became the first of Rank's West End cinemas.

War damage led to a nine-month closure in 1940–41, when Jack Buchanan's flat was destroyed. The direct hit led to a nine-month closure but repairs were allowed and it reopened (still as a cinema) on 11 July, 1941 with *The Flame of New Orleans* – a rather disappointing vehicle for Marlene Dietrich.

In 1946 the theatre came under Odeon control and has prospered over the years, but unfortunately not as the luxury Variety theatre originally envisaged by Walter Gibbons and Jack Buchanan. Incidentally, it is amazing to note that even after bomb damage and another reconstruction in 1968 a grid and a haystack lantern may still be seen over the stage area.

Syd Roy and the Lyricals, about 1930

We acknowledge Allen Eyles' and Keith Skone's book, 'London's West End Cinemas' as a source of film information. Also thanks to Barry Wolsey, of The Harry Roy Appreciation Society for information on Harry and Syd Roy.

Harry Roy – who never missed a publicity opportunity!

London Casino

22, Old Compton Street, Cambridge Circus

London Casino: exterior with Olsen & Johnson billed

The few years after WW2 are the ones that interest us most, when firstly Emile Littler presented pantomimes, then when Bernard Delfont briefly competed with the London Palladium in staging Variety bills. But this theatre has offered many styles of entertainment since its opening on 3 April, 1930 and is now a successful home for musicals.

Opening as The Prince Edward Theatre (the name under which it operates today) the theatre was designed by E.A. Stone and promoted by the Hay Hill Syndicate. The striking interior decorations were by Marc-Henri and Laverdet. Its first years were chequered to say the least as it was variously a theatre, a trade cinema, a cabaret-restaurant, a club and – later – a cinema. The opening production, *Rio Rita*, was not the success it had been on Broadway; neither was a string of other musical comedies, except for one starring Binnie Hale.

The world-famed Parisienne revue star, Joséphine Baker, was booked for a four-week season, opening on 3 October, 1933, but even she failed to fill the 1,800-seat theatre. Non-stop revue was tried, but did not attract either, so the building was leased as a trade film theatre giving day and evening showings. It was not licensed in 1934. Clifford C. Fischer's productions *Nuits de Follies* and *French Casino Show* were staged in 1937 and 1938, the latter with Lucienne & Ashour, Four Robenis, Ketty Mara & Chimpanzee, George & Jack D'Ormonde and Three Sophisticates.

In 1936 expensive conversion into a cabaret-restaurant, known as The London Casino, finally gave the lavish place the success it deserved. Tables and chairs filled the stalls, rather in the manner of an early music hall, with the stage extended forward into the audience. One of the four directors of the new enterprise was E.A. Stone, the theatre's architect.

There was no charge for admission, but for 15s 6d (17s 6d on Saturdays) one could enjoy a five-course Dinner or Supper, dance to Jack Harris' Band and see Clifford C. Fischer's 'intoxicating' New Revue, *Folies d'Amour*; there were two sessions nightly, with the show being staged at 8.15pm and again at midnight. Evening dress was compulsory for dancing after 11pm. The public flocked to Old Compton Street to enjoy the sumptuous venue.

Unfortunately, WW2 brought the show to a close in 1940 and two years later the theatre became the Queensbury All-Services Club. Once the hostilities were over, Tom Arnold and Emile Littler took over in 1946, revived the London Casino name and then somewhat surprisingly decided to re-open on 14 October. They transferred from the Prince of Wales a small-scale controversial 'problem' play, *Pick Up Girl* which had attracted considerable attention at the New Lindsey Theatre Club earlier that year. His name already on over a dozen West End and touring bills, as well as on numerous seaside ones, Bernard Delfont decided in 1947 to take a seven-year lease on the Casino. With the Holborn Empire (where he had earlier appeared as an eccentric dancer) put out of action by the blitz, only the Palladium was a serious rival in the West End. There was room, he felt, for the launch of a second top-flight Variety house. But he had not reckoned on the high cost of bringing over equally top-flight stars from America for a public starved of international performers.

He did well enough with Laurel & Hardy, Olsen & Johnson and Allan Jones – despite the latter's liking for the bottle. He also brought on newcomer Winifred Atwell, who came to him as a replacement performer for Carole his wife, who had fallen ill before a big charity concert. Two of his staff at the Delfont Agency, Billy Marsh and Keith Devon, were also excellent talent spotters. Marsh followed up a tip from Stan Laurel and 'discovered' Norman Wisdom in a show at the Victoria Palace; Wisdom had wangled a position in the second half of the bill by switching spots with Vera Lynn, pointing out that she could get home earlier by appearing before the interval. This saucy move appealed to Billy Marsh, who booked Norman Wisdom for the Casino.

Billy Marsh also saw the possibilities in Frankie Vaughan, whom he persuaded into top hat, tails and cane – the rest is history. Vivian Blaine ("The Strawberry Blonde") and Sophie Tucker were other stars who were at the Casino at this period. In November, 1950 Rex Ramer appeared, following a successful four-week ciné-Variety season at the Empire, Leicester Square; also that month we saw The Merry Macs and The Beverley Sisters.

However, Bernard Delfont had been called to Val Parnell's office and given a strong warning that his Casino shows were hurting the Palladium, ordering him to "stop this nonsense". When Delfont refused, Parnell – as new M.D. of Moss' Empires – banned his acts from the powerful circuit. Even worse, he began booking the biggest American acts at fees that Delfont could not possibly afford.

The Casino tried to keep going with British acts for a time, but there were just not enough Norman Wisdoms and Winifred Atwells. The battle with the Palladium raged on, but the position at the Casino was getting critical even before the big stars started arriving at Argyll Street. Delfont did very well with Chico Marx, who played to near capacity. There was then a good chance of closing the gap when Mickey Rooney flopped at the Palladium, finishing his four-week engagement a week early. But when Parnell followed up with Danny Kaye, who quietly and then zanily dominated the huge theatre for forty minutes, Delfont knew the game was up.

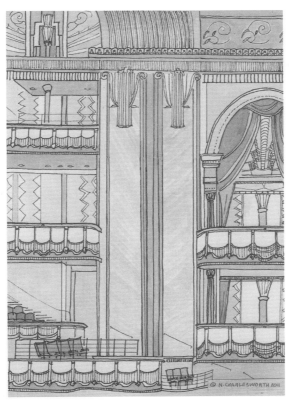

London Casino (now Prince Edward Theatre again), part of interior

Tom Arnold and Emile Littler returned to the Casino with Robert Nesbitt's French-style *Latin Quarter* in 1949. The show was sub-titled 'An Evening in The Naughty Square Mile' (the Casino is in the heart of Soho, of course). The third edition in 1951 displayed the talents of many British and international acts. Among them were Nat ('Rubberneck') Jackley, Jean Carson, the pianist Rolly Rolls, Halama & Konarski, Dick & Dot Remy and the ventriloquist Bob Bromley. There were also several Emile Littler pantomimes here, one of which was the 1946 production of *Mother Goose*. This had Nat Mills in the title role, with his partner Bobbie as Tulip a dairy maid. The strong cast included Stanley Holloway as Squire Skinflint, Dave & Joe O'Gorman as Cup & Saucer ('Two snakes in the grass'), Roberta Huby as Jill, Con Kenna in his flying helmet, Celia Lipton as Colin and a young Jasmine Dee as Fairy Snowdrop.

After a further revue and Jack Hylton's *Wish You Were Here*, set in a holiday camp and giving the young Dickie Henderson a success, the London Casino became the home of Cinerama in 1954. Henderson went straight into a show at Her Majesty's, further advancing his reputation. The conversion of the theatre into a full-time cinema, with its 64ft wide curved wide screen, took some time and some stalls seating was inevitably lost. Part of the upper circle had to be taken out of use, due to poor sightlines. With its three separate projector booths at the rear of the stalls, it opened with *This Is Cinerama* on 30 September, 1954. We enjoyed *Cinerama Holiday*, a later presentation, but when the supply of suitable product dried up, the Casino fell back on conventional 70mm films. These, too, were in short supply and the seating capacity was reduced to 1,175.

Bernard Delfont was back in 1974, when his EMI organisation became the owners of the theatre. At first it was run as a cinema with an occasional Christmas pantomime; but with its original name, The Prince Edward Theatre, it rejoined the live fold in 1978. The Peron musical *Evita*, with Elaine Page and Joss Ackland had an eight-year run. It was followed by *Chess*, another big hit for the theatre.

Later Cameron Mackintosh became joint-owner of the building with the now Lord Delfont in 1992 and the theatre was immediately closed for complete refurbishment at the cost of £3 million. In the event it was well worth it as his chosen architects (Renton Howard Wood Levin) turned in one of their most astonishing pieces of work – the re-built auditorium looking even more convincingly 1930ish than the original. It re-opened and continues happily today.

Nat ('Rubberneck') Jackley in *Latin Quarter*

London Coliseum

St. Martin's Lane

The London Coliseum: exterior in 1910

Largely forgotten by the theatregoing public today, the name of Stoll is connected in most people's minds with the London firm once controlling a dozen West End theatres – as well as with a former theatre which once stood in Kingsway. But Sir Oswald Stoll was a great patron of the arts and showman for nearly forty years at The Coliseum – for twenty-five of those years presenting Variety of the highest standard in the West End's biggest theatre. Apart from conceiving the vast building itself, which occupies an area of more than an acre, Stoll commissioned plays and music specially for his theatre; put on Sarah Bernhardt and Ellen Terry in Variety; brought Diaghilev's Russian Ballet back to London; introduced Max Reinhardt; produced replicas of The Derby, Wimbledon tennis, Rodeo and Terrier Racing on stage; presented the great clown, Grock; and even had Sir Henry Wood conducting the Coliseum pit orchestra in Wagner! Enough to ensure that any man's name should be gratefully remembered.

Exterior name panel facing May's Court

Built on the site of ramshackle tenements at the southern end of St. Martin's Lane (an area which is said to have inspired Dickens' Tom-All-Alones in his *Bleak House)*, the Coliseum was conceived by Oswald Stoll as a vast Variety theatre, deliberately exceeding in size and luxury London's biggest theatre, the Theatre Royal, Drury Lane. Designed by Frank Matcham in the Italian Renaissance style, its most notable external feature is the massive square tower, guarded by lions and surmounted by what was originally a revolving globe, spelling out the word C-O-L-I-S-E-U-M in the night sky. The London authorities early on forbade a moving sky sign, so the globe was immobilised and flashing lights were installed to give the impression of movement. After the recent renovations the globe is, once again, moving properly and makes a lasting impression when seen from the street. The theatre occupies one of the outstanding positions of any West End house.

The original seating capacity was 2,358 in stalls, dress circle, grand tier and balcony, all upholstered and with arm rests. The unique feature was a railway car to convey royalty to their seats in the Royal Box, sited centrally under the dress circle at the back of the stalls. There were tea rooms on every level and such amenities as an information desk offering postal services, together with commodious cloak- and 'retiring', rooms. The revolving stage, in three sections, was able to revolve at twenty miles per hour. It was on this mechanical marvel that a version of *The Derby*, complete with crowds and book-makers appeared – sadly a jockey was killed at one performance. The revolve ran on the DC power supplied for the London tramways and was only taken out when Sadlers Wells Opera took over the theatre. The drop curtain, depicting theatre and music hall personalities, was painted by Byam Shaw.

Interior from balcony towards the stage

Before he reached the planning stage Stoll himself made an extensive study of the crowds at Charing Cross Railway and Underground stations. He calculated that visitors from the suburbs and country would welcome light entertainment before or after their shopping, sightseeing and lunch and the expanding Underground system would bring ever more people into the heart of the West End. He decided that an early show at, perhaps, 12 noon would be an attraction to people who might well balk at patronising the more racy Oxford, Pavilion or nearby Tivoli, and that he would then present three further shows during the day. The ambience of a club rather than that of a Music Hall, could well build up what Stoll considered would be a special following.

The Inaugural Season

Opening on 24 December, 1904

1st Programme, at 12 noon and 6pm

Decima Moore in *Barney in Connemara*; Sylvia Sablanc and J.G. Piddock in *The Last Load*; Sisters Meredith & Co. in *The Banks of The Ganges*; Sylvia Sablanc & Co. in *The Pickle Girl*; May Edouin and Fred Edwards in *A Bachelor's Dream*; The Boissetts (The Bricklayers); The Troubadours (Vocalists); Reiff Brothers (American Step Dancers); De Breans (Juggling and Shadowgraphy); Allan Morris & Co. in *Bluebell*, an illustrated song; and *The Derby*.

2nd Programme, at 3pm and 9pm

Madge Lessing in *Goodbye, Little Girl*; Eugene Stratton and Bessie Butt in *The Black Pearl*; Millie Hylton in *Monte Carlo Belles Parade*; Bertha Palliser & Co. with J.G. Piddock; R.A. Roberts in *Dick Turpin*; Tina Clementa with her Looping The Loop Boys; Three Bounding Pattisons (trampolinists); Bertha Palliser in *Missouri River*, an illustrated song; Cooke & Miss Rothert; and *The Derby*.

Each programme ran for two hours, with a break of one hour between each house.

After well over a year in the building, the theatre opened on 24 December, 1904, with four shows a day: these involved two different programmes, with the first programme at 12 noon and 6pm, and the second at 3pm and 9pm. However, it became obvious that Stoll had overreached himself and after eighteen months the theatre closed. After some fairly controversial financial reconstruction, it reopened in December, 1907, when with twice-nightly Variety it ran uninterruptedly until 1931 with virtually every notable star of Variety there – Wilkie Bard, Albert Chevalier, Cinquevalli, Chirgwin, Datas the memory man, Gus Elen, George Lashwood, Harry Lauder, Billy Merson, G.H. Elliott, Will Evans, Harry Fragson, Jack Pleasants, Arthur Roberts, Harry Tate, Little Tich, Cecilia Loftus, Billy Williams and – still imitated today – Robb Wilton. There were others which I had the good luck to see elsewhere in their later years, such as George Robey, Gertie Gitana and Hetty King. There were also many stars from America, notably Marie Dressler, The Marx Brothers, W.C. Fields and Layton & Johnstone; and from the Continent, such as Yvette Guilbert and Grock.

Sir Oswald Stoll persuaded stars of the legit to appear at The Coliseum, sometimes in one-act plays that ran over two or three weeks; these included George Alexander, Gladys Cooper, Cedric Hardwicke, Lily Langtry, Ellen Terry and Irene Vanbrugh.

The Imperial Russian Ballet played seasons, as did Markova and Anton Dolin, with dancing of a less serious type being contributed by Maud Allan. The Beecham Opera Co. was a triumph, while purely physical attractions were demonstrations of badminton, golf, lawn tennis and a full-stage excerpt from the Highland Games; for a massive Rodeo the steers were stabled in sheds behind the theatre, while cowboys galloped up a ramp from Bedfordbury to reach the stage. All these acts posed considerable problems for the stage management, but pulled in excellent audiences. The legendary Vesta Tilley gave her last performance at the Coliseum on 5 June, 1920, before becoming Lady de Frece; while the Irish comedian Jimmy O'Dea first appeared in 1930.

Interior showing the Royal Box and Circles

In 1931 talking pictures sent Variety into decline and forced a change of policy on Sir Oswald Stoll, who had held out against the inevitable. As late as 1926 Variety had been doing good business at The Coliseum, but the final week took place in a theatre filled with gloom. The top of the bill, Nellie Wallace was ill and could not appear, while Clapham & Dwyer had fallen out for some reason. The unlucky thirteen acts on the bill were received by a tiny unresponsive audience. The theatre was already being converted for its next show. This was *White Horse Inn*, for which Stoll had virtually imported the Austrian Tyrol and decorated the auditorium as well as the stage itself; the £40,000 production ran initially for 651 performances. It was followed by *Casanova* (429), *Blackbirds of 1934* and the ice spectacle *St. Moritz*.

Variety had not completely disappeared from St. Martin's Lane however, as there were short seasons during the intervening weeks. There were also ballet seasons and The Coliseum's first pantomime. I saw Alice Delysia and formed the opinion that the theatre was too large for Variety.

Pantomimes appeared most Christmases, often presented by Francis Laidler from Bradford. The first was in 1936, when *Cinderella* with Duggie Wakefield, Lupino Lane, Edna Best, Madge Elliott and Wallace Lupino, ran for 123 performances. The same subject was repeated three years later, with Patricia Burke, Leslie Holmes, Fred Emney and Leslie Sarony as Buttons. Other Laidler pantomimes included *Aladdin* (1940), *Jack & The Beanstalk* (1941), *Mother Goose* (1942), *Humpty Dumpty* (1943) and *Goody Two Shoes* (1944). Popular performers included Norman Evans, Iris Sadler, Jean Colin, Betty Jumel, Naughton & Gold and Jimmy Plant. Revivals of musicals, such as *Maid of the Mountains*, *Belle of New York* and *The Quaker Girl* filled the rest of the time: the average run was around 250 performances.

Sir Oswald Stoll died in 1942 and was succeeded by Prince Littler, who welcomed the end of the Second World War with two fine revues – *The Night and the Music*, starring Vic Oliver (686 performances) and *The Night and the Laughter*, with Bud Flanagan, which did not do so well. In 1947 the theatre had one of its biggest successes ever, *Annie Get Your Gun* with 1,304 performances. This was followed by an outstanding series of musicals: *Kiss Me Kate*, *Guys & Dolls*, *Can Can*, *The Pajama Game*, *Damn Yankees* and *Bells Are Ringing*.

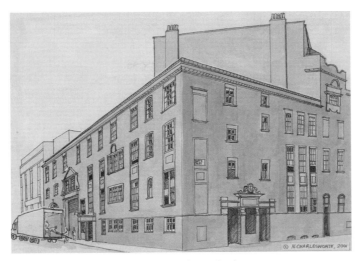

Rear exterior with get-in doors

At this time two 'American' pantomimes were presented with tremendous success. Rodgers & Hammerstein's *Cinderella* (Christmas 1958) had an amazing cast drawn from the world of revue, pop music and Variety. Tommy Steele made his West End debut as Buttons, a part incorporated especially for the London production and Yana as Cinderella. The Ugly Sisters were Kenneth Williams and Ted Durante while Betty Marsden was a pioneering 'ironic' Fairy Godmother. Bruce Trent brought his firm tone to the part of The Prince who in this version had a father – played by Jimmy Edwards. A rare handful kept mostly in their places by the experienced director of spectacular variety – Freddie Carpenter. Two years later Christmas 1960 saw one of the most colourful pantomimes ever presented in London – Cole Porter's *Aladdin* with sets and costumes by Loudon Sainthill and a cast headed by Bob Monkhouse, Doretta Morrow, Ian Wallace and Ronald Shiner. Directed by Robert Helpmann, it ran for 145 performances.

There followed a period during which the Coliseum was occupied by dance companies and films; it began to look as if the theatre might well close, like the Stoll and The London Hippodrome. However, a new novelty, Cinerama – already in occupation at The London Casino – took over theatre for a number of years, which saved the building, but not the Royal box and its accessories which were removed to accommodate the projectors.

Exterior looking down St. Martin's Lane

Theatre lovers rejoiced when in 1968 Sadler's Wells Opera Co. went into permanent occupation, changing its name in 1974 to The English National Opera. The building, rapidly wearing out, was purchased from Stoll Moss Theatres in 1992 for some £10 million, with government help. It was later suggested that the company might move to a part of London with more room for expansion, but in 2001 a radical programme of restoration and improvements was started to bring the Coliseum up to date, after many years of neglect. Apart from the reinstatement of the revolving globe, the long-absent lions on the tower and the splendid curved and glazed roofs flanking the tower were replaced; the former had simply worn away, while the roofs had been removed for safety during WW2.

The vast theatre has a stage some 120ft deep with 60 lines; the audience is accommodated in stalls, dress circle, upper circle and balcony, the fronts of which are constructed of marble. The orchestra pit will hold some one hundred musicians for opera performances, although there are many who say that the Coliseum is too large for anything but dance.

Duggie Wakefield as 'Buttons' in *Cinderella*

London Hippodrome

Cranbourn Street

The London Hippodrome: exterior from Charing Cross Road

The London Hippodrome, designed by Frank Matcham and built by Holliday & Greenwood, stands on an island site at the junction of Charing Cross Road and Cranbourn Street. It backed onto Newport Street, which was widened by 10ft at Edward Moss' expense. The enormous site – too large for merely the theatre – also houses shops, flats and the headquarters offices of Moss' Empires Ltd. in Cranbourn Mansions. Later, an entrance to Leicester Square underground station emerged from one corner of the building.

The theatre was originally built in order to carry out a long-cherished ambition of Edward Moss to give London a circus, combined with elaborate stage spectacles. Beneath the circus arena was a huge water tank, holding 100,000 gallons of water supplied by the Cran Bourn which still runs beneath the theatre. The hydraulic works were carried out by Whitford & Co. and were said to have cost £43,000, enabling the stage to rise and sink as required. But in spite of all the wonderful building and engineering, the LCC would not grant a refreshment licence, even though two public houses had been demolished to make room for the new building!

The Hippodrome finally opened on Monday 15 January, 1900 after three postponements, not only to the lack of a drinks licence but also that still familiar problem: the intricate stage mechanism would not work properly. The commemoration stone had been laid on 29 December, 1899 by Alfred de Rothschild. The new building was hailed as 'Stupendous, even in these days of magnificence'; one reviewer even prophesied that 'The London Hippodrome is likely to rank with Westminster Abbey as one of the sights of London'. The General Manager of the new theatre was Frank Allen, while the Acting Manager was T. Aynsley Cook. Prices were quite cheap for the West End, at 1s, 2s, 3s, 5s and 7s 6d, with boxes at one or four guineas.

The programme of the opening show was presented twice daily at 2pm and 7.45pm, opening suitably with *Light Cavalry* played by the band, conducted by Georges Jacobi, late of The Alhambra. One of the principal items was The Lawrence Svengali Trio, a thought transference act which caused characters to be presented, or tunes played on stage, from whispered instructions passed to one of the members placed in the stalls. The other main attraction was *Giddy Ostend* (or *The Absent-minded Millionaire*), the leading role played by Little Tich. This sketch ran for an hour on opening night, but was cut back to 35 minutes by Frank Parker, the resident Stage Manager.

Apart from the two main items, the programme comprised no less than sixteen circus and Variety acts. One of these, Mr. Goodnight, was a horse dressed as a man. Mr. Goodnight took off his own clothing, made his own bed, lit and blew out a candle, got into bed and went to sleep. Prior to opening night the management received a telegram from Herr Julius Seeth, requesting accommodation for his '21 boys'. These turned out to be 21 Forest-Bred Lions in six big travelling cages, which Seeth moved up and down Newport Street in an attempt to secure rooms. Not surprisingly, he was unsuccessful both for himself and his charges. The *Giddy Ostend* segment ran until early June, with frequent changes among the supporting acts, when Albert Hengler's mammoth water spectacular *Siberia* opened, running through until 15 December. The first pantomime at the new house, *Cinderella*, opened two days later and even this had nine circus acts in support! Thus was The London Hippodrome launched.

During the first decade other similar water shows, with titles such as *The Flood*, *The Earthquake*, *The Redskins* and *Zuider Zee* were staged. Lupino Lane made his first appearance in the latter, nearly losing his life in a torrent of water. Men dived into the tank from the ceiling colonnade, elephants slid in from ramps and fountains spurted up from the arena, while snow storms and other effects were also produced from the ceiling. For dangerous animal acts a nickel silver grille arose from below to protect the audience.

Acts that played during this period included Cinquevalli, Chung Ling Soo, Loïe Fuller, Happy Fanny Fields, Fragson, Yvette Guilbert, Seymour Hicks, Clarice Mayne, Mrs. Langtry, Ada Reeve, Lafayette and Irene Vanbrugh – all really first class acts. Pantomimes were presented regularly during the early years, *Aladdin* and *Dick Whittington* being seen in 1901 and 1902.

In 1909, with the public perhaps tiring of water shows, the Hippodrome's auditorium was altered to make it into a normal Variety theatre. Frank Matcham returned to supervise the necessary works. The proscenium arch was moved into the auditorium to give the stage a new depth of 40ft. Wing space was increased and the arena was removed, being replaced by a conventional orchestra pit and additional stalls seating. Operetta, ballet, Variety and one-act plays now replaced circus. The first performance in London of *Swan Lake* was given in 1910. Leoncavallo conducted his opera *The Gipsies* on the same bill as The American Ragtime Octette.

Interior towards the stage

Then, from December 1912, Albert de Courville's revues were in occupation for over a decade. The Octette had started a craze and *Hullo, Ragtime*, starring Billy Merson, was a brilliant success. It was followed by *Hullo, Tango!* with Harry Tate as its star. These were followed by a production by Ernest Rolls, one of the pioneers of revue, entitled *Push and Go*. In 1916 Little Tich returned in *Flying Colours* and another success during WW1 was the revue *Business As Usual*. There were ten big shows in ten years – others including *Joyland*, *Zig-Zag*, *Box o'Tricks*, *Joy-Bells*, *Jig-Saw* and *Round in Fifty*. The stars of these included George Robey, George Clarke, Stanley Lupino, Ethel Levey, Shirley Kellogg and Teddie Gerard.

The success of revues was followed by an equally impressive array of musical comedies: *Mercenary Mary*, *Sunny*, *Hit The Deck*, *That's A Good Girl*, *Mr. Cinders*, *Sons o'Guns*, *Stand Up and Sing*, *Mr. Whittington*, *Yes Madam*, *Please Teacher* and *Hide and Seek*. Artistes associated with some of these were Jack Buchanan, Binnie Hale, Bobby Howes and Cicely Courtneidge.

As war loomed again, revue returned to Cranbourn Street under George Black, with the topical *The Fleet's Lit Up*. This was followed by *Black & Blue* (described as George Black's Intimate Rag) and *Black Velvet*. It was good to see Variety artistes such as Vic Oliver, Pat Kirkwood and Max Wall featuring in Hippodrome shows.

Detail of proscenium arch

During WW2 musical comedy alternated with revue and we enjoyed *The Lisbon Story* with Patricia Burke and *Perchance to Dream* with Ivor Novello. Maurice Chevalier played a season, presented by Jack Hylton, while The Royal Canadian Navy, in collaboration with ENSA, presented *Meet The Navy*, the profits going to British charities. An outstanding show, still talked about, was Robert Nesbitt's *Starlight Roof*. The stars were Vic Oliver, Pat Kirkwood and Fred Emney; however, it is especially remembered for the introduction of twelve years old Julie Andrews and for the amazing comedy antics of Michael Bentine with the broken back of a chair.

Despite its lavish decoration in the Flemish Rennaisance style, The London Hippodrome was stuck with its slightly peculiar stalls area, still influenced by its earlier circus role. In 1952 during the run of one of the successful *Folies Bergére* revues, Moss' Empires requested the architect E.M. Lawson to prepare plans for completely rebuilding the Hippodrome auditorium on a different axis, with the main entrance front on Cranbourn Street. Apparently, the large fan-shaped auditorium was to have been in a dull 1930s cinema style with two, very deep balconies. No doubt the idea was also to increase its capacity, which at the time was barely 1,300; but the scheme came to nothing and five years later the theatre was closed. While The London Palladium had a sensationally profitable decade, from 1948 to 1958, with a succession of big American bill-toppers, its sister theatre hosted an extremely mixed bag of shows. Once the long run of *Folies Bergére* revues had ended, there seemed to be no firm policy at the Hippodrome, something that has let down many a theatre. The show *Wonderful Time* completed its Palladium run there, with Billy Cotton & his Band, Ted Ray, Joy Nichols and George & Bert Bernard. Arthur Askey starred in a musical, *Bet Your Life*, following *High Button Shoes* and *Wedding in Paris* starred Evelyn Laye, Anton Walbrook and Susan Swinford. These were mixed in with plays such as *The Caine Mutiny Court Martial* with Lloyd Nolan, David Knight and Nigel Stock, ice shows, Variety bills and revue.

Exterior side wall to Little Newport Street

Not only The London Hippodrome, but many big theatres in the West End were feeling the pinch. The Stoll Theatre was demolished, The London Casino was converted for *Cinerama* and The London Coliseum went over to films, but The Hippodrome managed to return to its roots with seasons of Variety. One bill was topped for four weeks by Lonnie Donegan and Alma Cogan, followed by two weeks each of big bills headed by Shirley Bassey, then Charlie Gracie, the American singer. Max Bygraves fronted *Meet Me On The Corner*, really a named Variety show. He was strongly supported by the magician Channing Pollock (who, for his sins, was named the most beautiful man in the world in a poll at the time), The Nitwits, Louie Ramsay, Joan Winters & Guy Fielding, Katherine Feather, Latona, Graham & Chadel, with singers and dancers. Prices were 4s to 15s 6d. The show then toured some of Moss' Empires in the provinces, including Manchester Palace.

The Dave King Show had the doubtful honour of being the Hippodrome's final attraction as a theatre. King had already topped the bill in Variety at The London Palladium, but this latest show was interrupted by his illness, Benny Hill having to take over. The leading lady was Shani Wallis, with others on the bill including The Andrea Dancers, Howard Jones & Reggie Arnold, Los Gatos Trio, Jimmy Lee, a line of sixteen girls and The Fabulous Fountains of Rome – an interesting echo of the very early days of water spectacle at the Hippodrome.

When the Hippodrome closed on 17 August, 1957, conversion work got under way to make it into a Theatre Restaurant. A second E.M. Lawson scheme was passed over in favour of a more modest one carried out by another architect for Trust House Forte. Dining, a floorshow, dancing and a late cabaret were offered at the new Talk of The Town, which opened on Thursday, 30 July, 1958. Reviewers found the 700-seat restaurant, with its ex-Savoy Hotel director A.B. Amanda in charge, to be intimate despite its size. Indeed, the evening was wonderful value at 42s 6d a head, including a first-class three-course dinner. An excellent wine cellar was kept. The floorshows were lavishly staged, usually under the direction of Robert Nesbitt.

Exterior from Coventry Street, while 'The Talk of The Town'

Newspaper cutting for 'Talk of the Town' Opening, 1958

Over the twenty-four years of its operation as The Talk of The Town, the old Hippodrome presented every top-line cabaret star from the United Kingdom and overseas, but at its closure in 1982 it was stated that the cost of engaging the star cabaret artistes had become too high in relation to what could be gained in ticket revenue. Some of those who appeared included Judy Garland, Shirley Bassey, Cliff Richard, The Beatles, The Seekers and many, many more. The venture had played itself out and the historic theatre passed into the hands of Peter Stringfellow, to be converted yet again, this time into a theatre-discotheque. The theatre has now re-gained its old name of The London Hippodrome and is now a successful casino, together with facilities for staging Cabaret or conferences.

London Palladium

Argyll Street, Oxford Circus

The London Palladium: exterior in Argyll Street with Laurel & Hardy billed

Situated on the site of Hengler's Circus, originally The Corinthian Bazaar, The Palladium opened on 26 December, 1910, being the brainchild of Walter Gibbons and cost around £250,000 at that time. On the site before the Bazaar arose stood a house of 1744, occupied by one of the Dukes of Argyll, a rambling building whose cellars remain below the Argyll Street front of the Palladium and formerly used by wine merchants.

The Palladium was designed by Frank Matcham and retained most of the façade of The Corinthian Bazaar (the work of Owen Lewis in 1868), cleverly converted into one of the best theatre frontages ever built in London. With seating in stalls and two tiers, the new theatre held 2,325 in great comfort – only The Coliseum holds more. Decorated in white and gold, with Rose du Barry hangings and coloured marble in profusion, the auditorium presented a magnificent sight. Strangely, it was Matcham's future father-in-law, J.T. Robinson, who had been engaged to carry out conversion work for Hengler's Circus forty years earlier.

The opening show was headed by Nellie Wallace, Whit Cunliffe, Ella Retford, Ella Shields and John Martin Harvey in a one-act playlet – a popular 'act' at the time. The show was overlong at 4½ hours, but the theatre had been well launched on its illustrious career.

In 1911 Walter Gibbons offered something new in the scena *Mexico*, with horses, a water tank and a plot involving the detective Nick Carter. But Gibbons, who had been responsible for building up The London Theatres of Varieties (LTV), made injudicious financial arrangements and in 1912 had to hand over control to Charles Gulliver. The latter brought prosperity to the house with bills such as The Beecham Opera Company, Little Tich, George Robey, Eugene Stratton, Ruth Vincent and Irene Vanbrugh in *The Twelve Pound Look*. In those pre-WW1 years 'Tango Teas' were served in the foyer.

The Palladium has some of the most generous foyers and bars in any London theatre, with most of their original ornament intact. In recent years the new, big Val Parnell Bar has been installed, completely designed in the Matcham style by the architects Renton Howard Wood Levin. The theatre later absorbed older adjoining buildings as dressing rooms and, at the left of the entrance a superb box office has been created. The auditorium, although badly in need of restoration now, is – at once – huge but intimate: it is designed so that the audience wraps around the performer. Many artistes over the years have enjoyed and commentated favourably on this close contact with the audience – a contact absent in some other large theatres. It is in a style described as 'French Rococo' when built and is full of atmosphere.

Pantomime appeared early in The Palladium's career and in the 1914 production Clarice Mayne and Harry Weldon starred, the principal girl being May Gibson, George Black's daughter. A typical Variety bill for the week commencing 18 February, 1918 was: Jack & Evelyn, Coram, Maidie Scott, Whit Cunliffe, Fred Barnes, Wish Wynne, together with five supporting acts.

When WW1 broke out The Palladium instituted a three-a-day policy and business was good. During the early 1920s a series of spectacular Revues had long runs: Harry Day's *Rockets* (490 performances), Albert de Courville's *Whirl of The World* (627) and *Sky High* (309) and Maurice Cowan's *Life*. *Whirl* had an outstanding cast in Nellie Wallace, Billy Merson, Tommy Handley and Nervo & Knox, while in its successor Nellie was teamed with George Robey and Lorna & Toots Pounds – regulars at the time. Between runs, traditional Variety held the fort, prominent being Billy Merson, Will Evans, G.H. Elliott, Wilkie Bard, Marie Lloyd and Albert Whelan. The run of Revues was broken by the pantomime *Cinderella*, with Clarice Mayne, George Mozart and Charles Austin.

In the mid-twenties new Variety stars were few and, apart from Nora Bayes and Cissie Loftus (making a come-back), The Palladium had to try something new. Charles Gulliver yearned for something entirely different, which the burgeoning cinema was about to offer with The Talkies. Gulliver sold out and LTV reverted to Walter Gibbons, who was also a cinema pioneer, interested in sound tracks; he, with George Black and others, formed The General Theatres Corporation (GTC). The new management turned The Palladium into a Ciné-variety house, which quickly proved a failure. Disagreements led to Gibbons' second departure, with GTC coming under the complete control of Black in 1928. Gibbons eventually died penniless.

George Black declared his intention to reinstate Variety, but of the 'High-Speed' type, using more acts but cutting out a lot of the running time. Following the opening night on 3 September, 1928, the new format was hailed an overwhelming success, with 55,000 people seeing the show in its first week and over 4,000 people turned away before the second house on opening night. Shows were at 6.10 and 8.45pm. The bill included Gracie Fields, The Seven Hindustanis, Dick Henderson, Ivor Novello, Billy Bennett and others. Sophie Tucker, who was in the audience, was introduced and persuaded to perform a number. The Newsreel on screen had to be passed up, as the show was over-running.

Interior showing the circles

Black's *Crazy Shows* (starting with a *Crazy Week* and eventually lasting many months) were enormously successful. His Crazy Gang was formed, changing its personnel from time to time, becoming almost resident, with the audience being assaulted as soon as it entered the theatre. These shows, *Life Begins at Oxford Circus*, *Round About Regent Street*, *O-Kay for Sound*, *London Rhapsody* and *These Foolish Things* were fast-moving and gave Variety a much-needed boost. Touring versions were sent out to provincial theatres controlled by GTC.

Variety stars favoured by Black were Layton & Johnstone, Will Fyffe, Will Hay and Max Miller; and certain draws during this period were the Big Bands. I saw Harry Roy, Ambrose and Ray Noble, while jazz was also the basis of *The Cotton Club Revue*. With his Booking Manager Val Parnell, George Black provided a superb array of talent in the form of 'Fats' Waller, Carl Brisson, Burns & Allen, Louis Armstrong (making his first English appearance in July, 1932), Hutch, Sandy Powell, Jack Buchanan, Ramon Novarro, Cab Calloway and Jack Benny to name just a few.

Black's last pre-Second World War show was *The Little Dog Laughed*, but it was suspended for a few weeks when war loomed, as all the international artistes, including Willie, West & McGinty ('A Billion Building Blunders') had to return home. As soon as he could, Black opened without the American acts.

Shortly after the outbreak of war, *Garrison Theatre* with Jack 'Blue Pencil' Warner and his 'Littel Gel' Joan Winters ran for 225 performances, allowing the public to see their radio idols in person. The following show, after a Variety season, was *Top of The World*, but this folded after four performances, when a bomb fell through the roof of The Holborn Empire and the government closed all the theatres. The management lost £30,000, although some of this was recouped when *Apple Sauce*, the Max Miller vehicle at Holborn, was later transferred to The Palladium. It ran for 462 performances, to be followed by *Gangway* (525). Then Tommy Trinder, the man of the moment, occupied the star spot in *Best Bib & Tucker* (490 performances) and *Happy & Glorious* (938), a run broken only by the US Army show *This Is*

The Army. This had a company of 160 strong and was produced by Irving Berlin, who also appeared in it singing his own song, 'Oh, How I Hate To Get Up In The Morning', wearing his 1918 battledress.

Variety seasons in between were notable for appearances by Max Miller (even today holding the record of 28 consecutive weeks for straight Variety), Cyril Fletcher, Arthur Lucan (Old Mother Riley) & Kitty McShane and Geraldo. Sadly, George Black died on 4 March, 1945 having guided the famous theatre's destiny for sixteen years.

Val Parnell, Black's innovative successor, launched The Palladium's first post-Second World War show, *High Time* with Tessie O'Shea and Billy Cotton, and the Skyrockets Orchestra in the pit. Following this success – and bills headed by George Formby and Laurel & Hardy – Tommy Trinder (Black's last home-grown star) was back in *Here, There and Everywhere*. For 1948 Val planned a season of Hollywood stars, with the Skyrockets Orchestra on stage, interspersed with long-running Revues and pantomimes. The first act booked, Mickey Rooney, did not distinguish himself, but he was followed by Danny Kaye, whose triumph was described by Hannan Swaffer as 'unequalled in the annals of the London stage'. Many other Hollywood stars were to set the Thames on fire over the next ten years, with Lena Horne closing the series. We were able to see Martha Raye, Carmen Miranda, Duke Ellington, Jack Benny, The Andrews Sisters, Bob Hope, Frank Sinatra, Judy Garland, Benny Goodman, Dean Martin & Jerry Lewis, Mel Tormé, Dorothy Lamour and many more, playing for two or three-week seasons.

Among all this American talent, the only notable British bill-toppers then were Gracie Fields, Donald Peers and – when not barred by Parnell – Max Miller. Revues alternated with Variety: *Out of This World* with Frankie Howerd, Binnie Hale and Nat Jackley, *Fun & The Fair* with Billy Cotton, George Formby and Terry-Thomas, and *To See Such Fun* were some of them.

Pantomime usually occupied the stage at Christmas, with big spectacular productions; the first after the war was *Cinderella* starring Tommy Trinder, Evelyn Laye, Zoe Gail and George & Bert Bernard. The last-named became fixtures in the theatre for years. Home-grown stars were few at the time, but for one nostalgic fortnight *Thanks For The Memory* occupied half the bill, also being featured in The Royal Variety Performance that year; and notable support-acts at this period included The Arnaud Brothers with their bird courtship, Michael Bentine, Frank Marlowe and the great juggler, Rob Murray.

Interior showing proscenium and dome

The 1950s brought many new stars, including Winifred Atwell, The Beverley Sisters, Max Bygraves, Tommy Cooper, Bruce Forsyth, Tony Hancock, Arthur Haynes, Des O'Connor, Harry Secombe and Frankie Vaughan. Visitors from the USA included Sammy Davis jnr., Guy Mitchell, Johnnie Ray and Liberace. A typical pantomime was *Turn Again, Whittington* starring Norman Wisdom.

During the 1960s Leslie A. MacDonnell was Managing Director of Moss' Empires Ltd., who had taken over The Palladium from GTC in 1947. He continued with much the same policy, even when all the other Variety theatres had closed. Even The Palladium itself was threatened with take-over by developers in 1960, but this was firmly resisted by Prince Littler, the long-serving Chairman. The situation was resolved by a merger between Moss' Empires and Stoll Theatres, which eventually became known as Stoll Moss Theatres.

More new stars were emerging, notably Charlie Drake, Tom Jones, Larry Grayson, Roy Castle, Cilla Black, Cliff Richard, Dickie Henderson, jnr., Morecambe & Wise, Jimmy Tarbuck and Mike Yarwood. Among the ladies were Shirley Bassey, Joan Regan and Alma Cogan. But the most outstanding individual talent was Ken Dodd who, backed by The Bluebell Girls, had sensationally successful seasons in a decade not outstanding for its Revues. Of these, three worth mentioning were *Large as Life* with Harry Secombe and Adele Leigh, *Here and Now* with Des O'Connor finally topping, supported by Los Paraguayos, The Rockin' Berries and The Ukranian Cossacks, and *Let Yourself Go* in which Harry Secombe again topped, with strong support from Roy Castle, Marion Ryan, Eddie Calvert, Audrey Jeans and Jeremy Hawk.

The 1970s were the last decade when The Palladium could call itself 'The Ace Variety Theatre of The World'. For a time it presented Variety bills, among them Vic Damone with Millican & Nesbitt, Arthur Askey, Roger Kitter, Bobby Crush, Val Doonican, Moira Anderson, Norman Vaughan, Dailey & Wayne, Trio Athénée, Des Lane & Company, and an American bill with Johnnie Ray, Billy Daniels, Frances Faye and The Ink Spots – all on one evening. But where were the specialities? Another successful Variety-type show was *The Comedians*, a group of club comics who gained stardom via television. On one bill were Ken Goodwin, Charlie Williams, Jos White, Bernard Manning, Mike Reid, Dave Butler, together with Shep's Banjo Boys, a singing group and a line of dancers.

A few new stars hit the headlines – Freddie Starr and Les Dawson (a throw-back to the great days of Variety) were among them, but real Variety bills were almost non-existent, consisting, when they existed at all, of one big star and two or three perfunctory supporting acts. It was rather disappointing – unless you were a fan of the big star.

Grayson's Scandals in 1972 was, in fact, the last true Variety show that I saw at The Palladium; supporting Larry Grayson were George Carl, Noele Gordon, Keith Harris and two old-timers, Eli Woods and Bill Lynton – a company of twenty-six in all. Performances were still twice nightly, at 6.15 and 8.45pm with prices ranging from 85p to £2.50. *The Two Ronnies* (Ronnie Barker and Ronnie Corbett) brought their own show into The Palladium for a season: it had merit, but some items were familiar from television exposure and only Corbett was really at home on such a big stage. However, Leslie MacDonnell presented some fine pantomimes, notably *Dick Whittington* with Tommy Steele and *Jack & The Beanstalk* with Frankie Howerd, but he caught a cold when he tried a Space Musical. MacDonnell's tenure was fairly brief and he was followed by Louis Benjamin. On the death of Prince Littler, Lew Grade (later Lord Grade) took over. He obviously made good use of his international show business connections, and in 1976 persuaded the 'old groaner' Bing Crosby to appear live for the first time (apart from wartime shows for the forces) since his distant youth. He insisted on being surrounded by his children, but he also brought Rosemary Clooney with him. Louis Benjamin also dragged Ethel Merman out of retirement to shake the rafters in her inimitable manner; brought Julie Andrews back to Variety for the first time since she had become an international musical and film star and gave London the chance to see Shirley MacLaine at her peak.

But without a screen or recording reputation, hardly anyone could draw: even the great Joséphine Baker did only mediocre business. Sadly, the big headliners had disappeared, while the faithful twice nightly audience had dispersed. Even Louis Benjamin, steeped as he was in the business, could not sustain Variety, except spasmodically. Some lovers of Variety yearn for a West End house to be established where they could enjoy their favourite entertainment. A smaller theatre, but with a distinct 'Music Hall' feel, would be the Apollo on Shaftesbury Avenue – should it ever become available.

There have been the occasional Sunday shows, with stars such as John Denver, Captain & Tenniel, Glen Campbell, The Carpenters, Petula Clark and Neil Diamond; but for an increasing percentage of its time The Palladium became host to record-breaking musicals. *The King and I* (two seasons), *Hans Christian Andersen*, *Singing in the Rain* (both with Tommy Steele), *Barnum* (with Michael Crawford), *Joseph and The Amazing Technicolor Dreamcoat* and – not the anticipated success – *La Cage aux Folles*.

Pantomime made a welcome return for the 1985/86 season, with a big production of *Cinderella* starring Des O'Connor as Buttons, with a strong company including Paul Nicholas, Anna Neagle, Hope & Keen and Sarah Payne. However, it is impossible to break into long-running musicals to stage pantomime for a relatively short season as it would have been with Variety bills, so sadly London misses out on its once plentiful array of pantomimes. As recently as 1949 there were no less than thirty-three pantomimes and Christmas shows to choose from in the London area – not including seasonal films.

Prince Littler, Chairman of
Moss' Empires Ltd.

True Variety last saw the light of day on Sunday 11 September, 1988, when The British Music Hall Society celebrated its Silver Jubilee at The London Palladium. The sparkling bill was topped by Roy Hudd, Bert Weedon, Bruce Trent and The Southlanders, with strong support from Margery Manners, Stella Starr, Jenny Maynard, Terri Carol, Chubby Oates, Joan Hinde, The Cox Twins and Pauline and Joe Church. From Canada came Kirk McMahon, one of the hits of the evening with his acclaimed recreation of Danny Kaye, having flown in especially for this one night. The Edinburgh and South London Gang Shows completed the bill; in the pit The Don Shearman Orchestra played in great style, while Jack Seaton, then Chairman of The British Music Hall Society, suavely compered the show.

The London Palladium has been the venue for very many Royal Variety Performances over the years, and attending a show there is very much of an occasion. Variety may have taken a back seat, but London's greatest Variety Theatre still exerts its pull and brings the public the finest attractions available – but fully-geared to modern, not nostalgic, taste. The whole front of house was revitalised by the Arts Team at RHWL between 1996 and 1998. The London Palladium was owned by the Holmes à Court family from Australia for several years, until – with the rest of the group's theatres – it was bought by The Really Useful Theatres.

As we go to press a new show entitled *Sinatra – The Man & his Music* is due to be staged at The Palladium in July 2015, with multi-media footage from Sinatra's private archive and a live 24-piece band with 20 dancers.

Sir Andrew Lloyd Webber is investing in considerable refurbishment of the theatre, following his sale of the Palace Theatre on Cambridge Circus. The Palladium can look forward to many more years of success.

London Pavilion

Formerly in Tichborne Street, later rebuilt at 3–5, Piccadilly

The London Pavilion: exterior of the original building in Tichborne Street with Arthur Lloyd billed

In 1859 Loibl & Sonnhammer opened a cheap sing-song saloon attached to a public house, The Black Horse Inn. In 1861 this saloon was converted into a music hall named The London Pavilion, which opened on 23 February as 'the first music-hall de luxe' in the West End.

In 1879 the lease passed to Edward Villiers, but in the meantime the building – at which G.H. Macdermott had sung his famous 'Jingo' song – was acquired for road-widening and was demolished on 26 March, 1885, when Piccadilly Circus was enlarged and the building of Shaftesbury Avenue begun. On the present triangular site the second Pavilion, designed by Saunders & Worley, was built by Villiers and opened on 30 November, 1885. Under the personal management of Edward Swanborough, the new building had a ground floor resembling a continental café, occupied by marble tables at the head of which sat the Chairman.

After a year the Pavilion was taken over by Syndicate Halls, who reconstructed it, dispensed with the Chairman and replaced the tables with luxurious tip-up seats with ledges for holding glasses. In 1900 the interior was rebuilt under the architects Wylson & Long, decorated in the Louis XV style, with the floor raked. It was now a pioneer of the more palatial music-hall. Swanborough was succeeded in management by Frank Glenister in 1897, and he remained in control until 1934, living in a flat above the theatre.

Frank Glenister, the long-serving Manager

A particular type of comic singer ensured the early success of The Pavilion. Arthur Lloyd and George Leybourne were followed by Charles Coborn, William Lingard and Dan Leno. Following the latter's appearance before King Edward VII at Sandringham in 1901, the Pavilion's box office was besieged for days by thousands wanting to see Leno. It was said that what was good enough for the King was good enough for them. Many had not visited a music-hall before.

Exterior of the new London Pavilion building with Harry Tate billed

The Pavilion was a favourite haunt of members of the Conservative establishment, many of whom had taken cabs up Whitehall to hear Macdermott sing 'Jingo'. Much was written by Sir Louis Fergusson, KCVO in his book *Echoes of The Older Music Halls*, extracts from which have been printed in the BHMS *Call Boy*. He described the programme on Saturday, 18 June, 1898, when he and his father occupied standing room close to the small stage and gazed obliquely at the front-cloth depicting 'The Centre of The World'. The 24-act bill included: James Fawn, Alice Lloyd, Pat Rafferty, Sisters Wright, T.E. Dunville, Chirgwin, Brothers Griffiths, Dan Leno, Vesta Tilley, Eugene Stratton, Leo Stormont, Harry Ford, George Robey, The McNaughtons and The Brothers Harloe!

Interior as in 1885

The Pavilion ceased to be a music-hall in 1918, when it was again re-modelled and reopened as a theatre under the direction of C.B. Cochran, who had the façade lit with electric signs proclaiming 'The Centre of The World'. Apart from his spectacular revues, films were shown by arrangement with Cochran and these included *The Taming of the Shrew* with Fairbanks and Pickford. Under Cochran's management stars like Evelyn Laye, Jessie Matthews, Hermione Baddeley, Anna Neagle, Florence Desmond, Dorothy Dickson and Max Wall were made or found there. The music of Cole Porter and Rodgers & Hart was heard in London for the first time at The London Pavilion. Noel Coward's greatest songs, such as *Poor Little Rich Girl* and *Dance Little Lady* were heard there. After Cochran's reign, Variety artistes made a welcome return to The London Pavilion, when John Southern presented the new craze, Non-Stop Variety for two years.

Then, in 1934, Londoners were shocked to learn that the hallowed building was to follow The Empire and become a cinema. Closure came on 7 April, 1934 and the interior underwent complete internal reconstruction to plans by F.G.M. Chancellor, of the Frank Matcham office. The three levels of stalls, circle and upper circle were retained, the boxes removed, with the auditorium and stage widened – not that the stage has served any purpose since the transformation.

Interior as cinema, the auditorium of 1934

The distinguished theatre remained a cinema of no distinction whatsoever. The original, decorative stalls saloon did, however, remain in its underground position to give some idea of the old theatre. The London Pavilion was reopened on 5 September, 1934 by United Artists, becoming their West End showcase; they continued to operate it until its closure on 26 April, 1981. The final seating capacity was 1,004.

Despite a vigorous effort by The Save London's Theatres Campaign, the Pavilion was later gutted to house divers facilities. The freehold had been held by The LCC, while some of the offices on the outer part of the building were occupied by Variety Theatres Consolidated Ltd., successors to Syndicate Halls. No better site for a live theatre exists in central London. We can be grateful that the fine neo-classical façade has been retained, at least below roof level. Several theatre managements were keen to return the Pavilion to live use, but they were rebuffed.

Lyceum Music Hall

Wellington Street, Strand

The Lyceum Theatre: exterior as restored in 1996

I remember the Lyceum best at Christmas, when Walter and Frederick Melville presented their splendid pantomimes. They engaged big names from the worlds of musical comedy and Variety, while we marvelled at the wonderful transformation scenes – especially the astonishing 'House of Cards' set, which always quite literally brought the house down in *The Queen of Hearts*.

The Lyceum's time as a Variety theatre was very short and it must have taken some filling, but a 'dry' music hall did not endear itself to Londoners – even though it was surrounded by public houses of all sorts. One thing must be remembered: the house that staged Variety was *not* the one made famous by Sir Henry Irving – only the portico and shell remained from that era. The theatre had been rebuilt, specifically for Variety, in a highly flamboyant style by Bertie Crewe.

The first Lyceum was opened (not on, but near, the present site) as the headquarters of The Royal Incorporated Society of Artists in Great Britain on 11 May, 1772. It contained a concert room as well as art galleries, but when the much grander Royal Academy of Arts was given its own rooms in the new Somerset House almost opposite in 1776, the S.A.G.B.'s fortunes ebbed and its rooms were rented out. Anyone wanting to put on virtually anything – from debates and acting lessons to art sales and boxing matches – could hire space at the Lyceum. Things changed in 1794, when an attempt was made to challenge the power of the Patent Theatres. This failed and the building became Handy's

New Circus. The content of an advertisement dated 10 February, 1795 is included in A.E. Wilson's delightfully written history of the Lyceum and includes the very interesting phrase 'the following series of novelty and variety'. This is significant, as the bill was made up of all those speciality acts later so popular in circuses and Variety: balancers, slack wire and tightrope dancers, tumblers and performing horses. Also on view were a clever pony, and a man dancing a hornpipe over and around twelve eggs!

Interior as it appeared in Sir Henry Irving's time

In 1802 Madame Tussaud's waxworks made their British debut there and then, on 20 April, 1809 the Lyceum opened as a theatre, having got a special licence so that it could house the company from Drury Lane Theatre, burnt down on 24 February. When the new Drury Lane Theatre opened on 10 October, 1812, the Lyceum reverted to its former status. Then Samuel Arnold obtained the lease of both the Lyceum and some adjacent buildings and built a new Lyceum (to designs by Samuel Beazley), still with its entrance on The Strand. On 16 February, 1830 this new theatre was lost in a fire, together with a lot of nearby buildings. The opportunity was taken to widen the Strand and build Wellington Street over the original site.

Another Lyceum (designed again by Beazley) was built with its entrance on the new Wellington Street through the famous portico. It opened on 12 July, 1834 but from then until 1871 a continuous stream of managements attempted to run it, but all were unsuccessful and in the profession it became known as an 'unlucky' theatre. Even the early ventures of the truly remarkably-named American manager, Hezekiah Linthicum Bateman, failed when he opened the theatre under his banner on 31 August, 1871. Then on 25 November he had that 'little bit of luck' about which all managers dream: his new leading man became the instant talk of the town in a psychological drama, *The Bells*. The actor's name was Henry Irving and the rest (as they say) was history.

Incidentally, it is probably worth mentioning in passing that Irving's clique later included a lot of musical comedy and music hall performers and that his notorious 'mannerisms' provided impersonators, both professional and amateur, with ample material for their acts. In fact, Irving did so well that he took over the lease of the Lyceum himself on 29 September, 1878 and immediately commissioned the actor-architect Alfred Darbyshire to undertake extensive structural and decorative alterations to the building – retaining the portico.

THOMAS BARRASFORD TOUR.

CALLS for MONDAY, JANUARY 30, 1905.

PAVILION, GLASGOW.
Zutka, Edna Groves, Pollo Jerome, Sid Bandon,
Josephine Casaboni, Raffelo Trio,
Larry Lewis, Harry Drew, Pictures, Barra Troupe.

HIPPODROME, BRIGHTON.
Harry Ford, Vi Dell, Mr and Mrs Lucas,
Miss Du Barry, Toch and Tard,
Erwins, Pictures, Leonard and Francis.

HIPPODROME, BIRMINGHAM.
Arthur Roberts, A. Aldridge, Ida Ross, Bros. Forrest,
Young American Quintet, Paxton Trio,
T. Nelson Downs, La Belle Wilma, Starr and Jerome,
Pictures, Jack Haggerty.

REGENT, SALFORD.
W. F. Frame, Fred Curran, Aladina, the O'Learys,
Alexander, De Henau, Ted Cowan, Pictures,
the Densmores.

HIPPODROME, GLASGOW.
Myaki Wrestlers, Florence Hill, Blind Man, the Toreadors,
Brinn, Chas. Morritt, Chas. Vandyke and Co.,
Sydney James, Pictures, Mr and Mrs Gene Hughes.

ALHAMBRA, PARIS.
Bonhair Gregory, Nora Emerald, Vansart, Juno Salmo,
Les Five Purroscoppis, Carl Reinsch,
Les Yumeaux Australiens Anderson, Ricardo et Salving,
Jules Kellar, Yamamoto, Vues Animees,
Donaldson Frères and Ardel.

PAVILION, NEWCASTLE.
Colonel G. Bordeverry, Lily Flexmore, Mdlle. Haydee,
Marquis Ito, Mdlle. Marvelle, Permane Brothers,
Henri Abdy, the Athlones, Burton Joyce, Pictures,
May Edouin, and Fred Edwards.

ALHAMBRA, HULL.
Keen and Waller, Nancy St. John, Harry Leybourne,
Alice Ormonde, Alix Lokos, Fred Earle, Gus Harris,
Edith St. Clare, Pictures, Vaudeville Trio.

EMPIRE, BRISTOL.
Six Brothers Luck, Frank Hutchings,
Emma and Victor, Clarus Brothers, Francis Letty,
Dan Llewellyn, Mons. Slippere, Pictures, Four Cliftons.

HIPPODROME, LIVERPOOL.
Hebburn Band, Lily Seville, Maud Oswell, the Arleys,
Alfred Barker, Philippi Bros., Chas. Steuart and Co.,
Gardner, Griffin, and Gardner, Amiel, Pictures,
the Yiulians.

PALACE, GLASGOW.
Banker, Mollie Doon, Pichel Troupe, Carina Sisters,
Charles Baron, Bennecelli Troupe, Melaine,
Beattie Kent, Pictures, Leo Dryden, Tom Collins.

TIVOLI, LEEDS.
Lottie Lennox, the Evalos, Lillian, Mountford and Walsh,
Schutzenlieserl'n, R. Judges, Bob Hamilton,
Flora Lumière, Pictures, Sandor Trio.

PALACE, MANCHESTER.
Harry Clifford, Boissets, Prof. Thornbury, Florence,
Ethel May, Bros. Ashley and Co., Tambo and Tambo,
Apollo, Pictures, Laares Troupe.

HIPPODROME, OLDHAM.
Due notice will be given of the Opening.

GRAND, MANCHESTER.
Chapender, Jennie Reeve, Wallace Whitney,
Beattie Foster, King and Delane, Bessie Lind, Reklaw,
Comical Walker, the Three Henriques, Pictures,
De Marse.
Matinée every Monday and Thursday.

LYCEUM, LONDON.
Lyceum Operatic Company, including Mons. Ansaldi,
Mons. Rey, Mdlle. Van Parys, Mdlle. Dardinac, Mdlle. Nervil,
Harmony Four, Michele and Sandro, the Cattaneos,
Al. Lawrence, Walton and Miss Ella, Ed. F. Reynard,
Thos. E. Finglas, Pictures, Browning and Wally,
Staig, Norman French.

HIPPODROME, ST. HELENS.
Chas. Majilton and Co., Geo. Neno,
Lachie Thompson's Topweights, Tom and Neil,
the Hamiltons, T. W. Royal, Ambey Brothers,
Pictures, George Formby.

HIPPODROME, MANCHESTER
Due notice will be given of the Opening.

Artistes please note which Halls they are booked for in Manchester and Glasgow.

All communications to be addressed to the London Office,
11, LEICESTER-PLACE, LEICESTER-SQUARE, W.
Telephone—6,824, Gerrard.   Telegrams—"Barrasford, London."

Advertisement for w.c. 30.1.1905 on the Thomas Barrasford Tour

LYCEUM, LONDON.
Lyceum Operatic Company, including Mons. Ansaldi,
Mons. Rey, Mdlle. Van Parys, Mdlle. Dardinac, Mdlle. Nervil
Harmony Four, Michele and Sandro, the Cattaneos,
Al. Lawrence, Walton and Miss Ella, Ed. F. Reynard,
Thos. E. Finglas, Pictures, Browning and Wally,
Staig, Norman French.

The calls for w.c. 30.1.1905, relating to The Lyceum Music Hall

The first season under Irving's management (with Bram Stoker of *Dracula* fame as his 'Acting Manager') opened on 30 December with himself as Hamlet and Ellen Terry as Ophelia. A legendary partnership was formed and the most memorable twenty years in the building's stage history commenced. It is also worth noting that Ellen Terry had even closer connections with music hall. Two of her friends were Marie Lloyd and Vesta Tilley, joining the former at a Benefit Matinée in 1911 at the St. James's Theatre, in aid of the Three Arts Club. They presented a fan of palm leaves and the 'People's Tribute' (a book containing over two million signatures collected from audiences on her Farewell Tour) to Vesta on stage at the Coliseum in June, 1920 after her last performance. Vesta Tilley then retired to become the full-time Lady de Frece

During the 1885 summer break the Lyceum's interior was again reconstructed to designs by C.J. Phipps. The roof over the stage was also raised, but Beazley's portico was untouched except for a new coat of paint. Irving's fame reached its height in 1895 when he received a knighthood, but thereafter things started to go wrong. A fire destroying a lot of scenery and properties in store in Southwark was a crippling blow to Irving, both physically and financially. Then, on 4 April, 1899 the London County Council condemned the Lyceum's antiquated fabric. Irving passed the management to a syndicate which continued to stage plays at the theatre, including on 19 July, 1902 *The Merchant of Venice* with Irving as Shylock – his last appearance there. But by now the structure of the Lyceum building was in such a dangerous state that the L.C.C. refused to renew the syndicate's licence. On Shakespeare's birthday in 1903 the house was sold at auction and by March, 1904 had been demolished, except for a retaining wall at the rear – and the portico.

Interior as redesigned by Bertie Crewe

A music hall, designed by Bertie Crewe, was erected on the site for Thomas Barrasford who opened it on 31 December, 1904 – very speedy builders in those days. He optimistically thought he could make a success of it, even though the well-established Tivoli was just along the Strand, the Palace Theatre was now doing well as a Variety theatre just up the hill in Cambridge Circus, the Alhambra and Empire were still going strong in Leicester Square and – to cap it all – Stoll had at last managed to open the gargantuan Coliseum at the far end of St. Martin's Lane only the previous week. Barrasford should surely have known better! He did, after all, control a chain of fourteen theatres –

including the Alhambra in Paris. To improve business, in desperation he even tried a full-length ballet, *Excelsior* in October, 1905, but this was a disaster and it came as little surprise to his rivals when he was declared bankrupt in December, 1906.

Henry Smith took over the licence in January, 1907 and with his partner – Ernest Carpenter – ran the Lyceum as a pretty successful theatre. They were especially lucky as they gave a chance to a 29-year-old up-and-coming Canadian actor-manager Matheson Lang, but now almost completely forgotten. Son of a clergyman and related to the then Archbishop of Canterbury, Cosmo Lang, he was destined for the church until as a student he fell under the spell of Irving and Terry.

Many other melodramas and pantomimes were presented but, although nearly all the shows were profitable, Smith decided to sell up when Ernest Carpenter died in 1909. In spite of paying the then remarkable sum of nearly a quarter of a million pounds for the lease, Walter and Frederick Melville quickly turned the Lyceum into one of the most 'Popular Playhouses' (the name of their holding company) in London.

The Melvilles came from a theatrical clan which had been in the business since the reign of George IV, working its way up from Penny Gaffs to the Lyceum. They were always astutely in touch with the audience at which they aimed and rarely, if ever, made mistakes. They presented an astonishing array of shows, from high drama to the notorious 'Bad Women' melodramas with titles such as *A Girl's Crossroads* and *The Worst Woman in London*. They took in the Carl Rosa Opera Company, Sir Thomas Beecham's Opera Company, a sensational Diaghilev Ballet season and two plays with Variety connections: Bransby Williams in *David Copperfield* and (after a four-year provincial tour) Albert Chevalier in a tear-jerker worked up from his hit song, *My Old Dutch*. They also put on Edgar Wallace thrillers, and revues starring names from the new-fangled world of wireless, such as Gillie Potter, Stanley Holloway and Flotsam & Jetsam.

All these shows broke even, but it was from the pantomime season that the Melvilles made their biggest profits. I can still recall the long matinée queues of ordinary Londoners, mainly from south of the river. The present Queen, then Princess Elizabeth, saw her first pantomime here in 1934, followed by Princess Margaret the next year. The pantos, which they staged for thirty-two consecutive years, with the exception of one year when a hit play ran through the festive season, would seem extremely staid today with their rhyming couplets, were written and produced, like many of their shows, by the Melvilles themselves and it is said that they always took a show off once it had made a profit of £30,000. The shows were then revived at The Brixton Theatre, which the brothers also controlled.

Some of the many Variety artistes involved in these spectacular pantomimes included Dave & Joe O'Gorman, Naughton & Gold, 'Monsewer' Eddie Gray, Florrie Forde, Clarkson Rose and George Jackley. The latter, with his rasping voice, began in Variety with The Jackley Wonders, an acrobatic troupe who did amazing somersaults over piles of tables. As a solo act he was billed as 'The Indignant Comedian'. Stanley Lupino made one of his earliest appearances at the Lyceum as the Cat in pantomime, eventually leading to a memorable Buttons in a production of *Cinderella*. He had that wonderful gift for getting on familiar terms with audiences – a huge asset in pantomime. He was, of course, related to Lupino Lane, whose aunt was Sara Lane of the Britannia Theatre, Hoxton.

With the death of Walter Melville in 1937 and of his brother the following year, the future of the theatre looked uncertain. It was run for a year or so by Bert E. Hammond, but had to close in 1939, as the site was purchased compulsorily by the L.C.C. for a new approach road to Waterloo Bridge. The final show was a star-studded production of *Hamlet*. John Gielgud, with Fay Compton as Ophelia, was supported by Harry Andrews, Glen Byam Shaw, Jack Hawkins, Andrew Cruickshank and Marius Goring. Only H.M. Tennent could have brought such an enviable cast together to mark what all concerned feared was the end of one of the most famous theatres in London.

The outbreak of WW2, however, stopped the demolition plans and in 1945 the theatre became a very successful dance hall, run by Mecca until 1985, entertaining over ten million people. 'Come Dancing' was regularly broadcast from the theatre by BBC Television, as was 'Miss World' hosted by Eric Morley. An Edwardian Music Hall season was presented by Eddie Kennedy and John Martin for the summer in 1971. The producer was Duggie Chapman and the show was staged four nights a week, twice nightly at 8.30 and 11.15pm. This 'Phantasmagoria of Fun, Frolic and Frivolity' brought Variety artistes back to the Lyceum after nearly seventy years, in the persons of Mr. Bruce Trent, Miss Violetta ('Direct from Paris'), Shek Ben Ali, Mr. Barry Craine and Miss Julie Fisher, who got the show a lot of publicity with her male impersonations. The Chairman was the comedian Mr. George Raymonde, with Miss Zena Cooper and Mr. Roger Dene at the pianofortes. Typical Edwardian food and drink was served at tables and at times the Chairman's attempts to retain order were rendered in vain. A good time was had by all!

Exterior showing old stage house in 1964 with TV crew covering "Come Dancing"

In the 1980s Bill Bryden's NT production of *The Mysteries* was presented here, using a platform erected in the stalls. But for the rest of the time the Lyceum continued as a dance hall and the broadcasts went on, until 'Miss World' became politically incorrect – as have so many other formerly 'innocent pleasures'. Mecca closed the building in 1985, having run Bingo there, and once again its future looked bleak until a 150-year lease was sold by The London Residuary Board (LRB) who succeeded the GLC. When the buyers, Brent Walker, planned to open a London version of the Paris Lido – a cabaret theatre – there was an outcry from theatre (but not Variety) people! The figure of £9 million was rumoured to have been paid. There was great frustration in the theatre community, as a number of managements were anxious to return the Lyceum to a live theatre – among them Maybox, Stoll Moss and London Festival Ballet (dance at that time not having its own London home).

Protests were made and numerous plans mooted until, in 1988, the LRB indicated its intention of transferring the freehold of the Lyceum to The Theatres Trust. This had been the original intention of the old GLC all along. To cut a long story short, the Trust eventually became the theatre's landlord and the Apollo Leisure Group, now the leaseholder, carried out extensive refurbishment of the auditorium and complete rebuilding of the stage house and dressing rooms, the architects being Holohan Architects. Despite improvements to legroom, the number of seats still exceeded 2,000, making the Lyceum one of the top lyric theatres in the West End. A vacant site alongside the auditorium was also developed to provide seven floors of new accommodation, including bars, a restaurant and hospitality suites. The decorations in the newly-painted auditorium may have appeared overly bright to some eyes, but the return of this important theatre to the fold was welcome and unexpected. The Lyceum reopened on 19 November, 1996 with a new production of *Jesus Christ Superstar*.

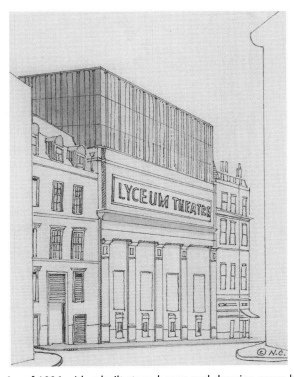

Exterior of 1996 with rebuilt stage house and dressing room block

Your compiler saw a good revival of *Oklahoma!* but his legs suffered badly after two hours in the cramped upper circle seat. Since then Disney's *Lion King* has had a long run here, meaning that over two hundred years of entertainment on, or very close to, this site would happily continue. Maybe one day we shall enjoy the return of pantomime.

LYCEUM THEATRE.

Sole Lessee - - - - - - Mr. HENRY IRVING.

Every Evening, at a quarter to Eight o'clock, "MACBETH."

Macbeth - - - - - - - Mr. HENRY IRVING.
Lady Macbeth - - - - - - Miss ELLEN TERRY.

Box-office (Mr. J. Hurst) open 10 till 5. Seats can be booked by letter or telegram.

Pantomime time at The Lyceum Theatre

Middlesex Music Hall

167, Drury Lane

Middlesex Theatres of Varieties: exterior facing Drury Lane, formerly The Mogul Tavern, with Marie Lloyd billed

Variety entertainment had long since departed from The Middlesex when I first arrived in London in 1930, although the most recent building on the site, The Winter Garden, was functioning as a successful theatre. The site of this theatre had been associated with entertainment since Elizabethan times. Nell Gwynn, who lived nearby, has been linked with the tavern here, which by the end of the 17th Century was known as The Mogul's Head, from which eventually developed the famous Middlesex. It is said that not only the bloods of the period, but even King Charles II frequented the neighbourhood in those days.

Archibald Haddon relates the history of the area in 'The Story of The Music Hall', maintaining that only The Canterbury Music Hall could claim older historic associations. The Canterbury's claim rested upon the fact that its adjoining tavern, The Canterbury Arms, reached back into pre-Reformation times, whereas The Mogul's Head was established only around the period of James I.

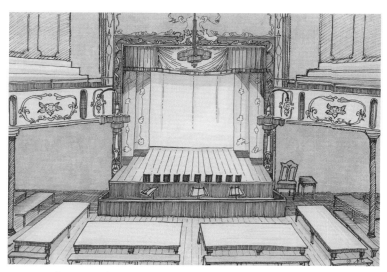

Auditorium of The Mogul Saloon based on a drawing of 1847

Glee clubs met and sing-songs were held in the hall adjoining the tavern during the 1830s and 40s. The establishment attracted a respectable class of tradesmen and mechanics – unlike The Coal Hole and The Cider Cellars! (This was in the opinion of J.L. Graydon, who later ran The Middlesex for many years. Other sources report that the place was extremely rowdy.) With its glees and comic songs The Old Mo' was a place of Variety entertainment by the 1850s. In 1847, after alterations, W. Edwin Winder had opened the place as The Mogul Saloon with a capacity of 500 and here true Music Hall gradually evolved. By 1851 Winder had renamed it The Middlesex Music Hall, and there he remained until, in 1865, he went to The Metropolitan.

At this time The Middlesex had no stage – merely a raised platform at the back, and a small band on the platform. The oldest surviving bill, dated Wednesday, 18 January, 1860, includes the names of Madame Elise, who topped as 'The Favourite Soprano', Mr. Sam Collins (later of Collins' Music Hall fame), Mr. J.H. Stead ('The Cure') and Mr. Charles Sloman ('The only English Improvisatore'), as well as 'A Full and Efficient Band' on a bill of twenty-six items. Prices were Upper Hall 1s and Lower Hall 6d. H.G. Lake, another prominent and popular licensed victualler, ran the hall for a time until, in 1875, J.L. Graydon became manager.

Interior of the Middlesex Theatre of Varieites looking towards the stage

From this point until 1910 The Middlesex enjoyed thirty-four years of enormous success. The hall underwent some reconstruction in 1872, when scenery and footlights were first introduced, and again in 1891, the latest work costing some £12,000. But The Mogul Tavern still existed and even when the theatre was completely rebuilt by Frank Matcham for Oswald Stoll in 1911 the tavern was incorporated into the bar at the back of the stalls; the street entrance was then bricked up when The New Middlesex became The Winter Garden Theatre.

Bills of the 1870s show the names of George Leybourne, Macdermott, Marie Loftus, Alice Lloyd, Arthur Roberts, Ada Lundberg, Jenny Hill ('The Vital Spark'), Bros. Griffiths, Bessie Bellwood (her first and last appearances were here), Charles Godfrey, Tom Coyne and J.M. Rowley ('Over, Rowley'), as well as a great many others forgotten today.

Undoubtedly one of the most popular and picturesque of the numerous Chairmen at The Middlesex was the famous Harry Fox, who served for twenty-five years, dying in 1876. Apparently a charming man, he knew exactly how to handle an unruly audience, his awesome, thunderous rebuke of 'Order, gents!' never being ignored. Chance Newton dwells lovingly on Fox's marvellous visage – purple-hued, thickly-veined, and emphasised by a big bulbous 'conk'. Evidently there was an affinity to Bacchus, god of drink.

Chairman Harry Fox would often oblige with a comic song of his own; two which were famous with the Mo' pit and gallery habitués were *The Warbling Waggoner* and *Jolly Nose!* Fox was followed as Chairman by Gus Leach.

Exterior of the Middlesex Theatre of Varieties (as rebuilt by Frank Matcham)

By the 1880s bills featured Charles Coborn, The Great Lupino Troupe, Vesta Tilley, Herbert Campbell, Harry Rickards (who went to Australia to build Tivoli Theatres), James Fawn, Bessie Bonehill, Lottie Collins, Harry Randall, Mellie Farrell and many more familiar names. The great Dan Leno made his first London appearance here during the week of 5 October, 1885. He had appeared earlier in the evening at The Foresters' and, following The Middlesex, moved onto other halls that night. By November, 1891 he topped a bill here which included 'The New Comedian' George Roby (sic).

Regular Benefits and Anniversaries offered large numbers of artistes: Graydon's 31st on 20 November, 1902 included Marie Lloyd heading a bill of 105 acts! The show commenced at 6.30pm and must have lasted all night. Prices were 6d, 1s, 2s 6d and 5s.

In 1910 the famous 'Old Mo' was closed and a new one arose the following year as a result of a partnership between J.L. Graydon and Oswald Stoll. But, for various reasons, the venture could not be counted a success even though it was another Matcham masterpiece. Was the proximity of the notorious Seven Dials area to blame? Had the local population of the Drury Lane district moved away? Was Music Hall on the wane? Did Oswald Stoll make the hall too respectable? Whatever the reason, in less than ten years The New Middlesex Theatre of Varieties, as it had become, was disposed of. In the new hall the Chairman had disappeared and the atmosphere resembled that of a regular theatre: despite the magnificence, the 3,000-seater, fully-upholstered building struggled to pay its way. Somehow, misfortune dogged the venture from the beginning. Graydon, still a director, tried quick-fire Variety – years before George Black used it as The Palladium – and in time the theatre became simply The New Middlesex Theatre with Revues, many of them touring French ones, filling the bill.

Eventually Stoll disposed of The Middlesex to George Grossmith and Edward Laurillard, who spent a lot of money on its interior redecoration and reopened it as The Winter Garden Theatre. No sooner had they done this than the place became a fashionable success as the home of Musical Comedy. Perhaps a firm policy helped, but in any event (thanks to Leslie Henson as the headliner) each of a whole series of musical plays in succession was a huge success. The reopening attraction was *Kissing Time* (430 performances), followed by *A Night Out* (309), *Sally* (383), *The Cabaret Girl* (462) and *The Beauty Prize* (214). Names always associated with the house during the Musical Comedy years include George Grossmith, Guy Bolton and P.G. Wodehouse as writers and Dorothy Dickson. Following *So This Is Love*, which in 1928 notched up 321 performances with Laddie Cliff, Cyril Ritchard and Madge Elliott, The Winter Garden was sold for £200,000 freehold.

The theatre, now controlled by The Winter Garden Theatre Ltd., was redecorated, recarpetted and reseated, but success was only spasmodic, with a number of transfers and revivals. Time and again in the theatre the lack of a firm policy has been a recipe for poor results. During WW2 the Winter Garden's biggest successes were *It's Time to Dance*, with Jack Buchanan and the play *No Room at The Inn* (425 performances).

In 1947 the theatre fell into the hands of The Rank Organisation (perhaps as a possible site for a new Odeon, or maybe as a live showcase in the West End for some of their stars), while Agatha Christie's *Witness For the Prosecution* held the stage. Another success was *Hotel Paradiso*, a farce with Alec Guinness, Irene Worth, Irene Browne, Douglas Byng and Frank Pettingell, presented in 1956. An important play a couple of years later was The Arts Theatre production of *The Iceman Cometh* by Eugene O'Neill. A show with perhaps a flavour of the old Middlesex was *Ah! Quelle Folies,* which came to The Winter Garden in 1958 – the comedian Gerard Sety having a big success with turning all his garments inside-out and impersonating a dozen male and female characters. In August of the same year it was rumoured that the theatre was to become the venue for a season of Lunch Hour plays in the West End of London, each to run for two weeks. But the end was approaching.

The Matcham Interior of the New Middlesex Winter Garden

At least the old Middlesex/Winter Garden finished with a Variety artiste topping the bill, as Frankie Howerd (the Mock Turtle) headed the cast of *Alice in Wonderland*, supported by Richard Goolden, in the theatre's final show. The theatre closed in 1959, being sold by Rank to a property development company. After much argy-bargy the old building was demolished in 1965 for the erection of the latest building on the site – The New London – which opened on 2 January, 1973 with *The Unknown Soldier and His Wife*, starring Peter Ustinov. The complex incorporated a theatre, restaurant, shops, showrooms, flats and a car park. Its big success has, of course, been the musical, *Cats*.

Exterior of the rebuilt New London Theatre

Number 167 Drury Lane is unique in the London entertainment scene, having seen Tavern life; the rise of the Music Hall from the Glee Club; its evolution into Variety, then Revue; the change to

Musical Comedy; Plays; Pantomime and finally Dance Drama. Cabaret is covered – in The London Room and even Pop is covered by the dive clubs in the basement.

MIDDLESEX MUSIC HALL,

DRURY LANE.

Proprietor and Responsible Manager   -   -   Mr. J. L. GRAYDON.

OPEN EVERY EVENING AT 6,30.   COMMENCE AT 7.

FOUR HOURS' CONTINUOUS FLOW OF AMUSEMENT.

CHANGE OF PROGRAMME EVERY WEEK.

THE SMARTEST VARIETY ENTERTAINMENT IN LONDON.

Managing Director   -   -   -   *Mr. Gus LEACH.*

Oxford Music Hall

Corner of Oxford Street and Tottenham Court Road

Interior, circa 1861

The Oxford was built at the corner of Oxford Street and Tottenham Court Road by Charles Morton, the Father of the Halls, who had already built and successfully launched London's first purpose-built music-hall, The Canterbury. It opened on 26 March, 1861 with a Grand Inaugural Concert for which the conductor was the ubiquitous Mr. Jonghmanns, and the magnificence of the hall, with Corinthian and Ionic columns, its promenade and its supper room, was universally admired. Unfortunately the auditorium was partially destroyed by fire on 11 February, 1868.

When the rebuilt hall reopened on 9 August, 1869, it was noted that the carpet was no longer laid on the floor. Presumably it was felt that such materials had contributed to the fire. Morton had relinquished the management, which was now under Maurice R. Syers and W. Taylor. The inaugural programme included a cantata *The Apple of Discord*, conducted by J.H. Jennings – the resident Musical Director.

A second fire occurred on 1 November, 1872, after which the hall was again rebuilt in part with certain improvements. For instance the boxes at the back of the balcony were replaced by another promenade. When it reopened on an enlarged site on 17 March, 1873 it was still under the management of M.R. Syers, but J.H. Jennings became acting managing in addition, and eventually proprietor. For this reopening a fine programme included Jenny Hill and for nearly twenty years the hall ran successfully without more disasters.

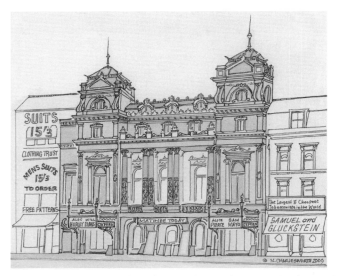

The Oxford Music Hall: exterior of the final building of 1893 with Alec Hurley billed

On 4 June, 1892, by which time the older halls were giving place to buildings the styles of theatres, constructed on the cantilever principle, the Oxford was closed and demolished. A completely new building rose on the site, which opened on 31 January, 1893 under the management of the Newsom-Smith Syndicate. Charles Morton was brought back to perform the laying of the foundation stone.

Final interior, closed in 1926

Excellent cloths had been furnished to decorate the stage and an 18-piece orchestra was in attendance. But, after twenty years the traditional music-hall bills provided by the Oxford were losing their appeal and by 1913 the fare was diversified by musicals and touring revues.

In 1917 C.B. Cochran took over the Oxford, where he presented Bruce Bairnsfather's *The Better 'Ole* which ran for 811 performances with entrance, foyer and auditorium stacked with sandbags to provide a suitable front-line environment. During its run the hall's name was changed to the Oxford Theatre. But after several successful shows the theatre closed in 1920 and underwent alterations, reopening as the New Oxford in January, 1921 with The Dolly Sisters in *The League of Notions*, which ran for 360 performances.

At Christmas, 1922 Cochran presented his first pantomime, *Babes in the Wood*, again with the Dolly Sisters. Following the revue *Mayfair & Montmartre*, Jack Buchanan had a success in *Battling Butler*, but after that there was a succession of short runs, apart from *Little Nelly Kelly* (265 performances), including experiments with serious drama, until the theatre closed in May, 1926. It was replaced by a Lyons' Corner House.

THE OXFORD,

14, OXFORD ST., LONDON, W.

Open every EVENING at EIGHT,

and every SATURDAY MORNING at HALF-PAST TWO.

To the Morning Performances the Profession, both Musical and Theatrical, are admitted Free by previously writing to the Manager.

Musical Director and Manager - - J. H. JENNINGS.

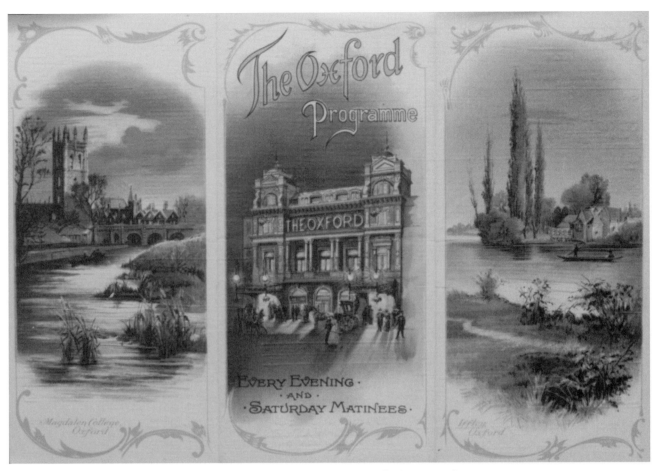

A programme cover used at The Oxford Music Hall

Palace Theatre of Varieties

Shaftesbury Avenue

The Palace Theatre of Varieties: exterior with Arthur Roberts billed

Shaftesbury Avenue was cut through Soho in 1886, providing numerous sites for development and The Palace was opened on Saturday, 31 January, 1891, as The Royal English Opera House. It was the dream of Richard D'Oyly Carte, son of a flautist and born in nearby Greek Street. He was by now well-established as a successful theatrical entrepreneur, having presented most of Gilbert and Sullivan's comic operas and having built The Savoy Theatre on The Strand to house them.

D'Oyly Carte's new theatre, designed by G.H. Holloway and T.E. Colcutt, was intended to house home-grown Grand Opera and the opening attraction was Sir Arthur Sullivan's only venture in that field, *Ivanhoe*. Based on Sir Walter Scott's novel, it ran for 155 performances and was followed by André Messager's *The Basoche*, but this failed and was followed by a season of French drama presented by Sarah Bernhardt and her company.

Unfortunately for D'Oyly, in less than two years from its opening his beautiful opera house was sold to a company headed by Sir Augustus Harris, of Drury Lane. After a few minor alterations, Harris reopened it as The Palace Theatre of Varieties on 10 December, 1892. However, the engagement of Charles Morton as Manager was necessary before the Palace was successful. From then until 1914 the new hall retained a reputation for providing the very best in entertainment. Morton had of course made his name at The Canterbury and, later, at The Oxford and was known as "The Father of The Halls"; when he died in 1904, the management passed to his assistant, Alfred Butt, who built on Morton's high standards until he departed in 1921, to take control of Drury Lane Theatre.

The Palace was to become one of the most famous Variety theatres in London and it was there, on 1 July, 1912 that the first Royal (and only truly 'Command') Performance was held, inspiring Oswald Stoll to declare: "The Cinderella of the Arts at last went to the Ball". In the presence of King George V and Queen Mary Variety became "respectable" and the beginning of the end of true 'music hall' began.

Most of the established stars of the halls appeared at the Palace on ordinary bills, as well as at the Command Performance – the likes of Gus Elen, Vesta Tilley, George Robey, Lottie Collins, G.H. Chirgwin, Herbert Campbell, Arthur Roberts, Albert Chevalier, Marie Lloyd, Little Tich and Harry Tate to name but a very few.

Numerous visitors from America, France and Australia were also engaged, including The Keatons (who caused great controversy in the press, as part of their act consisted of hurling their young son Buster at the scenery), Fanny Brice, Mistinguette, Gaby Deslys, W.C. Fields with his amazing juggling routines, Will Rogers, Yvette Guilbert and many more.

Various forms of dancing were always a main ingredient of the bill, including such "exotics" as Loïe Fuller and Maud Allan, who created a sensation with her *Vision of Salome* in 1908. Can Can dancers from The Moulin Rouge included Jane Avril, whilst John Tiller's Palace Girls were constant favourites. High points were reached with the engagements of Anna Pavlova for long seasons each year from 1910 to 1913 and Nijinsky the following year.

Interior showing part of the grand staircase

Over 1,200 different music hall bills are estimated to have been presented between 1892 and 1914, including, of course, a myriad speciality acts – ventriloquists, jugglers, acrobats, aerial artistes, illusionist and trick cyclists. Every type of animal act also appeared on the Palace stage, from elephants and monkeys to snakes, birds and crocodiles. Tableaux Vivants were popular, despite problems with moralistic vigilantes.

Herman Finck became Musical Director in 1900, a position he held for twenty years – having already been associated with the Palace as pianist, violinist and leader of the orchestra since it opened.

In 1914 the Variety format was abandoned, when the revue craze hit London, although for a time the evening commenced with two or three unrelated Variety acts, changing weekly, and was rounded off with the Bioscope. Successful Palace revues included *The Passing Show* (1914), which ran for 351 performances, Gertie Millar in *Bric-a-Brac* (1915) and *Vanity Fair* (1916). Maurice Chevalier made his first London appearance at the Palace in 1919.

Then, out of the blue in May, 1920 the theatre was bought by Sol Levy and C.B. Cochran, who opened it as a 'Luxury Cinema' in February, 1921 – incorporating a stage prologue. But, in spite of a massive hit with Rudolph Valentino in *Four Horsemen of the Apocalypse* in 1922 (it ran for a hitherto unprecedented 22 weeks), the project was abandoned and the Palace returned to full-time live use in 1923; although, as Allen Eyles and Keith Skone explained in *London's West End Cinemas* (1991), it was regularly used for day-time trade shows right up to the 1950s. MGM used it intermittently for premiere runs of special attractions: *Grand Hotel* (1932), *Dinner at Eight* (1933), *Gone With the Wind* (1940), etc. Alfred Butt's departure in 1920 was not quite as clear cut as it seemed on paper – as apparently it was he who lent £200,000 of the £345,000 he was asking for the freehold to one Sol Levy, who was anxious to acquire the Palace as a cinema to support his bid to become Britain's leading film exhibitor.

Levy had very ambitious, not to say complicated, ideas on film presentation and to help him achieve his aims he enlisted the help of C.B. Cochran as Chairman of the separate company he set up to run the Palace. Cochran's involvement meant that some of Levy's ambitions for spectacular film presentation could be achieved. It also meant that live shows also continued. Thus, early in 1921 Harry Lauder appeared for an eight week season supported by a weekly change of Variety bill, the second half of the evening being entirely devoted to a selection from his own extensive repertoire of songs.

Interior towards the stage

But by then the Palace had become home to a successful sequence of revues and musical comedies. Three of these were by that prolific team of R.P. Weston and Bert Lee, so brilliantly documented by Roy Hudd in *Just a Verse and Chorus* at Greenwich Theatre in 1981. Just a reminder of some of the songs they wrote – *I'm 'enery the Eighth, I am*; *The End of My Old Cigar*; *What a Mouth* – as they say, the true gold of music hall. Weston and Lee's shows at the Palace were *No, No, Nanette* (1925) which ran for 665 performances; *Princess Charming* (1926) and *The Girl Friend* (1927).

Other successes of the 1930s included *The Cat and the Fiddle*; Irene Vanbrugh in *Dinner at Eight*; Fred Astaire in Cole Porter's *Gay Divorce*, just before his departure for Hollywood; and C.B. Cochran's famous revue, *Streamline*. During the run Larry Adler made his London debut. Cole Porter's *Anything Goes* was only moderately successful, while Rodgers and Hart's *On Your Toes* transferred to The London Coliseum after a brief run. (The show was revived at the Palace in 1984 for a sixteen-month run). The highly popular comedy duo, Jack Hulbert and Cicely Courtneidge, were almost permanent residents at the Palace from 1938 to 1944 in their shows *Under Your Hat*, *Full Swing* and *Something In The Air*, the first with music by Vivian Ellis.

In September, 1940 bombing became so bad in London the The Palace Theatre was closed until July, 1941. During this period the old Shaftesbury Theatre, which stood opposite the Palace on Shaftesbury Avenue, was completely demolished by a direct hit; damage at the Palace was repaired and it reopened, when *Chu Chin Chow* returned from a forced tour.

Emile Littler had joined the board of The Palace Theatre in February, 1946, becoming Chairman on the retirement of C.B. Cochran two months later. Tom Arnold shared Littler's control of the theatre for five years. After some misfortunes, success returned in 1948 with *Carissima* and in 1949 *Lilac Time*, both shows starring Bruce Trent. Unfortunately, Ivor Novello died in 1951 during the run of the last show in which he starred as well as wrote, *King's Rhapsody*. Later that year George Formby made a big hit in *Zip Goes a Million*, Reg Dixon taking over during the star's illness. Anna Neagle held the stage in Robert Nesbitt's *Glorious Days* for most of Coronation Year, 1953.

From 1955 to 1957 Peter Daubeny presented one-off productions and International Seasons, anticipating his later World Theatre Seasons at The Aldwych Theatre. Other visitors included Les Compagnons de la Chanson, Antonio and his Spanish Ballet and Maurice Chevalier. For three months in 1955 John Gielgud and Peggy Ashcroft led The Shakespeare Memorial Theatre Company in *King Lear* and *Much Ado About Nothing*. After visits by Chinese and Spanish companies, Emile Littler broke new ground by presenting a pantomime.

For many years Emile Littler presented pantomimes all over the country and became known as 'The King of Pantomime', even having a pantomime factory in Birmingham. He presented only two at the Palace – in 1955/56 David Nixon starred in *Cinderella* and in 1956/57 George Formby was in *Dick Whittington*. Littler personally supervised every aspect of the pantomime and both of these bore the credit: 'written, presented and produced by Emile Littler'. His shows were praised for their domestic qualities.

At this time Littler was convinced that the theatre business was in decline and that the Palace, its fabric deteriorating, was ripe for redevelopment. The Palace Theatre was nearly lost, its site being earmarked for an hotel. As it happened, great prosperity lay ahead, but a glance through the records indicates that shows came and went with worrying regularity – in one case as many as a dozen in a single year. Around this time the Palace was sold to a finance company with a limited lease-back arrangement, half of which Littler sold to EMI: thus, Bernard Delfont gained joint-control of the theatre.

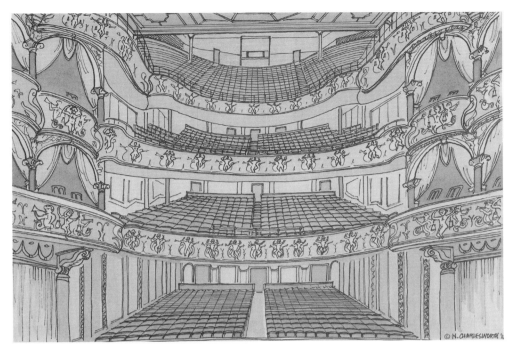

Interior towards the circles

Variety had returned briefly to the Palace in 1931, when C.B. Cochran presented The Marx Brothers, but they were not to the taste of Londoners at that time and no further attempts were made to present pure Variety at the theatre, although vaudeville performers such as Flanagan & Allen, Wilson, Keppel & Betty and Cyril Fletcher did appear here in musicals and revues.

For Variety fans the most important production of 1957 was John Osborne's *The Entertainer*, starring Laurence Olivier with Joan Plowright, which transferred from the Royal Court in September. For this show Olivier and Osborne did their preparations by attending Collins' Music Hall in Islington, by now in its penultimate year. The production at the Palace ran through to January, 1958, with a four-week break in November for a Soviet film season.

Variety, having regained a toe-hold (as it were) at the Palace with Osborne's satire, the real thing was back early in 1958, when Bernard Delfont presented a Season, headed by Frankie Vaughan. Also on the same bill were Petula Clark, Bernard Miles, Hetty King and Harry Worth, while the inclusion of one of Covent Garden's star ballerinas, Nadia Nerina, and The Tiller Girls were a happy throwback to earlier Palace traditions. Norman Wisdom then rocked the roof to its rafters in *Where's Charley?* – a musical version of *Charley's Aunt*.

Delfont presented a second Season of Variety in 1959, this time for ten weeks, with changes of bill every fortnight. I enjoyed a good bill topped by Johnnie Ray, supported by The Three Monarchs and Des O'Connor. Other headliners were Connie Francis (making a hit with *Stupid Cupid*); Alma Cogan; Lonnie Donegan and Max Miller, making his last London appearance, on a bill with Georges Ulmer and Oreste Kirkop.

I then had the good luck to see one of Benny Hill's infrequent live appearances there in *Fine Fettle* – 'a musical romp in cloth cap and tails' – in which his unlikely co-star was the immortal Robertson Hare, while Shani Wallis and Pip Hinton also shone.

In the 1960s the Palace echoed to the music of Rodgers and Hammerstein – first in *Flower Drum Song* and then in *The Sound of Music*, before Judi Dench invited us to the *Cabaret* 316 times. Betty Grable did an incredible job in keeping *Belle Starr* going against all the odds and Stanley Baxter mesmerised us in the much-underestimated musical *Phil the Fluter*. In *At The Palace* Danny la Rue held the stage in revue for two years, supported firstly by Roy Hudd and then Joe Church, before the modern musical well and truly took over there – *Jesus Christ Superstar* for the then staggering 3,358 performances.

Exterior view as a very successful musical theatre

A revival of *Oklahoma!* then filled-in successfully and enjoyably with a cast headed by the Australians John Diedrich and Madge Ryan. Another surprise success was *Song and Dance* – introduced as a stop-gap, it was eventually withdrawn after 795 performances. This was another 'modern' musical from the pen of Andrew Lloyd Webber. *Song* consisted of a series of inter-related songs (with lyrics by Don Black), presented in the form of a pop concert by Marti Webb; while *Dance* was a ballet performed by Wayne Sleep to 'Variations on a theme by Paganini' played by a group of 'cellists. During the run, Andrew Lloyd Webber bought The Palace Theatre. Another classic musical, *On Your Toes*, was revived before being withdrawn to allow for the arrival of *Les Misérables* in December, 1985. 'A fine, if somewhat downbeat, show' with little of the traditional musical comedy or Variety ethos, it is evidently popular with modern audiences, as it is still running!

In the meantime, the exterior of The Palace Theatre was rescued from its years of neglect and in 1989 was revealed again, when the lights came on in Cambridge Circus to the delight of all. Sir John Betjeman's heart would have been warmed, as it was he who described the building as 'the only theatre architecture of the last sixty years in London, or for that matter the provinces, which climbs into the region of a work of art'.

Prince of Wales Theatre

Coventry Street

Exterior of the old Prince of Wales building that was pulled down and rebuilt in 1937

The first theatre, designed by C.J. Phipps, was opened on 18 January, 1884 under the management of Edgar Bruce, who played in the curtain-raiser which preceded W.S. Gilbert's *The Palace of Truth*, in which Herbert Beerbohm Tree played the lead. Plays and comic opera each took their turn – Marie Tempest, Charles Hawtrey, John Martin-Harvey, Mrs. Patrick Campbell and Johnston Forbes-Robertson being frequent visitors. The Edwardian era saw numerous musical comedies, which increased the reputation of Paul Rubens; and after 1918 André Charlot presented a series of revues.

In the 1930s business was bad and the theatre was bought by Charles Clore, who in 1934 brought in Alfred Esdaile to manage it. In 1937 the old theatre where, like any right-thinking young man, I had attended the current revue *Encore Les Dames*, was demolished and rebuilt, the work being completed in nine months – the building industry was still efficient in 1937. The architect was the famous Robert Cromie, who produced a clever design. He managed to increase the capacity to 1,358 (now 1,133) with a large, comparatively shallow, balcony. This brings the audience seated there apparently right on top of the stage – ideal for viewing spectacular revues featuring scantily-clothed girls and solo performers of all sorts. It also works well for musicals and plays, incidentally.

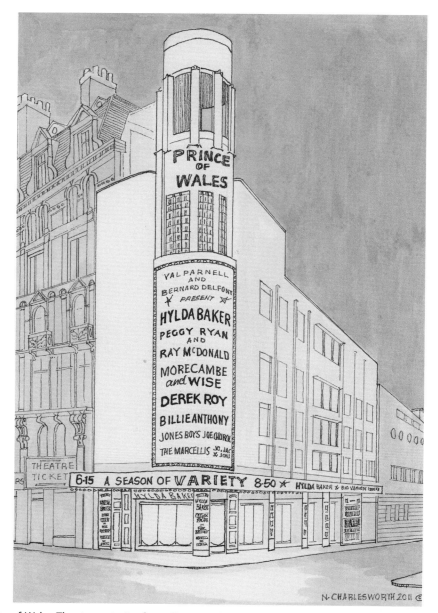

The Prince of Wales Theatre: exterior from Coventry Street, new building of 1937 with Hylda Baker billed

I had the pleasure of viewing the new theatre shortly after it opened. I tend to prefer the old to the new, but I am forced to say that this delightful auditorium is an improvement on its four-decker predecessor. With vastly improved stage and back-stage facilities, the first two revues surpassed even those at the old theatre.

Prince of Wales revues, such as *Caprice Parisienne* and *Revue Folies de Can-Can*, were splendid productions and each starred a comedian of the calibre of Ronald Frankau, Gillie Potter or Naunton Wayne. Other interesting features of the original 1937 building, for which Gracie Fields laid the foundation stone, were the absence of footlights (very unusual for the time) and the presence of a glass panel, illuminated from underneath, on which the chorus could promenade. This was an ideal arrangement for the revues now presented at what was billed as 'London's Folies Bergère'. Incidentally, after her efforts with the ceremonial trowel 'Our Gracie' climbed a ladder in wedge heels and tight skirts and sang to the workmen, equally insecurely balanced on the scaffolding. A typically impulsive gesture on her part.

The theatre returned to musical comedy with the wartime *Present Arms*, after which George Black took over, presenting *Happidrome* and the occasional Variety season. Typical bills were topped by Flanagan & Allen and Max Miller. In later years The Prince of Wales came under the direction of Moss' Empires Ltd., becoming their fourth West End showcase.

In 1943 the outstanding talent of Sid Field was belatedly recognised in the West End when the posters announced: George Black and the Younger Generation present *Strike a New Note*. Sid was so successful that they had to *Strike It Again* and, when peace returned, had to star as their hottest property in *Piccadilly Hayride* and the play *Harvey*. The latter ran for 610 performances, but unhappily Sid died during the run – he was a worrier and had taken to the bottle in an attempt to control his fears about holding his own in the business. He was mourned by both members of the legitimate and illegitimate sides of the business.

Although there are some films of old stars, it was usual in pre-TV days for a star's act to die with him; but luckily in Field's case his best material was documented in an otherwise routine musical, *London Town*.

During Sid Field's tenure straight Variety bills appeared spasmodically, of which this is a good example: Flanagan & Allen, Florence Desmond, Wilson, Keppel & Betty, Tommy Fields, Noni, Nita & Dody, Scott Sanders, Newman Twins, Artemus & Co., Bert Wright & Zena, and The Prince of Wales Dancers.

Interior of 1937, as it looked in 1972

After the American revue *Touch & Go* in 1950, spectacular Folies Bergère-style revues filled the bill for the next decade, with such stars as Frankie Howerd (*Pardon My French*), Norman Wisdom, Winifred Atwell, Tommy Trinder and Benny Hill. The sequence was broken by *The World of Suzie Wong* and Variety bills headed by, among others, Bob Hope, Nellie Lutcher and, in 1961, Sammy Davis jnr. Shirley Bassey also starred in the spectacular revue, *Blue Magic*.

Do-Re-Mi and *Come Blow Your Horn*, with Bob Monkhouse, had long runs until, in 1963, stage alterations were made preparatory to the opening of *Round About Piccadilly*, which scored 408 performances. It was also in 1963 that The Prince of Wales hosted the annual Royal Variety

Performance. These Performances always bring a new star, or group of stars, to the attention of a national TV audience: this was no exception, as it was a group called The Beatles who stole the show completely from Marlene Dietrich and Tommy Steele. For those interested in such things, they sung four songs – 'She Loves You', 'Till There Was You', 'From Me To You' and 'Twist and Shout'.

Barbra Streisand in *Funny Girl* was followed by a long-running revue, *Way Out In Piccadilly* in 1966. The next big success was *Sweet Charity* (484 performances), followed by a Feydeau farce and the long-running *Promises, Promises*. Bruce Forsyth appeared in *Little Me*, but not much happened until Anthony Newley opened in his own show, *The Good Old Bad Old Days*, in 1973. This was followed by *The Danny La Rue Show* and then by James Stewart in a revival of *Harvey*, which seemed a much bleaker play than it did with Sid Field.

Various short-lived plays and musicals were staged before Tommy Steele appeared at The Prince of Wales at the peak of his career in 1979. Roy Hudd brought his wonderful tribute to Flanagan & Allen here in 1982: this was *Underneath The Arches*, which had been staged at The Chichester Festival Theatre. However, the usual fare has not been Variety but musicals, such as Andrew Lloyd Webber's *Aspects of Love*.

Important alterations were being made to improve the theatre as we went to press, including better circulation areas and more exit doors, so the theatre has now been fully restored to its 1930s glory.

Marlene Dietrich, who was here in a Royal Variety Performance

Stoll Theatre

Kingsway, corner of Portugal Street

The Stoll Theatre: exterior on Kingsway (former London Opera House) with Rawicz & Landauer billed

This huge theatre, with its 52 private boxes (many positioned under the dress circle) and capacity of nearly 2,200 opened in November, 1911 as The London Opera House. It was promoted by Oscar Hammerstein II, who had already built several enormous theatres in New York. Intended for Grand Opera, the new theatre – designed by Bertie Crewe – was certainly that. It had a 272ft frontage to Kingsway and an auditorium that was both sumptuous and cavernous.

The Grand Opera season opened with *Quo Vadis*, but within a year it became apparent that Covent Garden held an unassailable position in London and the vast new opera house failed, like The Royal English Opera House (the Palace Theatre) before it. It went over to lighter entertainment with a revue, *Come Over Here*, which included a sensational scene where a car raced a train on stage. The pantomime which followed the revue was not a success, nor was the patriotic drama, *England Expects*, staged early in WW1. The excellently-equipped theatre tried further revues and Variety seasons, but it closed for long periods and only came into its own when bought by Oswald Stoll and reopened as a cinema in April, 1917.

The newly-named Stoll Picture Theatre became a very successful cinema, popular with families, for the next two decades. Its current films were prominently advertised in programmes at the Alhambra and London Coliseum, as well as those of the four Stoll Variety theatres in the London suburbs. There were still live acts to be seen between films. Sunday concerts were often presented as well, such as one with Mantovani and his Radio Orchestra.

Losses on the film operation started in 1936, but the Stoll continued as a cinema until the blitz forced closure in September, 1940. Sir Oswald Stoll, as he now was, had presented *The Merry Doll* two years earlier, but it was not particularly successful. Stoll died in January, 1942, with Prince Littler taking over his empire and returning the big theatre to the live fold. In 1942 Littler started a regular Variety season, but, possibly unsure of its reception, he still called the house 'The Stoll Picture Theatre'

Interior of the Stoll Theatre

The bill for the week commencing Monday, 6 April, 1942 seems to have been a happy mixture of new and old artistes. Rosie & Alice Lloyd and Billy Bennett from earlier years joined newer acts, such as 'The Jolly Americans', Nelson Clifford & Marie Marion, with Billy Cotton and his Band topping. Strong support came from Scott & Foster, Earle Bros. & Josephine ('Hot from Harlem'), and Chow Ding, a 'Chinese Wonder'. Jack Frere directed The Stoll Theatre Orchestra. West End prices applied of course – from 5s in the orchestra stalls to 1s 3d in the balcony.

The former bandleader turned impresario, Jack Hylton, became closely associated with the reopened Stoll, presenting many shows there. Various fugitives from The Crazy Gang featured in his shows, before and between their long runs at The Victoria Palace. *Hi-Di-Hi* was one of his "named" Variety bills during the war, with Flanagan & Allen, the impressionist Florence Desmond, the opera singer Gwen Catley, and "Monsewer" Eddie Gray showcased. Over the 1945 Christmas season Londoners enjoyed Hylton's *For Crying Out Loud*, which had Nervo & Knox, Billy Caryll & Hilda Mundy, and Will Hay in the twice daily production. Later, Naughton & Gold and Charlie Kunz headlined in Leslie Grade and George A. Smith's show, *To See Such Fun*. This also featured London's Dancing Stars, Gold & Cordell. Back from the war, serving men and women were avid for live entertainment and for two weeks in the summer of 1945 Hylton presented the Aircrew ex-P.O.W.s Revue, *Back Home*, which played nightly at 6.30 with three matinees.

A period as London's Ice Theatre began in 1948 with Tom Arnold's *Stars on Ice*. His second production was *Ice Revue*. There were usually twenty items in the programme, but wedged between the two intervals was a miniature Variety show, when we were invited to an 'International Cabaret'. Manley & Austin proved that 'Music Hath Charms', before we were entertained by Ted Ray. Finally, Arren & Broderick gave us *Opera in the Ruff*. In his own spot early in the show was our old friend Topper Martyn, in *Putting on the Top Hat*. A programme note on *19th Century Ball*, in the Third Act, told us that "the dresses worn in this scene are made of Irish Linen. The linen has been supplied by members of The Irish Guild of Belfast". This was clearly a boost for the province's economy in those early post-war years.

Stoll Theatre (the new Royalty Theatre), exterior

We were able to enjoy a number of Variety artistes in the third of the series, which was Tom Arnold's *Ice Vogues*. Cecilia Colledge again starred on the ice, but highlights for us were Richard Hearne's two spots. His well-loved *Lancers* never failed to captivate, but he also appeared as The Grand Prince in *Neapolitan Carnival*. Recalled to the Stoll, Ted Ray's spot was named after his current radio success, *Ray's a Laugh* and had his 'Radio Wife' Kitty Bluett. Also in this segment were Bob & Alf Pearson ('My Brother & I') and The Marie des Anges Quintette. The show had a skating chorus of 23 ladies and ten gentlemen. The Stoll Theatre Orchestra was directed by Reginald Swinney, with the show going on at 6.00 and 8.30pm.

The big Stoll was not an easy theatre to programme, or to fill. In the public's mind, Kingsway was slightly remote from the West End, particularly since a number of neighbouring theatres had gone; the Holborn Empire and the Kingsway Theatre had been lost in the blitz, while both the Gaiety and the Lyceum had closed for demolition in 1939. Even the Aldwych Theatre had been threatened in the 1950s. The centre of live theatre life was continuing to move westwards. However, Prince Littler persevered. There was a ballet season in 1950, when Julian Braunsweg presented The Festival Ballet, which included Alicia Markova and Anton Dolin. In 1954 came Jack Hylton's production of *Joan of Arc at the Stake*, and a season by The Ballet Rambert.

The Stoll was also used for big musicals to complete their London runs, freeing their main houses for incoming shows. One big show here was *Kismet*, a musical Arabian Nights based on themes by Borodin and – once again – presented by Jack Hylton, in 1956. The musical starred Alfred Drake and was a popular success. *Noddy in Toyland* was the children's show over that Christmas season for matinees.

Stoll Theatre (the new Royalty Theatre, built on part of the site), interior at opening

By the late 1950s the theatre business was becoming critical and a number of big houses went over to other forms of entertainment – The London Coliseum and London Casino to films and The London Hippodrome to Dinner, Dancing and Cabaret. The Palace nearly became an hotel. It was decided to close the Stoll, which had become something of a liability, and sell the site for office development. Prince Littler blamed the high rate of Entertainments Tax, the Stoll having paid over £100,000 to the Exchequer over the two years of 1955 and 1956. A large hoarding stating these figures appeared outside the theatre.

The final production was Shakespeare's *Titus Andronicus*, just returned from a triumphant European tour after opening at the Shakespeare Memorial Theatre, Stratford-upon-Avon in 1955. Directed by Peter Brook and starring Laurence Olivier and Vivien Leigh, it played to standing room only for its whole run, proving that audiences would go to the Stoll if there was something or someone there they really wanted to see. Closing on 4 August, 1957 it was soon just a very large hole in the ground. Had it survived a few more years, the Stoll would have been a great asset in today's era of long-running blockbuster musicals.

Following the tragic loss of the St. James's Theatre, also in 1957, the L.C.C. had introduced a new regulation forcing developers to include a theatre in any new building erected on a former theatre-site. The Royalty Theatre, designed by Lewis Solomon, Kay & Partners, was therefore built in part of the basement of the new office block. Opening on 23 June, 1960 it has had as varied a life as its predecessor, including providing a home for *Oh, Calcutta!*, an all-male revue *Birds of a Feather* – which introduced Larry Grayson (not in drag) to London – and a Paul Raymond show, *The Royalty Follies*. It has been bought by the nearby London School of Economics, who planned to run it as an adjacent lecture hall/theatre, so its future was lively. After renovation, the theatre re-opened under a new name – The Peacock Theatre, with links to Sadler's Wells Theatre.

Tivoli Theatre of Varieties

65–70½, The Strand

The Tivoli Theatre: exterior

On the site of the Tivoli Beer Gardens and Restaurant, which had opened in 1876, was erected a larger building comprising the Tivoli Theatre of Varieties and its Restaurant. The latter included the Palm Room and Flemish Room on the first and second floors and on the third floor a series of private dining rooms and a Masonic Room. The total cost of the building and site was over £¼ million. The theatre opened on 24 May, 1890.

Crowds gathered in The Strand outside for the official opening, when the opening bill included Vesta Tilley, G.W. Kenway, Jennie Williams, Florrie Leybourne, Kate Chard, J.W. (Over) Rowley, Millie Hylton, Sam Redfern, Sam Torr, The Bohee Boys, Tom Costello, Parker's Dogs and Harry Freeman. In the succeeding weeks the following great stars appeared: Charles Godfrey, Harry Randall, Harriet Vernon, Jolly John Nash, Arthur Lloyd, Lottie Collins, Billie Barlow, Albert Chevalier, Herbert Campbell, Harry Champion and Charles Chaplin, whose son was to appear there later. There were, withal, two young ladies destined for stardom: Vesta Victoria and Marie Lloyd.

Less than a year after opening business had declined and the theatre was put up for sale. The new Directorate of Colonel Newson Smith and G. Adney Payne approached Charles Morton to revive the theatre's fortunes and called in Frank Matcham to make structural alterations. Morton negotiated a booking arrangement with the London Pavilion and the Oxford, which was the foundation of the London Syndicate Halls.

Tivoli Theatre exterior, close-up

The Tivoli re-opened on 6 July, 1891, and among the twenty-five (yes, twenty-five) acts on the opening bill were Jenny Hill, Ada Reeve, Lydia Yeamans ('*Sally in Our Alley*'), Bessie Bellwood, George Beauchamp and the Jonghmanns Sisters. Business thrived, and Sandow (the Strongman) was engaged at a record £150 weekly. 1892 saw Lottie Collins introduce '*Ta-ra-ra-boom-de-ay*'.

While 1893 saw two newcomers – Gus Elen and George Robey – as well as Auguste Van Biene of '*Broken Melody*' fame, Paul Cinquevalli, Will Evans and the Sisters Duncan. And in 1894, when the Parisian star Jane May made her London debut, the Prince of Wales was present. Charles Morton having revitalized the Tivoli, transferred to the Palace, where he remained until his death in 1904, his place at the Strand hall being taken by his former assistant Vernon Dowsett.

Other tops at the Tivoli in the late 1890s were Joe Elvin, Bransby Williams and Lil Hawthorne, and a 'spesh' that was still working in the 1950s, Duncan's Scotch Collies. Charles Godfrey, with his patriotic and thrilling historical scenas, was a great favourite until his sad death in 1900. In addition, Florrie Forde, Wilkie Bard, T.E. Dunville and Ernest Shand all appeared before the century ended. While on Mafeking Night Ethel Levey, then aged 18, made an un-programmed appearance, but it was not until 1908 that she made her official debut at the Alhambra.

There were one or two unusual 'acts', for example the New Year's bill was headed by Rossi Ashton, the War Correspondent, who related his experiences in the Boer War, with illustrations and the Countess Russell, who had a rather unsavoury divorce case.

In 1901, with Marie Lloyd topping, Harry Lauder had a ten-minute spot and sang '*Killiecrankie*' and '*Tobermory*' with such success that a fortnight later he was accorded star billing. When Queen Victoria died the same year Bessie Bonehill introduced a new National Anthem which, despite its enthusiastic reception, passed into oblivion.

Interior looking towards the stage

R.G. Knowles, having played a record sixty-eight weeks, announced his retirement, which eventually materialised over a decade later. Marie Loftus, Queenie Leighton and Kate Carney were popular on the distaff side, as were the two Dutch rivals, Happy Fanny Fields and May Moore Duprez. Four newcomers who were to appear half a century later in *Thanks for the Memory* were Nellie Wallace, Gertie Gitana, G.H. Elliott and Hetty King. At the same time two long-lived sketches were being launched: Harry Tate's *Motoring* and Charles Austin's *Parker P.C.*

Other early stars at the Tivoli included Whit Cunliffe, Harry Weldon, George Formby, Sam Mayo, George Lashwood, Franco Piper and James Fawn (who was on the stage for sixty years). Of concerted items Pelissier's *Follies* were a recurring attraction, and of magicians Chung Ling Soo was outstanding.

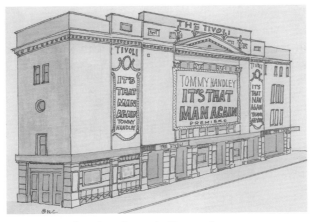
Exterior when rebuilt as a cinema

December, 1904 brought the Tivoli additional competition from the Lyceum, newly rebuilt as a Variety theatre and – fatally – the Coliseum. One of its biggest successes was Fragson, who in 1906 received £250 per week and stayed for fifteen weeks. Ladies who topped bills were Clarice Mayne, Daisy Dormer and Maidie Scott, while their male colleagues included Alfred Lester, Arthur Roberts and Neil Kenyon. Specialities of note were The Jackson Family of Cyclists and The Elliott Savonas, later The Musical Elliotts, relatives of whom were still working in the 1950s.

Interior when rebuilt as Tivoli Cinema after 1928 alterations

By 1910 Ragtime had become established, its finest exponents being The Two Bobs, Harry Williams & Nat D. Ayer, and The Hedges Brothers & Jacobson. Stars of the Tivoli's final years included Carlton, Malcolm Scott, Johnson Clarke, Jack Pleasants, Georgie Wood, Tom Clare, Dora Lyric, Betty Barclay and Beattie & Babs. One must not forget George Gray's long-running sketch, *The Fighting Parson*.

In 1914 the Tivoli had to close for purposes of road widening, but the site remained vacant until 1923 when part of it was redeveloped as The Tivoli Cinema – itself demolished in 1957.

Trocadero Music Hall

Great Windmill Street

The Trocadero Theatre of Varieties: exterior of the old building on the site

In Great Windmill Street was built in 1744 a tennis court and vaults which were used for miscellaneous entertainments. Later the premises were reconstructed as the Argyll Subscription Rooms, opened in 1849 under the management of Robert Bignell. Here 'soirees musicales et dansantes' took place nightly, but the place was little more than an up-market brothel and was frequently threatened with closure. When the blow eventually fell he tried to run the place as a restaurant and billiard saloon, but without success. Then he hit upon the idea of converting it to a music-hall. With a seating capacity of 600 the Trocadero opened on 30 October, 1882.

Reviewing the opening performance The Era commented on the comfort and amenities of the refurbished building and the excellence of the orchestra. Following the singing of the National Anthem by Alexander Lumsden ('The Sims Reeves of the music-halls'), Ferdinand Jonghmans sang *'The Gallants of England'* and the Toreador Song from *Carmen*. Another fine singer was J.H. Milburn (*'Romping in the Clover'*) and there were many specialities including Marie Gilchrist in her transformation dances, The Three Brothers Le Fre and The Kellino Troupe of acrobats. But the best-remembered on that lengthy bill was Marie Loftus. The manager was H. Hart and the musical director A.A. Asher.

After its promising opening the hall did not prosper, apart from the fourteen months in 1886 when Charles Coborn sang *'Two Lovely Black Eyes'* almost incessantly. In 1888 Bignell died and Sam Adams, from the 'Pav', took over. When he too died, Hugh Jay Didcott and Albert Chevalier took over until 1894, when their company went bankrupt and they closed. In 1895 Bignell's daughter sold the lease to J. Lyons & Co., who bought other adjoining premises and created the Trocadero Restaurant, with its entrance in Shaftesbury Avenue.

During the 1920s the Trocadero pioneered supper-time revues presented by C.B. Cochran under the title 'Trocabaret'. They included Variety acts and Mr. Cochran's Young Ladies. Massine danced there, Anna Neagle was discovered, and such old-time favourites as Charles Coborn and Wilkie Bard celebrated the restaurant's 40th anniversary.

When entertainment declined in the 1950s Mecca bought the lease and reopened it as Tiffany's, to which was added a casino and bowling alley. They couldn't even think of an original name for it. During the 1970s it began a steady decline and the change of ownership to the Brent Walker organisation did nothing to help. They did start to make alterations but they ground to a halt and eventually the receivers were summoned.

Recently an entrepreneur by the name of Nigel Wray paid £94 million for the site and he has begun working on transforming the property into a massive cinema/computer games and shopping centre with, unfortunately, no space at all for live entertainment!

TROCADERO PALACE OF VARIETIES,

SHAFTESBURY AVENUE, W.

Manager and Treasurer -   -   -   -   ..   Mr WALTER HEHL.

ALWAYS A FIRST-CLASS COMPANY.

Open every Evening at **7.30.**   Commence at **8.**

THE MOST LUXURIOUS AND COMFORTABLE CONCERT THEATRE IN THE METROPOLIS.

Prices from 6d to One Guinea.

Victoria Palace

Victoria Street, opposite Victoria Station

The Royal Standard Music Hall: exterior with a 1908 bill with Billy Williams billed

In 1840 John Moy, proprietor of a tavern at which Harmonic Meetings were held, obtained a music and dancing licence. He enlarged the premises and presented regular Music Hall bills. Gradually a more structured form of entertainment evolved, with the room becoming known as Moy's Music Hall. In 1863 his successor, Robert Brown, reconditioned the hall and reopened it as The Royal Standard Music Hall, its stage jutting into a room on the first floor. Three years later, on the arrival of Victoria Station, it was entirely rebuilt by a new owner, with electric lighting and a handsome grill room being installed. The last owner, Thomas S. Dickie, took over in 1896. In 1910 he sold Alfred Butt what was then the oldest premises to hold a music hall licence in London.

As it had been strongly been criticised on safety grounds, Alfred Butt demolished the old Royal Standard and engaged Frank Matcham to rebuild a new theatre. The 1,565-capacity theatre has an imposing white patent stone exterior of classical design, topped with statues and a tower. This was originally crowned by the figure of Pavlova, but this was removed, so it is said, 'for safety' during WW2 and was sadly not seen again. The new theatre, costing £12,000 (half the cost of The Palladium) opened on 6 November, 1911 with a Variety bill including Lizzie Glenroy, Betty Barclay and Herbert Sleath & Co. in a one-act playlet, *The Deputy Sheriff*.

Interior of The Royal Standard Music Hall

Subsequently, all the famous names of the music hall took the stage, as well as luminaries of the 'legit' – like the matinee idol, Owen Nares. Artistes found the Victoria Palace audience to be one of the most relaxed and friendly in London. The bill for the week of 21 June, 1915 included Oscar Ashe & Lily Brayton, The Harlequinaders, the great Will Rogers, Dale & O'Malley, Wilson Hallett, Lily Hayes, Jack Sheridan and Van Dock. The following week one could have seen Phyllis Dare, Arnold De Biere, Tucker (the singing violinist), Frank & Vesta, Jock Whiteford, Arthur Ferris, Millie Ickson and The Jenkins Brothers.

Straight Variety was the order of the day, while the Christmas attraction for many years was *The Windmill Man*, with Bert Coote. In 1920 Alfred Butt was joined in management by R.H. Gillespie. A representative bill for the week of 22 February, 1926 offered Harry Lauder, Doris Dene, Hope Charteris & Eve Dickson, The Victoria Girls, Leslie Strange, Four Lafettes, Farlane & Mai and Jack Le Dair. A month later one could have seen Clarice Mayne, Wilkie Bard, Lillian Burgess and Gillie Potter in a strong bill. In 1929 Gillespie introduced revue to the Victoria Palace, with Gracie Fields in *The Show's the Thing*. A series of other revues followed, notably *The Chelsea Follies*.

In 1932 Charles Gulliver joined Gillespie on the board and by this time the fare had diversified somewhat, including the serious play that everyone laughed at, *Young England*. Gulliver was soon replaced by George Black, however, and Variety returned. Jack Hylton was later to present The Crazy Gang at this same theatre.

Seymour Hicks presented a season of plays in 1935, then Kurt Robitschek's revue, *Let's Raise the Curtain*, brought Florence Desmond, Elizabeth Welch and George Gee. When I mentioned to Miss Welch that I had seen this production on my first visit to the Victoria Palace, she confided that the cast knew their employer as 'Kurt Rubbercheck'. Another of his three revues was *All Fun and Folly*, with a big company that included Bebe Daniels & Ben Lyon, Nellie Wallace, Oliver Wakefield (The Voice of Inexperience), Dick Henderson, Lalace 'The Famous Aerialist', as well as Sherkot 'The Famous Goalkeeper'! The show was twice nightly at 6.30 and 9.00pm, with matinees on Wednesdays and Saturdays.

In 1937 *Me & My Girl* began its phenomenal run of 1,046 performances with the effervescent Lupino Lane, the most attractive Teddie St. Denis and George Graves. The most notable wartime show was George Black's *Black Vanities*, while Lupino Lane returned to that stage in a rare pantomime, *Babes in The Wood*, co-starring with Adele Dixon and Polly Ward.

Exterior of Victoria Palace, showing main entrance, with statue of Pavlova (and a 1926 bill)

In 1947 The Crazy Gang, up to that time connected with The Palladium, took possession of the Victoria Palace until 1962, their spirit still evident in this happiest of Variety theatres. The Gang had distilled itself into two doubles and two singles by this time: Nervo & Knox, Naughton & Gold, Eddie Gray and – their leader, Bud Flanagan. His partner, Chesney Allen, having had to take early retirement due to ill-health was running Reeves & Lamport theatrical agency. With interludes for short runs of other productions, including Jack Hylton's *Snow White & The Seven Dwarfs* in 1949 (one of thirty-three pantomimes in London that year), The Gang's shows were *Together Again*, *Knights of Madness*, *Ring Out The Bells*, *Jokers Wild*, *These Foolish Kings* and *Clown Jewels*. After an interlude for *Podrecca's Piccoli Theatre* and *Rose Marie* with David Whitfield, The Crazy Gang's final show was *Young In Heart*, after which most of them retired. Bud Flanagan commented in the last programme – "Retiring – the tread's gone". As The Crazy Gang's last night crashed to an end at around midnight on 19 May, 1962, one of the last bastions of British music hall crumbled. One of two of The Gang continued in pantomime for a few years, but an era had ended. The Gang's shows gave opportunities to many other Variety artistes, whose acts were interspersed between The Gang's own manic activities.

Productions seen in between The Crazy Gang's shows had included *Friends & Neighbours*, with Valentine Dyall, Glenn Melvyn and Danny Ross, as well as a give-away show, *Pot Luck*, hosted by Charlie Chester and panned by the critics. However, the Victoria Palace was to enjoy another long run, when *The Black & White Minstrel Show* opened. This fast-moving stage version of the television success, again employing Variety artistes such as comics, musical acts and ventriloquists, achieved an outstanding run of 4,344 performances, to be followed by its successor, *The Magic of The Minstrels*; these shows ran for around eight years until 1970.

Victoria Palace, interior looking towards the circles

Max Bygraves and his Variety company filled The Victoria Palace in 1972 while *Carry on London* with Sid James, Barbara Windsor, Kenneth Connor, Bernard Bresslaw, Jack Douglas and Peter Butterworth was just the show for this theatre. Pantomime also returned with stars such as Arthur Lowe and John Inman, while Basil Brush headed a variety-Revue, *Boom! Boom!* – surely one of the few times that a bill has been topped by a dummy on his own!

Proscenium arch dressed for 'The Black & White Minstrel Show'

Since then the Victoria Palace has been forced to follow the pattern of its sister Variety house, the London Palladium, and the stage has been occupied by *Annie*, which ran for three years, *Windy City* with Dennis Waterman, an Ice Spectacular, the musical *Sweet Charity* and the long-running *Buddy*, the story of Buddy Holly. Under the direction of Moss' Empires for many years, the Victoria Palace is now in the hands of Sir Stephen Waley-Cohen who has carried out a whole series of improvements, including most recently a new Dressing Room block. Excitingly, the figure of Pavlova has been gloriously restored to its rightful place on the tower. The current success is *Billy Elliott*.

ROYAL STANDARD MUSIC HALL,

ESTABLISHED OVER 50 YEARS.

OPPOSITE VICTORIA STATION, S.W.

Sole Proprietor and Manager - - - R. WAKE.

The above HALL is now one of the Best in London.   New and Enlarged Stage.   Luxurious Private Boxes and Stalls.

OPEN EVERY EVENING WITH THE MOST POWERFUL COMPANY IN LONDON.

A CONSTANT CHANGE EVERY WEEK.

REFRESHMENTS of the FINEST QUALITY.

POPULAR PRICES OF ADMISSION.

Basil Brush topping the bill in *Boom! Boom!*

Windmill Theatre

Great Windmill Street, Shaftesbury Avenue

The Windmill Theatre: exterior

Tucked away in a side street, this 322-seater theatre is on a site occupied from Charles II's time until late 18th Century by one of those handsome buildings that give it its name. One of the first West End cinemas, the Palais de Luxe opened here in December, 1909. Surrounded by bigger and better cinemas, it did not succeed and was bought by Mrs. Laura Henderson, who, with her associates, converted it into a theatre, remodelling its exterior on the style of a real mill.

The opening play *Inquest* on 22 June, 1931 was only a mild success and soon films returned. Then Mrs. Henderson gave her manager Vivian Van Damm carte blanche to try and help the depressed Variety profession by bringing back live entertainment. Van Damm brought in an American manager, Teddy Elbin, who suggested a British version of American burlesque.

On 3 February, 1932 *Revudeville* – continuous non-stop Variety like that already practised in Paris – was launched and was an instant success. The show ran from 2.30 to 11pm, but at first the prices were too low for it to pay; but with increased prices and reputation the corner was turned and the theatre was a commercial success. During the war it remained open continually, apart from twelve days of compulsory closure in 1939, and proudly boasted – "We Never Closed". During the worst nights of the blitz beleaguered artistes often slept in the theatre.

After the death of Mrs. Henderson, Van Damm and his daughter Sheila carried on the business, and after 1945 they were responsible for giving their first chance to scores of young aspirants. It was the only theatre consistently offering this service. For decades a roll of honour outside the 'Mill' recorded the beginners who had 'arrived'. Unfortunately, since Sheila Van Damm had to relinquish the theatre in the face of competition from more explicit nudity, some later owner has had the board removed. For the record, the future stars who were blooded at the 'Mill' included Kenneth More, Alfred Marks, Harry Secombe, Michael Bentine, George Martin, Jimmy Edwards and Arthur English.

Van Damm (the girls called him V.D.) was, like his opposite number Alfred Esdaile at The Prince of Wales, a producer of talent and taste. His shows always contained a strong element of subtle humour. I remember a trio of gigolos who sang:

> *"We're the chaps who sit around all day,*
>
> *And look like tailors' dummies,*
>
> *Hoping all the time that fate*
>
> *Will send us sugar mummies"*

I should not have remembered these lyrics if my mind had been centred *entirely* on the nudes!

Interior from the circle

The pattern of the Windmill shows did not change during the theatre's thirty-year run of *Revudeville*. The cast of about a score was accompanied by a seven-piece orchestra. There were several well-choreographed production numbers in each programme, the immobile nudes lending glamour to most of them. The comedy was sophisticated – too clever for many of the audience. It is an unfortunate fact that most males went only to see the nudes, and when early-comers left the auditorium there took place the notorious steeplechase of men moving forward to closer seats.

In the face of more explicit nudity all around, the last *Revudeville* closed on 31 October, 1964. Some of the Windmill Girls toured the Tivoli Circuit in Australia a year or so later in *The Windmill Revue*, together with a number of good specialities. Like so many of my favourite theatres, the Windmill became a cinema, and unfortunately like many of its suburban and provincial contemporaries specialised in 'X' films. Attendances gradually declined and there was talk of a buy-out by a group of ex-Windmill Girls to prevent its becoming yet another strip joint. But this failed and it was purchased in 1974 by the King of Soho, Paul Raymond who, after spending some £200,000 on cleaning the place up, reopened it with one of his typically-titled shows – *Rip Off*.

Raymond closed it in 1982 and reopened it after a £1,250,000 re-fit as a dinner-theatre, La Vie En Rose. The opening show on 9 January, 1983 was *Bizarre*, in which to meet the even more 'sophisticated' demands of the day, the shapely girls were joined by equally shapely men in drag. Somewhat surprisingly, there was no nudity! This project soon failed and La Vie En Rose closed in 1985.

After another expensive re-vamp, it reopened as Paramount City on 30 April, 1986 with a Variety show headed by Hale & Pace. It was also used as a TV studio – Derek Jameson's *Sky TV Show* came from there. This one lasted until 1995 when it changed use yet again and, after one more make-over, became Big Country – 'London's First Country & Western Saloon'. When I passed the theatre the famous frontage bore three signs: Big Country, Paramount City and The Windmill Theatre. More recently the venue has become a 'Gentleman's Club'.

The West End Halls

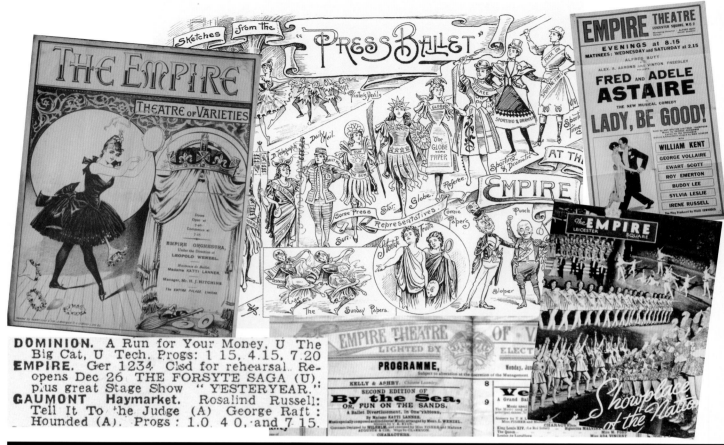

DOMINION. A Run for Your Money, U The Big Cat, U Tech. Progs: 1 15, 4.15, 7.20
EMPIRE. Ger 1234. Clsd for rehearsal. Reopens Dec 26 THE FORSYTE SAGA (U), plus great Stage Show "YESTERYEAR."
GAUMONT Haymarket. Rosalind Russell: Tell It To the Judge (A) George Raft: Hounded (A). Progs: 1.0 4 0, and 7.15.

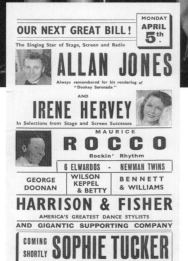

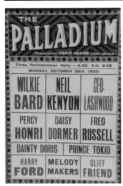

WINTER
GARDEN

Evening 7-45
TUESDAY
Nov. 4

DRESS
CIRCLE
14/6 Inc. Tax

A22

To be Retained

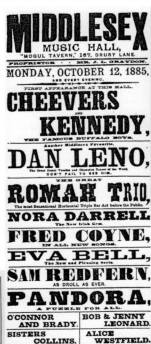

MIDDLESEX
MUSIC HALL,
"MOGUL TAVERN," 167, DRURY LANE.
PROPRIETOR · · MR. J. L. GRAYDON.
MONDAY, OCTOBER 12, 1885,
AND EVERY EVENING.
FIRST APPEARANCE AT THIS HALL.

CHEEVERS
AND
KENNEDY,
THE FAMOUS BUFFALO BOYS.
Another Middlesex Favourite.

DAN LENO,
The Great Comic Vocalist and Champion Dancer of the World.
DON'T FAIL TO SEE HIM.
THE GREAT

ROMAH TRIO,
The most Sensational Horizontal Triple Bar Act before the Public.

NORA DARRELL,
The New Irish Gem.

FRED COYNE,
IN ALL NEW SONGS.

EVA BELL,
The New and Pleasing Serio.

SAM REDFERN,
AS DROLL AS EVER.

PANDORA,
A PUZZLE FOR ALL.

O'CONNOR | BOB & JENNY
AND BRADY. | LEONARD.
SISTERS | ALICE
COLLINS. | WESTFIELD.

BROS. HARRISON,
The Clever Little Variety Artistes and Dancers.

MONDAY NEXT, OCTOBER 19th,
First Time at this Hall. A Sensational Entertainment, entitled THE

BRIDGE!
By POLLY RANDALL, CHARLES WILFORD, and
EDIE FRENCH.
ENTIRE NEW SCENERY.
CHAIRMAN · MR. GUS. LEACH.

ARCHIE PITT   GRACIE FIELDS   TOMMY FIELDS

Three of the many stars in "THE SHOW'S THE THING,"
the New Musical Production, now at the WINTER GARDEN Theatre, Drury Lane.

GRAND EASTER PROGRAMME.

For the week ending Saturday, May 9th, 1891.

NOTICE.

The Number on each side of the Stage corresponds
with that in the Programme.

1	Overture - - "Guy Mannering" - Sir H. R. Bishop
2	JEANNIE VENOI — Ballad Vocalist.
3	GEORGE LEYTON — Characteristic Comedian.
4	THE MAYNE QUARTETTE — In their Charming Entertainment.
5	J. MANHILL — Funny Patterer.
6	TENNYSON & O'GORMAN — Eccentric Comedians.
7	JEAN ROLLON — The All-Round Athlete in his Marvellous Athletic Performance. Combining the Skill and Suppleness of the Greatest Gymnast to the Strength of a Modern Hercules.
8	ELSA JOEL — Bravura Soprano. Miss JOEL and Mr. CURTIS D'ALTON will Sing "What are the Wild Waves Saying?"
9	BELLE BLACK — Vocalist.

WEAR
DUNN'S
FAMOUS HATS,
ALL ONE PRICE,
3/9
Latest Shapes   Newest Colours.

7, Tottenham Court Road.
(opposite the Horse Shoe).
Branches:— 259, Edgware Road.
32, Liverpool Street.
27, Eastcheap.
28, Stoke Newington Road.

The Oxford Programme

THE OXFORD

EVERY EVENING &
SATURDAY MATINEES.

10	CURTIS D'ALTON — The Eminent Baritone, will sing the following : "Sons of England," "Hunting," and "That Awful Ye Ho," by Ed. St. Quinten.
11	MISS MARIE LLOYD — The charming Serio-Comic Vocalist and Dancer.
12	CHARLES COBORN — The Celebrated Comedian and Vocalist.
13	HARRIETT VERNON — The Popular Favourite.
14	ZÆO
15	FLORRIE LEYBOURNE — Serio Comique.
16	DAN LENO — The Inimitable.
17	VIOLET HARLEY — Serio Comique.
18	LOTTO, LILLO & OTTO — Bicyclists.
19	FREDERICKS & DREW — Knockabouts and Dancers

Conductor of the Orchestra   ...   .   Mr. E. BOSANQUET

Open at 7.30, Commence at 8.

Grand Morning Performance every Saturday at 2.30.

Sole Manager, Mr. C. R. BRIGHTEN

The order of this Programme is liable to alteration.

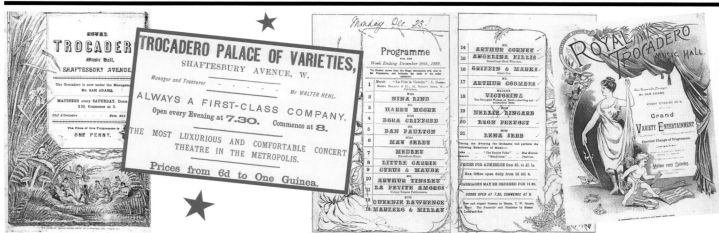

WINDMILL THEATRE

Licensed by the Lord Chamberlain to Mrs. LAURA HENDERSON

HOLD UP WHEN AUDITORIUM LIGHTS ARE OUT

"GLOWGRAMME"

REVUDEVILLE 95th EDITION

1. **OVERTURE**
WINDMILL THEATRE ORCHESTRA
(Under the direction of Alan D'Albert)
"Selection from Revudeville"
Arranged by Alan D'Albert

2. **THE EMERALD ISLE**
Paddy ... ... **MEGGIE EATON**
Pat ... ... **DICK MONTAGUE**
Mike ... **KENNETH BIRRELL**
Colleens ... **WINDMILL GIRLS**
and **REVUDEBELLES**

3. **"IRONWORKS"** *(Bert Lloyd)*
GUS and **ERIC WOODBURN**

4. **DANCING FOR JOY**
(John Stevens and Dick Hurran)
The Boy ... **JOHN STEVENS**
His Friend ... **DICK HURRAN**
The Girl ... **MOLLIE HALLEWELL**

5. **BALLET** ... "MASQUERADE"
RITA DELL and the **WINDMILL GIRLS**

6. **THE SILENT DRAMA** *(Dick Montague)*
Compere ... **DICK MONTAGUE**
The Wife ... **MOLLIE HALLEWELL**
The Husband ... **ERIC WOODBURN**
The Artist ... **KENNETH BIRRELL**

JUGGLING ... **ANITA MARTELL**

N.B. All scenes presented at this Theatre are fully protected and must not be reproduced without the written consent of the Management.

8. **AT THE COURT OF OLD KING SWING**
(Boyle, Bristow and Rose)
King of Swing ... **G. LARSEN**
His Guests... ... **MEGGIE EATON**
JEAN CARR
RENEE JOLLIFFE
ANGUS WATSON
DICK HURRAN
Heralds ... **MARIE and JEAN**
Dancers ... ... **WINDMILL GIRLS**

9. **"COALIE"** ... **ERIC WOODBURN**

10. **"GETTING BETTER"** *(Gus Chevalier)*
The Doctor ... **JOHN STEVENS**
The Nurse ... **MOLLIE HALLEWELL**
The Patient ... ... **GUS**
The Undertaker ... **DICK HURRAN**
Blind Man ... ... **J. LARSEN**
Wife ... ... **JEAN**

11. **"LEGS AND FACES"** *(Bristow and Rose)*
THE WINDMILL GIRLS

12. **"SIXES AND SEVENS"** *(Angus Watson)*
Jack ... ... **ANGUS WATSON**
Mary ... **MOLLIE HALLEWELL**
Daisy ... ... **JEAN CARR**
Uncle ... **ERIC WOODBURN**
Lift Girl ... **BRENDA WILKINSON**

13. **TABLEAU** "THE CURSE OF THE PHAROAHS" *(Paul Boyle)*
KENNETH BIRRELL
JOHN STEVENS
REVUDEBELLES
Dancer ... ... **MARIE**

14. **LARSEN BROTHERS**

15. **"CRUISING"**
(Watson, Hurran, Boyle, Bristow and Rose)
Head Stewardess ... **MEGGIE EATON**
Sailors ... **DICK MONTAGUE**
and **ANGUS WATSON**
Captain ... **KENNETH BIRRELL**
Steward ... **DICK HURRAN**
Stewardesses ... **WINDMILL GIRLS**
and **REVUDEBELLES**

FINALE ... For all who have seen from Item 1

Printed & Published by TRIBE BROS., Ltd., Dalston, N.1

Halls North of the Thames

ROYAL FORESTERS' PALACE OF VARIETIES,

CAMBRIDGE ROAD, MILE END, E.

PROPRIETOR - - - - - MR. WILLIAM LUSBY.

OPEN EVERY EVENING FOR VARIETY ENTERTAINMENTS.

PROGRAMME FOR THIS EVENING.

NOTICE.—It being the desire of the Proprietor that the Entertainments offered at this Establishment should be at all times absolutely free from any objectionable features, he invites the co-operation of the public to this end and would feel obliged to anyone who will inform him of anything offensive upon the stage that may have escaped the notice of the Management.

1. Overture by the Band.
2. HARRY LEMORE, Comic Vocalist.
3. KATE CARNEY, The Irish Serio-Comic.
4. TOM VINE, Comic and Topical Vocalist.
5. CLARA NISBETT, Descriptive and Serio-Comic.
6. TOM and LILLY ENGLISH, American Musical Variety Entertainers.
7. JENNY VALMORE, The Talented Serio Comic.
8. The Popular Extempore Vocalist and Author
ARTHUR WEST,
Who will sing TWO NEW SONGS every week. The subject to be chosen and given in by the audience for Arthur West to write the words, compose the music and sing the songs on the following night.
9. Selection by the Band.
10. FOLLOY AND HARVEY'S
NIMBLE NIPS Will appear in an Entertainment, entitled A Row in McGuinnis' Kitchen.
11. GEORGE RIPON, Character Comic Vocalist.
12. The Gifted Artiste
VESTA TILLEY,
The London Idol.
13. POOLES MINSTRELS (Male and Female Artistes), Five in Number.
Will introduce Ballads, Choruses, New Sayings, Conundrums, and their great Champion Acrobatic Machine Dance
14. GOD SAVE THE QUEEN.

THIS PROGRAMME IS SUBJECT TO ALTERATION AT THE DISCRETION OF THE MANAGEMENT.

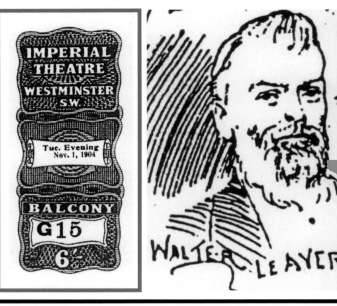

Crouch End HIPPODROME

Telephone No.
420 HORNSEY

One Performance Nightly

Doors Open 7.30.   Commence at 7.45.

EALING HIPPODROME

EALING BROADWAY, W.

Twice Nightly at 6.30 & 9
Saturday First House Commences 15 mins. earlier.

MONDAY, OCT. 19th, 1908

THE GREAT

GEORGE ROBEY

IN ALL HIS LATEST AND GREATEST SUCCESSES

3 SAN REMO Girls

Bert BRANTFORD

RICH & RICH

KITTY TAYLOR

HARRY COTTON

JACK PLEASANTS
The Popular Star Comedian in His Latest Successes

ANNIE BRADDAN

Patty Yole

BARTON & FRANKLYN

Imperial Bioscope

POLUSKI BROS.
WILL & SAM - In their Latest Successes. PICTURES.

REDUCTION IN PRICES!!

BOXES	Faut'ils	CIRCLE	PIT	Gallery
10/6	1/-	6D.	4D.	2D.

Booking Fee for Fauteuils and Circle, 2d.

EALING HIPPODROME

EALING BROADWAY, W.

TWICE NIGHTLY AT 6.40 & 9
SATURDAYS (FIRST HOUSE) COMMENCES 15 MINUTES EARLIER.

MONDAY, JANUARY 10th, 1910.

THE QUEEN OF COMEDY

MARIE LLOYD

In Her Latest Successes

G. W. FOSTER ✶ HANID ALEXANDER

RAY ESPINOSA
The Celebrated Premier Danseuse from the Lyceum Theatre in a Novel Terpsichorean Scene

PHILLIPS & MERRITT
THE POPULAR COMEDY COUPLE

MARLO The Incomparable Juggler

THE BIOSCOPE WITH NEW PICTURES   **PHIL BRANSBY**

A Twisting Twirling Jumble of Comedy

| **3 LAURELS** | **DICKSON MOFFATT & CO.** |
| Acrobatic & Comedy Trampoline Speciality | **SIX & EIGHTPENCE** |

BOXES	Fauteuils	Gr. Circle	PIT	GALLERY
7/6 & 5/-	1/6	1/-	6d.	3d.

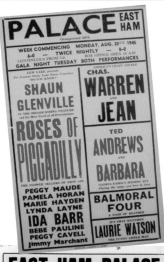

PALACE EAST HAM

WEEK COMMENCING MONDAY, AUG. 20TH 1945

SHAUN GLENVILLE

CHAS. WARREN AND JEAN

ROSES OF PICCADILLY

TED **ANDREWS** AND **BARBARA**

PEGGY MAUDE
PAMELA HORAN
MARIE HAYDEN
LYNDA LAYNE
IDA BARR
BEBE PAULINE
PEGGY CAVELL
Jimmy Marchant

BALMORAL FOUR

LAURIE WATSON

EAST HAM PALACE

MONDAY, JULY 9TH. 1951

MAX BACON

NONI NITA AND DODY

THE OLD PHILOSOPHER
SCOTT SANDERS

'SUSIE'
EDDIE WHITE
NORA FORD
REG RUSSELL
VAN DUSEN
VALEE
SAM LINFIELD & CO.

22.12.54.

7766

East' Ham Palace

O. Stalls 3/9
Inc. Tax

1st Perf.. 6.30
Wednesday

This portion to be retained

PALACE EAST HAM

MONDAY, 7TH JUNE 1937

DEVITO & DENNY
with DOROTHY STEVENS

IN A RIOT OF FUN

MRS. O'HARA'S BIRTHDAY PARTY

RANDOLPH SUTTON

EDMUND **BOYS**

DAVE **SEED**

WALKER & RAY

KARLSON 4

CHICK ELLIOTT

EVERY SUNDAY   TWO BIG FEATURE FILMS

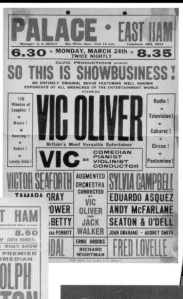

PALACE · EAST HAM

6.30 MONDAY, MARCH 24th 8.35
TWICE NIGHTLY

OLVIC PRODUCTIONS present

SO THIS IS SHOWBUSINESS!

AN ENTIRELY ORIGINAL REVUE FEATURING WELL KNOWN EXPONENTS OF ALL BRANCHES OF THE ENTERTAINMENT WORLD

STARRING

VIC OLIVER
Britain's Most Versatile Entertainer

VIC as COMEDIAN PIANIST VIOLINIST CONDUCTOR

Radio !
Television !
Cabaret !
Circus !
Pantomime !

VICTOR SEAFORTH

SYLVIA CAMPBELL

EDUARDO ASQUEZ
ANDY McFARLANE
SEATON & O'DELL
FRED LOVELLE

PROGRAMME

PALACE THEATRE EAST HAM

PROGRAMME 3d.

EAST HAM PALACE

BOX OFFICE OPEN FROM 10 a.m.

WEEK COMMENCING MONDAY, AUG. 3rd, 1953

TWICE NIGHTLY

A MODERN HIGH SPEED SHOW

DICK EMERY

KAREN GREER

DUKE DIAMOND

PAULINE & EDDIE

CHARLIE DRAKE

Continued on page 271

HALLS NORTH OF THE THAMES

Bethnal Green: Foresters' Music Hall

Cambridge Heath Road (formerly Dog Row), Bethnal Green

The Foresters' Music Hall: exterior as the Artichoke Tavern with The Great MacDermott billed

This hall opened on the site of the Artichoke public house at 93–95, Cambridge Heath Road in 1889. William Smith was mine host at the Artichoke in the early nineteenth century when it was just one of the 109 (yes, 109) ale-houses and inns all open at the same time in the parish of St. Matthew's. The coming of the railway had completely altered the area, with its rural atmosphere giving way to some of London's worst slums.

In about 1850 a Mr. Buckhurst became the licensee and was granted a licence for music and dancing in a hall he had built at the back of the Artichoke. The street at the back of The Foresters' is still called Buckhurst Street. It was fairly successful, but it was William Lusby who started the hall's real prosperity between 1890 and 1904, with assistance from G.H. Macdermott and W.H. Pannell.

In 1891 the Foresters' was reconstructed inside, as shown by the drawing below. In 1906 the new manager, Frank Macnaghten, wanting to keep up-to-date, introduced cinematograph apparatus into the theatre and in fact the hall was licensed as a cinema in 1912, becoming one of London's earliest cinemas.

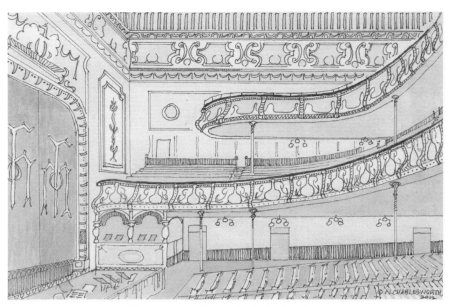

The Foresters' Music Hall: the Interior

But it was the take-over of the Foresters' by the Macnaghten Vaudeville Circuit in 1906 that led to a period of prosperity. This concern had control of so many of the London and provincial halls that they found it to their advantage to institute the famous 'trial turns', which took place at the Foresters' on one matinee during each week. The public were present at the performance and any artiste having aspirations towards the music-hall stage could present himself for audition. The audiences were extremely critical and, if they were not pleased, the curtain was very quickly rung down upon the unfortunate performer. In this way the circuit was able to acquire talent for their many theatres. Indeed, the Foresters' audience had always been difficult to please. For example, when on 5 October, 1885 Dan Leno made his London debut as a solo comedian and clog dancer, he died the death.

New exterior while a cinema on the Gaumont circuit

Films, which had originally been introduced to enliven this programme, took over completely until 1917. It re-opened as a full-time cinema in 1925, still as the Foresters' and it joined the Odeon circuit in 1936. During WW2 the area around the theatre was severely bombed, but the Foresters', although slightly damaged by incendiary bombs, kept open. It was structurally damaged, though, and once the war was over had to be closed for two years. Repairs were carried out, the theatre being redecorated and refurnished at the same time. There was a Grand Reopening on Monday, 10 October, 1949. New flats had meantime replaced the cramped and crowded housing bombed by the Germans, bringing a fresh audience and enabling the Foresters', now part of the Gaumont circuit (although never owned by them), to regain its local popularity for a few more years.

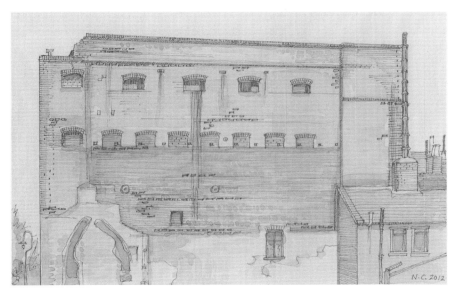

Rear of building in 1961, before demolition

Like many suburban cinemas, the Foresters' gradually lost ground, closing down on 20 August, 1960 with an appropriate last show: *The Chaplin Revue* (a compilation of some of his shorts) and *A Dog's Best Friend*, starring Bill Williams, Marcia Henderson, Roger Mobley, Charles Cooper and Harry Dean Stanton. I went to have a last look around and saw some traces of the old hall, which by then was pretty derelict. It was eventually demolished.

ROYAL FORESTERS' PALACE OF VARIETIES,

CAMBRIDGE ROAD, MILE-END, E.

Proprietor - - - - - - *Mr WILLIAM LUSBY.*

Open Every Evening for Variety Entertainments at Popular Prices.

SMART PROGRAMME.   NO WAITING.

ALWAYS A MONSTRE COMPANY WITH FREQUENT CHANGES.

Open at 7.   Commence at 7.30.

This Popular Place of Amusement, Handsomely Decorated, Carpeted, and well-seated, is pronounced by Press and Public to be the Most Comfortable Hall at the East of London.

General Manager - - - - - - Mr WILTON FRIEND.

MISS FLORRIE ROBINA,

BURLESQUE ACTRESS,

Engaged after first night at the OXFORD for long Engagement.

NOW APPEARING **LONDON** NIGHTLY, THREE HALLS.

Provincial Tour Commencing March 25th, 1889, for Seventeen Weeks.

On return to town will open at the EMPIRE, OXFORD, and METROPOLITAN.

Agent - - - - R. WARNER & CO.

HARRY RANDALL,

Alhambra,
Oxford,
Foresters.

PROVINCIAL TOUR, EASTER MONDAY.

AGENT - - - - - HUGH J. DIDCOTT.

MISS MINNIE CUNNINGHAM,

SERIO COMIC AND DANCER,

Prince of Wales' Theatre, Birmingham.

Sole Agent, Mr EDWARD COLLEY,

163 Stamford Street, Waterloo Road.

Miss CORA CARDIGAN,

THE GREATEST AND MOST ADMIRED INSTRUMENTALIST OF THE PRESENT DAY.

Unique, Brilliant, and Refined Performance.

Accorded the Highest Honours by the Entire British and American Press.

The only Lady Flute, Violin, and Piccolo Solo Artiste on the British and American Stage.

For Engagements see Weekly Papers.

ADDRESS—18 VARDEN'S ROAD, ST. JOHN'S HILL, WANDSWORTH, S.W.

Calling cards for artistes

Bow Palace (Eastern Empire)

156–8, Bow Road, Poplar

Bow Palace: exterior (formerly The Three Cups Tavern)

Another music hall to grow out of a public house, this hall started life in 1855 as The Three Cups Public House & Music Hall under William Ufindell, with a capacity of 300. The hall was at the rear of the tavern and in 1889 changed its name for three years to Bow Music Hall.

A company promoted by T.H. North on 12 January, 1891 acquired the building with adjoining land, demolished it and opened a new one with a capacity of 2,078 on 3 August, 1892. Now known as the Eastern Empire it was taken over by Frank Macnaghten in 1899, and he changed the theatre's name to the Bow Palace in 1903. In the London area he also controlled the Battersea Palace and – for a time – The Foresters'. At Bow he was succeeded by his manager, Fred Baugh. The 1899 bill (shown at the end of the chapter) was topped by a tear-jerking sketch, *Poverty Lane*, with My Fancy also billed; she was married to Harry Bawn, of the Edmonton Empire.

The interior of the Bow Palace was quite old-fashioned even for the time, with benched seating and a forest of supporting pillars; there were two balconies. As the years went by, the Variety shows gave way to cinema performances, although some turns were added between films. Just to add confusion, the theatre became known as the Tivoli Theatre, Bow between 1917 and 1918.

Interior of Bow Palace

The Bow Palace was remodelled to designs by George Ides at a cost then of £50,000 as a super-cinema and Variety theatre. It was officially opened by George Lansbury, M.P. (Angela Lansbury's father), on Monday, 13 November, 1923 in the presence of the mayors of Poplar and Stepney, many borough councillors and several 'film artistes'. A full orchestra, a pipe organ and The Royal Bartle Quartette added to the pleasure of those attending the opening.

Variety turns continued to appear between films, even after the rebuilding, as shown on the December, 1926 press advertisement in the colour section, when Jack Wynne & Co. appeared in a sketch, *His Lucky Day*. There is very little mention of the Bow Palace in *The Stage*, *The Performer* or other trade papers, so it was clearly quite a minor date.

In 1934 the manager of the ciné-Variety house was murdered by the projectionist (we do not know the reason for this somewhat extreme action, but perhaps the poor man had not been paid). For some time after this the building was closed. Subsequently it was rebuilt to designs by Kemp & Tasker and reopened on 26 September, 1935 as the Regal Cinema.

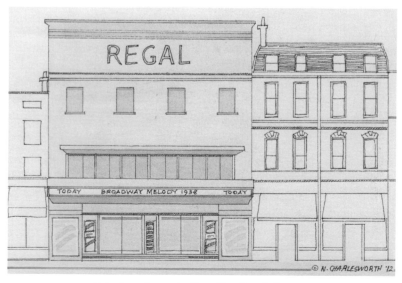

Exterior when rebuilt as The Regal Cinema

Closed by bomb damage during WW2 it was allowed to be repaired and reopened on 16 October, 1947, again as a cinema. However, as so often, business gradually fell away and it closed on 11 January, 1958 and demolished. Council flats and shops now cover the site.

With thanks to Alfred Chapman of Islington.

Josef Blank and Company

Bedford Theatre

93–95, Camden High Street, Camden Town

The Bedford Theatre: interior of the old Bedford building

This theatre was a music hall when I was a small boy. It came under a number of managements (including LTV), but went over to films in 1933 and reverted to Variety soon after the outbreak of WW2. It was often said to be the most beautiful music hall building in London, although its exterior could have been that of a bank. Inside it was quite delightful with its caryatides and fine plaster mouldings – the work of Bertie Crewe.

The site of what eventually became the Bedford Music Hall was originally The Bedford Arms Tavern and Tea Garden, which opened in 1824 and operated under a succession of managers until 1861. The Bedford Arms had been built on part of the estate owned by the Russell family, who later became the Dukes of Bedford. In the 17th century they inherited large tracts of land, now known as Holborn and Bloomsbury. The Tea Garden was built on what had been pastures and orchards.

In 1861 a proper theatre was built at a cost of £5,000, the first owner being R.C. Thornton, who opened the Bedford Music Hall himself in the September of that year. The theatre was managed at first by a man named Wilson. Later licensees associated with this first theatre proper were Edward Weston, Alfred Trotman and George Fredericks. The latter was a comedy and dramatic sketch writer and comedian.

I have researched back as far as 1878, in which year audiences heard Tom MacLean sing *The Good Time to Come* – a sentiment still current today! Alexander Lumsden won plaudits for his fine tenor and in the month of June the Sisters Waite and the negro duo Warde & Springley appeared. Camden audiences also saw Bessie Bellwood, Arthur Roberts, Jenny Hill and Bessie Bonehill, names that still resonate today. That summer a new Manager/Chairman, Fred Roberts, was appointed and was known to render, on request, his favourite song – *When I Took Our Nancy To Wed*. Among performers at the Bedford later in 1878 was Harry Rickards, singing several numbers, including *A Virgin Only 97 Years Old*.

Exterior of front of the rebuilt Bedford with 'Fanny Get Your Fun' billed

George Fredericks' Farewell Benefit was held on 25 July, 1878 and he was succeeded by Harry Hart. Notable acts at this time were Wheatley & O'Gorman the Irish comedians, singing *Pretty Peggy*; Charles Godfrey, with *On Guard*; The Flying Children, Dello & Zetti; and Keegan & Little Elvin. Another artiste who entertained here was the Extempore Vocalist, Charles Williams, who was later killed at the age of twenty-seven when his brougham overturned outside the South London Palace on 12 September, 1880.

Under Harry Hart the Bedford was rebuilt with a capacity of 1,168 to the designs of Bertie Crewe, following a fire. The old building was demolished in July, 1898 and work began early in August on its replacement. The beautiful new theatre, with its sliding roof and lightly-draped goddesses supporting the two stage boxes, was opened on Wednesday, 1 February, 1899 with a large private function held by the new proprietors, Messrs. Lucas and Johnson. After the memorial stone had been laid by little Miss Marguerite Lucas, luncheon was served at tables set up on the stage. The Bedford orchestra, under G.S. Thomas, played selections during and after luncheon.

The New Bedford opened to the public the following Monday with a strong bill, including The Craggs, Gus Elen, Slade Murray, Fred Russell, Texarkansas, The Collins Trio, Ernest Leader, Charles Milner, Marie Faudelle, The Leopolds, Wal Pink and Company in a sketch, Abel & Welsh, The Maddison Girls, W.F. Moss, The Dellers, Lizzie & Vinie Daly, Charles Seal, The Delevantis and other artistes. It was generally agreed that the spacious new hall, built by W. Johnson and Co., was a great improvement on its small and inconvenient predecessor, which could be entered only from a court that ran between Camden High Street and Arlington Road.

Auditorium looking towards stage box

Once launched, the New Bedford hosted the biggest stars of the day. Among them in May, 1900 were Kate Carney, T.E. Dunville, Tom Leamore, Vesta Victoria, George Lashwood, Austin Rudd and Lottie Lennox. The following month Dan Crawley, Bransby Williams, Tennyson & O'Gorman, Jenny Valmore, Harry Tate, G.H. Chirgwin, Harry Champion and both Marie Lloyd and her then husband, Alec Hurley appeared. In later years Marie Lloyd celebrated her 50th birthday in pantomime at The Bedford.

Summer vacations are nothing new, as the new hall closed for a holiday at the end of June in its first year, reopening on 17 September for the autumn season with a host of favourites. Among these were John Lawson, Fanny Leslie (*Words, Beautiful Words*), Pat Rafferty, George Robey, Arthur Rigby, Ada Cerito and Harry Anderson. Back again on £20 per week for the Christmas programme was Jenny Valmore, with Leo Dryden, Paul Martinetti (*A Duel in the Snow*), G.W. Hunter and Vento in an eleven-strong bill.

By the time the second anniversary of the new hall arrived in February, 1901 Queen Victoria had died and "a national gloom on amusements in general has been felt at this fine Camden Town Variety Palace as well as elsewhere" stated one newspaper reporter. But the celebratory programme was said to have "lifted the cloud of melancholy" with its three sketches and a company of more than thirty artistes. Galleryites delighted in Tom Leamore's rendering of *Since I've Come Into My Rhino*, while the whole house gave a great reception to Peggy Pryde, Charles Whittle, Kate Carney, Millie Linden, Amy Allnut and Katie Lawrence.

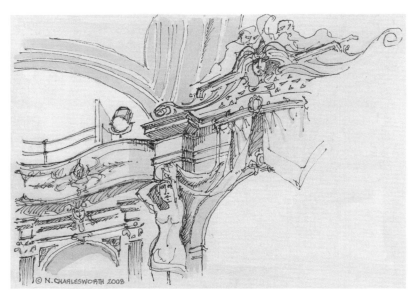
Interior showing top of a stage box and follow-spot in gallery

By 1903 Harry Day had become General Manager at the Bedford. Three years later he took a similar position at the Bristol Empire and there was to be a working relationship between the two halls later on. Col. Harry Day (1880–1939) was once a twenty-five shillings-a-week bill-sticker in Bristol, who later became Labour MP for Southwark Central. He was one of the great producers of British revues, whose *Spangles* is said to have been one of the best ever staged. A grand charity Variety show at the Bedford under Day's control was held at The New Year in 1903. It was enlivened by Lottie Collins, The Caledonian Boys, Lew Lake and Bob Morris in one of their many sketches and by "a capital speciality", The Leopold Troupe of acrobats, one of whom joined The British Music Hall Society in 1963.

The Bedford also played a small role in the arrest of Dr. Crippen, who murdered his wife Belle Elmore, a well-known Variety artiste. A short distance from the theatre were Goldington Buildings, built in 1904, where Crippen spent evenings with his mistress Ethel le Neve, while poor Belle was appearing on the stage of the Bedford. Crippen returned by sea to America after murdering Belle, but was arrested as he tried to leave the liner – as a result of a warning telegraphed to the captain. He was hanged in 1910.

A unique presentation took place at the Bedford in January, 1905 when the comedian Sam Mayo (*The Immobile One*) was given a silver cigarette case by B.P. Lucas on stage at the theatre. This was to mark Mayo's record of fifty-eight performances in a single week at London music halls – he had worked nine turns per night and four matinees. The actual appearances being:

Bedford 6.30pm, Euston 6.50pm, Royal 7.25pm, Tivoli 8.00pm, Gatti's 8.45pm, Euston 9.25pm, Standard 10.00pm, Royal 10.25pm and Bedford 10.50pm.

With four matinees, that made a grand total of fifty-eight performances in the week and all done by rushing around the capital by cab!

In 1912 both Gracie Fields and Charlie Chaplin are recorded as having appeared at The Bedford. So the good times rolled on, but with difficulties during the Great War and with the competition of early cinemas.

Moving forward to the 1920s, with the theatre under the control of Charles Gulliver of LTV for several years, we find that revues have largely ousted straight Variety bills in Camden Town. Following a week of the pantomime *Aladdin* in January, 1923, some of the lively offerings numbered J.M. Turner's *Shuffle Along*, Espinosa's *Oh, Lady, Oh*, Bertram Levy's *Search Me!* and Dick Ray's *Kick Off*. Lovers of Variety could enjoy Wish Wynne, Harry Champion, King & Benson and Ethel Newman when the diet of revue was relieved.

Exterior showing canopy for gallery queue

Revue produced its own stars and in 1924 Harry Day, whose production house was the Bristol Empire, gave London audiences their first viewings of his latest revues at the Bedford. His revue *Crystals* paid two visits that year, topped firstly by Kitty Collyer and secondly by Jimmy Leslie. He also brought *Spangles* with Fred Miller, *Ideas* and *Radios*, the latter featuring the 'dude' comedian, George Clarke, famous for his 'new car'. Masses of other producers had caught the revue craze and in just a few months the names of Alf Lyons, Will Garland, C.T. Lawrence, Moss' Empires, Webb & Page, Charles Gulliver and Ventom Swift were among the many whose shows brought enjoyment to local audiences.

In 1933 the Bedford Music Hall became an ABC cinema and the area was bereft of live entertainment for several years, as the Camden Hippodrome nearby had also become a picture house, albeit with a couple of live acts. Fortunately, the Bedford returned to the live fold in December, 1939 under Harry Goodson. Strangely, Goodson had 'three bites at the cherry', having been in charge earlier from 1920–21 and from 1928–32. Some good bills were presented under his management, including one headed by Billy Bennett and Afrique. A South African, who opened at the Windmill in 1934, Afrique had previously been over here in opera in the Vic-Wells Opera Company. He was a big success in America and at the Palladium. His act consisted of impressions, especially of Richard Tauber and of King Edward VIII. His career suddenly declined, but he attempted a comeback in 1948 at the London Casino and shortly after this he was at the Alexandra in Stoke Newington – not a great date. Afrique also appeared in the pantomime *Jack and Jill* for Emile Littler at Manchester Hippodrome for the 1948–49 season.

In 1941 F.J. Butterworth took over the Bedford, one of the first of his rapidly expanding chain of Number Two theatres (Boscombe, Southampton, Aston, etc.), presenting mostly touring revues. The theatrical agent Frank Pope also had his office at the Bedford Theatre. The theatre deteriorated however, under F.J.B.'s control and after WW2 it offered the usual array of Number Two revues, including Charlie Ellis in *Chase Me, Charlie* and Harold Walden in *Kick Off*. Tom Moss also appeared in *Laughter Offensive*. Steve Daniels managed the Bedford for a time and his show, *The Stars We'll Remember*, played there.

In December, 1949 Pat Nye and John Penrose took over the theatre as a repertory house, engaging among other distinguished actors, Dirk Bogarde. Plays included *The Silver King*, *Trilby*, *East Lynne* and other similar melodramas, which were initially supported by audiences from Hampstead, until the novelty wore off. Donald Wolfit took the theatre and for sixteen weeks presented 128 consecutive performances of Shakespeare at popular prices – 6s, 4s 6d, 3s 6d and 2s. The season was a terrific success, achieving seventy per cent capacity. A local market trader was one of the many to crowd the theatre, saying, "Shakespeare? Why not? I'll take a basin of Hamlet any time". Only a pre-arranged four week tour forced Wolfit to leave the Bedford, when a season of Bernard Shaw's plays that he had booked as an interim, failed to attract. As Hermione Gingold said, "Olivier is a *tour de force*, and Wolfit is forced to tour".

Melodrama returned to the Bedford, but despite national press publicity from Beverley Baxter and others, the brave venture failed. Variety was tried for one last time and I saw a bill headed by Renée Houston & Donald Stewart, Wee Georgie Wood and Jack Daly, but the management had lost thousands of pounds and the Bedford closed soon after in 1950. The beautiful hall, where artistes reported that they could almost touch members of the audience in the dress circle, became gradually derelict. It was regularly vandalised and the sliding roof left open, allowing rain to ruin the fine plasterwork. Most of the building was demolished in 1969, but not before it was immortalised by Geoffrey Fletcher in his various books on London. Even the remaining walls have now gone. Outside music hall circles the Bedford is one of the best-known halls, as Walter Sickert used it and the old Bedford as subjects for many of his paintings and etchings. As John Barber recalls, the film *Trottie True* opened in 1949, starring Jean Kent, Bill Owen and Lana Morris. It told the story of a young actress who is inspired to become a Gaiety Girl after visiting the Bedford Theatre. So its image lives on.

Joe Haynes, Chairman of the old Bedford

Camden Hippodrome (The Camden Theatre)

Camden High Street, corner of Crowndale Road, Camden Town

The Camden Hippodrome: exterior while on Ciné-Variety

The name 'Hippodrome' is slightly misleading, as it leads one to believe that this was a long-established Variety house, which it was not! Another hall built as a legitimate playhouse, the theatre was formally opened by Ellen Terry on 21 December, 1900, so can just be described as 'Victorian'. Its first public performance took place on Boxing Day, when E.G. Saunders presented *Cinderella* with Edwin Barwick and Ethel Newman, which ran for a month. Camden Town was a respectable district with its streets and squares inhabited by the prosperous middle classes, so W.G.R. Sprague's handsome free-classical exterior was fully appreciated. Its interior was – and is – in the Louis XIV style. The building is in a commanding position overlooking a busy road junction opposite Mornington Crescent. E.G. Saunders was already associated with the Brixton Theatre and the Coronet Theatre in Notting Hill Gate (the latter also still standing). Fifteen of Sprague's fine theatres already graced the metropolis and the builder of this new theatre was Walter Wallis.

The new playhouse got away to a good start, with changes of production weekly. These were largely touring versions of West End successes, but at much reduced admission prices. For example, a fortnight after the pantomime season finished Mrs. Langtry brought her 'London' Company to Camden Town for six nights in *The Degenerates* by Sydney Grundy, appearing herself in the role of Mrs. Trevelyan. The curtain rose nightly at 8pm and there was a Saturday matinee at 2pm. The programme announced the following week's play as *Lady Windermere's Fan,* starring Miss Marion Terry and Mr. Thalberg, supported by 'a Powerful Company'.

There was a competent orchestra at the Camden Theatre under James Philp, so visiting productions of light opera were well catered for. *The Geisha* was one such visitor, which played for six nights in November, 1901. In the early years the theatre was crowded, people even being turned away on many occasions. The programme was varied, offering new plays such as *Drink*, as well as revivals of plays such as *The Two Little Vagabonds* and Dickens' *Oliver Twist*. Whilst opening the new theatre Ellen Terry promised to appear there in a production when she was able and her promise was kept when she played Portia in *The Merchant of Venice*.

Unfortunately, the Camden Theatre's life as a playhouse was not a long one. There were some thirty suburban theatres ringing the capital – not counting Variety houses – many of which faced the competition of the cinema during and after WW1. Maybe this house was opened too late, but in any case it became part of Robert Arthur's circuit for a short time. In London Arthur ran the Kennington Theatre, Fulham Grand, The Coronet and The Camden, while in the provinces his interests included the Nottingham Theatre Royal and theatres in Newcastle, Aberdeen and Dundee. For a time he also ran the Royal Court Theatre in Sloane Square.

The theatre had an even shorter time under Walter Gibbons than under Robert Arthur, when he put on Variety at the house. In fact there was a court case in 1908, when the Crown objected to Arthur and Gibbons' move from drama to Variety and the defendants were convicted. At this time Gibbons was on the look-out for failing drama houses which he was buying up to form his Variety circuit, LTV. Had he succeeded here, the Camden Theatre (which was re-named Camden Hippodrome in 1914) might have joined such illustrious names as The Holborn Empire and The Palladium. But it was not to be, as there was strong competition from the top end of Camden High Street in the form of the well-established Bedford Palace. Other nearby halls such as The Euston, Islington Empire and Collins' Music Hall already had their loyal supporters. Charles Gulliver took over from Gibbons, but success still eluded the fine theatre. The managers changed yearly, trying Variety, melodrama and Ciné-variety.

The theatre achieved some sort of success as a cinema under Joseph Clavering, when it became part of his circuit in 1917. Then in January, 1928 the Hippodrome became one of nine halls in the newly-formed United Picture Theatres Ltd. (UPT), which quickly grew to sixteen – most of them outmoded former theatres and music halls.

Ciné-variety kept the stages of many old halls in use, with Camden Hippodrome usually having three acts among the silent films – an orchestra providing the accompaniment. Thus in July, 1928 we could have been entertained for the week by Mavis & Duval, Les Storks, and, cleverly imitating her late mother – Marie Lloyd jnr. Marie herself had died just six years earlier and there was great demand for her songs. Most of the acts seen at Camden in that era are forgotten today. For example, on view that summer were Charteris & Dickson, Caro & partner, and Tarzey & Scott.

The change from silent films, rented at flat rates, to sound films, booked on strict percentage terms, hit UPT hard. The company also had to wire up all its old theatres for sound, which added to its woes.

Interior towards the stage

However, Ciné-variety kept going for a while, often on a split-week booking, to maintain local interest. For three days in May, 1929 we could have enjoyed live Jean Andrews, Hart, Pender & Hart, and De Marr & James. If we still had spare cash left by the Thursday we could have gone again to see on stage three more live acts – Jones & Chase, Valliere & assistant, and Aubrey & Haye. During the split-week some of the acts working Camden were also to be seen at other UPT halls, such as The Shakespeare at Clapham Junction, Mile End Empire and the Hippodromes at Putney and Woolwich.

In April, 1930 the big Gaumont British circuit took a financial interest in UPT, giving it over 300 cinemas and the ability to book films at more advantageous terms. Ciné-variety gave way to films-only at Camden Hippodrome; and UPT off-loaded many of its poorly-performing halls from 1934 onwards. The blitz closed all the UPT houses, except three, as they were in target areas. Camden Hippodrome never re-opened, as Gaumont had a much larger and more modern cinema in Camden Town. From 1945 the Camden Hippodrome, now reverting to its old name of The Camden Theatre, operated as a BBC studio and concert hall. Perhaps its best-known programme was the weekly broadcast of *Friday Night is Music Night*, when the theatre's name always got a mention. Vilem Tausky, who often conducted the BBC Concert Orchestra at Camden, estimated that he had conducted more than 125 operas, but he was best known for his *Friday Night* work. The Moravian-born conductor and composer maintained that his work at Camden killed his career because 'people started looking at me as an entertainer'. After his ten years on these broadcasts, he was offered only popular concerts – 'There was always a Rachmaninov piano concerto, never symphonies'. It is said that, although he had the highest regard for light music and conducted it with immense flair, his gifts were largely wasted for a long period of his British career.

The Camden Theatre was sold in 1960, and in 1972 (when its studio days were over), it was converted into a discothèque, known variously as The Music Machine and The Camden Palace. Surprisingly, in 1973 there was a move by the The London Borough of Camden to reintroduce live theatre at the old house, when it was estimated in a report commissioned by Ian Albery that restoration costs would be in the region of £200,000. Unfortunately, the Council could not find all the necessary funds, so the plans lapsed. Luckily, the theatre is still in action as a music venue, so it could in theory be restored one day as a live theatre.

UNITED PICTURE THEATRES, LTD.

(Rehearsals Mondays and Thursdays, 11.30 a.m.)

CAMDEN HIPPO.—Jean Andrews, Hart, Pender, and Hart, De Marr and James. May 23, Jones and Chase, Valliere and Asst., Aubrey and Haye.

CLAPHAM.—Jones and Chase, Peter Fannan, Aubrey and Haye. May 23, Varney and Butt, Godwin and Roy, Leslie Trio.

DEPTFORD BROADWAY.— Masu and Yuri, Oliver and Mack. May 23, St. Denis Sisters, Sims and Sims.

KENNINGTON T.—Dekker and Pan, St. Denis Sisters. May 23, Dean and Ross, Oliver and Mack.

LEYTON KING'S HALL (AMUSE-MENTS (LEYTON), LTD.).—Fred Douglas and Sonny, Ley and Tonn. May 23, Dennis Duo, Huntley and Jutt.

MILE END EMP.—Videau and Kirby, Fred Culpitt and Jan Glenrose, Keith Gerrard. May 23, Jean Andrews, Hart, Pender, and Hart, Ella Logan.

OLD KENT PICTURE HOUSE.—Derry and Sloan, Ella Logan, Fred and Mirrie Hurdle. May 23, Dekker and Pan, Two Sharpes, The Kildares.

PALASEUM.—Gibbs and Doodles, Stevens and Him. May 23, Videau and Kirby, Russell and Vivian.

PUTNEY HIPPO.—Valliere and Asst., Godwin and Roy, Tommy Sandilands. May 23, Masu and Yuri, Peter Farnan, Keith Gerrard.

STAMFORD HILL KINEMA.—Vernon and Ford, Russell and Vivian, Sims and Sims. May 23, Keith and Joan Dingley, Gibbs and Doodles, Fred and Mirrie Hurdle.

UPTON PARK CARLTON CINEMA (R.E. CINEMAS, LTD.).—Fyne and Hurley. May 23, Sylverne and Olga.

WANDSWORTH PAL.—Dean and Ross. May 23, Leslie Elliott.

WOOLWICH HIPPO.—Varney and Butt, Keith and Joan Dingley, Two Sharpes. May 23, Derry and Sloan, Tommy Sandilands, De Marr and James.

Ciné-Variety at The United Picture Theatres Ltd. in 1929

Imperial Palace/Royal Albert

Canning Town

Victoria Dock Road, Canning Town, later in Barking Road

Royal Albert Music Hall: exterior while run as Relf's Music Hall in the Town of Ayr public house

Best remembered as having had the supposed last Chairman in a London music hall, the Imperial's history dates back to at least the 1870s. It started life as the Town of Ayr public house, with early photographs showing the hall in a narrow street and with its entrance embedded in the pub, near the railway. Road-widening in the area has destroyed that part of Victoria Dock Road.

The whole story of this hall needs a good deal more research, but it is known to have been enlarged into the renamed Royal Albert Music Hall in 1875 and it was under this name that this popular hall was best known. In January, 1891 it was closed for drastic rebuilding, including the addition of a second gallery, under the architect Walter Emden. Its new capacity was stated to have been 2,500, with a 30ft. deep stage, but using rolled scenery as there was no fly tower. According to *The Stage*, a new ventilation system involved the opening and closing of 'specially-placed ventilators'. Mr. Ward jnr. was said to have made the arrangements for the new stage.

The manager at this time was the long-serving Charles Relf, who gave his name to the music hall for a period. He took exception to demands from the Council in 1904 for a number of improvements before a licence could be issued. These were:

a) The gallery to be licensed to hold not more than 560 people and the upper circle not more than 540 persons.

b) A fire-resisting asbestos screen to be installed which shall be lowered and raised once during every performance. This is to be provided within twelve months.

c) Alterations to doors/staircases, etc., to be carried out to the satisfaction of the Borough Engineer.

Charles Relf was adamant that flimsy scenery and dresses were not used and that all his scenery was rolled and practically fireproof, therefore posing no danger. The Mayor announced that the Council had decided that the licence be renewed subject to the carrying out of the recommendations. It is not known whether Relf complied.

In early 1906 it was decided that the Chairman at The Royal Albert, following the pattern in all the other old suburban halls, had become an anachronism. So it was on 31 July that Walter Leaver stepped down from his dais – and the words "Order, Order" (encouraging the audience to re-charge their glasses, including his own) were no longer heard in a real London hall. In another move away from tradition, the hall obtained a stage play licence in the September of that year.

The Royal Albert drew its audience from an area dominated by factories, where one of the principal occupations was collecting 'gash' wood from various sources (known as 'toshing'). According to W. Pett Ridge, the Canning Town factory girl was the cheeriest and most exhilarated worker in all London. "The duties over, her relish of freedom and the joy of walking arm-in-arm with girl

Royal Albert Music Hall (Relf's), interior when rebuilt as the Imperial Palace

companions is un-disguised. She knows all the diverting songs, all the latest dance tunes and nearly all the sentimental melodies. She used to sing this snatch as a kind of chant – 'we haven't much money, but we do see life!' " A night at The Royal Albert would have been a ritual for those living beside Bow Creek.

A bill that they could have enjoyed was the one offered for the week of 7 January, 1901. Topping were Albert Athas and Lizzie Collins, who must have had their skates on that week, as they were also billed to appear at the Middlesex in Drury Lane and at Collins' Music Hall in Islington. Others to be seen in Canning Town that week were Fred Karno's Famous Company of Comedians, in *The Dossers*, Tom Maxwell and Virginia Francis, Conan & Doyle (what a clever name!), the Sisters Eugenio, Miss Louise A. Sydney's Imperial Sketch Company in *The Slave Chase (or, The Death of Uncle Tom)*, Edie Nicholls, Lance Linwood, Miss Maude Rivers, the Sisters Stewart and Alf Tate.

As the hall was conveniently situated opposite Canning Town station, to help entice the public in, the Royal Albert allowed a 2d discount to all persons travelling by rail, on production of their railway ticket. So there's nothing new in theatre marketing.

The departure of its Chairman was only part of the modernisation of the hall, for only three years later its interior was reconstructed again, this time using the entire auditorium from another London theatre.

The Imperial Theatre, Tothill Street, Westminster (on the site of the present-day Methodist Central Hall) was opened in April, 1876 and eventually closed and sold by the then owner, the notorious Lily Langtry in November, 1907. As it had been reconstructed by Walter Emden only in 1901, it was still quite new. The Royal Albert management bought the interior from the Wesleyan Methodists, carefully dismantled it in the late summer of 1908 and transported it over to Canning Town.

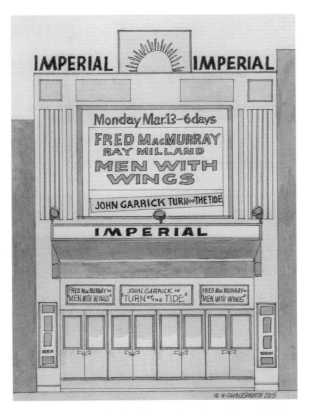

Royal Albert Music Hall (Relf's/Imperial Palace), exterior of new Imperial Cinema in Barking Road

The renamed Imperial Palace ('The Music Hall of Docklands') was opened in December, 1909. One wonders whether Emden, with his earlier dealings with the Royal Albert, was responsible for arranging this most unusual re-cycling of his own auditorium! However, a less atmospheric design for a music hall would be hard to find.

From its reopening to the end of WW1 the Imperial presented Variety in an era when films were a constant threat locally. Many of the bills gave audiences the lesser performers – among them Arthur Stevens, Violet Vandelle and Gertie Gascoyne's Dappy Dandy Girls – but there were occasionally some better-known names, such as The Six Brothers Luck, 'London Favourite' Lily Lassah and Will Burton among them. A typical bill was that of the week of 30 October, 1916 which offered The Ko Ten Icki Troupe, The Eight Daffodils, Four La Solo Girls, Cliff Barrett, George Hylton, Lily Lassah, Stacey & Tinney and The Four Gerbolas.

Shortly before live shows ended, Leonard Mortimer & Company appeared in *Deliver The Goods* in July, 1918. Films soon took over until, on Monday 16 March, 1931 a disastrous fire swept through the building, severely damaging the adjoining Town of Ayr public house; water also caused some damage to the Hallsville School nearby. According to *The Stratford Express*, it was eight hours before the fire in the congested area of houses and shops was finally doused by the West Ham brigade.

The rebuilt Imperial Cinema, now in Barking Road, opened in 1934. Further alterations and improvements, were carried out five years later to bring the building right up to date. The reopening of The New Imperial took place on Monday 15 May, 1939 with a personal appearance by Sandy Powell, then at the height of his popularity. The film programme included Boris Karloff in *Son of Frankenstein* and Bing Crosby in *Paris Honeymoon*, with Max Bruce manning the mighty organ.

The cinema survived the heavy bombing of dockland during WW2 and acquired a further new name, the Essoldo, in 1958; it showed films for another five years, until becoming a bingo hall in 1963. It was eventually demolished in the summer of 1967.

Additional information from Ted Bottle and John Earl, with many thanks.

ROYAL ALBERT MUSIC HALL,

VICTORIA DOCK ROAD, (Opposite Canning Town Railway Station).

Sole Proprietor - - - - - - - CHARLES RELF.

Best Ventilated Hall in or out of London, Capable of Seating 1,000 Persons.

Open EVERY EVENING at SEVEN. Commence at 7.30,

With a CONSTANT CHANGE of

LONDON AND PROVINCIAL STAR ARTISTES.

FOUR HOURS' CONTINUAL AMUSEMENT.

Prices of Admission from FOURPENCE to ONE GUINEA.

MANAGER AND CHAIRMAN - - - - - MR. WALTER LEAVER.
FULL BAND: DIRECTOR - - - - - MR. F. KNAPP.

Frequent Trains from Liverpool St. and Fenchurch St. to opposite the doors. Trams and 'Busses pass the doors

Chelsea Palace

Kings Road, on east corner of Sydney Street

The Chelsea Palace: exterior to Kings Road with Gladys Morgan billed

This commodious theatre, occupying a prime site at Nos. 232–242 Kings Road, was opened on 13 April, 1903 by Henri Gros, whose name is closely liked to the powerful Syndicate Halls company. The architects were Wylson & Long. From 1910 Ilford Ibbetson was in control, with the management of this and several other Syndicate properties, changing its name in 1925 to Variety Theatres Consolidated. At its height the circuit controlled a dozen music halls in London, including The London Pavilion, The Metropolitan and The Oxford. In later years the bookings were undertaken by Miss Leddington, almost as powerful a figure as Miss Cissie Williams of Moss' Empires Ltd.

With a seating capacity of 1,896 in stalls, circle and balcony, one felt that the Chelsea Palace could have presented consistently better bills. Nearly all the big names of Variety – Fred Karno, G.H. Elliott, Florrie Forde, Charles Coborn, Ernie Lotinga, Harry Lauder, Little Tich, Vesta Tilley, Gracie Fields and Max Miller – worked there at one time or another, but the bills were seldom as strong as those on the Moss and Stoll circuits. In later years there was actually a link, as Reginald C. Bromhead was on the boards of both V.T.C. and Moss' Empires Ltd.

Under the managership of Edward Swanborough, Fred Karno's company appeared in their 'Great Triumph' *Twice Nightly* at the end of January, 1905. Two curious items appeared on pre-WW1 programmes: 'The Charming Trentanovi – Lady Trapeze Artistes'. One wonders whether as they were billed as Ladies (not unusual and obvious in practice) they were really female impersonators. While the mind boggles at the possible contents of Joe Boganny's sketch – *Opium Friends* – obviously, especially in Chelsea, the second word of the title should have had one letter less – but presumably the censor would not allow it! Throughout the Great War one could expect to see nine or ten acts on a typical twice nightly Chelsea bill; names remembered today included Lily Morris, Grock and Victoria Monks.

Among sketches on otherwise rather dull bills in the latter part of WW1 one could see Stanley Cooke in *The Weekend* and Ida Crispi & Fred Leslie in *Tony's Luck*, which doubled with The Oxford. Joe Peterman's company offered *The Harem Girl*, while S. Bransgrove's company presented *The Prince and the Beggar Maid*. Straight Variety bills in the 1920s and 30s were hidden away between plays such as *Two White Arms*, *The Murder on the Second Floor* and M. Barry O'Brien's production of *The Man Who Changed His Name*. The Hamilton Deane Repertory Company, on a four-year tour of Britain, appeared for one week at Chelsea Palace in 1930. While in the London area they also appeared at The Borough Theatre in Stratford, Brixton Theatre and Watford Palace, also a V.T.C. theatre at that period.

More to my taste were *Nuits D'Amour* and *The Revue of The Moment*. In April, 1934, as part of an extensive tour, Chelsea patrons were able to enjoy *The Third London Crazy Show*. An attempt at being topical – the presentation of *This Year of Carnival* put on in 1936 to celebrate the succession of King Edward VIII – backfired through no fault of the management! Plays still got a look in and two at this period were *Ten Minute Alibi* and Ernie Lotinga in *My Wife's Family*. As an added attraction the Chelsea Palace offered All-in Wrestling on Sundays at this time.

By the summer of 1936 Variety theatres were starting to close for a vacation, presumably for lack of strong draws; V.T.C.'s Chelsea Palace and Walthamstow Palace were among those that closed that summer – ostensibly for 'painting and redecoration'. Their Brixton, South London and Metropolitan theatres were still playing Variety, while their East Ham Palace was showing films; Watford Palace had left the group to become a straight drama house.

A year of two before the outbreak of WW2 there was a welcome return to full-blooded Variety. In September, 1937 Ivor Moreton & Dave Kay headed a strong bill, including Reco & May, Hope & Ray, The Emberts, Lewis & Lawn, the illusionist Demain and Claude Lester in the company.

The momentum continued into 1938. Toward the end of January, Jane Ayr and Eddie Leslie topped a bill largely comprising multiples! There were Twenty Singing Scholars, Three Knaves and Six Harmonists. Keith Wilbur and Russ Carr were also on the bill, the latter was of course related to Val Parnell of Palladium fame.

In October of that year The Western Brothers (Kenneth & George) doubled Chelsea Palace and Brixton Empress twice nightly, supported by Don Philippe & Marta, Archie & his Band, Trio Tobas, Gordon & Rosina, Billy Rhodes & Chika Lane and Maisie Weldon. The cycling act of V & F Browning footed the bill, having just appeared with Fats Waller at The London Palladium.

On my first visit to Chelsea, in about 1938, a revue pretentiously entitled *International Cavalcade*, with comedian Dick Montague and ragtime singer Eddie Fields, was the not-very-strong attraction. One wartime bill that I saw included Peter Brough with, of course, Archie Andrews – just making their names – Bartlett & Ross and Peter Bernard. The great Austrian tenor Richard Tauber appeared for a week in 1944. *Artists & Models* with Gaston & Andrée was another wartime offering, including Stanelli, Low & Webster (Educate Yourselves) and Clifford & Longley. Wartime performances were at 6.00 and 8.00pm.

Chelsea Palace: the interior as in 1903

On VE Night a good bill was headed by Jack ('Blue Pencil') Warner, supported by Eve Drury & Co. and May Goring Thomas who, after the show, rushed down Whitehall to hear Churchill declare victory was won and to lead the singing of 'Rule Britannia'.

By 1950 some bills were being presented by outside managements. One in November of that year was F.J. Butterworth's *Hi-Diddle-Diddle* with Billy Whittaker & Mimi Law, Eric Marsh, The Clayton Sisters, Pat Hagan, Morgan & Manning and the Hi-Diddle Debutantes. The following month Tex McLeod's *Rhythm on The Range*, with Vera Cody's trained horse Araby and the Great Film Star Collie Dog, Colin, was the attraction. Another show in a similar vein was Big Bill Campbell & his Rocky Mountaineers with his *Hill-Billy Round-up*, although I remember being slightly disappointed by Big Bill himself.

My last visit to Chelsea was in August/September 1954 to see Clarkson Rose in *Twinkle*, which brought temporary prosperity to the Chelsea Palace. The company included the Dorset yokel Billy Burden, Douglas Quarterman, Doreen Lang, John Vicars, Stewart & Mathew and, of course, Olive Fox and Clarkie himself.

The V.T.C. management did its best to fight the tide of television with a typical bill to be seen in September 1956. Gladys Morgan 'With her Laugh and Company' topped, with performances now restored to 6.30 and 8.45pm. Other artistes appearing that week were Hackford & Doyle, magicians Pat Hatton & Peggy, Billy O'Sullivan, Levanda (Feats with the Feet), Kish & Valaire, Patsy Silva and Martin & Gaye. However, extra strength in the shows was too late.

By this time Syndicate Halls were down to three London theatres and in 1956 these were taken over by Granada Group. Variety continued for a few months, before Chelsea Palace and Brixton Empress were closed as live theatres in 1957, leaving only The Metropolitan. One of the final shows at

Chelsea was a Christmas production of *Alice in Wonderland* with twelve-year-old Mandy Miller in the title role: Chelsea Palace was, of course, nearly 'West End' with the nearest underground stations being Sloane Square and South Kensington.

Chelsea Palace became Granada TV Chelsea, a television studio, for about ten years. Audiences could watch *Chelsea at Nine*, *Criss Cross Quiz* and *Bootsie & Snudge* being broadcast or recorded, but it was a depressing experience I found, while sitting in the gallery one evening. However, many stars did appear, including – amazingly enough – Maria Callas.

The Chelsea Palace was finally pulled down in 1967, from the inside outward to avoid detection, after tentative plans to reopen it as a Variety theatre were abandoned by Granada. The company decided to concentrate their television production in Manchester, so eighty staff and technicians were laid-off or redeployed. *The Evening Standard* ran an article headed *VARIETY AGAIN AT CHELSEA PALACE?* But it never happened. Shops and flats stand on the site today, almost opposite Chelsea Town Hall.

Chiswick Empire

Chiswick High Road, Turnham Green

Chiswick Empire: exterior from Chiswick High Road on opening night, 2.9.1912 with The Great Rameses billed

The handsome Chiswick Empire, which seated 1,956 in stalls, circle, balcony and eight boxes, had one of Frank Matcham's best exteriors in a chaste, neo-classical style. It opened on 2 September, 1912, after a fight against local 'long-eared 'uns', who saw all sorts of social evils in a live theatre. As at other theatres on the Stoll circuit, The Empire's bills carried the message that summed up its aims: "tis not in mortals to command success, but we'll do more – deserve it" – a quotation from the eighteenth century essayist Joseph Addison. Chiswick Empire lived up to these aims throughout its life as one of Oswald Stoll's Theatres of genuine Varieties, presenting regularly Opera, Classical Music, Drama, Circus, Music Hall and Cinema. Stoll's theatres were certainly *not* just Music Halls – and the Empire still drew crowds.

The Chiswick Empire stood on the site of some cottages which had replaced a forge – the base for the many highwaymen waiting to pounce on travellers along the nearby Bath Road. When I went there a drawing of these cottages used to hang in the circle bar. The area was also famous for its gardens and nurseries, referred to in Gus Elen's *Nice Quiet Day (The Postman's Holiday)*.

The Chiswick Empire opened a week before its sister theatre, Wood Green Empire (also by Matcham) with a bill which included: The Great Rameses, Ella Shields, Billy Merson, Yorke Stephens and Margaret Moffat in *How Large a Woman*, Cornalla & Eddie and My Fancy. The two theatres had similar roof features (seen again at Willesden Hippodrome) – cupolas which held revolving illuminated signs, spelling out the name E-M-P-I-R-E.

During its first year a fire closed the theatre for three months, while its 'Jacobean' interior was restored. Chiswick Empire was a very successful theatre, mainly presenting Variety, although first-class touring Musical Comedy and Revue companies were also presented. The Carl Rosa Opera Company was also popular. The bill for the week of 11 June, 1917 comprised: *Poached Eggs and Pearls*, a Canteen Play by Gertrude E. Jennings, Neil Kenyon the Scots character humorist, *Music Awakes* by The Ryewodes Trio, George Hughes (late of Alexandre & Hughes) in a sketch set in a Matrimonial Agency, Australian Alberto – a magician, Kate Hughes, Carlton Trio with *Voice, Violin and Piano*, with *Up-to-Date Happenings* on The Bioscope. All very refined – Bedford Park was, after all, just over the road – at prices which ranged from 3s in a box to 3d in the Balcony. It is interesting to note that seats could also be booked at outlying Offices at Ealing and Richmond. There were reduced prices for soldiers and sailors in uniform, except on Saturdays.

Exterior of Chiswick Empire, seen across Turnham Green in 1955

The bill for Monday, 14 October, 1935 contained the names of Brookins & Van, Hetty King, Yvette & Rugel, Ivor Vintor, Talbot O'Farrell, Three Aberdonians ('Too mean to tell you what they do'), Eddie Gray, Eight Black Streaks and Donald Peers. The Chiswick Empire had recovered from a brief flirtation with films during 1932/3 but Variety was then mainly uninterrupted for the rest of the theatre's life. Other attractions in the 1930s included Bennett & Williams, George Jackley, Nina Mae McKinney, Five Sherry Brothers, Albert Whelan. One week a monkey escaped from a circus appearing at The Chiswick Empire and swung about on the window ledges of the building, to the delight of the crowds in the High Road; it was eventually caught when it dived through a balcony window.

The bill for the week of 25 January, 1938 was Ken "Snakehips" Johnson and his Swing Orchestra, Clapham & Dwyer, Ronald Frankau, Ivor Vintor (again), The Brasellos, Harrison Viney, Billy Whittaker and Sheila, Sutherland Felce, and Three Mighty Atoms. After a brief closure at the start of The Second World War, The Chiswick Empire reopened and offered such attractions as Arthur Askey, Jimmy James, Vera Lynn, Lucan & McShane (Old Mother Riley) and Jewel & Warriss in *Black Vanities* from The London Hippodrome. Circus was not forgotten either, as the bill for Don Ross's show illustrates; it must have been quite a tight fit on the 32ft stage.

Interior with proscenium, 1912

Managers included Messrs. Persich, Milne, Harbour, Merritt and Jack Christie; the latter was usually named on bills as J.H. Christie Jnr., to avoid confusion with John Christie. No, not the founder of Glyndbourne, but the long-serving Area Supervisor for Stoll Theatres Corporation. John (always known as Jack) Christie had come from Shepherds Bush Empire on its closure in 1953 and was later Manager at The Bristol Hippodrome. For its last six months the Empire's Manager was Raymond Lane, also associated with Derby Hippodrome and Her Majesty's Theatre in the Haymarket. The last Musical Director was Charles Henry, still heading an orchestra of twelve players.

In the 1950s, besides such established favourites as Max Miller, Tessie O'Shea, Norman Evans and Sid Millward's Nitwits, the Empire introduced a host of newcomers, including Alma Cogan (who also starred in one of its pantomimes), Ken Dodd, Dave King, Joan Turner, Arthur Haynes, Mrs. Shufflewick, Dick Emery, Joan Regan (in the final *Cinderella* pantomime with Hylda Baker and MacDonald Hobley), Harry Secombe, Terry-Thomas and Dickie Valentine. I saw a wonderful show there at this time – *Rhythm is their Business* starring the live-wire Lita Rosa.

By 1958 Chiswick Empire was one of the only three remaining London suburban Variety Theatres – and the last London date on the Stoll tour. However, it still presented top-class shows, including bills headed by Tony Brent, Stan Stennett and The Hedley Ward Trio, Earle & Vaughan with Reg Dixon, Penny Nichols and Iris Sadler, Anne Shelton, Russ Hamilton and Jill Day, Nat Jackley, Robert Earl, Jimmy James, Audrey Jeans and Sally Barnes.

When artistes of this calibre were not available, the odd Strip Tease show appeared. One fairly dire one which I saw in November, 1958 was *The Astor Club Glamour Strip Show*, when those in the big Circle numbered around thirty. Artistes who stood out were Johnny Silver with his 'sophisticated humour' and Andy & The Bey Sisters. These shows simply drove away the remaining family audience and did not attract those at whom they were presumably aimed.

Interior towards the circles

Cliff Richard with The Drifters appeared at Chiswick Empire in May, 1959, on a strong bill with the Five Dallas Boys, Des O'Connor, Jean & Peter Barbour, Ray Alan, Kay & Kimberley and Tommy Wallis & Beryl, who later became The Plummers. There was almost a riot amongst Cliff's teenage fans and, after a fire extinguisher was thrown from the balcony, the curtain was dropped. That same night, following two houses at Chiswick, the star performed a late-night show at The Davis Theatre, Croydon.

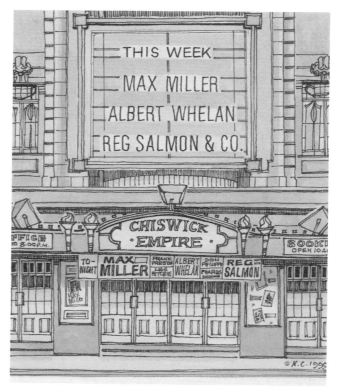

Main entrance with Max Miller billed, 1950s

Following the final pantomime, 1959 had opened with *The Max Wall Show* with Howard Jones & Reggie Arnold, Jill Summers and company. Some shows had now been reduced from eight to seven acts. Audiences were becoming thinner and *The Stage's* critic, on following a hearse into the Empire's car park one Monday night, remarked "Surely business can't be that bad". But it *was*, and he reported that Hal Monty, the comic in that week's show, cracked jokes while the Good Ship Variety sank beneath him. In a desperate attempt to find what the public wanted and would support, Stoll Theatres began to present touring Musical shows, amongst them *Me and My Girl*, with Lupino Lane, Lauri Lupino Lane and Valerie Tandy. Posters carried the exhortation: "Don't sit at home in the dark! Put on your 'Tifter' and come and see A Real Live Show". Other Musicals were *The Lilac Domino* and – the penultimate show – *Bless The Bride*.

Variety still had a look-in, however, with bills headed by The Marino Marini Quartet ('Volare'); the ever-popular Billy Cotton and his Band; and The Mudlarks. In April, 1959 Bruce Forsyth, fresh from his triumphs in Sunday Night at The London Palladium, did wonderful business heading a bill called *I'm in Charge*, which included The Skylons, Tino Valdi, Nennette Mongadors & Ann, Ron Parry and Suzy Miller. In his main spot Brucy had to break the sad news of the Empire's forthcoming closure.

The most famous figure ever to appear on the Chiswick Empire's stage was that of Liberace, who topped the closing bill for the week of 15 June, 1959 and for whose benefit three dressing rooms were redecorated. His own act, featuring vocalist Janet Medlin, was excellent value, while the others on the bill included Peter Dulay, Allan Kemble & Christine, Johnny & Suma Lamonte, Nelson Brothers, George Meaton and The Embassy Girls. Prices were more than doubled for the week, with a top of 10s 6d, but long-absent audiences returned in force to give the old girl a good send-off. On the Saturday night the curtain fell for the final time about 10.45pm, without any ceremony.

Stage house as seen from Chiswick Park Underground Station

The Chiswick Empire was the nineteenth Variety Theatre to close down in Greater London since 1945 and the site was sold to Town & City Properties for office development. In early August the breakers moved in and by January, 1960 the foundations were laid for the new building. There was criticism from a member of the Stoll Theatres board, who felt that the company should have developed the Empire site themselves, rather than sell it. At the time Stoll were disposing of their theatre interests in Derby, Leicester and Cardiff, and had closed and demolished The Stoll Theatre in Kingsway. Their Empires in Shepherds Bush, Hackney and Wood Green had all been lost to television, while their London Coliseum flagship had gone over to films. Only the Hippodromes in Manchester and Bristol remained open as living theatres. In November, 1960 Stoll Theatres made a £5,700,000 bid for Moss' Empires Ltd., which eventually resulted in a complete merger between the two companies.

The Chiswick Empire fitted perfectly into the architectural scheme of Turnham Green, whose unity has been completely destroyed by its replacement, in the 1960s, by an ugly sea-green office block, which – incidentally – is strongly rumoured to be haunted! Opened in the year of The Royal Command Peformance at The Palace Theatre, the Empire was a mere forty-seven years old when it closed down and was considered by artistes as very comfortable to work, with plenty of dressing rooms and an excellent stage and front-of-house staff. For the record, it had a stage almost identical in size to that of The London Palladium. There were fifty-eight lines, three follow spots and permanent steps from stalls to stage on each side of the 44ft wide proscenium. Unusually, the theatre had "carnival" front tabs, drawing up into the top corners of the proscenium arch. During demolition a few posters were rescued by a future member of The British Music Hall Society; a pelmet from one of the stage boxes lives on in a private cinema in Somerset; while three gas lamps from the Circle and Manager's office grace a house in West Sussex. A large poster of the final bill is displayed in a house in Wiltshire.

Programme Logo, 1950s

Crouch End Hippodrome (Queen's Opera House)

Topshill Parade, Hornsey Lane

Crouch End Hippodrome: exterior while on Ciné-Variety with Russ Carr billed

An almost forgotten place of entertainment, the Crouch End Public Hall, or Queen's Hall, was built by James Edmondson, of Highbury, and originally opened in 1896. The following year it was converted into a proper theatre by Frank Matcham, reopening as The Queen's Opera House. There was an elaborate, though fairly narrow, entrance with a large rounded window on the first floor; the front was topped with an ornate gable and urns. It had a steep mansard roof directly behind it, crowned by metal work and a flagstaff – certainly eye-catching in the street of shops. The adjoining terrace hints at the hand of the same architect, with similar curly pediments over the second storey windows.

Behind the façade lay quite a large gold-and-cream auditorium and a 54ft wide stage, with an orchestra pit and raked stalls floor; there were eight dressing rooms, a smoking and refreshment room and a well-equipped kitchen designed to cater for functions. Two floors over the main hall were given over to The Crouch End Athenaeum; a gentleman's club which even before opening had a membership of over 400. A few years later Edmondson also constructed the impressive Muswell Hill Athenaeum in Fortis Green Road.

The house opened on 27 July, 1897 with an ambitious production of *The Geisha*, which apparently came almost up to West End standards. Later that year, under the management of Morell & Mouillet, the Queen's built up its name by booking major companies and stars such as Ellen Terry, Lily Langtry and Mrs. Patrick Campbell. At this time it seems that seats were often sold out ten days before performances, at least for weekend performances.

Competition was fierce between drama houses, especially from the Grand Theatre, Islington, a larger and longer-established house, which was only a bus ride away. Standards inevitably declined, bemoaned by the local press. Morell & Mouillet, although a company with a score of theatres, sold out to the de Groot family of South Africa, H. de Groot becoming manager.

The new owners quickly converted the Queen's to a music hall, changing its name to Crouch End Hippodrome, with immediate success. Harry Champion and Harry Lauder were presented regularly, with crowds often turned away. By 1912 the theatre was being booked by Harry Day, later an MP and a famous Revue producer, in conjunction with his established tour, which included Bristol Empire. The proprietors were officially Crouch End Hippodrome Ltd., with Percy Calder as resident manager and Harry Day as general manager. However, Finsbury Park Empire's opening the previous year rapidly killed the Hippodrome's hopes of being one of North London's leading centres of entertainment. The Empire had an enormous capacity and, of course, had the booking power of Moss' Empires Ltd. behind it. Finsbury Park was, in addition, well-served by all forms of public transport, whereas Crouch End was (and still is) rather cut off from the rest of London.

Crouch End Hippodrome: the interior

Not surprisingly, given Harry Day's involvement, revues soon occupied most of the Hippodrome's programmes, with an overture and a couple of Variety acts to complete the evening's performance. Shows tended to be once-nightly at 7.45pm. There were appearances by local amateur dramatic and operatic societies, but its flurry of success had been short-lived.

In 1915, for example, the theatre presented Leonard Mortimer and company in the revue, *Don't be Silly*. Later that same year the Crouch End Hippodrome became a cinema, albeit with a 'theatre' feel about it. My friend Stanley Smith, who attended film matinees there with his mother, vividly remembered the plush carpeting and exotic smell on entering the vestibule and the tea and biscuits served in the interval. While the cinema was under the direction of The General Theatre Corporation during the 1920s some live acts leavened the film presentations. Over the years these included Russell Carr (related to Val Parnell), Florence Oldham, Two Canadians, The Carlier Sisters, Fisher & Ariani and The Ohio Three.

The Crouch End Hippodrome came under the Gaumont-British banner in May, 1928. Various improvements were made to the auditorium, but its end came in 1942, when it was badly damaged by bombing. A dancing school operated in part of it from 1948 to 1950, when the remains were largely cleared away. The stage walls are said to remain in a replacement commercial building. The theatre makes a ghostly reappearance for a week or two each autumn, when its exterior is shown on the cover of 'The Woodlands Hippodrome' programme in Somerset.

Harry Champion – 'Boiled Beef and Carrots'

Joanne Lisa, juggler

Ealing Hippodrome

22, Ealing Broadway

Ealing Hippodrome: exterior with Little Tich billed

Designed by Walter Emden with G.H. Pargeter as The New Ealing Theatre and opened in 1899, this theatre's spire was a prominent landmark in the busy shopping street. There was a large restaurant as part of the development, later a ballroom. The theatre is not well documented, but over the years carried a bewildering number of names. As a playhouse it was known for a time as The Lyric Theatre, or – even more grandly – as The Lyric Opera House, presenting touring plays once nightly with a Saturday matinee at 2.30pm. The manager at this time was Thomas J. Noble.

Even as a Variety house, it masqueraded for a period as The Ealing Empire Palace, although its best years were as part of the LTV circuit under Walter Gibbons, when it was called The Ealing Hippodrome. Under this title it was able in the years immediately before WW1 to present some really big names, but I suspect that its limited seating capacity, of less than 1,300, made it an unattractive proposition for LTV. However, such was the booking power of the circuit that George Robey, Little Tich, Jack Pleasants and The Poluski Brothers all appeared, but business cannot have been promising, as in October, 1908 a reduction in prices was announced. Fauteuils came down from 1s 6d to 1s and the Grand Circle from 1s to 6d, with similar reductions in the pit and gallery.

Things looked up by the time the great Marie Lloyd topped the bill in January, 1910 because seat prices had all gone up, maybe to meet the fees of The Queen of Comedy in such a small theatre. There were two houses, at 6.40 and 9pm, but few of the other nine acts on the bill are recalled today. They included Ray Espinosa, 'The Celebrated Premier Danseuse from The Lyceum', comics Phillips & Merritt and Marlo, 'The Incomparable Juggler'. A special note on the bills invited the public to hear the General Election results in a cosy stall, rather than waiting in the cold street for a paper. *The Daily Mail* had arranged to telephone the theatre as soon as the results were known. It was mid-winter, after all.

As part of the LTV circuit, Ealing Hippodrome was involved in the music hall strike of 1907, when the Variety Artists' Federation ordered many stars not to appear at those halls operated by Walter Gibbons and George Adney Payne until the dispute was settled. Among other demands, the big circuits had attempted to force artistes to fulfil extra performances and matinees, but without acceptable extra payments. Some halls remained open, presenting inferior acts (or even sending acts on several times during the evening) to beat the strike, but Ealing was reportedly 'Out'. Some local people remember Gracie Fields in Archie Pitt's show, *Mr Tower of London* and Fred Karno's company in *Mumming Birds* – a street urchin's idea of putting on a music hall show. The cast included the future Stan Laurel (Arthur Stanley Jefferson).

Interior, often used as a film set

In around 1923 the 1,260-seater Ealing Hippodrome was again re-named, this time as The Palladium, Ealing, and was taken over by the Scala circuit as a cinema. Further acquisitions, by Provincial Cinematograph Theatres and, in 1927, Associated Provincial Picture Houses, led in 1929 to its incorporation into the powerful Gaumont-British circuit, with whom it remained for the rest of its days. Unusually, the building retained its "theatre" ambience and furnishings, which led to its extensive use in films where music hall scenes were needed. One of these was *Champagne Charlie*, starring Tommy Trinder. The theatre was very close to Ealing Studios, which made it ideal as a ready-made set.

The Lyric Restaurant, now the Montague Ballroom, was retained even during the Gaumont years and was situated alongside the circle. The cinema was closed in 1958, demolished, and replaced by a branch of W.H. Smith.

East Ham Palace

High Street North (corner of Burges Road), East Ham

East Ham Palace: exterior showing entrance with Fred Karno's Co. billed

Situated next to the L.M.S. railway (i.e. London, Midland and Scottish Railway) Station (the train sounds permeated the stage – just as Southern's did the Players'), the East Ham Palace opened on 17 December, 1906 on the site of a former domestic garden. It was designed for The United Varieties Syndicate by their usual architects, Wylson & Long, and gave local people pleasure for fifty years. Its capacity after WW2 was just over 1,500 in stalls and two circles, so it was one of their smaller halls. The names of George Adney Payne, Henry Tozer and Joe Davis were among the original directors.

The Brothers Luck, Tom Leamore, Clarice Mayne and G.H.Chirgwin headed an 'all-star' bill at the opening performance, getting the East Ham Palace off to a flying start. Also on that bill were Lily

Burnand, Carlton, Miss Elsworthy (in a sketch), The Two Whites (comedy), Sibb & Sibb (trapeze artistes), Gilbert Gerard (animal mimic), Florence Zeatman (coon singer) and The Stella Troupe Dancers: all the elements of a well-balanced Variety bill, in fact. Ruffell's Bioscope completed the twice-nightly programme – a foretaste of the complete take-over by films 25 years later.

The company controlling the East Ham Palace's fortunes included at this time the Tivoli, the Oxford and The London Pavilion in the West End, giving it access to the top names for its growing suburban circuit. The comfortable East Ham theatre had the advantage of a large seafaring population in its neighbourhood, eager for rest, recreation – and the occasional pint – after returning to dry land.

Variety artistes seen here in the early years included Will Evans, Chas. Austin (doubling Walthamstow Palace in 1914), Fred Karno's Company in *The Casuals*, Ben Albert and Bransby Williams. Names now largely forgotten were Mark Melford & Co., Nellie Wigley, Max Waldon and Katie Marsh; but who could overlook Jack Dawe or Dusty Rhodes! Audiences were hard to please, so straight Variety was no means the staple here. Revue nationally came into vogue during and after WW1, and thrillers and dramas increasingly found a warm welcome at the East Ham Palace. The house was one of the first said to have run a full-length movie during a Variety programme.

A glance through theatrical trade papers shows that Harry M. Vernon's *The Case of Johnny Walker* (a great play on words) was the attraction here in September, 1915 on a bill that included Lucille Benstead. The next year *two* sketches appeared in the same programme – *Too Late* and *In The Trenches*, followed in 1917 by Lee Ephraim's offering, *Isadore You Tell Her* – obviously aimed at another key element of the audience. Another attraction to catch the eye was *Confessions of a Wife*, which took the stage in July, 1918; one hates to imagine what the 'confessions' were in this obviously topical offering as war ground to its end. So within a decade of its opening the Palace was already moving away from its Variety roots.

Exterior showing stage house

The more familiar names of Gertie Gitana, Jack Barty, Collinson & Dean and Eddie Gray appeared on bills during the 1920s, alongside John Morrison's *Dreambirds* and M. Barry O'Brien's production of *The Squeaker*. Bunny Doyle, one of my favourite comedians, had an excellent review of his work in *Full Speed*, "A Rollicking, Racy Revue" in July, 1929. *Encore* noted that: "First-rate fooling, comical capers and breezy burlesquing are Bunny's comical specialities".

Sadly, East Ham Palace succumbed to the talkies for around six years from 1934, being known for a time as The Regal Palace. When we passed the theatre in the late 1930s, however, the House Full boards were out for Tom Gamble in *Traffic Jam*. Also about this time *The Stage* favourably reviewed Mrs. Jack Hylton and Her Boys during the week at East Ham. The return of the Palace to the live ranks of V.T.C. Theatres went some way to replacing the old 'Sarf' (South London Palace), which was put out of action in the Blitz. *Old Soldiers Never Die*, with Ernie Lotinga, pulled 'em in for the week of 13 May, 1940.

As elsewhere, business was brisk during and immediately after WW2, whether for good Variety bills or for such controversial plays as *No Orchids For Miss Blandish*, staged in April, 1944. Stephane Grappelly and Max Miller topped in April, 1947. Audiences were still there for Bunny Baron in *Fun's A'Buzzin'*, with Billy Nelson, Chuck O'Neil & Co. in 1950 and for a strong bill topped by Max Bacon, Noni and Scott Sanders in Festival Year, 1951. Acts after the war were accompanied by an orchestra of nine musicians.

Soon, however, commercial television came to the London area and it became a struggle to fill seats. Artistes who were to become big names later on, such as Dick Emery and Charlie Drake, as seen on the bill shown, came too late to register on the suburban stage. By the mid-1950s the East Ham Palace was reduced to staging No.2 or No.3 shows, like *Kiss Me Goodnight, Sergeant-Major* (revived for the benefit of soldiers returning from Korea) and *Harem-Scarem*, described as 'A New High-Speed Revue', in 1955.

The Palace briefly became a playhouse, known as East Ham Theatre, but it was not a great success. This same idea was also being tried at Walthamstow, Camberwell and other halls that had fallen on hard times. In September, 1956 the theatrical paper *The Performer* announced the takeover of V.T.C. by Sidney L. Bernstein's Granada Theatres. There were promises of improved acts, a new lighting rig and fresh orchestral arrangements at the three remaining live halls on the V.T.C. circuit. Although £20,000-worth of work was mooted for the Brixton Empress, Chelsea Palace and the Metropolitan Theatre, East Ham Palace, which had closed in June that year, was earmarked for sale. In the event, only the Metropolitan continued to present shows for a few more years, while the other two gave way to films (at Brixton) and use as a television studio (at Chelsea). The East Ham Palace was itself demolished in 1958. We regret that we cannot depict the inside, as unfortunately no record of the splendid interior seems to have survived. However, we do have a box-office plan, which is shown below:

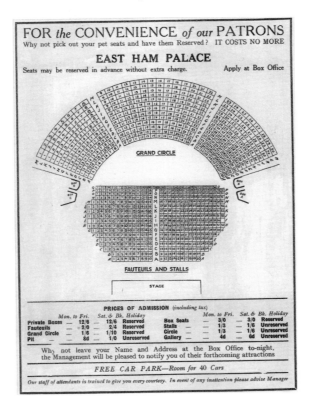

THE SYNDICATE HALLS.

BRIXTON EMPRESS (rehearsal, 12).— Connor and Maxon, A. D. Robbins, Jock Whiteford, Terence Byron and company in "William 'Enery's Wedding," Ko Ten Ichi Troupe, Bi-Bo-Bi, Elsie and Eddy Foy, Albert Foster, Ninon Oste.

CHELSEA (rehearsal, 12).—Joe Peterman's company in "The Harem Girl," Omega Trio, Trio, Charles Mott, Ida and Grace June, Five Hollanders, Ethel and May.

EAST HAM (rehearsal, 12).—Lee Ephraim's "Isadore You Tell Her," Yorke and Leonard, The Mongadors, the Three Scamps, Lydia and Francis, George Newburn, Tom E. Finglass, Jean and Josie, Maisie Rowlands.

EUSTON (rehearsal, 12).—Mark Sheridan, the Kratons, Dumond's Minstrels, Oswald Bemand, La Belle Nello, Queenie Finnis, Arthur Stroud, Frank Maura.

LONDON PAVILION (rehearsal, 11.30).— Mark Sheridan, Max Darewski, Gems from "Pick-a-Dilly" and "Honi Soit," the McNaughtons, Dumond's Minstrels.

METROPOLITAN (rehearsal, 12.15).—Jake Friedman and company in "The Dutch Hussars," Leonard and company, Charles Mott, Marcelle and Rose, Charles Sugden.

OXFORD (rehearsal, 12).—E. C. Rolls's "Seeing Life," T. E. Dunville, Ethel and May.

SOUTH LONDON (rehearsal, 12).—David Ponder and company in "The Dollar Rattlers," Connor and Maxon, Torino, Burr and Hope, Munroe and Robbins, Joy Wattle, Mlle. Hendricka, Joan Deering.

TOTTENHAM (rehearsal, 2).—Ginnett's War Horse, Harry Champion, May Henderson, Dolly Elsworthy, Little June and Joan Goode, Nelson and Maynard in "A Lame Excuse," Morton and Bowman, Les Altos.

WALTHAMSTOW (rehearsal, 1).—The Four Swifts, Benedetti Bros., Little June and Joan Goode, Norman Field, Eva Elkin, Marjorie Shepherd, Ernest Sims.

WATFORD (rehearsal, 1).—Arthur Gibbon's company in "The Rotters."

The Syndicate Halls in January, 1917

Edmonton Empire

Opposite Great Eastern Railway, Lower Edmonton Station

Edmonton Empire: full exterior

The greatest claim to fame of Edmonton Empire is the fact that in 1922 Marie Lloyd made her last appearance on its stage. Edmonton, lying alongside the Lea Valley, was a poor area and seats at the Empire were correspondingly cheap: stalls 1s, circle 6d and pit 3d; boxes for four were 7s 6d; on the other hand the management was able to boast that the Empire was the only theatre in the United Kingdom with upholstered tip-up seats throughout – including the gallery – and that cycles were stored free of charge – 'green' before their time!

The foundation stone for London's most northerly music hall was laid in 1908 by My Fancy, the wife of Harry Bawn who, together with James Sparrow, was a co-director of the enterprise. Alexander Bernstein, the father of Sidney Bernstein (one of the founding fathers of Independent Television) was in fact the power behind the building of the Empire – renting it to Bawn for £900 a year. The theatre advertised its Grand Opening on Boxing Day, 1908 and received a splendid send-off. The hall (a lot less pretentious than Tottenham Palace opened a few months before) was designed by Bertie Crewe, assisted by Cecil Masey.

The opening performance began with Hamilton Hill, the Australian baritone, singing the National Anthem, 'the large audience applauding him to the echo'. Other turns 'enthusiastically received' included My Fancy – described as the 'world's greatest dancer', (but as I said, she was the wife of one of the owners) and the programme was seasonably completed by a tabloid pantomime. The house manager was A.B. Hollands and the M.D. was Angelo A. Asher.

Subsequently several of the biggest stars played Edmonton, including Eugene Stratton, Charles Austin and Kate Carney. Reporting on Neil Kenyon, the 'Postman of Dunrobin', the press said that he was 'accorded a rousing reception. The points of his Scottish jokes are readily seized'. Peggy Pryde, the queen of low comedy and daughter of the late Jenny Hill (The Vital Spark) was here in the first season. One-act playlets were then a feature of Variety bills. One such was *The Sorrows of Satan*, a 'mystic episode'. Leo Dryden appeared in *The White Man*, obviously one of his patriotic imperial song-playlets. A longer piece was the sporting comedy-drama, *Rogues of the Turf*, which brought three thoroughbreds onto the stage.

Four more great stars played the Edmonton Empire soon after its opening. Victoria Monks gave her regards to Leicester Square on the same bill that Sam Mayo confided his sardonic humour. T.E. Dunville, 'The Long, Lean, Lorn Loon', made an exclusive and undoubtedly expensive first appearance, while Bransby Williams made a seasonable visit with his Dickensian studies. G.H. Chirgwin, the 'White-eyed Kaffir', starred in 1910, as did Gertie Gitana, already billed as 'A Star that never fails to Shine'.

Early in 1911 Carl Hertz baffled with his illusions and other magicians who wove their spells in Edmonton included The Great Rameses and Cecil Lyle, the Magical Milliner. The following year the girth of Ernie Mayne was in complete contrast to the long shanks of Carlton, the Human Hairpin. Described by C.B. Cochran as one of the quickest extemporaneous wits he had known, Arthur Roberts had been on stage for sixty years by the time he came to Edmonton. Joe Elvin, a prime mover in founding The Grand Order of Water Rats, as well as The Variety Artistes' Federation, was sixty when he brought one of his sporting sketches here in 1913.

Edmonton Empire exterior in 1922, Marie Lloyd's final date

Towards the end of 1913 the Middlesex County Council instructed the theatre to stop selling liquor. Harry Bawn pleaded that he had never had a police court case against him, and that for five years it had been a struggle to make the Empire pay in such a poor area; without an excise licence it would be forced to close. Fortunately more reasonable counsels prevailed.

Gus Elen paid his first visit to the Empire in 1914. A later bill advertised Chinko, 'a wonderful young juggler': he later grew up to be Teddy Knox, of Nervo & Knox fame. Following the great success of Albert de Courville's ragtime-oriented shows in the West End, revues were appearing in the suburbs, at first occupying only half the programme. Snappy titles like *Find the Lady* and *I Should Say So* were typical offerings. Not surprisingly, from 1914 onwards there was a plethora of military dramas. The Edmonton Empire was quick off the mark with *Second to None*, the story of the Scots Greys. When good old Harry Champion paid his umpteenth visit in March, 1915, it was to sing his topical success 'Harry with his old Iron Cross'. Dave & Joe O'Gorman, sons of Joe Snr., appeared that same year, but revues were more frequent now – such as *All the Nice Girls*.

In 1916 the halls suffered a blow by the imposition of the entertainment tax. This was small at first – a penny on the gallery and twopence on the stalls and circle. It was, of course, only a temporary wartime measure: tell that to the marines. As the war progressed, the management found difficulty in getting attractions as most of the male performers were on military age and were conscripted into the army. This situation enabled a local comedian named Dan Harlow to make a bit of a name in the area, but he never gained the fame of a later local lad, Bruce Forsyth. Once WW1 was over bills improved, however, and one strong bill included Vasco, The Mad Musican, whose son Bert later managed The Metropolitan. Fred Karno's Companies appeared at least three times at Edmonton, while Clarkson Rose and Olive Fox, just making their names, called in regularly. The orchestra numbered no fewer than sixteen at this stage.

In 1920 there were two pantomimes, followed by the biggest success the Empire ever had – paying four return visits. This was Archie Pitt's *Mr. Tower of London*, starring Gracie Fields. The next year a unique attraction was presented, being Datas, The Memory Man. Athas & Collins, whose posters long decorated the Players' Theatre, were supported by Howard Rogers, the Popular Padré. But bad times were to follow in 1922 with the deaths of two big music hall personalities.

In August Harry Bawn, who had guided the fortunes of the Empire since its opening, sadly died, and his widow, My Fancy, sold her lease back to Sidney L. Bernstein. Variety continued with sound bills headed by G.T. Pattman at the Mammoth Organ, and by The Hedges Brothers & Jacobson, together with Queenie Leighton and Whit Cunliffe. Then occurred the tragedy felt beyond the narrow bounds of the theatre.

On Monday, 2 October Marie Lloyd opened at the Edmonton Empire. She was known to have been unwell for fifteen months, but she sang her numbers, including 'The Cosmopolitan Girl'; and 'I'm One of the Ruins' with her usual flair at both houses that evening. On Tuesday she got through her performance at the first house, but collapsed on stage at the second house. On Saturday, 7 October she died. Never before has the passing of a music hall artiste evoked such sympathy from the general public.

Harry Day's *Spangles* was just as successful here as at other halls, returning later. Also in 1923 was seen Thomas F. Convery's *Zip*, introducing Caryll & Mundy, who were to remain at the top for thirty years; more active was Fred Ginnett's enactment of *Dick Turpin's Ride to York*. He had, of course, passed through Edmonton on his way north. A new name in the firmament was Talbot O'Farrell. The following year a big Palladium success, *Rockets*, reached Edmonton, while the Depression, now under way, was celebrated by *Unemployed*, and *Pledges* while the longest-running of the genre was *On the Dole*. More optimistic was *Tons of Money*, which had notched up 737 performances at the Aldwych.

Another rare appearance by a truly great star, Little Tich, marked the quarter century. Destined for longevity was Randolph Sutton in *Spare Parts*, and forerunner of scores of similar attractions was John Bitmingham's Band; but revues, alternated at the Empire with straight Variety. Good middles on Variety bills included child impressionist Wilson Hallett and the comic with bagpipes, Jock McKay.

The rebuilt interior looking towards the stage

In 1926 the press commented on the success that Mr. Bernstein had brought to the theatre, and certainly Layton & Johnstone, Jack Hylton and his Band, The Houston Sisters and Noni the clown were big attractions. Also worth mentioning are The Two Bobs, Arthur Prince and Gaston & Andrée. The next year, following an attractive revue with Tommy Mostol, *The Golden West* and a good one with Percy Honri, Variety lovers were in for a shock. On 6 April the theatre was closed for alterations: when it reopened it was as a ciné-Variety house.

The Edmonton Empire pursued a fairly consistent policy of booking accredited acts – if the names of Albert Whelan, Herschel Henlere ('The Mirthful Music Master'), Fred Barnes and The Lloyd family are anything to go by. In 1933, by which time the Talkies were well-established, the theatre was completely rebuilt (to designs by Cecil Masey, now an eminent cinema architect); it reopened on 28 August, 1933 – surprisingly not with film, but with stage presentations until WW2.

Since then live entertainment occurred only spasmodically. Its name was changed to The Granada, Edmonton on 1 January, 1951 before it finally closed on 13 July, 1968. Miss Regan, from the Metropolitan, had been transferred here to handle advance bookings. It soon reopened on Bingo, but was demolished in 1970 for redevelopment as offices and shops. The Wurlitzer 3/10 organ was preserved and is now in St. Albans Organ Museum.

Sidney Bernstein, whose father, Alexander, built the Empire

Finsbury Park Empire

Corner of St. Thomas's Road and Prah Road

Finsbury Park Empire: exterior with Vera Lynn billed

Finsbury Park Empire was opened at St. Thomas's Road on 5 September, 1910 and remained a theatre under the management of Moss' Empires Ltd. right up to its closure in 1960. It was their No.1 suburban hall, being the first date out of the West End on their premier tour. Licensees were, in turn, Sir H.E. Moss, Frank Allen, R.H. Gillespie and Val Parnell. It was constructed to the plans of Frank Matcham at a cost of £45,000. A condition of the building permit was that Moss's nearby Holloway Empire should cease to be a music hall, so Variety ended there on 3 September with George Lashwood as top.

The opening bill was headed by Fanny Moody and Charles Manners, the opera and concert singers, and Bert Coote & Co. in *A Lamb on Wall Street*, supported by The Poluskis and Helen Trix. The following week's top was Captain Raymond Phillips' Airship, which demonstrated wireless telegraphy, of interest through the recent arrest by that means of Crippen, the then notorious wife-murderer. Other early attractions included Marie Lloyd, Vesta Tilley, George Formby, Little Tich, Vesta Victoria and W.C. Fields. From the 'legit' we welcomed Ellaline Terriss & Seymour Hicks, Gladys Cooper,

Irene Vanbrugh & Edmund Gwenn in a playlet by Barrie, and Lily Langtry in another sketch. Other West End stars included George Graves, Nelson Keys and Owen Nares.

Magicians were also popular and it is strange to think that although Jasper Maskelyne and John Calvert died normally, three other popular visitors to the Park (The Great Lafayette, Chung Ling Soo and Houdini) all met tragic ends – burnt to death in a fire at the Edinburgh Empire, in May, 1911; accidentally shot on stage at the nearby Wood Green Empire in 1918; and after an attack on him at the Prince's, Montreal in September, 1926 Houdini died from poisoning following an unsuccessful operation to remove his appendix, ruptured by three punches from a student in his dressing room.

In the 1920s revue reigned supreme, with Albert de Courville and Harry Day pre-eminent in the field. More Americans arrived including Sophie Tucker, Burns & Allen, Herb Williams, The Duncan Sisters and the American Ragtime Octet. But traditional Variety had not been displaced and on my first two visits to the Park in 1929–30 I saw Harry Lauder and Gracie Fields respectively. Less traditional was *Shanghai Nights*, an allegedly daring revue which Wallace Parnell presented. Stage bands were enormously popular from the 1920s; many with their own signature tunes and nearly all of them appeared at The Park. One can name Jack Payne (*Say It with Music*), Roy Fox (*Whispering*), Harry Roy (*Tiger Rag*), Jack Hylton (*Come Listen to the Band*) and Billy Cotton (*Somebody Stole my Gal*). Vocalists often broke away from their bands to make their own names and among these were Lita Rosa and Dennis Lotis from Ted Heath's Orchestra, Dickie Valentine, Vera Lynn, Michael Holliday and Anne Shelton.

Interior looking towards the stage

In 1935 I was able to attend regularly and the first bills I saw then were headed by Flanagan & Allen, Max Miller and The Boswell Sisters. Other great pre-war attractions were Florrie Forde, Florence Desmond, Revnell & West, Tommy Trinder, Fats Waller and The Mills Brothers.

Immediately after the war an exceptional bill of past favourites, including George Robey and Percy & Mary Honri, with Peg Leg Bates in support, provided a foretaste of the nostalgic show that played two record-breaking fortnights in 1950–51 – Don Ross' *Thanks for the Memory*. Many American acts absent during the war returned in these post-war years, notably the Deep River Boys, the Delta Rhythm Boys and Chico Marx. Besides which there was an influx of new acts whose experience had been gained in the forces, some of whom, like Tony Hancock, Reg Dixon, Reg Varney and Harry Secombe, proved an asset to Variety.

When the London Palladium came under the control of Moss' Empires, from 1947, Finsbury Park Empire took a lot of big names straight from their West End seasons. Among these were Laurel & Hardy, Tex Ritter, Mae Barnes, Billy Eckstein and Dean Martin & Jerry Lewis from America. British stars included Shirley Bassey, Tommy Cooper, Ted Ray, Michael Holliday, Joan Regan, Billy Cotton, Elsie & Doris Waters, Jimmy Wheeler and – usually twice a year – Max Miller. Roy Hudd made one of his earliest appearances on a Max Miller bill, alongside G.H. Elliott and Hetty King in 1959. Perennial favourites were The Beverley Sisters.

A good M.D. in the pit is an essential in a successful Variety theatre and in Syd Kaplan Finsbury Park had one of the best. He came in from Lewisham Hippodrome on that hall's move to films in 1952, his arrival even being billed on the box office cards that week. Kaplan had been the popular conductor for many years at the Holborn Empire before it was bombed.

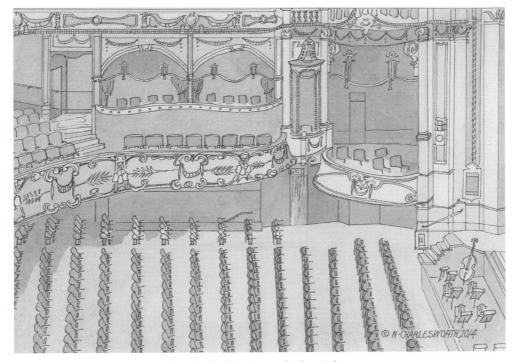

Interior looking towards the circles

A most enjoyable show in later years was *Cap & Belles*, featuring Max Wall and Company. After this week I did not find much to attract me. The star did make other appearances here, notably with Howard Jones & Reggie Arnold (also off-shoots from a big band) and The Tanner Sisters on the bill.

The Finsbury Park Empire declined, as did all the music halls, during the 1950s and it finally closed on 7 May, 1960. The last show starred Emile Ford & The Checkmates, The Lana Sisters (one of whom became Dusty Springfield) and Chas. McDevitt & Shirley Douglas. Even in its last years it was immaculately managed by David Wilmot, who moved on to the London Palladium.

There was an outcry when, in the spring of 1960, it was rumoured that the Empire was to close. Plays and musicals were staged to keep the theatre open. Rock 'n' Roll stars sustained it for the last few weeks, but one thing that these shows lacked was...Variety. Marty Wilde, Craig Douglas and Duane Eddie were among those who topped. Cliff Richard and The Drifters (later the renamed The Shadows) filled the place; in fact, Moss' Empires promised to keep the theatre open if Cliff would appear for two weeks a year. Unfortunately, the singer had too many other commitments and was unable to sign a contract.

Exterior of the stage house

As the weeks ticked away to closure, letters from the public appeared in *The Stage* listing all the acts that had not appeared at Finsbury Park for years. Others from agents lamented the reluctance of big names to appear, except at fees well beyond their drawing power. Remember that seat prices were 9d in the gallery to 4s 3d in the best stalls. An appeal and Anti-closure meeting was held at Beale's Restaurant in Holloway Road, addressed by Ted Gollop of Moss' Empires; the company even offered the theatre to the profession, with a gift of equipment, but the offer was not taken up.

After closure the curtain rose again only once, when the Empire played its part in the theatre sequences of the successful film *The Young Ones*, starring Cliff Richard in 1964. The theatre was demolished in March, 1965, its place eventually being taken by Vaudeville Court, a block of flats. And so ended a well-built, well-equipped, comfortable theatre (only 50 years old,) which any continental town would have cherished as a state theatre.

Thanks to Albert Ralph Ginn for memories of the stage bands.

Golders Green Hippodrome

North End Road

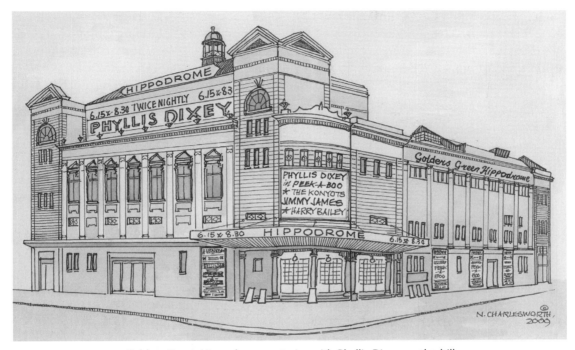

Golders Green Hippodrome: exterior with Phyllis Dixey on the bill

Although out of use as a theatre for some twenty years, the Golders Green Hippodrome is still standing and in use as a BBC concert hall. It is fondly remembered for its excellent Christmas pantomimes and as the home of the London area Scouts' *Gang Shows*. Occupying a large site adjacent to the Underground and bus stations, the theatre was designed by Bertie Crewe and is the most distinguished building in Golders Green. Opening on Boxing Day, 1913 under the management of Walter Gibbons, the Hippodrome held around 2,250 in stalls, dress circle and upper circle. It arrived on the scene very late for a Variety theatre, so it presented this style of entertainment for barely ten years, with revue making inroads practically from the start. A typical early example was *Splash Me!* in August, 1914, on a bill that included The Paulastos, Gladys Huxley, Visto, Albert Wyndham & Capt. Spalding. The independent house continued with similar bills until the early 1920s. When built, the Hippodrome was adjoining open countryside, so arrangements had to be made for late transport to take patrons home after the show; later, of course, it was extremely well-served by busses and trains. Stars who appeared in the early years included local resident Marie Lloyd.

The first real breakaway from the established music hall programme was in April, 1922, when *The Merry Widow* was revived, with Evelyn Laye and George Graves in the principal parts. Then towards the end of that year the theatre was taken over by Golders Green Hippodrome Ltd., under the direction of J.C. Clavering – a name familiar until the mid-1960s. F.R. Goodman was in partnership for the first two years, while James W. Perry and Claude Withers were others who served for a long period.

The Hippodrome, after considerable refitting, became a first-class touring house and in 1925 its excellent acoustics were appreciated when it became the temporary home of The British National

Opera Company. The policy then became the staging of West End plays and musical comedies, either prior to or at the end of their runs. One was grateful for the chance to catch a good show at Golders Green before it departed on its provincial tour. Shows generally included the leading West End artistes. All the Charles B. Cochran shows were staged at the Hippodrome. There was a first-class pantomime each Christmas.

During February, 1926 the famous show *The Co-Optimists* paid a visit, with Davy Burnaby, Stanley Holloway, Mary Leigh, Melville Gideon, Doris Bentley, Aust Melford, Gilbert Childs, Marjorie Spiers and Sheila Rawls in the cast. Stanley Holloway was later to appear in a long-running pantomime at the Hippodrome. Another local resident (in fact she lived just across the road) Anna Pavlova, made her last London appearance here in December, 1930 with a week's season of Ballets and Divertissements. There were in fact, fifteen different items, Pavlova being partnered by Pierre Vladimiroff.

For a number of years during the 1930s T. Arthur Russell presented his *Brighter Sunday Series*, a Variety concert, at the Golders Green Hippodrome with seats from 1s to 3s – "At a price you can pay!" One such concert gave us Don Sesta and his Gaucho Tango Band, Tessie O'Shea, Clifford Guest, Ronald Frankau and six other acts; while on another Sunday we enjoyed Bransby Williams, Talbot O'Farrell, Dorrie Dene, Nan Kenway & Douglas Young, Harry Hemsley, 'Musaire' and Arthur Askey. The last named was a perennial favourite here in pantomime after WW2.

During the summer of 1935 the Hippodrome tried a short Variety season with such acts as The Diamond Brothers, Max Miller and Nat Gonella's Georgians. In September Gracie Fields topped the bill, with strong support from Griffiths Bros. & Miss Lutie, Payne & Hilliard, Presco & Campo, Jack Hart and his Broadcasting Band, Leslie Strange, George Hurd and the Six Zio Angels. Shows were twice nightly at 6.30 and 9.00pm. Gracie Fields was back the following September, with Naunton Wayne among the supporting acts. Vic Oliver, Troise and his Mandoliers – and Banjoliers – Billy Bennett, The Charladies, Al & Bob Harvey, Bobby Wright & Marion and company provided another most enjoyable week, also in 1935.

The theatre then reverted to touring productions until the outbreak of WW2, when it once again became a Variety house until around 1950 – although there were of course weeks when a play or a star personality took the stage.

Interior looking towards the stage

Wartime spirits were certainly given a lift by weeks of well-balanced and entertaining Variety bills, often under the *"V for Variety…"* banner and it might make sense to list some of these good bills, which were normally staged twice nightly at 6.00 and 8.15pm. In June, 1942, just a year before his first West End triumph, Sid Field starred in *How's About It*, presented by William Henshall; Field appeared in no fewer than six sketches, while others in the show included The Western Brothers, The Avalons, May Mills, the American dancing stars Tracey & Hay, Bert Nichol, 'The Blonde Bombshell' Evelyn Taylor, Uriel Porter and Henshall's Young Ladies. Nat Jackley and Jack Clifford followed Sid Field into the Golders Green Hippodrome in Leslie A. Macdonnell's *Funny Bone Frolics*, supported by Jack Stanford, Three Musketeers, Bettina Richman, The Dolinoffs & Raya Sisters, Jean Shaw and The Glamourettes.

In August, 1942 Bertram Montague presented *All in Favour* with Caryll & Mundy and May Goring Thomas. Others 'in favour' were Syd Makin, the impressionist Mary Bland, Gwen Farrar teamed with Lisa Lee, Reg Redcliffe with his Super-Rumbaphone and The Betty Fox Globe Girls. The finale was a 'Potted and Potty Pantomime' – *Cinderella*.

At the height of his film career, George Formby topped in March, 1943 with Beryl assisting him in his spot and in a sketch; the company also included Sirdani ('Don't be fright'), Eve Drury, Peter Brough & Archie Andrews and the pianist Renara. Younkman's Famous Czardas Band headed another Variety bill, before a musical production, *No, No, Nanette*, took the stage twice nightly with Hazel Jennings, Hugh Rene and Barrett Lennard in a big company. A more familiar type of show came in the following week, however, with George Black's *Black Vanities*: this had Jewel & Warriss and Tommy Jover as headliners. About this time bookings for the Hippodrome were handled by Archie Parnell & Co.

Before Variety gave way to the old policy of touring West End productions, a couple of popular bills came to Golders Green. The ever-welcome Phyllis Dixey in *Peek-A-Boo* visited in February, 1949 with Phyllis's husband, 'Snuffy' Jack Tracey, in support as usual; comedy was in the capable hands of Jimmy James & Co., in two sketches, and 'The Irish Ambassador', Harry Bailey. In June of the same year America's Chico Marx topped a bill with Cyclo Bros., Frank Raymond, Jack Billings with Diana, Lionel King ('Joker, Ace High') Grafton Sisters & Jacques, Joe Ortnes & partner and Dick Henderson, jnr. Performances had by then reverted to 6.15 and 8.30pm. Master of Magic, Jasper Maskelyne, led a Variety company which included Sam Browne & Mary Naylor – also in June, 1949.

The Golders Green Hippodrome may have reverted to straight productions again, but there was no reduction in the quality of the shows staged. For example, *A Streetcar Named Desire* in 1950, Prince Littler's production of *Guys and Dolls* with Lizbeth Webb, Sidney James and Edward Devereaux in 1954, and *The Doctor's Dilemma* with Ann Todd, Michael Hordern, Lewis Casson and Anthony Ireland in 1956. Among star personalities to make solo appearances at Golders Green was Marlene Dietrich.

Full houses were the rule at the annual *Gang Show* staged by Ralph Reader at the Hippodrome for the Scouts movement in the London area and for others their only visit to the theatre was to see the Christmas pantomime – one of the best in town. A selection will prove what a magnet the Golders Green house was at this time of the year, giving Variety lovers a chance to see many of their favourites in action. Prince Littler's *Cinderella* (1941–42) brought Duggie Wakefield as Buttons with his Gang (Billy Nelson, Chuck O'Neil and Jack Butler), Lilian Keyes, Johnny Kavanagh and Norah Chapman; Emile Littler's *Puss in Boots* (1960–61) had Norman Caley as the dame, Tommy Trinder, Margaret Burton, Lauri Lupino Lane & George Truzzi, together with Brian Hewitt-Jones; Prince and Emile Littler combined to present *Aladdin* with Cora Goffin and Stanley Holloway; Arthur Askey appeared in *Humpty Dumpty* (1956–57) with his daughter Anthea, old-timer George Betton and Billy Gray, in *Dick Whittington* with Eve Lister, Eddie Molloy and The Lynton Boys, and in *Cinderella* (1961–62) with Elizabeth Larner, Dawkes & Webb and Erica Yorke; *Babes in the Wood* gave us Terry Scott and Hugh

Lloyd with Norman Caley, Laurie Lupino Lane & George Truzzi and – just retired from The Crazy Gang – Charlie Naughton, in 1962–63.

Pantomime continued on its merry way, with Jimmy Wheeler, Tommy Fields, Desmond & Marks, Jimmy Clitheroe, Albert Burdon, Hughie Green and – a record-breaking show – Danny la Rue. Variety lovers had one last chance to savour their favourite entertainment when in April, 1964 Audrey Lupton and Arthur Lane brought *Nights at The Tivoli* to the Hippodrome for a week, with The British Music Hall Society mounting an Exhibition of Early Music Hall Souvenirs in the Centre Lounge. The show was more of a Music Hall Revue than a straight Variety bill, but we enjoyed seeing Randolph Sutton, Hetty King, Don Smoothey and Nat Gonella in action. Younger talent included June Marlow, Barrie Gosney, Fergus O'Kelly, Terry Doogan, The Gladstone Harmony Four and Jasmine Dee; The Tivoli Belles quickened our pulses throughout the evening, while Robert Probst conducted the orchestra.

Things were not quite so happy for the weekly changes of plays. With dwindling audiences, the Hippodrome was acquired in the 1960s by Marfield (Theatre Enterprises) Ltd., whose project was to turn the theatre into a bingo hall. To start with, the usual weekly change of shows continued and we enjoyed *West Side Story* straight out of Her Majesty's Theatre; but when the application for bingo use was made the local authority – not wishing to attract bingo players into the area – opposed the scheme. Sadly, the Hippodrome's sister house Streatham Hill Theatre succumbed.

Eventually, in 1968, the theatre closed, but it is worth noting that even in its last year it made a small profit. There was a Farewell Charity Show on 18 February to mark the Hippodrome's closure as a live theatre and among those who took part were Vera Lynn, Bud Flanagan and Ralph Reader with *The Gang Show*.

The following year of 1969 saw the theatre's acquisition by the BBC as a concert hall and recording studio, from which *Friday Night is Music Night* and similar programmes were broadcast. The theatre was carefully converted and well looked after, despite the temporary loss of the upper part of the flytower and the stage wings to rehearsal and band rooms and offices. Present use is as a church, while live performances could be staged. Reconversion to a theatre is a possibility.

Hackney Empire

Mare Street, Hackney

Hackney Empire: exterior frontage in 1905

Occupying a large and prominent site at 381–391 Mare Street, Hackney Empire was designed by Frank Matcham and at its opening on 9 December, 1901 had seating for 2,132 in stalls, dress circle, balcony and gallery. It was owned by Oswald Stoll and, after his death in 1942, was managed by Prince Littler until its closure in 1956. The beauty of its design, with its perfect sight-lines and its compact arrangements, makes it the ideal music hall. We are very fortunate indeed that such an exciting theatre has survived the slaughter of the 1950s and 1960s, and is in use again.

Widely considered to be one of Matcham's most perfect and sensual creations, the Empire's fine plasterwork was carried out by *two* specialists, due to the tight schedule involved: Felix de Jong (possibly the greatest of the theatrical decorators) was responsible for the auditorium, while J.M. Boekbinder did the front of house. The appearance of the exterior was radically altered after the building contract had actually been let, as Stoll required the addition of shops on the Mare Street frontage. Drawings show that the original theatre frontage was to have been massive and far less attractive than that eventually completed. The kinship of the finished frontage to The Metropolitan, Edgware Road, can clearly be seen.

The first production at Hackney was *Two for Three Ha'pence*, starring Joe Elvin, Wilkie Bard and Marie Kendall, and during its long life practically all the 'Greats' of Music Hall and Variety played there: Marie Lloyd, Dan Leno, Vesta Tilley and Little Tich in the early days; Billy Bennett, Tommy Handley and The Houston Sisters in the 1920s; and Max Miller, Vic Oliver, Louis Armstrong and Sandy Powell in the 1930s.

A typical bill will give a flavour of those far-off, early years:

For the week of Monday, 28 April, 1902 – just four months after opening – the Empire offered twice nightly at 6.45 and 9.10pm: Herbert Campbell (the Drury Lane Comedian), Mora & Lola (Burlesque Musical Melange), O'Connor & Brady (Roars of Laughter), The Selbini Troupe (Acro-cyclists and Musical Head Balancers), New York Zouaves (the Wondrous Quick-Drill Squad), Little Gitana (Gertie, then described as Dainty and exceedingly clever Petite Artiste), James Grant (Vocal Comedian), Amy Allnut (Character Vocalist), the strangely-named Ben Nevis (Concoction of Character Creations) and S.H. Unthan (the Armless Wonder). The last-named would, of course, be considered in pretty poor taste today!

The Acting Manager at this time was the very long-serving John Christie, who was to survive until the theatre's closure in 1956, while the Conductor was W. Johnson. Prices were: Fauteuils 2s, Grand Circle 1s 6d, Stalls 1s, Pit 6d, Balcony (later re-named Upper Circle) 4d and Gallery 3d.

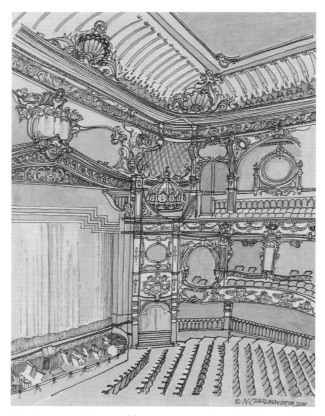

Interior proscenium and boxes as seen from the Upper Circle

By the time Monday, 26 February, 1912 had come round, John Christie has been promoted to District Manager, the Acting manager was Chas. Marte and John Russell had taken over the baton.

That week's bill ran as follows: Overture (from 'Lohengrin'), Mdlle. De Dio, The Bioscope with topical and 'Other Interesting Events', Whit Cunliffe, Arthur Slater (The Whistling Man in White), McConnell Trio, Little Zola (probably Claud Zola, who later played Cat in *Dick Whittington*), Annie Schuberth (Vocalist), The Kratons (America's Foremost Hoop-rolling Artistes in 'Hoopland'), Heely & Meely (The two Comedy Acrobatic Tramps in the Hayloft), Eily Adair and Charles Whittle.

The Bioscope had a place in all the early programmes and in fact a 'Bio' box was installed at Hackney Empire from the outset, running for about six to eight minutes during the programme. When the number of local cinemas increased during WW1, the Bioscope gradually became obsolete.

Although most of the great Music Hall stars trod the boards at Hackney, they did not do so in quick succession, for the Empire was quite a way down the league table, which comprised some two hundred and fifty Halls. The competition then – and later – for top names was intense, so there were many weeks of mediocre attractions. Many of the bill-toppers, such as J.B. Milburn, Cruikshank, Penrose & Whitlock and Harry Claff, meant more than they do now. However, others made big names for themselves later on: The Delfont Boys (Bernard Delfont and Albert Sutton), Flotsam & Jetsam, Will Hay, Ted Ray and Flanagan & Allen were among these. Notable bills in the 1930s were headed by The O'Gorman Brothers, Syd Seymour and his Mad Hatters, Jimmy O'Dea (the Irish comic) and Macari and his Dutch Accordion Serenaders.

On my first visit to Hackney Empire, around 1936, the top was Geraldo and his Gaucho Tango Band. Stage bands were all the rage at this time and in fact audiences complained that there were too many of them presented. Gracie Fields made frequent appearances over the years, to say nothing of such magnificent Revues as *Leicester Square Looks Round*, starring Sid Field. When nudes did appear they were such tasteful performers as Gaston & Andrée and Phyllis Dixey. Performances at this time were 6.40 and 8.55pm. Seat prices (in the cheaper parts) had increased by 2d – 3d since the early days.

Up to the outbreak of WW2 Hackney Empire ran Sunday Pictures, with a double-feature programme. Doors opened at 5.15pm and a typical evening offered Johnny Weismuller and Maureen O'Sullivan in *Tarzan Escapes*, together with Stuart Erwin and Edmund Gwenn in *Country Bumpkin*. Stoll's other Variety Theatres in London ran similar programmes, so were open seven days a week.

Forthcoming stage and screen attractions at the Empire were advertised weekly in their own publication, at one time entitled 'The Stoll Herald', but later just carrying the Theatre name boldly on the cover. Pictures of the following week's star and supporting acts, together with breezy and enthusiastic descriptions, were published from Stoll's headquarters at The London Coliseum.

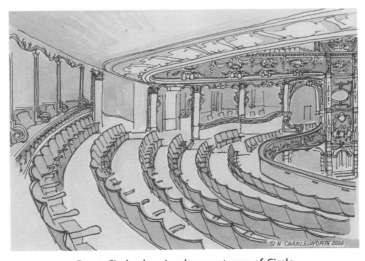

Dress Circle showing boxes at rear of Circle

These publications also pushed the attractions at The Stoll Picture Theatre in Kingsway, which sometimes ran a stage or Ice Show as well as two films. Sir Oswald Stoll had taken over this theatre when it had failed as The London Opera House, making it a very popular family cinema.

Unlike other Halls on the Stoll circuit, such as Wood Green Empire and Ardwick Empire (later New Hippodrome) in Manchester, Hackney Empire did not surrender to the cinema during the week. The bill for the week of Monday, 27 March, 1939 (just six months before the outbreak of war) was: Cliff Martel (the Comic on the Keys), Jim Emery in a comic sketch, The Four Smith Brothers (Harmony Singers), young Hughie Green with his girlfriends Sadie Corrie and Jean Ray, Velda & Van, Alf Powell & his Banjo Octet, comedian George Betton, Ivor Moreton & Dave Kaye (The Original Tiger-Rag Pianists) and Four Winclairs (Dancing Stars). It is interesting that the bill-topper (Hughie Green) closed the first half of the programme, as did Max Miller later on. The Cheekie Chappie always caught the last train back to his home in Brighton every night without fail. The Sunday Pictures advertised that week were: George Formby in *No Limit* and Bing Crosby and Madge Evans in *Pennies From Heaven*.

Interior showing the circles and stage boxes

Sir Oswald Stoll died in January, 1942 and was succeeded by Prince Littler, who continued to run Hackney Empire as a successful Variety Theatre. Littler also brought back live shows to The Stoll Theatre, Kingsway, whose attractions were printed alongside those of The Coliseum or The Theatre Royal Drury Lane in the Hackney programmes.

Wartime conditions led to strange performance times at West End Theatres (2.30 and 6.30pm daily at The Coliseum, 2.15 and 6.15pm daily at The Stoll Theatre), but left Hackney Empire relatively unscathed at 6.25 and 8.30pm. The bill for the week of Monday, 19 July, 1943 was topped by Britain's finest Clarinet Player, Harry Parry and Radio Sextet, supported by Hetty King, The Three Stooges, Ernie Gerrard & Co. (Magical Moments), Len Williams, De Bear & Du Bray and The Muldoon Four.

To indicate the richness of live entertainment available locally, my friend Harry Greatorex lived in Clapton and reached Hackney Empire for a 3d bus fare, although he usually walked. A 4d ride in the opposite direction would have taken him to Finsbury Park Empire, while the same fare would have allowed him to see Variety at Walthamstow Palace or Collins' Music Hall on Islington Green. However, Hackney Empire always seemed a lot friendlier and less formal than Finsbury Park Empire, although the latter had a bigger orchestra and drew larger audiences than Hackney. Harry remembers seeing Max Bygraves twice at Finsbury Park, but not at Hackney. Bygraves was a big draw in the 1950s, but was choosy about where he played. He did work for Stoll at Chiswick Empire in 1955. Names that did appear at the Mare Street house included Tony Hancock and Des O'Connor, but neither made a great impression at the time: Harry Worth and Reg Varney, however, showed great promise.

Strong Variety bills alternated with touring Revues at Hackney Empire in the 1940s and 50s (some of them rather weak). Tommy Trinder starred in his own show for the week commencing Monday, 14 June, 1948, appearing in no fewer than five spots. He received good support from The Ganjou Brothers and Juanita ('A Romance in Porcelain'), Woods & Jarrett ('Those Two Dark Gentlemen'), a melodrama – 'The Wooing of Hun Lang Wo', Young China, The John Tiller Girls, Jerry Allen & his Organ, as well as several sketch artistes. Times had altered slightly to 6.30 and 8.40pm now that the war was over.

Interior showing full proscenium during performance of "Little Miss Muffet", 1954–55 Season

In *Showboat Express*, for the week of Monday, 1 October, 1951 could be seen two sets of drag double-acts, Bartlett & Ross and Ford & Sheen, in a fifteen-item *Pleasure Cruise of Laughter and Song*. The programme showed that Fredk. J. Creasey had now become Manager at the Empire. Other Revues of the period included Joe Waxman's *Here Comes Fifi* and Sidney Burns' *Paree for Me*, with Des Dale, Dickie Arnold, Valerie Walsh, Maurice Stoller and (believe it or not) Eva May Wong.

After WW2 the Hackney Empire ran short Pantomime seasons, often following a season at Chiswick Empire. The companies worked hard, with three performances daily, at 2.30, 6.40 and 8.55pm. Frequently the Mayor of Hackney entertained the entire Pantomime company to tea during their season.

The young Shirley Bassey made a big impression during the week of 26 April, 1954 in *Hot From Harlem*, an All-Coloured Revue that included Harold Holness, Woods & Jarrett, Cyril Lagey (fondly remembered from The Nitwits) and Amos Gordon. A month later Albert Burdon featured in *Alamein to Petticoat Lane* along with Frank Richards, Geo. Rex, Alec Foster, Noel Talbot and the double-act Noble & Denester.

Straight Variety bills did quite well, headed by Archie Robbins, Carole Carr, Max Miller, Penny Nichols, The Beverley Sisters, Jack Durant and Dorothy Squires, but audiences had begun to slip away soon after the Empire had celebrated its 50th Anniversary in 1951. *Rising Stars of 1953*, an attempt to introduce new blood into Variety, was poorly received by sparse houses. Many of the twelve acts failed to 'get over' or, like a ballroom dancing act, were not seen by audiences as suitable for Music Hall. The managership had passed by this time to Philip Merritt.

Exterior rear wall of auditorium facing Town Hall

Big trouble arrived in September, 1955, when commercial television was launched in the London area. Hackney Empire had closed for a 'Summer Vacation', as business had not been good, but the new competition proved fatal for the theatre within six months. A rare packed house assembled on Saturday, 4 February, 1956 to witness the last night of Variety at Hackney Empire, but to loyal supporters it seemed to be a case of being 'in at the death', despite the excitement and the singing of 'Auld Lang Syne'. The final bill was topped by G.H. Elliott, Tod Slaughter and Morris & Cowley. I was not there, but Harry Greatorex reported that true lovers of Variety had paid their silent respects the previous week, when Issy Bonn had topped a wonderfully entertaining bill.

Two days after the final curtain Hackney Empire passed to Associated Television for conversion to a television studio; sadly, being part of an audience, even in such a magical theatre, was *not* like a night at the Varieties. ATV produced TV shows at the Empire until about 1966, when Mecca acquired it as a bingo hall.

In December, 1986 the Empire was reopened as a theatre under the aegis of The Hackney Empire Preservation Trust. Mecca had removed the decorative terracotta domes and figure of Euterpe in 1979, but when it became a Grade II listed building by the time of its reopening, they were forced to replace them, at a cost of some £250,000. The driving force behind Hackney's renaissance was Roland Muldoon, who, together with a number of Variety and Cabaret artistes from the theatre group CAST, formed a charitable trust with the intention of providing a wide range of performance artistes – with the proviso that they should not be racist of sexist.

Exterior showing flank wall and old stage house from Sylvester Road

The British Music Hall Society staged a sparkling bill of Traditional Variety, headed by Roy Hudd and Margery Manners on 28 January, 1987, when crowds packed the pavement outside the Empire as in the days of big-time Variety; seats were £4, £3 and £2, with around 1,000 capacity at that stage, the rear part of the stalls given over to a bar and promenade, with the gallery closed. The Society put on two further bills the following year, topped by Cavan O'Connor, ('Only a Strolling Vagabond') and by Joan Regan. Since then Variety stars such as Lenny Henry, Chas. & Dave, Frankie Vaughan, Ken Dodd and Julian Clary have appeared, relishing the chance to perform in a real Variety theatre again. 'The Hackney Empire is like a breath of fresh air', said Frankie Vaughan, following his appearance.

Jazz, circus acts, classical and folk music have also been presented, but alternative comedians have been the speciality of the Empire. Pantomime, long absent from Mare Street, has made a welcome return, with names such as Peter Duncan, Colin Devereaux, Gary Hailes, Pauline Quirke, Linda Robson, old-timer Ben Warriss and Dolly Henry scoring well in five-week seasons.

The Hackney Empire has been used by many film and television companies, both in drama and as a background for commercials; it has offered training for numerous students from local schools and colleges, a facility that the theatre wants to expand; and it has attracted members of nearly all the ethnic groups in the area to a very wide range of shows – grand opera to Jamaica farce – as well as Variety. Several million pounds have been invested in bringing the theatre up to date in recent years, but financial problems still threaten.

Hammersmith Palace

82 King Street, Hammersmith

Hammersmith Palace: exterior (formerly Temple Palace of Varieties) with Wilkie Bard billed

Originating as part of the Town Hall, the theatre which was to become the Hammersmith Palace was first licensed in 1880, under Donald Sinclair Watson, with a live existence of just under 50 years before becoming a cinema; but even then it still often presented Ciné-variety. From 1885 to about 1897 it was known as the Temple of Varieties – before being reconstructed by the architect W.M. Brutton, giving the hall a capacity of 2,815. The builders were Messrs. Godson & Sons and the audience was accommodated in stalls, balcony and gallery. For a period the Temple was directed by Acton Phillips, who was also associated with the nearby Lyric Opera House.

It was then known as Hammersmith Theatre of Varieties. On view were ten individual acts, principally Herbert Campbell from Drury Lane pantomime, Walter Stockwell (billed as 'The Old

Favourite') and the quaint Australian comedian, Johnny Gilmore, together with two sketches. The Musical Director was C.A. Wareham. Interestingly, the Lyric was offering *Trilby* that same week under Samuel T.T. James's management.

A reviewer of a bill in January, 1903 regretted the absence through muscular rheumatism and influenza (poor man) of Mr. Fred Reeves, the manager; but he was enthusiastic about the fare on offer in J.C. Coe's fine house. G.H. Chirgwin was 'enshrined in the hearts of Londoners, who never fail to appreciate the quips and cranks, the puns and witticisms of this most versatile of entertainers'. He waxed lyrical about the light-hearted Lily Burnand, who 'lets herself go in a comedy selection and in a chorus song', as well as George D'Albert with his descriptive songs. However, on Bransby Williams he rather despaired of finding anything new to say! There were no fewer than twelve other acts on view, with excellent business reported that week.

Alterations were made in 1910 under Frank Matcham and just three years later the hall – now known as Hammersmith Palace – came under the control of Charles Gulliver's London Theatres of Varieties. A typical bill of his era comprised: Ernie Mayne, Tom Edwards, Vasco (the Mad Musician), Gus Harris, Will Collinson, Murray & Holbein, Amac and Jen Latona.

The Palace was a popular Variety theatre under its powerful new owners, who presented all the big names – Ella Shields, Marie Lloyd, Sammy Shields, Arthur Reece, May Henderson, T.E. Dunville, Morny Cash and Talbot O'Farrell; magicians included Rameses and Chung Ling Soo. An October, 1916 bill gave audiences Billy Merson, Harry Champion, Wilson Hallett and the interestingly-named Grace Brothers! In July, 1918 the Sisters Sprightly offered *Looking For Lodgings* and *Pitching A Tent* in their act on a bill topped by Wilkie Bard, Gus Harris and the popular northern comedian, Dick Tubb.

Interior looking towards the stage

It should be remembered that the Hammersmith Palace had strong opposition from two large Stoll halls at Chiswick and Shepherds Bush, both only short bus rides away and, of course, cinemas were springing up everywhere. Admittedly LTV presented attractive bills up to the time that the circuit crashed, but it has been suggested that the public tired of seeing the same acts too frequently. Illustrated in the colour section is a bill for January, 1924 containing four top names.

On the dispersal of the seventeen LTV halls, Hammersmith Palace became largely a cinema under seven different managements, the first of which was the Summers Brown circuit. It still presented live acts between the films such as Nellie Wallace in *Love and Money* and Willy Pantzer's Midgets on a full Variety bill. In May, 1929 British Musical Productions' *Lumber Love* was staged, then in June Percy

H. Holmshaw's Novel Musical Production, *Speed and Sparkle* played for a week. May Royal's comedy and burlesque spots were very well revued in *The Encore* that week. Pantomime had a place in the programmes as well, with Holmshaw's *Babes in the Wood* being staged for the 1929–30 season.

There were frequent change of management and booking agents during the 1930s, but live acts never completely disappeared. De Frece's Agency booked Petulengro's Band, while Mario Lorenzi, Fred Brand and The Gordon Richards Four also appeared. By 1936 the big new Gaumont Palace had opened in Queen Caroline Street nearby and in July of that year offered Pop-Eye the Sailor, Elizabeth Welch and Five Cleveres in support of its extensive film programme. Twentieth Century Cinemas Ltd. were managing the theatre when George Black (of the London Palladium) decided to revive Variety at four suburban halls, including Hammersmith Palace. It was a brave attempt, but the experiment lasted only about six weeks – despite some very strong bills such as that for the week of 14 April, 1939 which was topped by non other than The Cheekie Chappie himself, Max Miller. He was aided and abetted by "Monsewer" Eddie Gray, Ivor Vintor and Co., Wright & Marion, Three Dudes & Rita, Will Duffy & Pearl, the musical act Reg Redcliffe, Peter Fannan in his parson's act and Van Delfts – enough to stop the drift to Chiswick! With the four additional houses, the Calls in *The Stage* listed twenty-six Moss' Empires theatres at that time, only seven of which are still operating today.

After this disappointment, Hammersmith Palace was controlled by various managements during WW2. In 1944 it was under Surburban Century Cinemas Ltd. and Archie A. Shenburn, who controlled several No. 2 halls in the London area. It suddenly closed when the rear of the theatre sustained damage, caused, it is thought, by a bomb falling on the Underground line behind the building. The theatre was never restored, being demolished after the war.

Once so well catered for with three theatres, the Palace, the Hammersmith King's and the Hammersmith Lyric, the borough now boasts now only the latter, albeit in reconstructed form. Fortunately, the huge Gaumont Palace (now the Hammersmith Apollo) has helped to maintain the balance since it switched from films to live shows.

HAMMERSMITH THEATRE OF VARIETIES,
WITHIN A FEW YARDS OF ALL THE HAMMERSMITH RAILWAY STATIONS.
Proprietors and Managers - - - - *MESSRS ACTON PHILLIPS AND SON.*
Open Every Evening at 7.30.
On Saturdays at 7, with Extra Artistes of well-known ability only. No trial turns.
Always a Grand Company. Changes Every Week and a Quick Programme.
ALL REFRESHMENTS FIRST-CLASS, AND AT MODERATE PRICES.
PRICES: Orchestra Stalls, 1s. 6d.; Stalls, 1s.; Area, 9d.; Balcony, 6d.; Gallery, 3d.
On Saturday, Stalls, 1s. 6d.; Area, 1s.; Balcony, 9d.; Gallery, 6d; Private Boxes, 7s. 6d. to £1 1s.
DIRECT ENTRANCE FROM MANSION HOUSE STREET.

The Street Singer (Arthur Tracy)

Harrow Coliseum Theatre

Station Road, Harrow

Harrow Coliseum: exterior with Variety billed

It was never a full-time music hall, but this theatre did present Variety and revue during and just after WW2. Most of its life it was a playhouse, mainly staging straight hit plays, occasionally acting as a home for repertory companies. It was built and opened in 1920 and operated at first as The Electric Cinema. The property was bought in 1923 by Enrique Carreras in his move into the entertainment world; minor films and re-issues were screened here. William Hinds, who later joined Carreras, had created Hammer Productions. He had named this after his stage act from the days when he was part of a Variety double-act, Hammer & Smith. The architect of The Harrow Coliseum is not known, but he produced a striking white building with two open-sided minarets – not unlike those atop the old Alhambra Theatre in Leicester Square.

The Electric Cinema became a live theatre in the later 1920s, changing its name to the Harrow Coliseum and presenting a mixed programme of attractions – plays, revues, Variety and pantomime. An edition of The Harrow Observer & Gazette dated 8 January, 1926 shows that a production of *The Merry Widow* was playing at the Coliseum that week. The theatre is probably best remembered for its years under the direction of Alfred Denville, J.P., known as 'The Actors' M.P.', but his attitude to his theatre may be judged by the Coliseum's entry in The Stage Guide (1946). Whereas most entries gave the number of seats under 'capacity', Alfred Denville, J.P. (he was very proud of that distinction) gave the potential box-office take instead; e.g. 'Capacity: £256; twice nightly: £156' – presumably at each house. Alfred Denville founded The Denville Home for Aged Actors; it was later run by Mr. & Mrs. Prince Littler.

The Harrow Coliseum was quite a modest theatre, but well-served by public transport, just one minute's walk from Harrow-on-the-Hill railway station, with Harrow Wealdstone and Kenton not too far away; plenty of busses passed the door. It had a stage 31ft x 52ft deep, with twelve principal dressing-rooms and three chorus rooms. However, Denville took the opportunity to re-equip the theatre in 1939, when the Gaiety Theatre in The Aldwych was being stripped, prior to its planned demolition. He bought many of the furnishings, including the house tabs, to up-date the Harrow theatre. A bargain was three rows of Gaiety stalls seats for a total of £3.00.

During WW2 Harrow Coliseum sometimes presented Variety, as shown in the colour section. After the war there was the occasional touring revue, but the theatre was probably best-known for its plays, including a well-remembered production of Terrence Rattigan's *The Deep Blue Sea*. A revue of 1945 was Harry Pringle's *Over to You*, which was staged for the week commencing 23 July, twice nightly at 6.25 and 8.25pm. The Harrow Light Opera Company, which was founded in 1944, staged its productions at the Coliseum until the house closed. The Company then moved to the Dominion & Granada cinemas in the town, and later to the vast Kilburn Gaumont State. At the time of writing the HLOC has performed well over 100 full-scale musical shows. The Harrow Coliseum closed in 1955 and was demolished the following year. By comparison, nine local cinemas had closed by 1964 – leaving seven in 1968. The Harrow Arts Centre now caters for live performances in the area.

Holloway Empire

564 Holloway Road (North Corner of Manor Gardens), Upper Holloway

Holloway Empire: exterior with Carl Hertz & Co. billed

Holloway Empire opened on 4th December, 1899 and had a short life of about ten years as a Variety theatre before being used for other entertainments – none of them hugely successful. There had originally been several local objectors to the scheme for a new hall, but most of these were overcome on a second application. One had been the Y.M.C.A., but it was suggested by one supporter of the Empire that – if the moral climate was as bad as predicted, then the Association might well have fertile ground on which to work!

The theatre had a seating capacity of 1,210 in stalls, circle and gallery, being designed for the Moss-Stoll coalition by W.G.R. Sprague; Oswald Stoll later left to run his own circuit. Matcham designed most of the Moss' Empires, but this one and those at Stratford and Swansea were exceptions as originally built. Matcham did, however, make some alterations to Holloway in 1901. The theatre had a magnificent exterior, slightly spoiled by an all-round canopy, fitted sometime after the opening. Inside, the theatre had an Indian flavour, hooded stage boxes and extravagant plasterwork by The Plastic Decoration Company, hinting at Frank Matcham's work: Sprague had, of course, spent time working in Matcham's office during his training. There were eight boxes at the rear of the dress circle and behind them refreshment rooms; a Crush Room in Indian style had marble steps leading to luxurious lounges. The stage had a depth of 35ft and a width of 70ft.

An early Variety programme of 1903 is worth looking at in detail, as it conveys a rare flavour of the Empire's short career as a live house. It was said to be one of the first to embrace the 'Twice Nightly' system of working, a claim also made by New Cross Empire! A future star and impresario, Lupino Lane, was on the bill in support of Carl Hertz, the great magician. Shows were at 6.50 and 8.55p.m.

Following the overture ('L'espoire de L'Alsace' by Hermann), the bill-topper was first on. Carl Hertz presented his latest illusion, entitled *Iris, the Levitation Mystery*; he was assisted by Mddle. D'Alton. Lizzie Kirk was the first of two consecutive comedians, the second being Frank Leon, who combined 'the most intricate dancing on earth' with his sallies. The Bovis Brothers from Australia were billed as 'The Counts', boasting vocal and comic skills in addition to their dancing. The Sisters Garetti thrilled with their 'wonders on trapeze', before a Bioscope intermission. One of the films was on *Bee Culture*, which would have interested local people. Holloway was then quite smart, with city workers in houses with large gardens, where there would have been room for hives!

Following the interval the house was then regaled with the latest successes of comedian Jack Camp, followed by the eccentric acrobats Wertz & Judge, billed as "Champion Trick Leapers of the World". Then back again came Master 'Nipper' Lupino Lane, combining Comedy, Song & Dance – as he did throughout the rest of his long and illustrious career. The programme then wound up with the Farce Comedy Sketch *The Professor and his Pupils*, with Dan Burke, Molly Moller and Maud Denny Teller. Keeping everyone in control was the Musical Director, Thomas Grey. After a frantic five-minute dash by the cleaners, the curtain went up for the second house and they all went through it all over again.

Interior towards the stage

During those early Variety years most of the stars of the day appeared at Moss' Holloway Empire, a link in a chain of houses nearly forty-strong in its heyday, with enormous booking power. Paul Cinquevalli, The Brothers Griffiths, Little Tich and Fred Karno's Companies were just a few. At the end of this chapter is a list of the headliners for one typical year at this Empire.

Perhaps because of its success – and therefore its limited capacity – Moss' Empires planned a 2,000-seater Variety theatre at St. Thomas' Road in Finsbury Park, about a mile away. However, the development of the latter was only sanctioned on condition that Holloway Empire should cease to trade as a music hall. This was agreed and when Finsbury Park Empire opened on Monday, 5 September, 1910, Holloway Empire started life as a drama house, with a stock company. The final bill-topper there the previous week had been George Lashwood, famous for his song *Twi-Twi-Twilight*.

The Holloway Empire jogged along for a few years on plays, competing with the nearby Marlborough Theatre, but it was not a great success. Pantomimes did better, as did a series of Wild West plays, presented by George Ballanger. (The Marlborough had been opened as a playhouse and at the time was considered Frank Matcham's best work).

Films had inevitably taken over by 1923, although Gibbons' Bioscope had played a large part in the earlier Variety programmes. The Empire came under the Gaumont-British banner eventually, with Ciné-variety bringing it back into the live fold. Its 35ft deep stage hosted two or three acts between the pictures. In May, 1929 Gandy's Comedy Circus was featured, together with Juliette Vedey and Eileen Evelyn. A split-week in January, 1930 saw The Three Remmos for the first three days, followed by Graham & Douglas for the second half of the week. When sound pictures arrived, the Empire boasted that – as a live theatre – it had been designed for the spoken voice!

Former live theatres like The Holloway Empire did not always make ideal cinemas and it limped along, eventually losing its live acts to Gaumont-British's Marlborough Theatre. In 1938 the spectacular 3,000-seat Holloway Gaumont opened just down the road offering as many as five live acts with a full film programme and orchestra – and the Empire was mortally wounded, closing in August, 1938. It was really outmoded against the plush and comfortable new picture palaces opening throughout the district. The building changed hands in 1947, coming under the control of the Bloom Brothers and two years later was in the hands of the Official Receiver.

The Empire was shorn of its decoration and, with its front modernised, it was let as a warehouse. It was later demolished. Had Moss' Empires continued to run it as a Variety theatre (and not built Finsbury Park Empire), it might just – like New Cross Empire – have survived the war; but obviously Finsbury Park, with nearly twice its capacity, was a better proposition. Empire Yard remained, until quite recently, alongside the site of the old cinema as the only reminder of those confident Variety days before WW1.

With acknowledgements to Bill Manley and Maurice Friedman.

On the next page can be seen "A year in the life of Holloway Empire"

A year in the life of Holloway Empire: Headliners throughout 1900:

JANUARY: 1st – Emma Pollock; 8th – *Cinderella* with Maud Ross and Bros. Webb; 15th – Glinseretti Troupe; 22nd – Miles Stavordale Quintet; 29th – *Roscoe's Porcine Pantomime.*

FEBRUARY: 5th – Will Evans; 12th – Dutch Daly; 19th – The Poluskis, Harry Champion; 26th – Vesta Tilley, Dan Crawley, Chas. Bignell.

MARCH: 5th – Bessie Bonehill; 12th – Charles Morritt; 19th – Little Tich; 26th – Dumond's Minstrels.

APRIL: 2nd – Dan Leno; 9th – Letty Lind, Florrie Forde; 16th – Marie Loftus, Morny Cash, Geo. D'Albert; 23rd – A.C. Lilly, Maggie Duggan; 30th – Ernest Shand, Harry Anderson.

MAY: 7th – Wilke Brothers; 14th – Prinz's Lions, Bears, Hyenas & Dogs; 21st – Ugo Bondi; (24th – Special Annual Matinee for The Great Northern Hospital, one of the objectors to the opening of the Empire!); 28th – T.E. Dunville.

JUNE: 4th – Original Leopolds; 11th – Gibbons' Bioscope Tableaux (Scots Guards at Bloemfontein), with George Lashwood, Cliff Ryland and Fred Earle; 18th – Gus Elen; 25th – Gibbons' Bioscope with Harriet Vernon.

JULY: 2nd – Carl Hertz, Frank Seeley; 9th – Peggy Pryde, Harry Freeman, Lawrence Barclay; 16th – Harry Randall, Boisset's Bricklayers, Harry Tate; 23rd – Little Tich return, Arthur Lloyd; 30th – Fred Karno's "Love Birds".

AUGUST: 6th – Vesta Tilley return, Wal Pink; 13th – Chung Ling Soo; 20th – Minnie Palmer, Kate Carney, Millie Hylton; 27th – Sandow, Rosie Lloyd.

SEPTEMBER: 3rd – Cissie Loftus, Austin Rudd; 10th – Talma, Alice Maydue; 17th – Stuart, Bros. Edgar; 24th – Eugene Stratton, Tennyson & O'Gorman.

OCTOBER: 1st – Woodward's Seals, W.J. Churchill; 8th – G.H. Chirgwin; 15th – Okabe Family ('Happy Japs'); 22nd – Donaldson Bros., Hetty King.

NOVEMBER: 5th – Leo Dryden; 12th – Griffiths Brothers, Florence Gallimore; 19th – Bert Gilbert and return of Dutch Daly; 26th – Albert Christian.

DECEMBER: 3rd – Ernest Shand; 10th – Joe Elvin; 17th – Walter Munroe; 24th – Phorte Pinaud, May Henderson; 31st – H.A. Moore, Maud Duprez.

Top names continued into 1901 with J.W. Rickaby, R.A. Roberts, Marie Collins, Bransby Williams, Lottie Lennox, R.G. Knowles, George Gray, J.W. Rowley, George Lashwood, Herbert Campbell, George Robey, Alexandra Dagmar, Brothers Edgar, Lottie Collins, W.H. Fox and the return of Vesta Tilley. There was no pantomime but the Variety bill on Boxing Day, 1901 was staged no less four times, at 1.40, 3.50, 6.50 and 9.10pm.

[From the archive of the late Bert Ross, former B.M.H.S. Historian]

Hoxton: Britannia Theatre of Varieties

188, High Street, (Pimlico Walk), Hoxton

Hoxton Britannia Theatre: exterior in 1855

An advertisement of 1841 proudly trumpets: 'Variety Entertainment – Talented Company – Grand Concert – Opera & Vaudeville – Rope and other Dancing – Ballet – Laughable Farce.' This was Samuel Lane's announcement of the Easter Monday opening of his Royal Britannia Saloon at The Britannia Tavern, Hoxton. It was a very early use of the word Variety relating to a form of entertainment – earlier even than its use at The Canterbury Hall by Charles Morton.

Lane had erected a spacious Saloon on waste ground at the back of the existing Tavern, to rival the neighbouring Grecian and Albert Saloons. In Elizabethan times the site had been occupied by The Pimlico, a hostelry and garden which was the resort of poets and players, including – it is said – William Shakespeare. Hoxton, it should be remembered, was close to the early playhouses in Shoreditch. In fact, the taste for dramatic shows was probably handed down through the generations, giving Lane an enthusiastic and receptive audience for his new venture. Pimlico Walk, on which Lane's property was built, still exists today.

Samuel Lane was born in Devonshire of humble stock, but prided himself on being descended from John Lane, who had accompanied Sir Walter Raleigh on his voyages of exploration. Samuel was apparently illiterate and throughout his life could only sign his name. Coming to London as a boy, he did not embark on his first theatrical venture until middle age, when he took on and ran The Union Saloon in Shoreditch as a drama house of sorts. This, of course, was prior to the passing of the 1843 Theatres Act, under which only the Patent Theatres (Covent Garden and Theatre Royal Drury Lane) could produce dramatic shows. Other houses were obliged to introduce songs and dances into any drama staged – even a Shakespeare play ended up as a sort of Variety show. Unfortunately, an informer caused the police to raid the Union Saloon and Lane was closed down.

Undeterred, Lane started afresh at the Britannia Saloon, while soon the passing of the 1843 Act freed up the multitude of minor London theatres. Again, the success of the new venture was brought to an abrupt halt when a long-eared magistrate refused to renew the licence; the theatre had to close and the dramatic company was disbanded. Only by forming a concert party and admitting the public free of charge did Samuel Lane manage to reopen, making his profits from the sale of drink and refreshments. Catering has always been an asset to a theatre and, in fact, generous victuals remained a feature of the Britannia throughout its history; meat pies, saveloys and enormous sandwiches were consumed in the auditorium – even being mentioned by Charles Dickens in *The Un-Commercial Traveller*. Lane got away with it and his licence was renewed the following year without any trouble.

Exterior of Britannia Theatre of Varieties, 1904

The Saloon's name soon became a household word, especially in North London. A new regular stock company was formed; one of the actresses, Sarah Wilton, later became Mrs Samuel Lane. It was quite common for actors to join the Britannia's stock company and to remain, playing older and older roles, for their entire careers, never appearing elsewhere. With the success of the Britannia Saloon, enlargements were made in 1850, without closing for a single night. Mdlle. Celeste Stephan was among the artistes engaged that year, as were Mr. and Mrs. Newham. But an even bigger auditorium became necessary and he purchased a number of cottages to enlarge the site. A huge new theatre was built at a cost of some £12,700 and opened on 8th November, 1858. The architects were Finch Hill and Paraire, while the decorations were by Messrs White and Parlby with W.Homann. The old Saloon had closed only in the June of that year.

Although officially a drama house, the Britannia offered a wide variety of entertainment for many years before it briefly became a Variety theatre proper in the period just preceding The Great War. It was notable in its 'drama' years for the large number of big names engaged. In fact this was truly an age of popular theatre, with programmes lasting several hours and providing a wide variety of items – no wonder that audiences had to be well fed and watered during the evening!

In 1851 Hoxton audiences saw Charles Rice and, for the start of an unprecedented 36-year engagement, Joseph Reynolds. Between that Great Exhibition year and 1856 audiences were privileged to see the great coloured tragedian Ira Aldridge, Clara St. Casse, The Great Mackney, Miss Sarah Thorne and (for sixteen pantomimes) the popular clown, Jean Louis.

Sam Collins, later the proprietor of the famous music hall in Islington, appeared in 1861, as did The Great Leotard. The following year the stalls were converted into an arena for Van Hare's Monster Circus. At that period G.B. Bigwood, later Stage Manager and Acting Manager, appeared for the first time. The year 1865 saw the engagement of J.H. Stead, who is famous for his song *The Perfect Cure*. He had made this famous at Weston's (later The Holborn Empire) in 1861, but his accompanying jumping dance was still amazing audiences four years later.

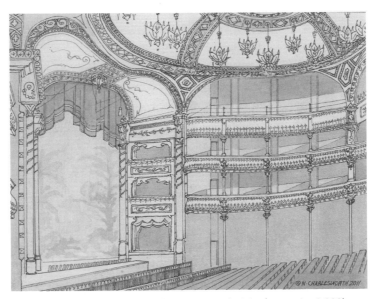

Interior of The Britannia Theatre, 1858 (original capacity 3,923)

The Britannia was now a well-established and successful theatre, but disaster struck just after Christmas in 1871, when Samuel Lane died. Mrs Sarah Lane took over the reins and until her death in 1899 made the Britannia even more famous, becoming known as 'The Queen of Hoxton' and revered by all. Notable names to appear under her management included J.B. Johnson, the champion swimmer; Marian, The Giantess; The Tichborne Claimant (soon to be imprisoned in Dartmoor) and G.H. Macdermott, who later ran The Hoxton Variety Theatre in Pitfield Street nearby.

Pantomime was first presented at Christmas 1841 and became more and more elaborate, until in 1891 the forty-ninth of the series, *The Spider and The Fly*, was staged. Another of the wondrous subjects was *The Magic Dragon of The Demon Dell*. Marie Lloyd appeared at the Britannia as Princess Kristina in a pantomime at this period.

Mrs Sarah Lane's death in 1899 really marked the end of a great era. Her funeral procession attracted many thousands onto the streets. Although several others did try to continue the tradition after her death, none was a great success. In 1904 the Britannia became a music hall, with Samuel Bury running the place for Thomas Barrasford, the new owner.

Barrasford's tenure was quite brief, however, and following his departure in 1908 Elles Brammall took the helm for just under a year. His was just one of many who attempted to revive the fortunes of the old theatre – another being George Oliver Conquest. In 1913 J.C. Vine carried out extensive redecorations, aiming to reopen as a music hall but films were now the new rage; the great days had gone and the Britannia operated mainly as a cinema.

There was one more attempt to bring back live entertainment in 1917 in the form of a pantomime, but its run was short and films returned for good. In November, 1926 the Britannia became part of the growing Gaumont-British circuit. It was bought from Biocolor Picture Theatres for just over £6,000; this was by far the cheapest of the fifteen properties acquired which included the Holloway Empire. Even then there were Variety acts to be seen between films on the great stage. For example, in May 1929 a split week was shared between Barclay & Schofield and Virginia Clay from Monday to Wednesday; with Salter & Hanlon and Vernon Harvey booked for Thursday to Saturday. Artistes appearing under similar arrangements in January 1930 included Marie Holt and assistants, Doris & Vick, Hawkins & Brooks and Alec Marden. The seating capacity remained enormous at 2,972, but over the years this cinema became of minor significance.

During WW2 the Hoxton Britannia was blitzed and a century of entertainment on this site was brought to an abrupt end. The bombing in 1940 caused a great fire which wrecked the theatre. The remains were demolished the same year, although two decorative pillasters remained for some years to mark the extremities of the frontage, while the shell of the gigantic scene dock housed a motor repair works.

BRITANNIA | THE GREAT | THEATRE,
HOXTON.

Sole Proprietress   -   -   -   Mrs. SARA LANE.

OPEN ALL THE YEAR ROUND.

TRAGEDY, COMEDY, DRAMA, FARCE, AND PANTOMIME.

THE BEST WEST END DRAMAS!
PRODUCED WITH WEST END COMPLETENESS!!
AT EAST END PRICES!!!

A SELECTED AND EFFICIENT CORPS DRAMATIQUE.
VOCAL, INSTRUMENTAL, AND ACROBATIC ARTISTS IN RAPID SUCCESSION.

Hoxton: McDonald's Music Hall

130, Hoxton High Street, parallel to Kingsland Road

Hoxton, McDonald's Music Hall: exterior to Hoxton Street, 1988

We are extremely lucky to have this rare survivor in London of an early music hall, although it operated as such for only a few years in the nineteenth century. The Hoxton and Shoreditch districts once bristled with theatres and pub halls both large and small, but Hoxton Hall is the sole survivor and stands almost opposite the site of the old Britannia Theatre, bombed in WW2. Those interested in early music halls should not miss a chance of attending a show there, for events are held regularly and a forthcoming programme is published by the theatre.

The hall was opened in July, 1863 and was known at first as Mortimer's, being designed and run by James Mortimer. His object was to combine instruction with entertainment, but the Hoxton audiences did not take kindly to this ideal after a hard day's work and the enterprise failed.

When it opened the auditorium had just one end balcony carried on two wooden columns. Heating was supplied by fireplaces, one on either side of the stalls. Francis Day and Joseph Sawyer were licensees in 1865, but James McDonald took over in 1866 and, having experience in music hall entertainment, made a better fist of running the hall. It seems that he was joint-licensee with Thomas Clark. McDonald enlarged the premises by raising the roof (literally) and inserting a second balcony to increase the capacity; both balconies were also given side arms and were supported on slender iron columns. There is quite a high stage, but it has been altered several times and now has an extension into the auditorium; steps lead down from either side of the stage into the stalls, as well as from the centre of the extension.

Interior towards the stage in 2006

James McDonald had only a modest success at Hoxton. According to Shoreditch sources, James McDonald and Thomas Clark were joined by James McDonald, jnr. in the management, but nevertheless the licence was refused in 1871. After being dark for a number of years, the hall was taken over by one John Clark – possibly related to Thomas Clark above – and then for three or four years by Thomas Henry Ellis. Use as a music hall finally came to an end in 1883; none of those involved having made much money there. Had the enterprise prospered, there is no doubt that the hall would subsequently have been rebuilt and enlarged as so many others, but its premature end as a music hall has left us a little gem of a building, now over 140 years old.

There is some disagreement about the dates, but in about 1885 the 'hall and premises' were taken in the name of William Goulding. He was chairman of a temperance organisation known as The Blue Ribbon Army and much of the social work done here was carried out by Robert Rae and his wife: she also founded the Girls' Club in Hoxton.

Detail of lower balcony rail

In 1895 McDonald's became the property of The Bedford Institute, a Quaker organisation; it was one of eight East London Quaker 'Settlements', offering local people a range of social and educational activities. Unlike James Mortimer's efforts, these worked and the building was doubled in size in 1910 – the additional space made available by the demolition of some nearby cowsheds (Hoxton, like a lot of suburban London at the time still retained traces of its rural roots).

During WW2 a programme of creative activities for young people, including art and drama, was set up. Then during the 1950s pensioners' activities and playgroups joined the thriving youth activities, so that gradually the hall moved back to its artistic roots.

The Warden at the time, May Scott, made a huge contribution to the hall's success in the 1960s: in fact, for period the hall became known as 'May Scott's', such was her reputation locally; others in charge more recently have been Terry Goodfellow and Chris Bowler. In 1963, to celebrate the Hall's Centenary, the newly-formed British Music Hall Society held a one-day exhibition at McDonald's, with a Variety show in the evening. The Guest of Honour was Ada Reeve, who had begun her theatrical career in 1878 at the age of four! She was the daughter of Charles Reeve, popular at one time at the nearby Britannia Theatre. Several hundred people visited the exhibition during the day, which gained a good deal of press coverage. The hall was packed for the evening show as Trevor Morton, Winifred Sabine, Splinters & Danny and a big company brought the place right back to life.

Betty Bray presided at the pianoforte, with fiddle and drums in support. Nobody present will ever forget the atmosphere that night.

The exhibition and show were such a success that the B.M.H.S. decided to repeat the event on 7 November, 1964, when Dorothy Ward was the Guest of Honour. The evening Cavalcade of Variety was presented by Don Ross, the Society's first president.

Interior from the stage in 2006

In 1976 the Quakers handed over the running of the centre to a group of community and arts workers. A major fundraising and restoration project, under the firm now known as Richard Betham and Associates, led to fresh programmes' being introduced, with adult education classes, arts projects and live shows being added to the existing pattern of community work.

There had never been a proper street entrance to McDonald's – merely a passageway. This was put right in 1982, with the purchase of a building in Hoxton Street, so that Hoxton Hall now has a street presence with the name of the hall painted in bold type. Adrian Betham oversaw this latest project. Earlier, a new ceiling had been constructed in the auditorium to replace the war-damaged one. The hall goes from strength to strength with its training courses in Theatre and Music. For those wishing to visit Hoxton Hall, Old Street tube station is the nearest to the theatre. Sadly, various factors (including increasingly Health & Safety and Licensing regulations) mean that McDonald's has now once again reverted to community hall use only – although Olde Tyme Music Hall shows are still presented for its clientele. In 2015 further restoration is being carried out, including the replacement of the stalls skylight, lost in WW2. In charge now is Carina Johnson.

Hoxton: Variety Theatre (Harwood's, or 'The Sod's Opera')

18–20, Pitfield Street, Hoxton

Hoxton Variety Theatre: exterior (formerly Harwood's Music Hall)

Having a life as a live theatre of around forty years, the Hoxton Variety Theatre was built in 1869 for Verrell Nunn, opening on 13 March, 1870, but was not a success under him. However, the next owner, George Harwood, is forever linked with this hall and his reign of nineteen years was the highlight of its history. Audiences were extremely rough, barking, cat-calling and throwing fruit from the market outside if they disliked an artiste. On one occasion there was even a fight between the Irish comedian, Pat Feeney and another performer in full view of the audience, who cheered them on.

There is some uncertainty about the actual architect of the hall. Some say it was C.J. Phipps, although it is strange that such an eminent figure should concern himself in such a minor work; others prefer J.G. Buckle, who certainly made alterations on two occasions later. Others who did work on the building were Wylson & Long (1903), Bertie Crewe (1909), Ward & Ward (1913) and George Coles (1927). The pub frontage was certainly like Phipps' work, with its four bays of round-headed windows, brick dentil cornice and capitals formed into bunches of fruit and flowers.

The theatre at the back of the pub resembled a Nissen hut on the outside, with a corrugated iron roof which I remember seeing in the 1960s. Inside, the theatre had a tall, narrow round-headed proscenium arch and two balconies, possibly with open metal fronts, supported on slender iron columns. There was a barrel-vaulted ceiling.

The theatre seated some 800 people and in later years the boxes and gallery were extended backwards into the first and second floors of the public house itself. George Harwood was said (among others) to have been the originator of the twice-nightly system for Variety theatres; it proved popular where he used it, but was not generally adopted for some years. Under his management, one enormous attraction for the Christmas holidays was billed as *The Greatest Combination of Comic Stars in London*. It opened with a Farce, *The Secret* and closed with a Drama, entitled *Honesty, or Merit Is Its Own Reward*. In between came a crowded bill of comics, trapeze artistes, topical singers, negro comedians and dancers and the first appearance of Miss Emma Thornton, The Celebrated Serio-Comic. All of this was offered for the top price of 6d.

George Harwood did very well here, bringing Harry Randall, Bessie Bellwood, Dan Leno, Fred Coyne, Sam Redfern and Jenny Hill to Hoxton's rough audiences. Even the big names suffered – George Leybourne being hooted off the stage on one occasion as his style was disliked here.

Part of the interior, towards the stage

In earlier times the Hoxton Variety Theatre had been known as a 'Trial House' because so many singers started here. The Great Macdermott appeared in his earlier days, making a big success with the political song *Carving the Turkey*, about the Great Powers in the Middle East – long before introducing *By Jingo*.

Harwood, having made a large fortune, sold the hall in 1889 to Gus Leach, formerly the long-serving chairman of the Old Mogul (later The Middlesex). After Leach's departure a succession of owners followed, some staying only a year or two and failing to attract much business. Not far away were The London Music Hall and The Olympia, both in Shoreditch and offering much bigger names. A notable manager who stayed for five years was G.H. (The Great) Macdermott, one of whose programmes is shown here. It will be seen that the two houses began at 6.25 and 9.10pm.

Interior, detail of roof rib

The Hoxton Varieties had as many titles as it had proprietors, one of them being the New King's Theatre, being forbidden by the Lord Chancellor in 1906. 'The Sod's Opera' had perhaps over-reached itself and was put firmly in its place!

One proprietor, Leonard Mortimer, managed to make the place pay for a time with dramas of the day on such subjects as immigration – once again a topical subject. A local benefactor, he ran Fresh Air Fund Matinees, raising money to send children away on holiday. He also funded free dinners for children from his proceeds – over 5,000 being fed in one season. These were served in the theatre itself. Despite his success, he departed in 1907 for the nearby Britannia Theatre with his entire company.

Two further proprietors, J.E. Stubbs and Matthew Raymond, battled on, Harwood himself having died in 1901. The Hoxton Variety Theatre then became a cinema – some say in 1910, others in 1913. It was operated by Denman Picture Houses Ltd. and later by Gaumont-British, who took over a lot of former theatres. The big, purpose-built cinemas gradually drained its audiences and the old hall closed down finally in 1923. In later years the hall was sometimes used as a club and social centre, but was often closed-up. A mezzanine floor was inserted just below the proscenium arch to make the area more intimate and manageable for modern entertainment. Amazingly, the building survived until 1981 and when demolished still carried the name Raymond's above its entrance.

GENERAL THEATRES CORPORATION, LTD.

Cranbourn Mansions, Cranbourn Street, W.C.2.
'Phone: Gerrard 2274.

BIRMINGHAM, Hippodrome (R. 11).—Harry Roy and his Band, Kimberley and Page, Mady and Cord, Howard Nichols, Dancing Dynamites, Donald Stuart.

BRIGHTON, Hippodrome (R. 11).—Unit Productions present " Radio Rodeo " (cast includes Harold Ramsay, Pop, White and Swagger, Armour Boys, Girl Friends Band, Six Clevettes, Sylvia, Jean Rodgers, Priscilla Wise, Billy Scott-Coomber, Buck (Warren) and Chic (Cooper).

HOLBORN, Empire (R. 10).—Max Miller, Billy Russell, O'Gorman Brothers, Ju-Lio-San, Ralph and Bob Darras, Angers and Waller, Libonati Trio, Winter Sisters, Wright and Marion, Levanda.

HOLLOWAY, Gaumont (R. 9.30).—Elsie Carlisle and Sam Browne, Herschel Henlere, Miriam, Murray and Miller, Low and Webster, The Globe Girls.

LONDON, Palladium (R. 11).—George Black's New Musical, " These Foolish Things " (cast includes Nervo and Knox, Flanagan and Allen, Naughton and Gold, Stuart Morgan Dancers, Sue Ryan, Ken Davidson and Hugh Forgie). (Mats. Wed. and Thurs. at 2.30.)

PENGE, Empire (R. 12).—Harry Hanson presents The Court Players.

PORTSMOUTH, Hippodrome (R. 11).—Jack Hylton and his Band, Peggy Dell, Freddie, Phyllis and Anne, Jack Woodroffe, Gerda and Ulrick Newman, Rebla, Hector and Pals, Billy and Idylle Shaw, Dennis Lawes.

WOLVERHAMPTON, Hippodrome (R. 11).—" Over She Goes ! "

The General Theatres Corporation Ltd, in October, 1938

Ilford Hippodrome

Broadway and Ilford Lane, Ilford

Ilford Hippodrome: exterior showing main entrance with Ambrose & his Orchestra billed

The only handsome building on the Broadway, the Ilford Hippodrome was one of Frank Matcham's finest creations – particularly the interior with its renaissance-style decorations. The odd-shaped Broadway, with its clock tower, was the centre of the town, with The Black Horse on one corner and The Angel on another. Right opposite the terracotta theatre entrance was the Westminster Bank building. The road layout in this area has been much altered, with the South Woodford-Barking Relief Road cutting through to the west of where the theatre stood.

It opened on 9 November, 1909 with seats for 2,500 as a sister theatre to Lewisham Hippodrome and The London Palladium, part of an order for four theatres given to Matcham simultaneously by Walter Gibbons for his London Theatres of Varieties; at the same time he entirely rebuilt the interior of The Holborn Empire and made improvements to Hammersmith Palace.

When Gibbons stood down, Charles Gulliver ran Ilford Hippodrome as part of his circuit. A typical week's Variety in those early years comprised: The Act Beautiful, Albert Whelan, Roxy La Roco, Arthur Brough (from the legit), Marie Kendall, Herbert Lee, Les Eldons and Grogie.

The Ilford Hippodrome ran very successfully for a number of years, until the cinema really became a menace. Stars such as T.E. Dunville, Joe Elvin, Ella Shields and Laddie Cliff graced its stage in the earlier days, with George Formby, Richard Tauber, Tommy Trinder, Gracie Fields, Flanagan & Allen, Vera Lynn, Max Miller and Wee Georgie Wood appearing later on. The latter of course usually appeared with Dolly Harmer as his 'mother'. Revues were legion, for example – *Hip, Hip, Hooray*, Arthur Whiteley's *Hullo, Darling*, Harry Day's *Made in England* and F. Rubens' *Mind The Step*.

The forgotten George E. Corum topped a Variety bill in August, 1915 with The O'Gorman Brothers, Phil Ray, Scotch Kelly, Patti Loftus and Ella Shields. While in February, 1918 Lew Lake presented *The House That Jerry Built*, with himself and Bob Morris leading a company of 22 at 6.20 and 8.50pm. The 'Colossal Comedy Company of Comic Carpenters, Perky Plasterers, Gay Gasfitters, Natty Navvies, Busy Bricklayers, Promising Plumbers, Pantomime Paperhangers, Lazy Labourers and Energetic Electricians' took over the entire programme, following the Overture. Not to be forgotten were Leo Cud's Six Musical Navvies – entertainment par excellence. And what brilliant bill matter!

After the crash of LTV in 1924, the circuit's various halls were dispersed, with Ilford Hippodrome becoming a cinema for a number of years, firstly under 20th Century Cinemas Ltd. (who presented Larry Adler and Gypsy Nina here in January, 1938), then later as part of Metropolitan & Provincial Cinematograph Theatres. A friend of mine, John Alexander, remembers Saturday morning "tuppenny rush" film shows but recalls that the atmosphere was completely spoiled for him by playground bullies operating in the seats around him. He was very pleased when it closed as a cinema and the return of Variety was announced in 1938. The advertising around the entrance – always fascinating – became even more so when the Variety photographs and colourful bills and banners began to appear.

Interior of auditorium

During the late 1930s George Black briefly took over the direction of the Ilford Hippodrome, which was booked by Moss' Empires, and some very strong Variety bills resulted. One terrific show which we enjoyed in October, 1938 was topped by Ambrose and his Orchestra featuring Evelyn Dall, Max Bacon, Denny Dennis, Vera Lynn – a very young local girl – and Les Carew, supported by Cresso Brothers, Elray and Lady, Leon & Kiki, Bob Lloyd & Betty, Marion Pola, Trixie & Jean and Eddy Bankey.

The following year an entertaining bill contained the names of Jack Edge, Stanley, Eddie & Mae, Donna Sisters, Leroy & Brown and Anita Martell – all in support of the headliners, *Carroll Levis and His BBC Discoveries*, a strong bill in itself. The Moss connection may have been quite short, but the momentum continued despite this, with morale-boosting wartime shows such as Lew & Leslie Grade's *Serenade to Fun*, staged for the week of 10 April, 1944. This starred Monte Rey, Billy Thorburn, Clapham & Dwyer, Jackie Trevor, Nicol & Merrill, Nora Moody and The Marietta Dancers. Also on the bill were The Dolinoffs & Raya Sisters, a very impressive American Black Art act, owned by Danny Dolinoff and his wife, Raya: they employed two girls and were all trained dancers.

The Black Art act is usually associated with magicians. It requires a completely black stage with "blinders" to increase the contrast: these are small bright lights shining toward the audience. All sorts of wonderful effects are produced by the magicians, dressed in very bright costumes. Things and people appear, vanish, float and do anything the magicians can think of. The magic effects are accomplished by invisible assistants wearing black suits and masks. Chung Ling Soo was very successful with a Black Art act before he became "Chinese". It is a lot of trouble to do, so there have always been one or two acts, but never very many. The usual scheme is to have a small stage on the stage proper, so that the blackout, lighting and angles can be controlled.

The Dolinoffs were unusual in coming from a dance background, rather than the magic fraternity. Their balletic training made their effects seem more magical than ever, with invisible aides lifting the girl assistants. There was quite a lot of comedy in the act and at the finish dancing skeletons seemingly disintegrated. As the Dolinoffs used the whole stage, they presumable carried the necessary black drapes for the entire stage with them, although many Variety theatres would have had black drapes hanging in any case. The 'blinders' used by The Dolinoffs were very bright and took the form of a large question mark at either side of the stage. The act was knock-out and played the best theatres in the U.K. the U.S.A. and on the continent. It is believed that they were around in the U.S.A. until the mid-1950s.

Exterior showing rear wall of auditorium in Ilford Lane

John Alexander's recollections of shows at Ilford Hippodrome are well worth recording, as they are so typical of Variety just pre-war:

"My father worked on Saturday morning, as was the custom then, so my mother left him a cold meal and we went off to the matinee at the theatre. I remember seeing a lot of old-timers, including Gertie Gitana

and Nellie Wallace on the same bill. Ernie Lotinga amused me by coming on with the costume worn by the previous act, a pretty dancer, in one hand.

One show was made up entirely of novelty acts, including a man who looped the loop on a bicycle on a contraption that looked none too safe, a girl who danced with leopards (shackled to the stage) and a line of 'Cossack' singers who were marched off one by one to be shot when they sang a wrong note! Another show included a 'Japanese' tight-rope walker (in full costume), who, after a couple of 'false' starts, walked up a rope stretched from the stage to the front of the circle: with a drum roll he slid back to the stage – over the heads of those in the stalls and without a safety net.

"I always enjoyed the magic acts, seeing Claude Cingalee several times; many years later he told me that his act was the same as his father's in Victorian times, except that his father took an hour over it, while he did it in twelve minutes. Jack LeDair was another magician with an entertaining act and two good illusions. A large marionette company appeared once with a proscenium and boxes within the real proscenium – I think it was the Barnard family, who toured the last of the big English marionette shows.

"An electric act that must have been similar to that of Walford Bodie terrified me: a row of lamp bulbs was lit between the mouths of two performers – I still wonder how this was done. It was all a bit serious and so as a finale, to inject some fun into the act, they bathed an "electric baby". This was a papier maché baby connected by wire to a big machine (mostly show). The bath tub was also connected and members of the audience were invited up to bath the baby. They suddenly received an electric shock and the baby flew all over the place. I was unaware that stooges were involved, thinking it might be my turn next. I was so frightened by all this that my mother had to take me to the Ladies' to dry off the damage!

"An animal act I saw several times and always liked was Pepino and his Miniature Circus. He was dressed as a clown and a monkey, dressed as a jockey, rode a very small pony. In another show there was a dog act with no humans in sight, Duncan's Collies I think, the dogs playing the parts of shopkeepers, pedestrians, policemen and postmen. Not much of a plot, but fascinating to watch".

Pantomimes of course played a season each Christmas and John remembers seeing Dorothy Ward playing Robinson Crusoe and singing *The Isle of Capri*, the latest song at that time. *Cinderella* was the subject for 1938, opening twice nightly on Christmas Eve, followed by three shows a day for the next week – an exhausting business for the company and stage crew. But it was production of *Robinson Crusoe* that closed the theatre for good. Renée Houston and Donald Stewart were the stars. The performance on 12 January, 1945 had barely started when a German V2 rocket fell on a row of cottages at the rear of the theatre. The stage was wrecked and the performers were blown off their feet, but the orchestra, under Syd Kaplan, continued playing and the audience filed out of the building. John had been in the audience the night before. Amazingly, there was no loss of life in the theatre, although fifteen died in the cottages. Sadly, a few days later the roof fell in bringing down the gallery and destroying any hope of the theatre's being repaired.

The shell of Ilford Hippodrome stood for just over a decade, before pieces of masonry hit a passing bus in 1957; orders were then given for its demolition. John could now only *dream* about girls dancing with leopards and Japanese tightrope walkers sliding from circle to stage. A painting of the demolition scene appeared in The Royal Academy Summer Exhibition in 1959 at Burlington House. Fortunately, live shows survive at The Kenneth More Theatre in Oakfield Road, Ilford – there has even been an occasional Variety show there.

With grateful thanks to John Alexander for his vivid memories of Variety at Ilford. He is, of course, the author of 'Tearing Tickets Twice Nightly', the tale of the last years of The Metropolitan Theatre, Edgware Road.

Islington: Collins' Music Hall

North side of Islington Green

Collins' Music Hall: exterior of original building in 1863 (The Lansdowne Arms)

What was later to be advertised as 'London's Oldest Variety Theatre' and even 'The World's Oldest Music Hall' – Collins' – was opened at 10–11, Islington Green behind the Lansdowne Arms public house. Sam Collins (born Samuel Collins Vagg) began life as a chimney sweep, but had a fine voice and secured an engagement at the Pantheon Music Hall in Oxford Street. Here he was observed by Mr. Winder, of the Mogul in Drury Lane, who, quick to recognise talent, secured Collins for his popular hall – later to become the Middlesex. The young Irish vocalist made an immediate hit with 'Paddy's Wedding' and 'Limerick Races'. Other engagements followed at the Canterbury, Weston's and Wilton's.

But Samuel was ambitious and, having saved money, he purchased the Rose of Normandy tavern at 32–3, Marylebone High Street, which he transformed into the Marylebone Music Hall in 1856, with a capacity of 800.

Ever optimistic, Sam Collins early in 1862 entered into negotiations with Mr. Montgomery, proprietor of The Lansdowne Arms & Music Hall at Islington Green. This establishment is said to have dated from 1790 and included in the premises was a singing room for the entertainment of its customers. Montgomery lacked the necessary business acumen to be a successful entertainment caterer and was glad to part with his interest in the concern. However, due to a slight misunderstanding with the licensing authorities, Collins was unable to have his Grand Opening until a year later, 4 November, 1863. He had sold the 200-year old Marylebone Music Hall to finance improvements at his new Islington hall.

The first Collins' Music Hall had a capacity of 600 and 'The Prince of Good Fellows' (his nickname) made a success of it. Unfortunately, it was to be a short-lived one, as Sam died on 25 May, 1865 at the early age of 39 years. However, his widow, Anne Vagg, carried on the business with the assistance of the manager, Harry Sydney, the song writer and vocalist.

The new 1897 exterior of Collins' Music Hall, with 'Bareway to Stardom' billed

After three years with Anne in charge there were changes of management, including that of Henry Watts, during whose reign Collins' acquired the nickname 'The Chapel on The Green' – because of its well-behaved audience and not because of the graveyard beneath the building. Stars such as 'Jolly' John Nash, George Leybourne and a local favourite – Arthur Lloyd – pulled in the crowds, particularly during the various shows at the nearby Agricultural Hall.

Herbert Sprake took over as manager in 1881 and his seventeen years in control were, perhaps, the best ones that this hall enjoyed. All the big names of the day appeared there, including Herbert Campbell and Kate Carney, who was still singing in the late 1940s. At this period the proceedings were still watched over by a Chairman, a particular favourite at Collins' being John Read, who died aged eighty-seven.

In 1887, under Herbert Sprake, the hall was rebuilt as a proper theatre with seating for 1,800, although this was later reduced to just less than 1,500. The new Collins' was quite palatial, the architects being Drew, Bear, Perks & Co. There were two circles and four boxes, although the under-stage dressing rooms are remembered as being quite basic. The public house remained at the front of the theatre, with entrances from both the street and from the stalls. On stage, the restricted height of the grid and shortage of lines did make life hard for some aerial acts, artistes recall.

The Box Office queue

Although renamed after its rebuilding as Collins' Theatre of Varieties, it was always known as Collins' Music Hall. Electric light was now installed and still more talent engaged: George Robey, Harry Randall and Wilkie Bard even appearing on one bill soon after the reopening. A January, 1901 bill, when the theatre was under the management of Richards, Burney & Co., had an even bigger array of stars: Gus Elen, Lily Burnand, Tom Leamore, Fish & Warren, Harry Champion, Katie Lawrence, Lotto, Lilo & Otto, Kate Carney, Austin Rudd, Athas & Collins, Celest, Lily Iris, F.W. Mills and Bransby Williams were all to be seen on one evening.

By 1908 and throughout the 1914–18 war Collins' was renamed as Islington Hippodrome, but the popular name was soon brought back. The two bills below date from this period.

Interior showing the proscenium arch

From 1919 to 1927 the theatre was in the hands of Charles Gulliver's London Theatres of Varieties Ltd., while during the 1930s it was run by John Southern and Worland S. Wheeler. It is worth emphasising that at no time did Collins' have the reputation of a leading hall (except perhaps briefly under Sprake), and even during the 1920s under LTV the bills were less prestigious than at other halls on the circuit. There was the occasional surprise, such as the appearances of Gwen Farrar and the swing pianist Billy Mayerl (in July, 1928), of Herschel Henlere, Balliol & Merton and Ella Retford (in March, 1933) and of Scott & Whaley, in that same year.

This was the period when I went there most frequently and the fare was very mixed. A good bill included Eddy Bayes ('The Basher'), Casa & Nova and Tom E. Hughes ('The Ragbag of Vanity'): they were mostly old-timers, but they seemed to go down well at Collins'.

A particular favourite of the locals were The Four Roadsters, genuine buskers who had been coached into a highly professional act. Later, Fred Barnes appeared, a gorgeous wreck of a man, but no longer capable of doing himself credit. I saw Lily Lassah in a pantomime there, which contained the erudite couplet:

> 'The Crew threatens to mutiny – if they do so,
>
> I will look after Robinson Crusoe'

Following Worland S. Wheeler's death, Collins' pursued an even less consistent policy, coming under the umbrella of Loughbrough Playhouse Ltd. (the Abrahams group of halls), who even ran it as a repertory theatre for a time, with dramas such as *Plaything of an Hour*. In 1941 Lew Lake took over. He had been Lessee under the previous management and his family had a long history of stage work and management, including that of the nearby Islington Empire.

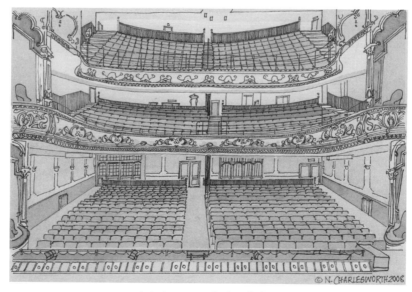

Interior towards the circles

Lew Lake soon brought back real Variety and on various visits after WW2 we enjoyed Nita Valerie & Alice Dey, Peter Bernard (husband of Nita) and Dudley Dale and his Gang ('schoolboys', who were seldom out of work).

But by this time most programmes were pretty thin, built around one or two nudes and an 'Archie Rice'-type comedian. In fact, John Osborn, Sir Laurence Olivier and Vivien Leigh attended Collins' shows several times in the preparation for *The Entertainer*. The management of Collins' tried to encourage a reluctant public to follow their example!

I attended less and less during the 1950s, few bills attracting me, but it was at Collins' Music Hall that Norman Wisdom made his first professional appearance after leaving the army, while others who cut their teeth there included Jimmy Edmundson, Peter Honri and Jimmy Patton, of The Patton Brothers.

It was of course from Collins' that Lew Lake launched his various Old Time Music Hall touring shows. These included *Roses of Piccadilly*, staring Shaun Glenville, and *Those Were The Days*, with Arthur Stott, Jim Jessiman and a company of twelve. Lew Lake, jnr. took over the management from his father; on Lew jnr.'s death, Eric H. Marshall was appointed manager, with Trevor H. Smith as booking manager.

Collins' carried on longer than most halls until, on 15 September, 1958 a disastrous fire in Anderson's timber yard to the rear of the theatre marked its final end. The Sunday papers carried stories of chorus girls rushing to save their costumes as the fire advanced. There were hopes that the hall would be restored and reopened and I well remember a 48-sheet poster in Farringdon Road encouraging us to 'Watch for Reopening Date'. However, water damage to the interior and scorched wiring made this impossible; there were rumours that the hall was under-insured. Although shows had finished, the public house at the front of the theatre continued in business for several more years and a member of the management could often be seen with a gin and tonic in his hand.

Suddenly an auction of the famous collection of autographed photographs, old playbills, mementoes, etc. was announced and it was obvious that Collins' would not be re-built. The auction was held on Shakespeare's birthday, 1963 under the 'gratuitous' prestigious auspices of W. & F.C. Bonham & Sons. The catalogue contains the note: 'The auctioneer, Mr. Leonard Bonham, proposes to call upon any willing stage personality in the audience to sell certain sections of the sale'. It was no surprise at all when the more than 'willing' Tommy Trinder, who had made his stage debut as an amateur at Collins', virtually took over. Although a very sad occasion, he made it a bit more bearable and a goodly sum was raised.

Bonham's had given their services free, as the proceeds went to 'the benefit of The Variety Artistes' Benevolent Fund and Institution'. Another organisation also benefited, as one of the keenest bidders was Ray Mackender, who later gave some of the material to The British Music Hall Society, of which he was one of the founders.

The front part of the Collins' building was converted into serviced flats, with the fire-damaged auditorium being completely demolished by Messrs. Gladdings; two side walls were retained and roofed-over for timber storage. Then in 1989 developers Ivory Merchant, fresh from their battle over proposals to build an office block on the site of the Elizabethan Rose Theatre, deposited a plan to build an office block on the site of Collins'! Equally vociferous protests came from the music hall fraternity. Their efforts were successful, as first Islington Council, and then The Department of the Environment threw out the proposals.

But in spite of fresh proposals to fill it with a theatre to have visits from the Royal Shakespeare Company and the Royal Exchange Theatre, Manchester, the actual site of the theatre is still used for storage – of commuters' cars this time. In 1994 Waterstones succeeded in the face of more opposition from music hall enthusiasts in converting the public house into a well-appointed bookshop. They have taken a lot of trouble to restore the frontage, including the reinstatement of the curved brickwork and stucco work above the rebuilt canopy – removed at the time that the auditorium was demolished. A plaque records the existence of the old music hall on the site, while a recording studio in part of the building maintains a precarious link with entertainment.

A 48-sheet poster seen in Farringdon Road following
fire at the adjoining timber yard, September 1958

COLLINS'S MUSIC HALL,

ISLINGTON GREEN, N.

| Proprietor and Manager | - | - | - | - | - | Mr HERBERT SPRAKE. |
| Assistant Manager | - | - | - | - | - | Mr C. S. BARNES. |

ONE OF THE MOST COMFORTABLE HALLS IN LONDON.

Having a Sliding Roof and every Modern Improvement.

THE BEST TALENT! THE BEST CIGARS!! THE BEST REFRESHMENTS!!!

PRICES FROM 6D TO £1 1s.

OPEN at 7.30.

Islington Empire

High Street, Islington

Islington Empire: exterior (formerly The Grand Theatre) with The O'Gorman Bros. billed

Nearly all the old Islington entertainment venues have gone, but the pub part of Collins' remains as a bookshop, the Rex survives as The Screen on the Green and Sadler's Wells still prospers. In their place there are a handful of fringe theatres, the most notable of which are the Almeida and the King's Head where, in the bar, the measures are still thankfully Imperial and the prices are tilled-up in real money.

None of these new ventures makes much of an impression to the passer-by – a criticism not possible where the impressive Islington Empire was concerned. This strikingly handsome building was excellently positioned at 40, High Street, close to The Angel. It opened in 1860 as the Philharmonic Hall, with a capacity of 1,500. The building had a history of fires – four in all – but survived to celebrate its centenary eventually. It was designed by Finch Hill and Paraire with a delightful frontage in neo-classical style. William Finch Hill and Edward Lewis Paraire were in partnership between 1856 and 1870, designing some seven London theatres, as well as public houses.

The Philharmonic Hall began by presenting concerts and operas, but soon had to inaugurate a more mixed bill of fare, including such artistes as Sam Collins and Harry Sydney, both later to be connected with 'The Chapel on The Green' just up the road. This was clearly more to the liking of Islingtonians.

There were frequent changes of owner at 'the spittoon', as it had come to be called, until, in 1870, Charles Morton from the Canterbury took over, cleaned the place up, rebuilt the stage, added a promenade and introduced 'opera bouffe' and a light opera company headed by Emily Soldene. The productions and the star were easily up to West End standards and Morton was soon regularly attracting a Society audience – including the Prince of Wales, a regular visitor. Incidentally it was here in *Genevieve de Brabant* that English audiences first heard that perennially favourite duet *Bold Gendarmes* – on the first night it got fourteen encores. Soon popular Gaiety stars such as Nellie Farren and Fred Leslie were doubling at what was now the Philharmonic Theatre, as it was known after redecoration in 1874.

In 1882 the theatre had its first fire; it was restored by Frank Matcham and reopened on 4 August, 1883 as The Grand Theatre under Charles Wilmot, with melodrama as the standard fare. Beginners engaged included Harry Hemsley (later a famous child impersonator on the wireless); A.E. Matthews and Seymour Hicks. Then, on 29 December, 1887 a second fire occurred. Again Matcham was responsible for the restoration. After this reopening on 1 December, 1888 a mixed programme prevailed, visiting troupes including that of George Alexander, later a famous actor-manager at the St. James's Theatre.

Charles Wilmot gained an enviable reputation for his magnificent pantomimes and recruited Harry Randall from the music halls as his star when nearby Deacon's Music Hall closed. Wilmot's fourth pantomime in 1891 starred Harry Randall as Idle Jack, Lottie Collins as Alice and Millie Hylton as Dick. Lottie Collins' repeated renditions of 'Ta-Ra-Ra-Boom-De-Ay', with its abandoned dance often causing her complete exhaustion, have gone down in history. She was even booked to perform the number at the Gaiety Theatre in the West End at the same time as the Islington pantomime; the cast often had to keep a scene going until her return!

The following year Tom Costello joined Harry Randall in *The Naughty Forty Thieves*: indeed, the Randall regime lasted a decade, with George Mozart taking over. For the rest of each year touring companies and a Grand Theatre stock company held the stage, visitors including the Carl Rosa Opera Co., Henry Irving in *The Bells* and Dorothea Baird in *Trilby*. Then, in February, 1900 a third fire took place. Frank Matcham, who by now must have been well acquainted with the site, was again called in. A Charles Dickens season was held during 1903 and *Oliver Twist* was among the productions staged.

In 1908 Walter Gibbons, who since 1902 had operated Berner's Hall, adjoining the nearby Royal Agricultural Hall, as the Islington Empire, transferred his business across the road to the Grand, taking the name with him. Most confusing for theatre historians to follow! Under Gibbons and his successor at LTV, the Empire – as it now was – followed a consistent policy of twice-nightly Variety. A typical bill was that for October, 1921 headed by Percy Honri and T.E. Dunville. Others who appeared over the years included Billy Williams, Gertie Gitana, Tod Slaughter, Clarkson Rose & Olive Fox and – as one of The Variety Three – the future Henry Hall.

Gibbons' successor, Charles Gulliver, presented the famous magician Chung Ling Soo in August, 1914 on a bill with Chirgwin, Rosie Archer, Bros. Hannaway and Roland Bros. In 1915 Fred Wilmot & Co. presented their sketch *Only a Rumour* on a bill that also included Morny Cash ('the Lancashire Lad') Kartella and Daisy Mead. Always welcome was Joe Elvin (doubling Ilford Hippodrome) in his latest laughter-raiser, as were The O'Gorman Bros., here for a week in September, 1915.

Interior whilst The Grand Theatre

Among Harry Day's many Revues was *Come Inside*, with Scotch Kelly and Rose Cambrey, and his 1921 offering, *Jingles*, said by some to have been his best ever. A lavish production was George Dance's touring version of *The Whip*, originating at the Theatre Royal, Drury Lane and making use of the Islington Empire's fully-equipped stage.

On the crash of LTV in 1924, the Islington Empire was one of seven halls to be taken over by the Summers-Brown circuit. Some of the shows presented at this period included Francis Laidler's *The Bull's Eye*, T. Elder Hearn's *Darktown Scandals* and Lew Lake's *What Price the Navy?* Lew Lake even took over the management of the Empire for a time, before his involvement with the nearby Collins's Music Hall.

The Empire as ABC Empire Cinema, exterior c.1963

Films, as everywhere, were making inroads into Variety audiences and in 1932 the Islington Empire staged its last proper Variety show, topped by G.H. Elliott. Four of the seven Summers-Brown halls were thereafter booked by De Frece's Agency, continuing to present live shows, but Islington was not one of them. In the 1930s live acts could be seen locally on a regular basis at the Carlton in Essex Road, at The Blue Hall, at Collins' Music Hall and – on special occasions only – at the Empire.

In 1960 the theatre, which had survived yet another fire, held a celebratory dinner at the Peacock Inn, opposite, to mark its centenary. For old time's sake, I attended a film show, when the second feature was *Nudes in the Snow* – entirely appropriate for a rainy winter's evening in North London. I was fascinated to see the safety curtain slowly lowered at the end of the performance – just in case of another fire! The interior of the building still had a strong 'theatre' feel about it, with the two circles and the eight boxes intact, but their surfaces quite plain and painted in gloss grey.

The ABC Empire closed on 10 March, 1962 and was soon demolished – the workmen remarking on how much timber came out of the fully-fitted stage. The handsome frontage survived for another nineteen years while the site of the auditorium was used as a lorry park; the façade was eventually demolished 1981. Some statues and other fragments are preserved in The Museum of London, as well as in private hands. A bank now stands on the site.

GRAND THEATRE, ISLINGTON.

SOLE LESSEE AND MANAGER   -   ·   -   ·   -   ·   - MR. CHARLES WILMOT.

Telephone, No. 7,571.   Open all the Year round at 7 o'clock.

CHARLES WILMOT'S SIXTH GRAND PANTOMIME, 1888-9.

"Cinderella," by GEOFFREY THORN.

Press and Public unanimously pronounce this New and Elegant Theatre to be one of the most Handsome and Complete in London; Lighted by Electricity; Seating Accommodation for 3,000 persons; No Fees.

PRICES—Private Boxes, £1 1s and £2 2s; Stalls, 4s; Dress Circle, 3s; Upper Boxes, 2s; Pit Stalls, 1s 6d; Pit and Amphitheatre, 1s; Gallery, 6d.

Mr. H. A. FREEMAN   -   -   -   -   Business Manager.

Islington Palace (St. Mary's Hall)

Royal Agricultural Hall, Upper Street

Islington Palace (formerly Mohawks Hall, later the first Empire): exterior onto Upper Street with Rosie Sismore billed

Few theatres have boasted such a string of names as the Islington Palace, which opened in 1869 and was converted into a concert hall by the architect Frederick Peck. Over the years the hall sported the names of Berner's Hall, Grand Concert Hall, New Concert Hall, Mohawks Hall, Empire Music Hall, Islington Palace, The Blue Hall Cinema, The Gaumont Cinema and Top Rank Bingo Hall. Different parts of the building were used, as we shall see. The Islington Palace has earned a place in the history books as possibly Britain's first full-time cinema: as such, it should rightfully have been preserved, but it was sacrificed to make way for a clearer approach to the Royal Agricultural Hall.

Fame first came in October, 1873 when James and William Francis, of the music publishers Hopwood & Crew, took a lease on Berner's Hall and introduced The Mohawk Minstrels: they were an instant success and performed in Islington for nearly thirty years. James Francis was one of the principal vocalists, as well as a principal comedian. William Francis was a flautist and composer. Other partners were Ottoway (lead Violinist) and Mowbray (bass), with the whole company numbering nearly twenty.

After only a year they took on Harry Hunter whose rival group, the Manhattan Minstrels, toured widely. Hunter wrote much of the show and quickly became a partner in the troupe. Very soon demand for seats was so great that a move had to be made into part of the main Hall, formerly used for the showing of pigs, but named St. Mary's Hall and with nearly three times the capacity of Berner's Hall.

The troupe did not concentrate entirely on American Deep South songs and material, as there were regular British shows – A Burns Night, a Nautical Night and even a Balaclava Night. Some of Harry Hunter's songs are still sung today, such as *I Can't Forget the Days When I Was Young* and *Your Best Friend Is Your Pocket*.

In 1877, with a growing library of popular music composed by three further members of the company, a music shop was opened in Oxford Street to sell copies of the songs. With the help of David Day (also from Hopwood & Crew), the music publishing firm of Francis, Day & Hunter was formed. With changes in taste, The Mohawk Minstrels merged with the Moore & Burgess Minstrels, moving in 1900 to the latter's venue at St. James's Hall in Piccadilly, but – apart from a series of tours – the combined troupe folded in 1904.

In the meantime, Mohawks Hall in Islington became a full-time cinema in August, 1900. There was an orchestra of sixteen and the place was packed, with audiences avid to see war films from South Africa and China, *Count Zeppelin's Airship* and street films made locally – some of them made just up the road at Alexandra Palace in fact. Crude 'Talkies' featuring music hall artistes like Vesta Tilley and Alec Hurley were also shown. Surprisingly, the place closed down in less than a year!

Walter Gibbons came onto the scene, acquiring Mohawks Hall in 1902 and opening it as the (first) Islington Empire, a Variety hall. The Bioscope featured in the programme, as was usual at the time. Stars who appeared during the following six years included Leo Dryden, Cissie Loftus, Dan Leno, Charles Bignell and Little Tich. In 1908 the hall reverted to full-time film shows, but under the name of Islington Picture Palace – Gibbons had moved across the road to the old Grand Theatre, taking the 'Empire' name with him.

Although the new Islington Palace was principally a cinema, quite a strong supporting bill of live acts was offered in the early years, although few are remembered today. In 1915, for example, one could see during the week of 23 August six acts – Four Olmares, Katie Weston, Fred Rose, Vi Romer, Dalver Duo and Learto with his Dog. There were even short sketches in between films – useful for re-winding or correcting breakdowns. One such was Graham & Harrington's Company in *Daughter of Pleasure*, which appeared on a bill with George James, Buchanan & Scott, Little Dando, Phyllis Court and Fred Zairenella.

Another name change came in 1918, when the hall was re-named The Blue Hall – still recalled today. Ciné-Variety was presented almost continually from that time until the outbreak of WW2. We were able to see Wright & Marion during the week of 16 July, 1928, when The Blue Hall was under the control of General Theatre Corporation (GTC). Split-weeks were soon the rule, with changes of live acts on Monday and Thursday – Jock McKay and Randolph Sutton each appeared for a half week in December, 1928. Others to make similar appearances were Four Brownie Boys and Austel in 1929, with Arthur & Rob Daymar and Fisher & Ariani in 1930.

Interior (formerly Mohawks Hall, Upper St.), later The Blue Hall and the Gaumont Cinema

By 1929 The Blue Hall was one of twenty-three houses on the GTC circuit, but the following year it came under the control of Gaumont-British Ltd. and for a time the new parent put live acts into only their more prestigious theatres and cinemas. Normal service had resumed by October 1935, when the Omega Trio and the Scottish comedienne Jean Kennedy appeared for a split week, with Blum & Blum (hand-balancers) and Robert Reilly with Mary Ann completing the second-half of the week. Rehearsals were held at the Canterbury Music Hall, another Gaumont-British house at that time. There was an occasional full week, as in July, 1936 when El Cubanos Tango Band set Islington afire. Among other names still recalled, Billy Whittaker & Partner, Michael & Arnova, Sherry & Kiel and Rome & Leonard were acts that we could see at The Blue Hall. By the late 1930s rehearsals were held at the new Camden Town Gaumont, only a short 'bus ride away.

Live entertainment came to an end here in 1939. After hostilities ended The Blue Hall became the Islington Gaumont Cinema in 1946. Gaumont combined with Odeon in later years, with further changes of name, but films ended at the old Palace in January, 1963; the last programme was composed of *The Millionaire* and *The Navy Lark*. A number of other houses closed around this time, including the ABC Empire (former Islington Grand Theatre) over the road. Soon the cry of "Eyes Down" was to be heard many times a day. Bingo lasted until 1975. For ten years the empty building – still in all its Victorian glory – became increasingly derelict. When The Royal Agricultural hall was to be refurbished, the Palace/Gaumont site was required for the provision of a new approach and entrance. The fine listed building, which would have made a splendid home the The British Music Hall Society, was sadly demolished in 1985.

229

Four Iles Rosetti

Islington: Sadler's Wells Music Hall

Rosebery Avenue, Finsbury

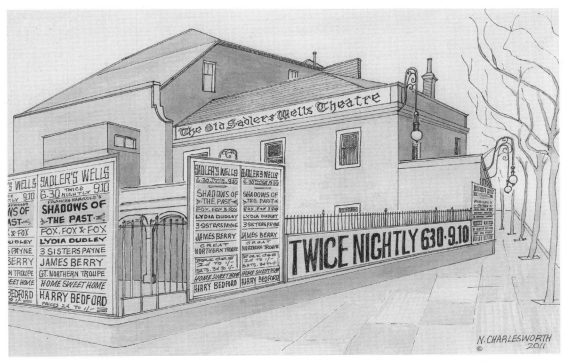

Sadler's Wells, Rosebery Avenue: exterior while a Music Hall, with Harry Bedford billed

Unlike all its old rivals, Sadler's Wells is still a working theatre. While not a music hall in the strict sense of the work, the Wells has been rescued by Variety entertainment a number of times during its long history. It has also provided a home for pantomime, most recently in 1994, shortly before its last major reconstruction.

Back in 1683 a well was re-discovered in the grounds surrounding the house of Dick Sadler, an inspector of highways in Clerkenwell. Finding that the waters were extremely popular with local folk, he and his partner Forcer, a dancing master, enclosed the gardens and on 3 June, 1683 opened a wooden 'Musick House'. Under Forcer's son, and then a Mr. Warren from 1743, the place became villainously disreputable. At this time there were four or five performances a day, the number and length of these depending on the number of people awaiting admission!

The old wooden theatre was replaced with a stone building by the manager, Thomas Rasoman, in 1765. Rasoman was also a builder and under his management a mixed programme was introduced, doing much to improve the status of the place. Following re-modelling in 1783, it even became fashionable – performing dogs being the big attraction that year. The opera singer John Hamilton Braham, who later built the lamented St. James's Theatre, sang at the Wells during the last quarter of the century – a particularly enjoyable time here.

The celebrated clown Grimaldi was a regular entertainer here until 1805 – even marrying one of the directors. Sadly, his later managership of Sadler's Wells was less successful than his stage appearances. In the meantime, the boy actor Master Carey (later the famous Edmund Kean) made his debut here and aquatic performances used a tank of water, fed from the New River behind the theatre. Under Charles Debdin these became all the rage, rather as ice-shows drew large audiences years later.

Exterior as in 1792

Exterior as in 1830

Exterior as in 1894

Managements came and went, as did plays, melodramas and further aquatic offerings. In 1832 there was a memorable run of *Black-Eyed Susan*, but two years later a thorough renovation became necessary after a fire caused by gas-lighting. Ballet-lovers should remember that on 23 August, 1842 the first production of *Giselle* was given in England at Sadler's Wells – once again featuring real fountains in the final scene, supplied from the famous water tank.

Perhaps the most important year at the Wells was 1844, when the theatre was let to Samuel Phelps and Mrs. Warren, although the latter departed after two years. Phelps produced thirty-four of Shakespeare's plays during his reign of nearly twenty years, making the theatre truly the home of the Bard. As Arthur Beales says:

> "It was a bold experiment to transform a theatre with a reputation extending over nearly two centuries for having the roughest audience in London and for being the home of the lowest forms of dramatic entertainment, into the home of legitimate drama, and Shakespeare at that. The same spirit was to be seen later in Lilian Baylis"

Phelps' revival of *Anthony and Cleopatra* in 1849 was the first for a century, while that of *Pericles* in 1854 was the first since the Restoration! By the time he retired in 1862 he had given well over 3,000 performances.

Following two more changes of direction – to light entertainment and then to further hydraulic displays and a skating rink – Sadler's Wells sank to its lowest depths in 1869 – it became a pickle factory and was even the scene of a prize-fight. Eventually condemned as a dangerous structure, it was closed and became derelict.

The new interior of 1879

Hope returned, however, with the sale of the theatre for £1,020 in August, 1875 to Mrs. Isabella Bateman from the Lyceum. It was reconstructed at a cost of £12,000 to designs by C.J. Phipps and reopened as a 2,500-seat theatre on 9 October, 1879 with a revival of Sir Walter Scott's *Rob Roy*, in an adaptation by Isaac Pocock. Even under Mrs. Bateman's control Sadler's Wells included Variety turns in its mixed programmes of Shakespeare, melodrama and burlesque. In 1886, under James Deacon's brief management, Variety artistes were also presented: perhaps he was testing the water at the larger house as his own music hall opposite was due to close for the construction of Rosebery Avenue in 1891.

Mrs. Bateman's daughter carried on for a while after her mother's death in 1893, and then in November of that year the Wells became a music hall. Other old drama houses, such as The Surrey,

The Britannia and The Old Vic followed the same path at this period. The change of use immediately attracted the attention of the authorities and a meeting of The Theatres and Music Halls Committee of the LCC required numerous alterations in doors, steps, handrails and backstage safety features; the WC and urinal under the stage was also to be removed and the connection with the drains properly made.

Astute manager, George Belmont, took Sadler's Wells into a new role with success, presenting Harry Champion, George & Nellie Lupino, G.H. Macdermott and Marie Lloyd (she was reputed to be working five halls in a night – the Hoxton Varieties and at the Poplar Queen's, followed by the Tivoli and London Pavilion in the West End and finally 'Merry Old Sad's' as Belmont used to call Sadler's Wells). *The Stage* reported that "The Sadler's Wells halfpenny programme is now adorned with a signed portrait of Mr. George E. Belmont, a very good likeness".

In 1897 George Belmont presented James Berry, the former public hangman who had despatched nearly 200 murderers. No doubt, a bloodthirsty audience packed the house that week, for – as a sequel – a lantern lecture was put on, showing prison flogging rooms. A fairly typical Variety bill, of January, 1899 is shown in the composite sketch by Sam Sibbitt, above. Other stars to be engaged at the re-launched house included Lily Morris, Gus Elen, Kate Carney and Tom Costello.

In 1898 some of Belmont's other bookings included Fred Karno's Company, Gertie Gitana, Roy Redgrave and G.H. Elliott, the latter still working sixty years later. 'Edisongraph' pictures were also shown as part of each programme. Redgrave was the patriarch of the Redgrave theatrical dynasty. He twice left for an acting career in Australia, dying in Sydney in 1922.

Business must have been brisk, as Belmont took over Sadler's Wells on a long lease from 15 October, 1900 and the following year redecorations were carried out under the architect Bertie Crewe. The ceilings of lath and plaster were removed and silicate cotton substituted. The work was carried out without the loss of any performances, as the scaffolding was taken down each night. The contractors were John Wevking & Sons, with some £2,000 being spent.

But all was obviously not well, as Frank Macnaghten, manager of Bow Palace and Battersea Palace, took over in November, 1902. Despite his continuing confidence in booking such luminaries as Dan Leno (towards the end of his career), Ella Shields and Florrie Forde, it was moving pictures that were attracting the crowds.

Macnaughten's reign was marked by complete redecoration of the auditorium in cream and gold, relieved by sky blue. The handsome stage curtain was heavily fringed with gold tassels. On the opening bill of 1 November, 1902 were Jack Foley (comedian), The Bob Hanlon Trio (gymnasts), Downs & Langford (eccentric comedians), Louise Herman (comedienne) and The Goldini Trio (acrobats) – hardly any of whom are remembered today. The bill was completed by Godfrey's British Bioscope.

An accident occurred on 6 February the next year during the pantomime, when Mr. Breton, an actor, shot himself in the hand with a blank charge, but courageously completed the scene. Passing out in the wings, he was rushed to the Royal Free Hospital. *The Stage* did report that *Aladdin* finished its successful run on Saturday, 7 February, 1903, so Breton probably only missed the two houses on the final day. Frank Macnaughten was fined £25 with costs in October that year, when poor lighting in the balcony caused an elderly lady from Islington Green to slip and fracture her arm – she had sued for £50!

As at other of his London halls, Macnaughten handed control at Sadler's Wells to his trusty lieutenant, Frederick Baugh, in 1912. But regime change followed quickly when in the following year the Wells ceased to be a music hall. Under H.T. Underwood's management the old theatre became a cinema of sorts for three years, much the same happening at The Surrey and The Britannia. On

19 December, 1914 Sadler's Wells was relaunched as 'North London's Popular Picture Theatre' – but to no avail, as it soon closed down. The theatre then became derelict once again and was used as a playground for children, having had its roof removed to avoid the imposition of rates. There were tentative plans by Ernest Rolls to turn the place into a cabaret theatre – reviving the Variety tradition – but nothing came of them and the rats remained undisturbed.

Exterior of the 1929 theatre

A fresh new era was ushered in during 1927, when Lilian Baylis and Sir Reginald Rowe launched an appeal for the rehabilitation of Sadler's Wells, with a view to making it the north London counterpart of the Old Vic. Under the Duke of Devonshire's leadership the committee raised the money necessary and the theatre was rebuilt to plans by F.G.M. Chancellor, of the Frank Matcham office. The exterior of the building was quite austere, relying chiefly on the proportion of its masses; there was a canopy over the principal entrance, with a group of three stone-dressed windows and a decorative panel by Herbert Cawthra above; he also designed a relief over the proscenium.

The new theatre opened on 6 January, 1931, under the management of Lilian Baylis in conjunction with the Old Vic with *Twelfth Night*. The cast was headed by John Gielgud and Dorothy Green; Gielgud hated the new theatre at first, describing its acoustics as "dreadful". Further improvements and extensions took place in 1938 in memory of Baylis, with the last of the old 1765 building disappearing. The architects were Stanley Hall and Messrs. Easton & Robertson, who designed a new frontage to Arlington Street and an extension to the frontage in Rosebery Avenue. After being used during WW2 as a rest-hose for people bombed-out locally, the theatre reopened on 7 July, 1947 with the production of *Peter Grimes*, the first opera to be composed by Benjamin Britten. For many years after that it enjoyed an excellent reputation as the north London home of opera and ballet with The Vic-Wells Association maintaining the link between the two theatres north and south of the Thames.

We attended several productions of operetta at Sadler's Wells, especially appreciating *Orpheus in the Underworld* and *La Vie Parisienne*, both starring June Bronhill. Having made her debut here in 1954, she made a big success in the title role of Hanna in *The Merry Widow*, which she sang over 200 times.

Eventually, the Sadler's Wells Opera Company moved permanently to the London Coliseum, becoming English National Opera (ENO), with the Wells becoming best known as a London receiving house for Dance, many overseas companies enjoying season there, despite its rather shallow stage. Stephen Remington was director here for a number of years.

Exterior of the new 1998 theatre

Financial problems increasingly affected Sadler's Wells during the 1980s, with closure seemingly inevitable by 1986. Parliamentary pressure led to an eleventh hour move to save the famous theatre. The Arts Council suggested that the three dance companies regularly performing there should increase their rents to the beleaguered theatre. The Arts Minister refused to fund the theatre directly – only the companies working in it. The crisis was temporarily resolved, with a smaller Lilian Baylis Theatre being added in 1988.

Interior of the new 1998 theatre, from a photo by Ian Grundy

Pantomime made a wonderful and unexpected return to Sadler's Wells for the 1994–95 Season. The spectacular comedy production of *Babes in the Wood* was the first such show in this part of London for many years and starred Roy Hudd, Geoffrey Hughes, Keith Barron and 'Britain's Finest Dame' – Jack Tripp. Others in the show, which was supported by The Evening Standard, were Lisa Hull, Julie Mullins, Howard Leader and Gary Lovini. It was written and directed by Roy Hudd, relishing the opportunity of appearing in such an historic theatre, with its history of Variety. The company repeated its success at Plymouth Theatre Royal the following year.

The shortcomings of the main theatre's facilities, particularly its stage – smaller than any other that the Sadler's Wells Royal Ballet performed on – became more acute. If it was to become a receiving house for international dance companies, something drastic would have to be done. Eventually money became available to radically reconstruct the house and the contractors Bovis were engaged. The new theatre, designed by Renton Howard Wood Levin (RHWL) with Nicholas Hare, opened in 1998 at a cost of £48 million. So a site used for entertainment for over 300 years happily continues in that role.

Billy Danvers, comedian

MISS MINNIE MARIO,

COMEDIENNE, BURLESQUE, AND OPERA BOUFFE ARTIST.

SPECIALLY engaged by Captain R. BAINBRIDGE to sustain the part of "Ganem," Principal Boy in the forthcoming Grand Christmas Pantomine "*The Forty Thieves*" at the THEATRE ROYAL, MANCHESTER.

LONDON, EASTER.   ARRANGEMENTS COMPLETE.

Special Starring Tour, August. 5th, 1889.

Sole Agent - - - - - - - - - - - - - *HUGH JAY DIDCOTT.*

Miss KATIE SEYMOUR,

BURLESQUE ACTRESS, VOCALIST, AND DANCER.

Christmas:

TYNE THEATRE, NEWCASTLE-ON-TYNE.

Communications to Agent—

Mr EDWARD COLLEY, 163 Stamford St., London, S.E.

THE ORIGINAL

LEOPOLDS,

ALL ARRANGEMENTS COMPLETE FOR 1889.

Winter—1888-9, Prince of Wales' Theatre, Birmingham.

SPRING .... EMPIRE THEATRE AND CANTERBURY PALACE.
SUMMER .... FOLIES BERGERE, PARIS.
AUTUMN .... FRIVOLITY TOUR, all the Principal Theatres in England.

Director - - - - - JOHN LEOPOLD.

Calling cards for three artistes

Kilburn Empire

Kilburn High Road and Kilburn Priory

Kilburn Empire (Essoldo, or Broadway Theatre): exterior with Chas. Austin billed

This large theatre, at 9–11 The Parade, High Road, Kilburn, was opened in 1906 with seating for nearly 2,000 in stalls, circle and gallery. There was a provisional licence for the years 1905–1908. Redesigned by W.G.R. Sprague, after an earlier plan by Frederick Hingston proved problematical, the New Kilburn Empire was built originally as a Variety theatre-cum-circus. There were modifications in 1908 and in 1910 to make the building into a Variety theatre proper, although the elephant pits from its circus days remained under the stage until the end of its life in 1994.

Joseph Pepper held the licence from 1909 to 1925 and a typical bill from that era comprised The Herman Darewski Ensemble, Hilda Glyder, The Poluskis, Thornley-Dodge, The Sutcliffe Family, Fred Curran, The Mafuziang-Manchu Troupe and Nellie Wigley. From an early date Kilburn Empire was managed by London Theatres of Varieties Ltd. (LTV), and under their aegis the theatre did well enough for two decades, hosting many of the great names of the period – in 1915 Joe Elvin & Co., Sam Mayo, James Fawn, May Henderson, Morny Cash, Jock Whiteford and May Moore Duprez; in 1916 Chas. Austin, Sam Stern and Harry Bedford; and in 1918 Daisy Dormer.

Interior towards the circles

In June, 1922 Marie Lloyd made one of her last appearances at Kilburn, dying in October that year. The Kilburn Empire became for a few years The Kilburn Vaudeville Theatre – an unusual name for a London house – reverting to its old name in 1928 on the crash of LTV. Most of the Variety theatres in that group then embraced films, with the Empire being no exception. It was at this time that the decorative statues and urns were removed from the frontage – presumably to make it more 'modern'. For a couple of years it was managed by the Summers Brown Circuit, touring productions and Variety being mixed with film fare. We could see such shows as Albert de Courville's *The Show World*, Will Murray in that long-running story of urchins who put on a music hall show – *Casey's Court*, M. Barry O'Brien's *Interference*, and Murray Mills' *Paris, 1919*. Another touring revue that played a week at Kilburn was C.B. Cochran's *The League of Notions*. From November, 1927 Variety was staged six nights a week, with regular film performances on Sundays.

Exterior while The Essoldo Cinema

When Metropolitan & Provincial Cinemas group ran the Kilburn Empire between 1931 and 1938, films became the mainstay, although there were some live acts: for example, in April, 1933 Eugene and his Magyar Izigane Band played a week. Full-time live entertainment was tried again in January 1938, when Will Mahoney could be seen in *Ride 'em, Cowboy*. Don Ross once told me that he and Gertie Gitana had had an interest in Kilburn Empire for a time, which he described as "a replica of The London Palladium", but I have not been able to locate details of any of the shows they presented there.

George Black tried unsuccessfully to restore No. 1 Variety bills to Kilburn during the late 1930s, during which time the Empire appeared in the trade press alongside such prestigious halls as Finsbury Park Empire and The London Hippodrome on The Moss Tour. There were some first-rate bills, such as that for the week of 26 September, 1938 when Ambrose and his Orchestra (doubling with The Holborn Empire) appeared for a week with Evelyn Dall, Max Bacon and a big Variety bill. And, again, a week later when Charles L. Tucker presented *Tops Everything*: this show gave us Hutch, Maurice Colleano (with Bonar and George, Tovia and Rubye), Max Wall, Jewel & Warriss and company. In November, 1938 Harry Roy and his Band appeared, but the leader collapsed as his signature tune ("Bugle Call Rag") opened their act. As *The Daily Express* reported at the time, women in the gallery screamed and Harry Mooney, of Mooney & Murray, rushed onto the stage and carried Harry Roy off. The bandleader was taken to his Mayfair home and his doctor advised him to rest for a few days. Cyril Fletcher also topped at around this period, so Kilburn had every chance to see the best. But, sadly, the experiment was short-lived and by 1939 Moss' Empires were no longer presenting shows at the Kilburn Empire, despite having better luck with their management of Croydon Empire at this time.

Interior while The Essoldo Cinema

During WW2 F.J. Butterworth ran Kilburn Empire as a No. 2 Variety theatre, part of his chain of nearly a dozen halls. During the week of 10 April, 1944 it was the only one to be showing films! Two years later the theatre staged a pantomime season with Syd Seymour as Buttons in *Cinderella*. Sadler's Wells Theatre Ballet Company also took in a week at Kilburn on its national tour: it is not recorded how well they were received at the North West London Variety house.

The last individual proprietor was Nat Tennens, who took over in 1947, presenting West End play successes and Variety, in conjunction with the Clapham Grand. The young Morecambe & Wise cut their teeth here, often apparently finding great difficulty in gathering sufficient material for two separate spots.

Exterior showing stage house and dressing room block

In 1949 the Essoldo group took over the Kilburn Empire, giving it their own name and running it as a cinema for around twenty years. Eventually it had become so run-down that the company gutted the Sprague interior and built a 'pod' inside to house a modern 471-seater cinema. This was done by extending the old circle down to the stage, the original stalls and gallery being abandoned. To raise its profile, the exterior was covered in blue metal cladding. It re-opened on 3 December, 1970 with *Catch 22*.

When Essoldo were themselves taken over it became the Classic cinema on 1 April, 1972. However, business declined and the cinema closed on 1 December, 1973. It remained empty for nearly three years when suddenly in 1976 Larry Parnes reopened it as The Broadway Theatre, with *Cycle Sluts*, followed by a touring production of *Pyjama Tops*. The venture soon failed, perhaps due to its situation, with films coming to the rescue again as they had repeatedly done over the years. However, the final closure came on 12 April, 1981, following the showing of (Idi) *Amin: the Rise and Fall*.

The old Kilburn Empire was boarded-up for the next ten years, becoming home to countless pigeons and its entrance a rubbish dump. There was final ignominy, when it became a Quasar Laser Games Centre for about a year. At least it was spared the cries of 'Bingo'. It held its last paying public in 1992 and demolition began in May, 1994. The site, together with the adjoining parade of shops, is now The Carlton-Plaza, an hotel and flats development.

I am grateful to Ken Roe for details of the Empire's final years.

Kingston Empire

Richmond Road, Kingston-upon-Thames

Kingston Empire: full exterior with James Fawn billed

In 1910 Kingston was an essentially suburban middle-class area, with some remaining farmland, when the much-loved Kingston Empire first opened. It was built on the site of the mid-eighteenth century Canbury House, home of the Roots family. W. Oldham Chambers of Kingston submitted the first plan, for a half-timbered 'Tudor' theatre in 1907. These plans were not to be adopted, due to the unfortunate bankruptcy of the firm. New designs by Bertie Crewe for a 2,000-seat Variety theatre were passed two years later. *The Era* certainly approved of the elevations, especially the 'verandah'; the plasterwork was by De Jongh and there were two circles and four boxes at circle level.

Mr Clarence Sounes, the proprietor and manager, promised performances 'kept entirely free from any suggestion of coarseness' and the Empire settled down to giving a fairly predictable night out over the next forty-five years. The theatre was considered to be a Number One Touring Date, offering what the public wanted – Variety shows at a reasonably cheap price, but in quite luxurious surroundings, with a twenty-piece orchestra. Backstage, of course, conditions tended to change; according to comments at differing dates they were described as 'dirty', 'primitive', 'cramped' and 'freezing'. There were only three washbasins for all the artistes to share.

Prices at opening night, when Dorothy Ward made her fist Kingston appearance, ranged from 3d in the gallery to 15s for the best box. After WW2 these had risen to 1s in the gallery, 3s in the circle, 4s in the stalls and £1 6s 0d for the best box – not an excessive increase over thirty-five years. A good supper at the small local restaurant was available at 1s 6d, or you could buy a bag of hot chestnuts from a man who was always outside the theatre. There were two bad fires – the first in April, 1914 and the second in mid-June 1919. Following the first fire Bertie Crewe was recalled and the theatre was miraculously restored in only three months. The damage from the 1919 fire was more severe and the repairs took six months. The re-opening bill of 1919 included Eric Randolph (who sang the National Anthem on both Monday houses), Frank Elliston & Co. in a farce entitled *Dear Old Bean*, Will Bland a magician, Peggy O'Hara a versatile entertainer, The Castillians in a frozen statuary act, comedian Tommy Davis, the well-known Sam Barton on his bike, Mr Maria conducting the Empire Orchestra and, of course, there was also the Bioscope.

Interior from the circle

Family audiences appreciated the familiar mixture of turns presented: a straight play, a circus turn, a sketch, a juggler, comedians, classical music and a knockabout double-act. Many established stars of the time came to Kingston Empire including Marie Lloyd, Harry Champion, Albert Chevalier and Ella Shields. During the 1920s, as elsewhere, revue became the popular and fashionable form of entertainment, with traditional Variety bills less often seen. In 1920 Stanley-Watson moved to Kingston from managing Aldershot Hippodrome, its sister theatre, and stayed until the Empire's closure. He was to see virtually every famous name in Variety on the Kingston stage; he ran a tight ship and the theatre was said to be his whole life. He was ably assisted by his larger-than-life stage manager, Percy Court, who ruled backstage with a rod of iron and expected a reward at the end of the week. Musical directors over the years included Alfred Ketelby, Mr Maria and Jack Frere from Penge Empire, but the greatest personality and showman was Olly Aston who stayed for ten years from 1933 and always made his flourishing entrance down a ramp from the stage.

Variety returned in the 1930s in a form more familiar to us and in 1935 Kingston Empire celebrated its Silver Jubilee with a month of special bills, including one topped by a huge favourite, Max Miller. In common with all places of entertainment, the Empire closed at the declaration of war in September, 1939, but only for a week. It was claimed that it was the first theatre in the suburbs to reopen after the declaration of war. During the first year of the war the Empire kept going with full bills; however, in the late summer of 1940, many things had to change. During September there were heavy raids and the Empire went dark until November, when advance notice was given of its pantomime, to open on Boxing Day. Again, it was claimed that the Empire was one of the first suburban houses to open after 'recent conditions'. The pantomime was a sell-out and extra performances had to be arranged at the end of its five-week run. In the summer of 1944, when the VI bomb campaign was at its height, the Empire closed again abruptly in July, but the opportunity was taken to do a thorough spring-clean and some re-decoration. However, it was triumphantly open for business again at the end of hostilities.

Interior: the stage as at opening in 1910

After WW2 a number of new performers gained popularity at Kingston, many of them coming from the armed forces. Others had been heard on the radio, which made them more familiar, and included Max Bygraves, Norman Wisdom and Frankie Howerd. Frankie Vaughan actually made his debut at the Empire in 1950, as a trial turn!

Exterior from Richmond Road

Variety, however, was not the only attraction, as twice a year a circus took the stage. The elephants were often stabled in the warehouse of Bentalls Department Store, wearing red lights on their tails when being led back from the theatre at night. Musical shows, touring after their London runs, were also popular at the Empire. *The Desert Song* and Ivor Novello's shows were some of them. There were also Ice Shows with their brilliant costumes and ice ballet sequences. Concerts of classical music were heard on Sundays, featuring the London Philharmonic Orchestra or local orchestras. Bernard Delfont often opened acts and shows at Kingston, for instance with Paterson & Jackson, the sensational coloured heavyweight American act in May, 1950. On the bill were Max Bacon (Britain's own heavyweight entertainer), Sunny King and six speciality acts. Kingston's Royal County Theatre had closed in 1920, so the Empire provided a home for local amateur dramatic, operatic and dance companies – a great asset to the town.

But by the early 1950s the whole presentation of Variety seemed tired. In the words of Barry Took: 'Music Halls were in decline... dying of their own incompetence'. The names of Bruce Forsyth and Spike Milligan do stand out in a list of quite mediocre Variety bills and nude shows. Audiences fell away, as they wanted 'something with a bit of guts in it', as locals reported. Even *The Billy Cotton Band Show*, normally a rip-roaring night, was a disappointment, as Billy was taken ill and the show had to use a substitute conductor. Some weeks the Empire had to take whatever show was available. The theatre closed on 26 March, 1955, with *La Vie Parisienne*, which was in fact a new show starting its tour at Kingston and led by Sonny Jenks. Others featured were Billy Nelson, Chuck O'Neil and Billy Morris in 'great form', with The Iris Long Trio, Stan Jay and Joan, with Douglas Maynard, who in addition to directing the orchestra, played the xylophone brilliantly. *The Stage* reported that, despite the sadness of the Kingston Empire's closure, 'the show set a much-needed new standard in touring revue'.

There was little interest in buying the Empire after it closed; in fact the building failed to reach its reserve at auction. Eventually it was converted into a supermarket, later becoming a Reject Shop. The old Empire still stands and in 1997 it was re-opened as a public house, The King's Tun, while displaying the theatre's name in large letters on the side wall. In time, Kingston gained the brand-new Rose Theatre, now making its name.

Adapted from a thesis by Claire Jones, with many thanks.

Mile End: Paragon Theatre of Varieties

95, Mile End Road, Stepney

Paragon Theatre of Varieties: the exterior with Ada Reeve billed

A theatre with a long history and still in use for entertainment, the Paragon Theatre is probably best remembered as the Mile End Empire, a name it acquired in about 1912. The Eagle public house was licensed as far back as 1848, gradually evolving into The Eagle Music Hall, under a series of licensees. It enjoyed prosperity from 1874 as Lusby's Winter & Summer Palace, under William Lusby and then attracted the attention of the proprietors of the Canterbury Hall in Westminster Bridge Road, eventually being controlled by a company known as The Canterbury & Paragon Ltd.

Under Charles Spencer Crowder and George Adney Payne, Lusby's was completely rebuilt after a fire in 1884 by Frank Matcham; it reopened as the Paragon the following year. The architect made his name with this commission, the building being particularly noted for its much-improved system of ventilation. Matcham had taken over the practice of J.T. Robinson, his late father-in-law, five years earlier. The architect was recalled in 1893 to supervise the redecoration of the hall and the installation of electric lighting; the work took one month, while the hall remained closed. The work included the building of an engine house to the east of the hall. The plans were approved by the LCC, who insisted upon the fitting of self-closing double iron doors at its entrance.

Business must have been brisk in the 2,480 capacity hall, as net profit of £6,700 was declared in September, 1891; a dividend of 7% was proposed. The programme for the week commencing 18 May, 1891 brought Paul Martinetti, the great pantomimist, in *Paris Night by Night*, his own creation in five scenes. Music was by M. Desorme of the Folies Bergeres and among the sixteen supporting acts were Jenny Valmore, the Brothers Poluski, Flo Hastings and Lily Burnand.

Interior towards the stage

A programme of 1893 shows on its cover pictures of Ada Reeve, who signed the original sheet years later in 1963, Little Tich and George Adney Payne, the managing director of the hall. It may be worth noting that Payne was born at the Curragh in Ireland in 1846, the son of a soldier. After some time in the army, he entered commercial life as a wine merchant, before joining Charles Crowder in the purchase of Lusby's Music Hall. At the time of his death in 1908, as a result of a motor accident, he was one of the most prominent figures in the music hall world. He was either managing director, a director or chairman of some eleven properties, collectively known as The Syndicate Halls and including of course The Metropolitan, The Oxford and The Canterbury. He was succeeded by his son, Walter Payne, later on the board of Moss' Empires Ltd.

The artistes in the June, 1893 programme include luminaries such as Katie Lawrence, The McNaughtons, Harry Anderson, Charles Godfrey, Paul Cinquevalli, R.G. Knowles and the above-named Ada Reeve ('the East-end favourite'), as well as the return of Paul Martinetti. So the quality of the entertainment remained extremely high.

The Paragon's attractions in the 1890s included a grill room and lounge, as well as a conservatory and crush room; the entrance foyer boasted statues of very lightly-draped females, which no doubt appealed to the Mile End lads. The place had a reputation as a fairly rough house, even later when it became a cinema.

The Paragon became a twice nightly house in 1902, commencing on August Bank Holiday that year. The length of some subsequent programmes sheds some doubt on whether this arrangement continued, or whether it later reverted to once-nightly presentation. Times were changing, even before WW1, with films making an appearance here as early as February, 1900. A short circuit, caused by poor wiring, caused a fire in the projector around this time, but happily the damage was confined to the iron housing required by the LCC, so no smoke escaped into the auditorium and no alarm was caused.

In 1903 plans were approved for the installation of a safety curtain, similar to that at the Canterbury. This was just as well, for a fire occurred again (this time on stage) the following February, luckily just after the theatre had closed for the evening. It was quickly extinguished by the stage staff helped by the local fire brigade.

Variety continued until just before WW1, but of course had included the Bioscope for some years, showing up-to-date news pictures. George Robey and Marie Lloyd appeared in October, 1908 on a 16-act bill that would have been hard to stage twice-nightly and included the Irish comedian Pat Rafferty, The Poluskis, Fred Elton, Dan Thomas (the famous "dame" comedian) and Frances Letty. The Paragon was a regular production date for Fred Karno's shows for many years thereafter.

Films largely took over from 1913 onwards, when the theatre became known as Mile End Empire and reports suggest that the management was still finding the audience a challenge! In 1928 the Empire became part of the catastrophic United Picture Theatres circuit (UPT) but live Variety acts (usually three acts for a split-week) continued to appear between films. In the 1920s one could have enjoyed seeing at various times Vernon Watson (later Nosmo King), Deen & Ross (Don Ross and his dancing partner), Fred Culpitt, Jean Andrews and Ella Logan. Ella was Jimmy Logan's and Annie Ross' aunt and the original Sharon in the first Broadway production of *Finian's Rainbow* in 1947. In April, 1930 Gaumont-British took a small financial interest in UPT, entering into a five-year management agreement. However, things went from bad to worse with UPT never showing a profit again.

Eventually, in 1934, six of the worst performing halls – mostly former music halls and theatres, including Mile End Empire – were sold off by the receiver at the best price he could get. The Empire property came into the hands of Associated British Cinemas (ABC) and even then continued to have some live acts to leaven the film programme. For instance, in July 1936 we could have seen Goldy and his Band, Cal & Nona Kay, Toledo and Elly & Joan. My travels did not normally take me to the East End, but I noted that the Mile End Empire was one of fifteen ABC cinemas in the London area to be staging Ciné-variety in the late 1930s.

Exterior when rebuilt as The ABC Cinema (formerly Mile End Empire)

In 1939 the old out-dated hall was demolished, rebuilt and opened as a brand-new ABC Empire, later known as plain ABC, Mile End. The cinema ran until around 1989, when falling audiences forced its closure. Latterly it was managed by another circuit and re-named the Coronet, Mile End. In 1999, after being empty for a decade, the former ABC was bought by a business family from Bow, East London, who planned to invest £2.5 million in a plush five-screen 1,100-seat cinema called Genesis. The interior was to be refurbished, retaining as many as possible of the original 1939 features. At the time of writing, the Paragon Theatre site has been connected with entertainment for well on 160 years.

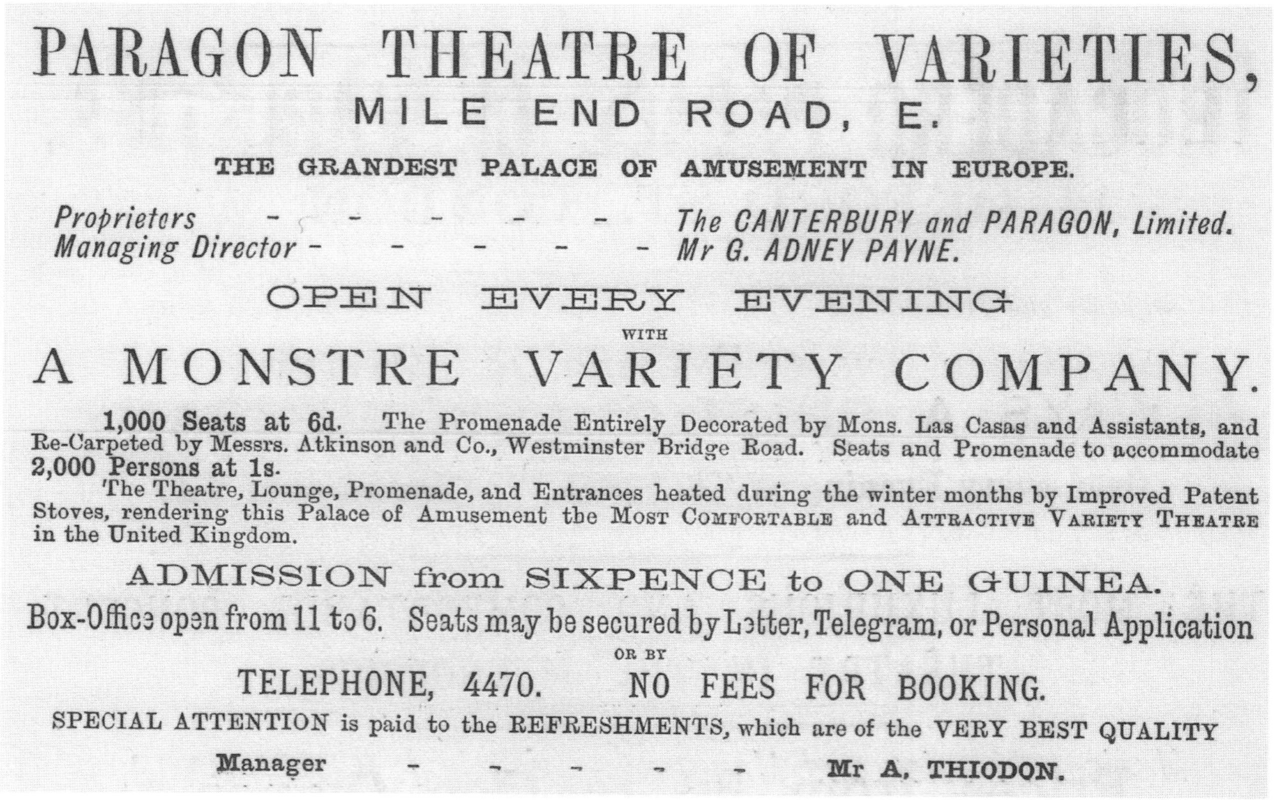

PARAGON THEATRE OF VARIETIES,

MILE END ROAD, E.

THE GRANDEST PALACE OF AMUSEMENT IN EUROPE.

Proprietors   -   -   -   -   -   The CANTERBURY and PARAGON, Limited.
Managing Director -   -   -   -   -   Mr G. ADNEY PAYNE.

OPEN EVERY EVENING

WITH

A MONSTRE VARIETY COMPANY.

1,000 Seats at 6d. The Promenade Entirely Decorated by Mons. Las Casas and Assistants, and Re-Carpeted by Messrs. Atkinson and Co., Westminster Bridge Road. Seats and Promenade to accommodate **2,000 Persons at 1s.**

The Theatre, Lounge, Promenade, and Entrances heated during the winter months by Improved Patent Stoves, rendering this Palace of Amusement the MOST COMFORTABLE and ATTRACTIVE VARIETY THEATRE in the United Kingdom.

ADMISSION from SIXPENCE to ONE GUINEA.

Box-Office open from 11 to 6. Seats may be secured by Letter, Telegram, or Personal Application

OR BY

TELEPHONE, 4470.   NO FEES FOR BOOKING.

SPECIAL ATTENTION is paid to the REFRESHMENTS, which are of the VERY BEST QUALITY

Manager   -   -   -   -   -   Mr A. THIODON.

Paddington: Metropolitan Theatre of Varieties

Edgware Road

Metropolitan Theatre of Varieties: the old exterior

The Metropolitan Theatre of Varieties as we remember it was designed by Frank Matcham and opened in 1897, with a jolly light classical exterior. It had a strong family likeness to this other theatres in Leeds, Sheffield and Leicester and was one of his finest creations. One forgets that its interior was constructed around Walter Emden's earlier building. Matcham's rebuild was cosy, despite its capacity of nearly 1,700, and highly ornamented. The rich plasterwork on the ceiling and two curving circles was by J.M. Boekbinder with the fine, tobacco-stained cove paintings depicting 'peasants rejoicing'. Due to the cramped site, the stage of the Metropolitan was almost triangular in shape. On the O.P. side a very large stock of cloths was held for every type of Variety act. After WW2 there was an orchestra of eleven, directed in later years by the popular Ivan Dozin – who was not averse to performing on the coach-horn occasionally. It was possible to see and hear the show from the Stalls Bar at the Metropolitan, in common with Collins' Music Hall and the Poplar Queen's. As it was on the verges of the West End, there were always lots of agents in the Metropolitan's audience during the week.

Metropolitan Theatre of Varieties, the new exterior of 1897 with Donald Peers billed

In 1836 the ancient White Lion at Paddington had been rebuilt with a concert hall attached and, from 1850, granted a music licence. The entertainment was extended to include such performers as J.H. Stead and T.D. Rice. In 1862 Turnham's Grand Concert Hall was built on the site to Edward Clark's designs, with a capacity of 2,000 and here Sam Collins, E.W. Mackney and Harry Clifton appeared, besides operettas and speciality acts. In 1863 Turnham sold out to James Miller, who transformed the hall into the Metropolitan. It opened on Easter Monday, 1864 with Charles Greville as both manager and M.D. The crowded house welcomed two great serios, Annie Adams and Jenny Hill, besides wire walkers, gymnasts, duettists and operatic singers. Later that year The Great Vance took the Met. by storm and, to a packed house of Italian expatriates, Garibaldi made his impassioned pleas for the freedom of their homeland. Among the favourites of the day who trod the Met's boards were 'Jolly' John Nash, George Leybourne, Arthur Lloyd and the Drury Lane pantomimists, The D'Aubans.

Full interior looking towards the stage

When they took over Syndicate Halls in the 1890s, Henri Gros and his co-directors, George Adney Payne and Herbert Tozer, determined to rebuild the thirty-five year old theatre, which gave its last performance on 29 March, 1897. The closing bill included George Lashwood, Kate Carney, Pat Rafferty, Alec Hurley, Marie Kendall, Harry Tate, Alice Lloyd and Duncan's Collies. Frank Matcham designed the new theatre with three floors instead of two, at a cost of £30,000. J.W. Edgar was retained as manager and Leon Turner was MD. It re-opened on 22 December, 1897.

The new century was welcomed by Gus Elen, Morny Cash and George Mozart, and on the distaff side by May Moore Duprez, Harriet Vernon and May Henderson. The theatre's profits in 1902 were £8,658 9s 9d and Harry Tate produced his immortal 'Motoring' sketch in the following year. Other stars of early bills included Hetty King, Neil Kenyon and King & Benson, while George Gray in 'The Fighting Parson' and John Lawson in 'Humanity' were sketch artistes at the time. When Vasco 'The Mad Musician' appeared, his wife and son did a bar act; the latter eventually became the Metropolitan's manager.

On 2 May, 1908 the Metropolitan gave its last once-nightly show with the lugubrious Alfred Lester topping the bill. Then Frank Matcham master-minded a £15,000 improvement, when the public house was removed from the centre of the main frontage and the Met. re-opened on 24 August, 1908. Shortly after, Percy Honri's *Concordia* was the first revue to be seen, and in the following year Madame Albani, the great operatic singer, created a sensation. Charles Chaplin made his last appearance at the Metropolitan in the week commencing 3 January, 1910 as Stiffy the Goalkeeper in Fred Karno's *The Football Match*. Four months later with some other Karno colleagues he was en-route to the USA.

Interior showing the Stalls and Circle Bars

Interior, close-up of plasterwork on Dress Circle

During WW1 most of the Metropolitan's favourites returned, although programmes tended to be limited to eight acts, rather than the previous twelve. More songs and sketches had a patriotic theme and there were far more revues. Producers included Harry Day (*Hullo, Everybody*, with George Clarke), William Henshall (*The Kodak Girl*, with Dick Henderson) and Fred Karno (*Parlez-Vous Francais?* with Syd Walker). But the most notable, which toured for six years, was *Bobo*, with Ida Crispi and the new star, Will Fyffe. Individual artistes making their names were Sam Barton ('He nearly rides a bike'), Lucille Benstead, Evie Greene, Nervo & Knox and Tex McLeod. There were musical acts galore, notably Alfredo, Max Darekski and The Elliott Savonas, as well as the famous musical clown, Grock. During the 1920s revues occupied over half the playing time, many with titles reflecting the hard times, such as *On the Dole*! with Albert Burdon and Florrie Forde's *Here's to You*, which introduced Flanagan & Allen. Single acts included Billy Bennett, Monsewer Eddie Gray, Will Hay and Ella Retford. Doubles were The Houston Sisters and Morris & Cowley.

The Metropolitan continued to prosper despite talking pictures – even presenting its own *Sunday Cinema*. The biggest attractions of the era were Gracie Fields, Max Miller, Sophie Tucker and Will Mahoney. Almost as popular were George Formby, Vic Oliver, Nat Mills & Bobbie, Five Sherry Brothers, The Street Singer and Hutch. Other musicians who scored were Charlie Kunz and the many bands, such as Roy Fox, Geraldo, Nat Gonella and Harry Roy. Outstanding specialities included The Ganjou Brothers & Juanita and Maurice Colleano & Co. Magicians were Jasper Maskelyne, Dante and Horace Goldin.

Interior view from the pit stalls

For its first wartime programme the Metropolitan had one of the best revues ever: Sid Field in *All the Best*. Fine comedians who followed were Jimmy James, Ted Ray, Billy Russell and Tommy Trinder. Comedy duos were Lucan & McShane, Connor & Drake, Revnell & West and Elsie & Doris Waters. The many stage bands spawned such singers as Adelaide Hall, Vera Lynn, Kitty Masters, Phyllis Robins and Anne Shelton. The American acts of Teddy Brown and Bebe Daniels & Ben Lyon provided strong tops, as did Tessie O'Shea, Issy Bonn and the enthralling novelty act of N'Gai. Daring for the times was Phyllis Dixey.

Interior of the Stalls Saloon Bar

In spite of numerous losses, after the war there remained over twenty Variety theatres in the London suburbs. Jack Warner, Rawicz & Landauer and Semprini were soon joined by The Deep River Boys and newcomers like Derek Roy, Morecambe & Wise and Mike & Bernie Winters. Many ex-service comics at this time included Max Bygraves, Charlie Chester, Tommy Cooper, Reg Dixon, Dick Emery, Dickie Henderson, Reg Varney, Harry Secombe and many others. New vocal stars were Frankie Vaughan and Donald Peers, with Sally Barnes, Alma Cogan and Winifred Atwell among the ladies. *Thanks for the Memory* was an outstanding attraction which played the Met. four times. Two rare revues were *The Best Years of Your Lives* and Renée Paskin's *Come to the Show*. A popular and regular visitor was Lancashire's Frank Randle.

Interior with stage box

In 1951 Billy Matthew was promoted and Albert Vasco became manager. In 1948 The Metropolitan Theatre of Varieties Ltd. had made a profit of £18,385, but by now the theatre had seen its best days and had lost its consistent policy. It out-lived Chiswick Empire and Finsbury Park Empire to become the last London suburban Variety theatre, closing after a series of once-weekly shows in

1962, for road widening. It re-opened for the one night of the VABF Concert on Good Friday, 1963, when your illustrator was present and the long-disused gallery had to be hurriedly re-opened. The excellent and extensive bill included many greats of Variety, including Ted Ray, who closed with 'Life is just a Bowl of Cherries'.

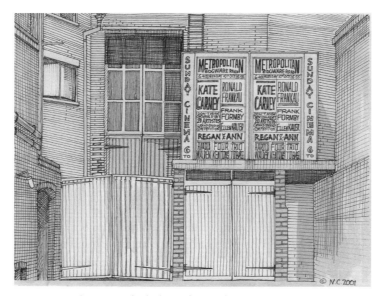

The Stage dock doors from White Lion Passage

It was with mixed emotions the crowd surged out into Edgware Road that night. There was wide coverage by press and television as a century of entertainment came to an end, but the event led to the formation of The British Music Hall Society. One final show, in aid of The Unity Theatre, Euston took place on Sunday, 26 May, 1963 when the statue of the girl in the niche outside the theatre was auctioned off. During the demolition of the Metropolitan that autumn quite a number of other items were salvaged, including the two stage box fronts and some of the cove painting. It is said that the stalls bar is intact under the pavement of Edgware Road, but this does seem like wishful thinking! The atmospheric and well-loved old hall was sadly missed when it came down to make way for a new road which didn't even cross the theatre site. Twenty years later this gem of a theatre would surely have been saved and fully restored.

The nameplate over main entrance

THE
METROPOLITAN,
EDGWARE ROAD.

Situated in the most fashionable part of the West-End of London, this

SPLENDID AND POPULAR PLACE OF AMUSEMENT

Is nightly crowded with highly *distingué* audiences.

THE ENTERTAINMENTS

Are of the most Varied and Refined Character, and comprise all the most Renowned Artists and Performers of the day. At the METROPOLITAN are nightly represented

SPECTACULAR, MUSICAL, AND BURLESQUE SKETCHES AND BALLETS.

Placed on the Stage in the most complete manner, Embellished with Elegant Costumes, and the best and most novel Scenic Effects.

Reserved Fauteuils, 2s; Stalls, 1s.
Private Boxes, to hold Four Persons, 10s 6d.

Manager - - - - - Mr. WILLIAM BAILEY.

A typical year's productions at the Metropolitan can be followed inside the front and back covers, compiled by Bert Ross.

Dalladas, acrobat

Poplar Hippodrome

East India Dock Road, corner of Stainsby Road

Poplar Hippodrome (formerly New Prince's Theatre): exterior with Sammy Shields, T.E. Dunville and Co. billed

This theatre had everything going for it, yet it failed. The Poplar Hippodrome had a main street frontage, was well-served by trams, busses and three railway stations and had a good large stage, 60ft wide by 41ft deep. In time, membership of the powerful LTV circuit brought all the stars of Variety to the area. Developed by Clarence Sounes, who had theatre interests in Kingston, Woolwich, Aldershot and Penge, the theatre opened as The New Prince's on Boxing Day, 1905 with the pantomime *Beauty and the Beast*.

Sadly, we do not have an illustration of the interior, although we know that at its opening it had a capacity of 2,500 in stalls and two circles; the dress circle and balcony formed the first tier, with the gallery and amphitheatre the second. The architects were Owen & Ward of Birmingham, whose exterior used the onion domes popular with Matcham at so many of his theatres. The theatre was built by Kirk and Kirk. The interior impressed with its canopied heads to the boxes and a broad-barrel arch over the proscenium opening, supported by massive columns; the French Renaissance decoration was by F. de Jong and Company.

It was planned for the New Prince's to offer opera, comedy and drama, as presented at Mr. Clarence Sounes' other theatres. He appointed as manager Herbert Leonard, who had held positions at The Surrey Theatre under George Conquest and more recently at The Terriss Theatre, Rotherhithe (later The Rotherhithe Hippodrome). Leonard was also a playwright and producer. His appointment was for one year, after which he was expecting to go to America as a producer for one of the big managers. While at Poplar he was to produce a comic opera written by himself, in collaboration with Rowland Carse (lyric writer) and Walter Slaughter (composer and conductor at The Coliseum). It is not known whether Leonard's opus ever reached the Poplar stage, although the whole idea sounds outlandish at this distance in time. However, another comic opera, *Les Cloches de Corneville* definitely was staged for the week of 30 April, 1906 by E. St. Alban's Opera Company. It was followed the next week by that old favourite, *East Lynne*.

Films made a surprisingly early appearance at The New Prince's, where they filled an entire programme in June, 1907. Included in the three-hour mixed show was a film of The Derby, run only a few hours previously. Houses were full, anticipating the theatre's appeal some twenty years ahead as a full-time cinema. A week later on 13 June, 1907, Walter Gibbons took over the theatre to add to his growing circuit, renaming it as Poplar Hippodrome. His policy at the time was to round-up as many as possible of the suburban theatres which in his opinion were not being well run and "had grown shabby – even derelict", although this could surely not have applied to the two-year-old Poplar house.

From then on the theatre was run for nearly twenty years mainly as a Variety house, although there were weeks of musical comedy and other entertainments – even a Boxing Tournament. For example, on August Bank Holiday, 1910 Albert Wyndham and his Company presented *Magna Charter*, or The Last Moments of Prince Arthur. "The Great Juvenile Actress" Mona Shepard was in the production on a set that depicted the Tower of London.

Again, in May, 1912 audiences enjoyed Harry Day and Edward Lauri's whimsical musical comedy, *Bill Adams, The Hero of Waterloo*, the music and costumes earning high praise from the local press. Generally, though, the Poplar Hippodrome prospered with strong Variety bills, with appearances by Sam Mayo, Joe O'Gorman, Will Evans (as 'The Gambler'), Billy French and Sammy Shields. Charles Gulliver took over from the failed Walter Gibbons in July, 1912, raising the Hippodrome's programmes to new heights, in association with The London Palladium. Gulliver was one of the most experienced managers in the field of Variety.

An attractive bill in August, 1915 was topped by the great magician Carl Hertz, Scotch Kelly and T.E. Dunville – a frequent visitor until he went out of fashion – together with H. La Martine, Cherry Girls, Geo. Benson, Daisy Stratton, Niobe and Dolly Varden. Revues that year included H. Grover's *Follow the Frill*, with Joe Elvin, Tom E. Hood and Dolly Danvers; and E.C. Rolls' *Good Evening*, with the ever-popular Sammy Shields, The Sisters Jerome and Ferguson & Mac.

Sketch comedian Joe Elvin was always heavily booked, appearing again at the Poplar Hippodrome in October, 1916 (doubling LTV's Rotherhithe Hippodrome), with The Diving Norins, Morny Cash, Laddie Cliff (doubling LTV's Ilford Hippodrome), Julien Henry & Co., Five Jovers, Monks & Manner and Florence Fulcher. The seeds of LTV's eventual crash could possibly be foreseen by the constant appearance of the same stars at their dozen or so halls in the London area. The public simply tired of them.

As a contrast, the powerful actor John Lawson appeared in July, 1918 in *Bully of Berlin*, which probably appealed to war-weary audiences; on the same bill were Stephanie Anderson, later to become a well-known producer of dance troupes, and the unusually-named act, The Grumblers.

In April, 1921 Nora Delaney topped an attractive bill which included Nellie Wallace, Sandy Powell (doubling LTV's Woolwich Hippodrome), Christine Ray, Harry Bedford and Manny & Roberts (doubling the distant Collins' Music Hall). The violinist Tucker, with Tom Stuart and Barker & Tarling also appeared that same year.

Clouds were appearing on the horizon, however, with the growing popularity of the cinema, making some Variety shows with over-familiar names look distinctly old-fashioned. Archie Pitt's Super Revue, *A Week's Pleasure*, was presented at 6.40 and 9pm for the week of 5 April, 1926; this starred Betty Fields (sister of Gracie), Walter Amner, Harry Gould and The Famous Busby Band, but the Poplar Hippodrome then closed down with the collapse of the LTV circuit, by now under the control of Sir Frederick Eley. After being shut for some time, the big theatre was re-launched as The New Hippodrome Super Cinema with a gala on August Bank Holiday, 1926.

The first films presented by W.S. Logan, the new manager, were *The Girl Who Would Not Work*, featuring Lionel Barrymore, and *Broadway Billie*, with Billy Sullivan in the leading role. Variety did not completely disappear, as Harry Claff and Winnie Wager were seen in the farce *The White Knight*, while The Eight Rooney Girls delighted with their dance routines. This pattern of films and Variety, sometimes with a full stage band, continued until WW2, as shown in the press advertisement below for November, 1932.

The story came to an abrupt end when the Poplar Hippodrome was completely wrecked by bombs during the war and not restored; the building was demolished in 1949, with flats being built on the site.

T.E. Dunville

Miss Rosalind Wade's Beautiful Girls

Poplar: Queen's Theatre

275–279, High Street

Poplar, Queen's Theatre: the old exterior with Scott & Whaley billed

It may have occupied a somewhat obscure site, but the Queen's Theatre had a proud history of exactly one hundred years as a house that entertained seafarers and residents in East London. It long out-lived its much larger rival, The Poplar Hippodrome.

The Queen's was first licensed in 1856, operating as The Queen's Arms, The Apollo Music Hall, The Albion Theatre, The Oriental, The Queen's Music Hall and Queen's Theatre of Varieties before acquiring the name by which it is best known. The original hall (built at the cost of £7,000) had a capacity of only 800, but in 1898 it was reconstructed by the architect Bertie Crewe with its capacity increased to 1,360 – much of it evidently standing room. The Queen's was one of the few London music halls from which patrons could view the stage from the bar at the back of the stalls.

The names of Robert Grimes and William Davis appeared on early bills as licensees, but by 1863 Frederick Abrahams – the first of three members of this family – had taken over the reins. There was still evidence in later years of a foundation stone laid on 4 September, 1873 by Frederick, clearly during one of the many re-buildings and reconstructions undertaken here. Michael and Morris Abrahams followed in management as the years passed. Works were carried out in 1904 and again in January, 1922 under the same architect, including the fitting of a new safety curtain; the contractors for the curtain were Frank Burkett of the Borough.

Exterior of the new building

The Queen's Theatre was where Gracie Fields first appeared in London. Stan Laurel, Charlie Chaplin (with Fred Karno's companies), Gertie Gitana, Harry Champion and Eugene Stratton all appeared on its stage. Artistes often seen here during WW1 included Dolly Vincent, Bert Terrell ('the popular Dutch comedian') and Jack Lorimer, father of Max Wall. A bill in October, 1916 boasted Arthur Lennard, Wager, Jack Lorimer, Manny & Roberts and Stella Stahl, Edis & Forbes and Tucker ('the singing violinist').

Being close to the three basins of the East India Docks, the Queen's had a ready-made maritime audience, in common with halls at East Ham, Woolwich and New Cross. The interior of the theatre appeared slightly archaic with its two circles supported on pillars and its frilly-arched boxes. Audiences in the late 1920s and early 1930s were regaled with revues. Straight Variety held its own largely until the mid-1920s, after which revues were the staple at the hall. Typical titles included *Free and Easy*, *Times Have Changed*, *Sherry Cocktail* and Joe Morrison's *Great Stuff This* – no doubt the presenter's opinion of his offering! In December, 1932 *The Wembley Circus* took to the stage, said to be one of London's deepest, while the Irish comedian Jimmy O'Dea appeared in *The Irish Sweep* in October, 1935.

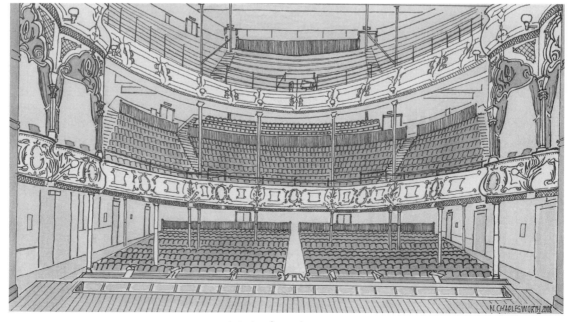

Interior from the stage

The procession of revues continued during the years leading into WW2. Offerings around this time included *Stars of Luxembourg*, with Billy Reid's Accordion Band, Jack Sonn's *Paradise on Parade*, Harry Dennis's *Time Marches On*, and a couple of increasingly spicy shows – Jack Sonn's *Show-A-Leg* with Jimmy Bryant, Billy Shenton Trio and Harry Blue in March, 1940 and Jack Gillam's revue *Strip, Strip, Hooray* two months later. Another similar wartime show was Elkan Simon's *Over the Top*, headed by Jimmy Malborn – often fêted as one of the funniest revue comics.

Hylda Baker's show, *Wild Women and Whoopee*, did its bit to lighten the burden on heavily-bombed dockland for a week in April, 1944, and Don Ross presented many revues there including *Don't Blush Girls* and *Eve Started It*, the latter with Jack Haig, Walker & Ray, Selkirk & Glyn and Joe Heritage among the company. *The Music Goes Round and Around* was emblazoned on Poplar hoardings around this time and for one glorious week *Thanks for the Memory* played the Queen's. Don Ross must have accepted a cut!

In the archives of The British Music Hall Society are two receipt books from the theatre covering the years 1937–1939 and 1943–1948, and a random selection of names would make an excellent bill anywhere; to mention a few – Sam Mayo and Ernie Lotinga in *Sanctions*, Charles Austin, Horace Goldin, Nellie Wallace, Issy Bonn, Kate Carney, Leon Cortez (who seemed to have been practically resident), Harry Tate, Scott & Whaley and Sid & Max Harrison.

Interior towards the stage

After WW2 the Queen's managed to keep going longer than some larger houses, although playing to meagre audiences – often three-quarters empty houses were the norm. However, the theatre had enormous character, as described by Geoffrey Fletcher in his book *London Overlooked*. Occasionally a proper Variety bill appeared, as in November, 1950 when Florence Oldham, Murray & Hinton and Johnson Clarke and the inimitable Adelaide Hall brought back lovely memories of the old days.

Astonishingly, Morris Abrahams served as manager for forty-nine years, a feat justly celebrated in an article in The Times on 24 August, 1955. Just achieving its centenary, the last bill at the Queen's was for the week of Monday, 13 February, 1956; Speedshows Ltd. presented *Let 'em Loose*, starring Tommy Hartley (The Perfect Inmate – Let Loose for You!). A fascinating inclusion on this final bill was Ted Rogers, later to make his name on television. He also made an excellent Buttons in *Cinderella*, which we saw at Worthing Connaught that same year.

After its closure, all sorts of hopeful ideas were mooted for the Queen's. It was planned to turn it into 'A West End theatre for the East End' when J. Baxter Somerville bought it for £15,000 in 1958; but this – and a scheme to turn it into a centre for modern dance – came to nothing. The large stage was used for a number of years for the building and painting of stage sets, including some for the Lyric Theatre in Hammersmith. The old caretaker, Fred Turner, sometimes allowed me to look around, giving me one or two old posters, which were filed on a nail in the gallery. The large poster of *Let 'em Loose* was discovered in a frame in the stalls bar during the demolition of the theatre. Finally the LCC bought the property for £9,750 and I was there in 1964 when the wonderful old theatre came down, the coat of arms over the proscenium arch reputedly going to the Theatre Royal, Stratford East. New flats were built on the site.

QUEEN'S PALACE OF VARIETIES,
HIGH STREET, POPLAR.
(Close to Railway, 'Bus, and Tram Routes.)

| Proprietors | - | - | - | - | PALACE OF VARIETIES CO., Limited. |
| General Managers | - | - | - | F. and M. ABRAHAMS. |

A West-End Music Hall in the East.
CONSTANT CHANGE OF PROGRAMME.
OPEN EVERY EVENING WITH THE BEST COMPANY OF ARTISTES IN LONDON.

The above Spacious and Magnificent Establishment, having been entirely Remodelled, Decorated, and Furnished Complete in the Latest Style, and a New Lounge and Refreshment Bar added, with every improvement for the Comfort of Patrons, is now one of the Largest and most Handsome Music Halls in London, with Seating Accomodation for 3,000 persons.

The REFRESHMENTS are all of the First Quality, special attention being given to this department, and the Prices the most Moderate charged at any Hall in London.

PRICES FROM SIXPENCE TO ONE GUINEA.
Doors Open at 7.30.   Commence at 8.

Acting Manager and Secretary - - - - R. WOODS.
Musical Director—WALTER LOOSLEY.   Chairman—FRANK ESTCOURT.

Richmond Hippodrome

Richmond Green, Richmond

Richmond Hippodrome (now Richmond Theatre), exterior

Here at last is a theatre that is still standing and open for business! The present Richmond Theatre is the fourth of its race, having opened on 18 September, 1899, but its time as a Variety house was quite a short one. It is worth noting that, over a period of nearly two centuries, the town was without some kind of theatre for only six of those years. For a very long time the town or suburb of Richmond has been favoured by Royalty, the aristocracy and thespians; the stretch of river between Hampton and Richmond has always attracted theatrical folk. David Garrick lived at Hampton, with Edmund Kean (as we shall see), among others, favouring Richmond.

The first Richmond Theatre, a timber structure, opened in June, 1719 on the rise of Richmond Hill. It served for some fifty years, before becoming a snuff warehouse, having lost its licence in 1756. It carried on, nevertheless, by charging the public for its snuff and throwing in the entertainment free!

A second and longer-lasting theatre was built and opened in June, 1765 by James Dance, who acted in the name of Love. It made a great impression in theatrical circles and even attracted King George III and Queen Charlotte, who paid a state visit a few years after it opened. The King and succeeding generations of Royalty continued to patronise the house, situated on the northern corner of Richmond Green. Mrs. Jordan acted here during several seasons and among the throng of other names who appeared here over a period of one hundred and nineteen years were George Colman the younger (who made his theatrical debut here), The Baddeleys, Mrs. Siddons, Liston, Benjamin Webster, Tom Matthews the clown, Buckstone, Macready, Mrs. Glover, Madame Celeste, Nellie Farren and George Alexander – in fact, a roll-call of the great names of British theatre.

Even Charles Dickens, in an amateur production of *Rent Day*, graced the stage, but the great actor Edmund Kean was, perhaps, the most famous to appear at Richmond. Well after his Theatre Royal, Drury Lane heyday and in broken spirits, Kean became lessee of Richmond Theatre, living at the adjoining house. He died there on 15 May, 1833 having collapsed on 25 March on stage at Drury Lane while playing Othello with his son Charles as Iago. The old playhouse, however, continued for many years until it became unsafe and was eventually pulled down in 1884.

After the closure of the 1765 theatre in 1884, there was an interregnum, which lasted until 1890, when F. C. Mouflet of The Castle and Greyhound Hotel converted an assembly room of the Castle into a bijou playhouse. The new theatre was managed for a short time by Horace Lennard, attracting Royalty once again and even becoming known as The Theatre Royal, Richmond. Mouflet later managed the theatre himself, with the help of Charles E. Hardy, until the present elegant and luxurious Richmond Theatre opened on 18 September, 1899. It was a sign of the confidence of the theatre business at that time that three other London theatres opened almost simultaneously in Balham and New Cross and on the Charing Cross Road.

Financed by Mouflet and designed by Frank Matcham, Richmond Theatre was constructed by W. Johnson & Co. of Wandsworth Common. It is one of the least altered of Matcham's works in London; the interior is one of his most satisfying. The exterior, with its twin towers, has similarities to that of other Matcham theatres, but as a playhouse is more respectable. The central figure of Euterpe is said to be identical to that atop his Hackney Empire.

The new theatre with its 34ft deep stage was well-equipped and ideal for visiting musical comedy companies, which were legion. However it opened with the Bard's greatest comedy – Sir Philip Ben Greet's Company in *As You Like It*. Pantomime, in the form of *Robinson Crusoe*, made its first appearance at the temporary Whittaker Avenue theatre and has since become a regular attraction at the new house.

Under the onslaught of the all-conquering music hall, the theatre became Richmond Hippodrome from around 1908, for some of the time under the direction of George Dance. Variety in all its glory *did* find a home at Richmond Hippodrome, but naturally many of Dance's musical comedies were staged here. In fact, "Hippodrome", conjuring up weekly Variety programmes, may have been a slight misnomer in this case, as the musicals filled many weeks in the year. The bill shown in the colour section does, however, prove that our favourite entertainment was actually presented. The names of Arthur Rigby and Lazern, the Australian magician, dominate the bill.

Continuing the musical comedy offerings, Dudley Bennett and T. C. Wray presented *The Country Girl*, from Daly's Theatre, with 'Powerful Chorus and Elaborate Scenery'; it had enjoyed 729 performances at Daly's in 1902. Even under the short-lived regime of Charles Gulliver, one of the great Variety pioneers, the attraction one week was *The Geisha*, though it was staged twice-nightly at 6.00pm and 8.30pm, suggesting that this was the norm here. It can be seen that Variety did not gain a foothold for long in Richmond, even though artistes of the calibre of Katie Lawrence did appear. For some time the booking agents were Reeves & Lamport, but their advertisements sought productions for Richmond, rather than Variety artistes.

Twice nightly performances of popular comedies, farces and West End plays continued under Joseph Mears Ltd., who took over during WW1. There were renovations and redecorations to the building in 1915 and again about ten years later. Many famous names of the legitimate stage, among them Violet Vanbrugh, Peggy O'Neil and Sir John Martin-Harvey, appeared at the 'Theatre on the Green', as it became popularly known.

Interior towards the boxes

The policy of presenting straight plays, with a profitable Christmas pantomime, has held for many years. Variety artistes could be enjoyed at festive periods in these productions, but the theatre settled down to being a playhouse, as originally intended. Harry Benet's resident production of *Cinderella* was here in 1935 and later Randolph Sutton presented his own pantomime. Sandy Powell also graced the Richmond stage, again in *Cinderella*, the cast including Jack Demain, the magician. F.J. Butterworth ran Richmond Theatre for a time during WW2, during one of his forays into the London area, which included the running of Kilburn Empire and the Bedford, Camden Town.

After WW2 the theatre continued with much the same policy, but once-nightly. For a time it was controlled by Louis I. Michaels, who also ran the Theatre Royal, Bath and Theatre Royal, Brighton until his unexpected death. Under his management the presentation of pantomimes with really big names and with first-class scripts by John Morley filled the gap left in the London scene by the disappearance of Golders Green Hippodrome and The Streatham Hill Theatre, former strongholds of the pantomime tradition in the suburbs. Leslie Crowther topped in *Jack & The Beanstalk* in 1977, with Arthur Askey, Avril Angers and the eccentric-looking Johnny Vyvyan. Two years later, Askey, a natural pantomime performer, was back in *Dick Whittington*, this time with Dickie Henderson, Barbara Windsor, Patrick Cargill and with Terry Doogan as the Cat. Another star-studded show which drew the crowds was the 1982 production of *Cinderella*, with Susannah York, Lionel Blair, Kenneth Connor, Rodney Bewes, Peter Sallis, Janet Mahoney and with a special appearance by the legendary Anna Neagle, as Fairy Godmother.

The ensuing history is a bit too complicated to go into here – I am supposed to be writing its use as a Variety theatre, but during her ownership in the late 1980s Sally Greene oversaw a major refurbishment, but continued the former mix of touring shows, all-star pantomimes and use as a film location during the summer break. Richmond Theatre goes from strength to strength, as the touring of plays has become profitable again.

Two stalwarts who appeared at Richmond Hippodrome
in its Variety days: Stan Laural and Charles Chaplin

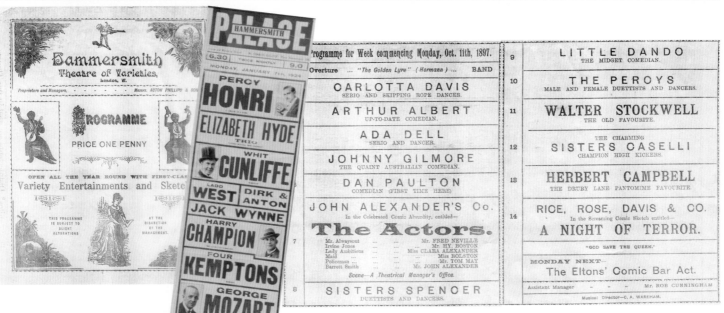

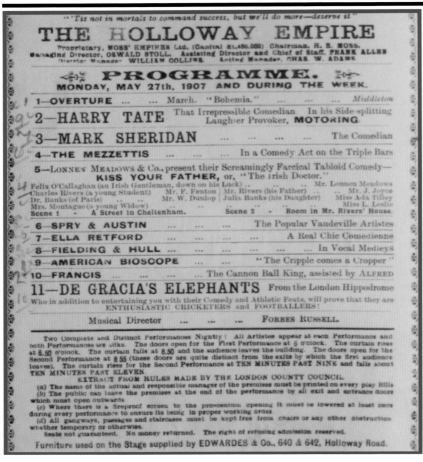

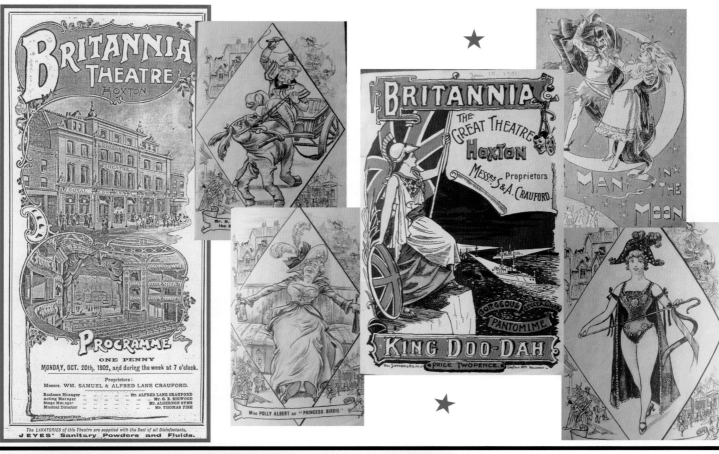

Variety Theatre,
PITFIELD STREET, HOXTON, N.
TELEPHONE, 5955 (Avenue).

Licensed by the Lord Chamberlain to Mr.
G. H. MACDERMOTT,
PROPRIETOR & MANAGER.

OPEN EVERY EVENING
A CHANGE EACH WEEK!

Yours truly, G. H. MACDERMOTT.
Musical Director - Mr. B. RODBOURN.

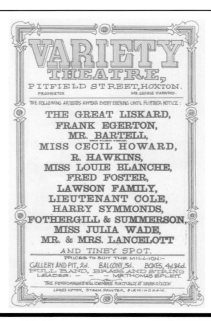

VARIETY THEATRE,
PITFIELD STREET, HOXTON.
PROPRIETOR — MR. GEORGE HARWOOD.
THE FOLLOWING ARTISTES APPEAR EVERY EVENING UNTIL FURTHER NOTICE:

THE GREAT LISKARD,
FRANK EGERTON,
MR. BARTELL,
MISS CECIL HOWARD,
R. HAWKINS,
MISS LOUIE BLANCHE,
FRED FOSTER,
LAWSON FAMILY,
LIEUTENANT COLE,
HARRY SYMMONDS,
FOTHERGILL & SUMMERSON,
MISS JULIA WADE,
MR. & MRS. LANCELOTT
AND TINBY SPOT.

PRICES TO SUIT THE MILLION:—
GALLERY AND PIT, 2d. BALCONY, 3d. BOXES, 4d & 6d.
FULL BAND, BRASS AND STRING

THE PERFORMANCE WILL COMMENCE PUNCTUALLY AT SEVEN O'CLOCK

PROGRAMME.
Monday, AUGUST 20th, 1900
And during the Week the following Company will be present

1 Overture at 6.25 and 9.10.
2 **CARL OSTEND** Female Impersonator
3 **DANDOE & NEAME** Comedy Duettists and Dancers
4 **DAISY DE ROY** Serio-Comic
5 **N. C. BOSTOCK** The Scotch Comedian
6 **THE GARTELLS** Musical Act
7 **EMMA DON** Character Comedian and Da
8 **SISTERS VESTA** Vocalists and Dancers
9 **FRANCISCO** The Juggling Marvel, introducing his Novel Tricks with Lighted Lam
10 **MISS ADA ALEXANDRA** AND HER COMPANY OF COMEDIANS IN
"THE MASON!"

Prices, 2d. to 1s.

ILFORD HIPPODROME
Broadway, Ilford
TWICE NIGHTLY AT 6.30 & 8.50
Saturdays 1st House commences Fifteen Minutes Earlier

MONDAY, SEPT. 25th.

PERCY HONRI
And his Colossal Combine, in a Reproduction of the Great
Musical Scenic Phantasy, entitled

CONCORDIA

THIRTY ARTISTES. EIGHT SUPERB SCENES

LITTLE JACK MARKS
Clever Boy Hebrew Comedian and Raconteur.

SISTERS TUDOR : THE BIOSCOPE

DEVON & EARLE
The Famous American Dancing Experts.

THE WESTWOODS
In an Entirely New, Original and Daring Cycling Act.

3 CAPE GIRLS 3
Comediennes and Big Boot Dancers.

FLO CECIL * WADE & LILLIAN

The CROMWELLS
Novelty Jugglers

BILLY MERSON
New Star Comedian in Original & Quaint Conceptions of Humour

FAUTEUILS 1/- Or. Stalls 9d. Gr. Circle 6d. PIT 4d. GALLERY 2d.

NEXT WEEK, MAY 25
AT THE
ILFORD HIPPODROME
Matinees Whit-Monday, Wednesday and
Saturday at 3.0 o'clock
FREE LIST ENTIRELY SUSPENDED

GEORGE FORMBY
And his Uke

BERYL ORDE
Famous B.B.C. Impressionist

McMURRAY THREE
BERYL assisted by GEORGE

DAMSEL & BOY

HAMILTON CONRAD
And his Pigeons

LORAIN

FRED BREZIN

NEWMAN TWINS

NEXT
H
3 PET
ROSS

CHRISTMAS ATTRAC
"CIN
Commencing SAT. EVE., DEC
ONE WEEK commencing DEC

The
THE HIPPODROME
NIGHTLY at 8.15
MATINEES: THURS. & SAT. at

"THE FLEET'S LIT UP"
FRANCES DAY   STANLEY LUPINO
ADELE DIXON   RALPH READER

ILFORD HIPPODROME
BROADWAY, ILFORD.
Twice Nightly at 6.30 & 8.50
Saturdays First House Commences 15 minutes Earlier
Monday, May 1st, 1911.
Special Engagement of the Distinguished West End Actor, MR.

LYN HARDING
In a Dramatic Episode, entitled
"HONOUR IS SATISFIED" by CHAS. KENYON
Supported by Mr. MONTAGUE LOVE & Miss FLORENCE JACKSON

Wilfred H. Benson's Co.
Including the Celebrated Versatile Actress
& MISS MABEL WYNN &
In a New Dramatic and Novel Episode, entitled

ROGUERY!
Written by Wilfred Benson. Music by the late Richard E. Lawson.

MAUDIE FORD
In Song and Dance

RUFFELL'S IMPERIAL BIOSCOPE
Showing the Latest Pictures

THE POPULAR IRISH RACONTEUR
JOE O'GORMAN
In Wit and Melody

THE MERRY PAIR
MILNER & STOREY
In an Act full of Vaudeville

ROSE CAMBRY
Australian Burlesque Artiste

RYDER SLONE
Character Comedian

BESSIE KNIGHT
Comedienne and Dancer

The Original Murderers of the King's English
LOWENWIRTH & COHAN
Britain's Premier Hebrew Comedians

PARK'S ETON BOYS

The Ilford Hippodrome

MONDAY, MAY 18th
AND ALL THE WEEK

A Feast of Merriment and Fun
MAD HATTERS OF 1942
Featuring the World's Craziest Conductor
SYD SEYMOUR
AND HIS BAND
And Full Supporting Cast

Programme • Price Twopence

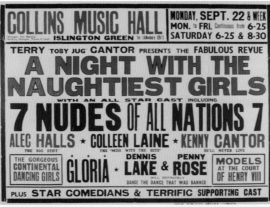

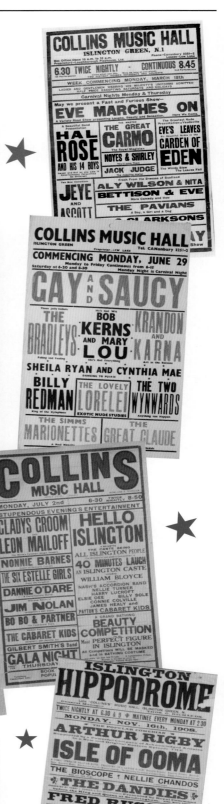

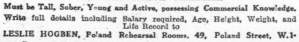

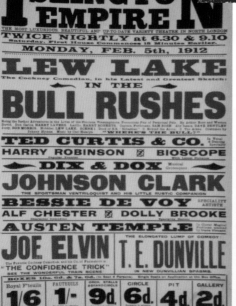

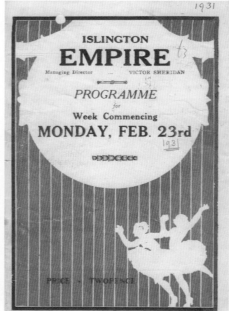

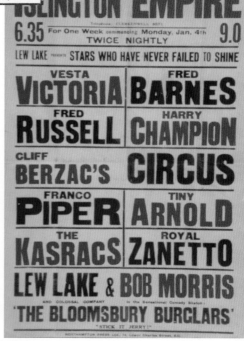

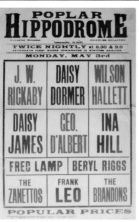

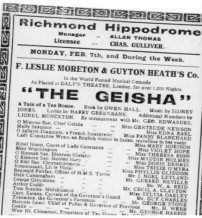

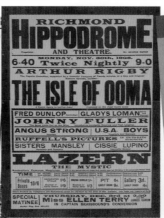

Continued on page 431

Shepherds Bush Empire

Shepherds Bush Green

Shepherds Bush Empire: exterior with Lily Morris billed, 5.12.1927

A favourite hall with artistes, having a large stage and plenty of good dressing rooms, Shepherds Bush Empire was run by Stoll Theatres from The London Coliseum throughout its fifty years as a Variety Theatre. The important main-street frontage on Shepherds Bush Green was shared with two other places of entertainment: the huge Shepherds Bush Pavilion and the small Palladium Cinema. In later years The Pavilion became an Odeon and finally a bingo hall; the Palladium became a night-club and at the time of writing all three are still functioning. Such a grouping of entertainments was typical in London suburbs at one time, though now unusual.

Shepherds Bush Empire and Hackney Empire came under a proprietary company known as Hackney & Shepherds Bush Empire Palaces Ltd. and – fascinatingly – both theatres survived their closure in the 1950s as Variety theatres and, after many years in other uses, reopened for live shows. So many other superb halls disappeared at this period. While Hackney was used as a commercial television studio, bingo hall and wrestling venue ('You can't go in – they're rehearsing for the wrestling'), Shepherds Bush became a studio theatre for BBC Television for some forty years before its rescue.

Exterior showing the art nouveau window

Designed by Frank Matcham, the Empire opened on 17 August, 1903 with a bill which included The Fred Karno Troupe, who were the first act on the new stage. The theatre's capacity was stated to be 2,332 with seats for 1,855 (later reduced to 1,650). Its interior was smaller than that of Hackney Empire, but architecturally was – and is – impressive, with a distinct *art nouveau* flavour. The exterior is asymmetrical, with a rough-cast tower, topped with a classical lantern and cupola. There is a delightful bow window, decorated with musical *putti* overlooking The Green. This, fortunately, survived alterations made by the BBC.

Both Wee Georgie Wood and George Formby (the son, not the father) made their first London appearances at The Bush, or 'Coliseum of West London', as it was sometimes known. For the week commencing Monday, 17 August, 1914 the bill included The Six Brothers Luck (one of whose members was Ernie Lotinga, married for a time to Hetty King), female impersonator Bert Errol, The Finney Sisters, Win & Windie, Les Videos, Bay Russell and Ray Hartley.

The Birmingham-printed programme for the week of 5 December, 1927 showed a fine bill that comprised Lily Morris, Clarkson Rose, Nervo & Knox (prior to their Crazy Gang days, in 'Fantastic Frolics'), Adrienne Peel proudly sporting her ARCM, Pierce & Roslyn, Wyn & Ivy, The Flying Flacoris and The Pierrotys. A film newsreel completed the show. John Russell conducted The Empire Orchestra, while the Acting Managing was Edward Fryer and District Manager John Christie. Performances were at 6.20 and 8.40pm. While the Stoll theatres had some difficulty in recruiting headliners, their bills in some respects gave better value, with a wide range of speciality acts.

Interior towards the stage

The famous Irish comedian, Jimmy O'Dea opened his show *Irish Smiles* at The Bush early in June, 1930. He had been obliged by the Stoll management to do a trial week at The Ardwick Empire (later The New Manchester Hippodrome), but within three days of opening in Manchester the show had been booked for the entire Stoll circuit. It was a resounding success at The Bush, once the company had persuaded Sir Oswald Stoll that his costuming of the theatre staff in exaggerated Irish attire was likely to cause an affray. It was said that Sir Oswald was sympathetic to Irish expectations.

Interior showing plaster feature at Gallery level

By 1933 I was going to shows regularly at Wood Green Empire, my local, but did occasionally visit other more distant halls, including Shepherds Bush Empire. I became more adventurous two years later when I left school and started work.

Jack Payne and his Band topped at The Bush for the week of 26 March, 1933 with Bud Ritchie ('*Where the laughs come from*'), Harry & Marjorie Ristori, Archie Glen ('*Still blotto*'), Lewis & Lawn and fast-steppers Earle & Eddie Franklyn among the supporting company.

Interior towards the circles

Jimmy O'Dea was back at Shepherds Bush for the week of 2 April of that year, together with Fred Sanborn, Dick Henderson, Rich & Galvin and four other acts. O'Dea was a regular in the London area during the 1930s in various sketches and revues. Among them were *Irish Revels* and *Mrs. Mulligan's Motor Car*, a sketch by Harry Donovan. His last London appearance was at The Metropolitan, Edgware Road in May, 1960.

We were able to see Charlie Kunz, the wizard of the keyboard, during the week of 14 October, 1935. Others on the strong bill were Percy & Mary Honri with their concertinas, Bob & Alf Pearson ('My brother and I'), Pat O'Brien, Haig & Escoe, Avon & Vale, Ringle Bros. & Renée, Len Young ('The Singing Fool') and Betty Jumel, who will long be remembered for her many pantomime appearances.

The previous week Jasper Maskelyne had topped at The Bush, supported by Coram (with Jerry), Ruth & Ella Myles, George Jackley – another pantomime favourite at The Lyceum, Van Dock, Peggy Rhodes and Madge Stephen (in vocal comedy numbers) and Miss Louise & her Dogs. In addition there were three acts making their first appearances at the West London venue, including Pat O'Malley, formerly the vocalist with Jack Hylton's Band. Frank Fletcher directed The Empire Orchestra at this period.

Exterior as a BBC studio

By 1936 the Stoll circuit was down to seven live halls, as a number were showing films. Shepherds Bush Empire stayed live, but with films showing regularly on Sunday evenings. In 1938 Wood Green Empire rejoined the fold, having turned its back on the silver screen. The same year saw The Bush presenting Ernie Lotinga's *Penny Soc-her Pools*, his latest revue, and Dante & Company in the Mystery Revue, *Sim-Sala-Bim*, the show that had closed Stoll's Alhambra, Leicester Square two years before. The magician was born August Harry Jansen in Copenhagen in 1883 and did his first hour-long show at the age of nineteen. He stayed three years in Britain before opening in Brussels in 1939.

Stage house, with additions when converted as a TV Studio

Shepherds Bush Empire played a valuable part in maintaining morale during WW2. A show that played a week in May, 1940 was *Very Tasty and Very Sweet*, with Harry Angers, Oswald Waller, Tom Ellis, Vi West and Company.

Variety and revues continued at The Bush until the early 1950s. Among shows thronging its stage may be mentioned *Why Worry?* with Johnny Lockwood, *Tell 'em All About It* with Syd & Max Harrison and Gaston & Andrée. Vic Oliver topped the bill during May, 1949, doing two spots and supported by Rex & Bessie and Fred Lovelle ('The Uncanny'), Tuppy Oliver, Lionel King ('Joker – Ace High'), The Stevie Sisters and a trio playing (somewhat surprisingly) selections of Edward Grieg's music. The Empire Orchestra was conducted by Jack Robson.

However, business was steadily declining, despite such excellent Variety fare and in 1953 – Coronation Year – Stoll Theatres decided to cease presentations at Shepherds Bush. The final bill, for the week of Monday 21 September, 1953 was Robb Wilton ('Still Muddling'), Hal Monty, Dawn White and her Glamazons, Stan Stennett ('Direct from his success at The London Palladium'), The Australian Songbird Tessa Smallpage, Allen Bros. & June, Krista & Kristel and The Two Condons. The bill was headed *Ring Down the Curtain*, in a tribute to The Empire's long career.

Exterior in 1994 as a music venue

The theatre was taken over by the BBC and the following week reopened as a Television Theatre. Once Variety had ended, I had no reason to travel to Shepherds Bush again. Transmissions continued at The Empire until 1992, including *Crackerjack* with Leslie Crowther, *Laugh Lines* and many editions of the successful feature, *This is Your Life*. The Empire was then advertised for sale in a lavish brochure.

After a while it was bought and partially-restored by Turner-Page Music, reopening as a live 'Rock' Venue on Tuesday, 22 March, 1994. Thankfully, the gross BBC signboard was removed, to reveal the four arches beneath it. The Stalls floor remained flat as it had during the studio years. The interior, with its three circles, was redecorated and the BBC's timber cladding removed; however, the two lower stage boxes are now missing, giving the theatre a slightly toothless look. It was heartening to see the name Shepherds Bush Empire appearing once again in newspaper advertisements.

Early programme logo

Shoreditch: London Music Hall

Holywell Street (later 95–99 Shoreditch High Street)

Shoreditch, The London Music Hall: full exterior with Kate Carney billed

I passed the London on a bus soon after arriving in the city in 1926, but unbeknown to me it was on its last legs: the next time I passed that way it was down, so I never had the chance to see a show there. I understand that it had a grand old-fashioned atmosphere. But I do remember that the building followed the curve of the street, where a warehouse was later erected.

Like so many of the early music halls which evolved from public houses, this one had started life as The Griffin in 1856 – a 'free-and-easy' public house and music hall where impromptu entertainments were given, the performers being drawn from customers in the bars, not professionals.

With growing prosperity, it was decided in the early 1890s to replace the old pub with a proper Variety theatre and Frank Matcham was engaged to draw up plans for a new building next door. Matcham was recalled in 1901 when extensions were made. Growing demand for liquor during the show had led to the conversion of the old Griffin into reasonably-priced refreshment bars and comfortable lounges; it – and a corner shop – were incorporated into the music hall. The architect had to make a submission regarding projecting stonework at less than the prescribed distance from the centre of Jane Shore Court. Permission was granted, with the work to be completed within 18 months. The father of Mr. A.W. Chapman, an Islington acquaintance of mine, was a potman at the London during its early years; Mr. Chapman himself went on to become a stage electrician at various halls, including the Bedford in Camden Town.

The opening performance of the new 1,329-capacity hall took place on 23 December, 1893, with the enormous expectant crowds having to be controlled by the police. Those lucky enough to get in (there were seats for only 901, the rest being standees) enjoyed a programme that included Charles Coborn, Daisy Wood (from the famous Lloyd family), Charles Bignell, Johnny Gilmore, Charles Gardiner, Nellie L'Estrange and T.E. Dunville. Prices ranged from 6d to one guinea.

At various times the hall was called The Shoreditch Empire, but was always popularly known as The London. Confusingly it was even called The London Theatre of Varieties for a time, but was not part of the LTV circuit – unlike its close neighbour the Shoreditch Olympia. For a period the London was booked in conjunction with Collins' and the Royal Cambridge, the general manager for the enterprise being Charles Hector. Those in the business knew it as the L.C.C. Less than half the size of the Olympia down the road, the London obviously could not book the strongest bills, although a glance at those illustrated here will show that many good acts did appear early on.

In contrast to the offerings only twenty-five years later, a July, 1900 bill gave audiences George Mozart, Harry Tate, Lottie Lennox (singing *Don't See The Fun Of It*), T.E. Dunville, Marie Kendall, Dorothy Royal, R.G. Knowles, Eugene Stratton, Tom Costello and no fewer than eight other acts! This may give the impression that the hall was a No.1 house, but a reading of Thomas Burke's *The Real East End* shows what dreadful acts did sometimes appear there. On the first air-raid on London in May, 1916 three bombs dropped from a German airship fell on the hall, but did little damage and it continued to provide entertainment throughout WW1.

Detail of plasterwork on proscenium arch

Apart from reviews of shows, *The Stage* sometimes carried reports of interest from the London. At one point the manager had his knuckles rapped, when an inspection team from the L.C.C. (the Council) found that the dressing room and stage exit doors were firmly locked during a performance. Illuminated electric number boards replaced the 'push-out' variety in May, 1901, to announce artistes' appearances; while in October, 1906 it was decided to revert from twice- to once-nightly performances – this was quite unusual at so late a date.

The London was at one time the home of M.D. Syd Kaplan, later famous at some of the foremost Variety houses in the capital; his name can be made out on the 1924 bill shown below. Orchestras played under his baton at Ilford, Holborn, Lewisham and Finsbury Park.

For the remainder of its existence shows at the London combined rising stars like Tommy Trinder and Nedlo the Gypsy Violinist (later to make a big name as Ted Ray), former stars such as Harry Claff and a host of unknowns to fill the bill. Hilda Glyder and Julian Rose each topped during 1928, while occasional revues included Lal Edwards' *Jingles and Smiles* and Will Garland's *Swanee River*. Other names still recalled, even if their acts are forgotten, are Devon & Earle, Sydney and Adelaide, Wraggs & Boans and – a family still working today – The Bouncing Dillons.

Exterior with the main entrance

Like its neighbour the Olympia, the London gradually lost ground to the cinema, so that by July, 1932 closure and possible sale were mooted in the press. Despite its having been in the hands of the Receiver in 1922, the hall had managed to struggle for a further decade. The final shows were given at this, London's second-oldest music hall, in 1934. At that time it held the record of being the only one that had presented continuously a programme of Variety for the previous thirty-nine years; Collins' was the oldest London hall. Demolition took place in March, 1935, a drapery warehouse being built on the site.

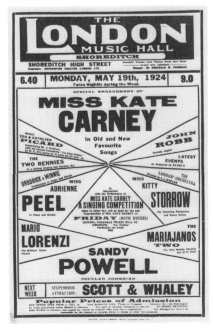

A Variety bill of 1924

The Eduardos rehearsing on a theatre roof

Shoreditch: Olympia

203–4, Shoreditch High Street (corner of Great Eastern Street, opposite Eastern Counties Railway Station)

An 1837 view of the National Standard Theatre that stood on the site

Although famed as a very popular Variety and Revue house until its conversion to a cinema in 1926, the Olympia of course had a long history as a drama theatre before its Variety days. I remember it from the 1930s only as a slightly archaic picture house. It opened as a place of entertainment known as The Royal Standard Theatre in 1835, as proved by the *Macbeth* bill shown below. As usual, comic songs and ballet interludes were included in the evening's programme, to get round the rules governing patent drama houses. These rules were not relaxed until 1843.

The theatre had a huge auditorium in horseshoe form holding 3,000 and having *four* circles. Under the management of John Douglass, to whom it was sold in 1845, it claimed to be 'the largest and most elegant theatre in Europe'. Douglass, who had been a showman for some years, would have appreciated that the stage and boxes were removable for circus performances. He went in for spectacular stage effects, with his pantomimes at the Standard running those at the Theatre Royal,

Drury Lane very close. In fact, Douglass always maintained that the Lane regularly "borrowed" his effects, to bolster its pantos.

The Standard's 1863 pantomime not only boasted twelve scenes but had one of those immense titles so beloved of producers at that time – *Cherry and Fair Star* or, *Harlequin The Dancing Waters, The Singing Apple & The Little Green Talking Bird!* No straightforward *Cinderella* or *Aladdin* for them! It was announced on the bill that on certain nights the pantomime would start at 8.00p.m., being preceded by another piece; so a lengthy evening's entertainment lay ahead – relieved, no doubt, by plenty of savaloys and pigs' trotters sold in the auditorium.

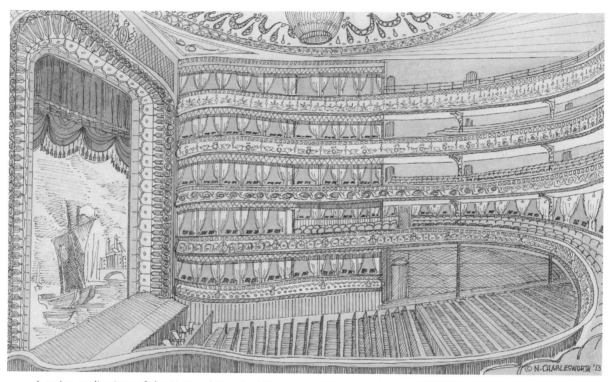

Interior, auditorium of the National Standard Theatre which was replaced in 1889 by a new Variety theatre

The Douglass family remained in charge for over forty years. It was said that, after the theatre was destroyed by fire in October, 1866, John Douglass rebuilt the house without the aid of an architect. It reopened the following year, again with a capacity of nearly 3,000 and now claiming to be 'the largest and most elegant theatre in the WORLD' – a claim not surprisingly challenged by The Illustrated Sporting & Dramatic News. A particular feature of the new Standard was a regular season of Opera, often by J.W. Turner's company. This might seem odd but it was always well supported by the large number of Jewish immigrants in the area.

Despite its situation on the edge of the East End, the theatre during the 1870s and 1880s attracted the top actors of the day in productions made famous by them: for example, Henry Irving pulled in the crowds with *The Bells*.

By now The National Standard, the theatre was completely rebuilt to designs by Bertie Crewe in 1876, with a slightly smaller capacity of 2,463 in stalls and a mere three circles. Crewe's exterior is shown below, but – sadly – there seem to be no extant illustrations of the interior. According to John Earl, Crewe specialised entirely in theatres, with a quite florid style, still to be seen at The Lyceum and The Shaftesbury (originally The Prince's) in London's West End; so it is likely that his work at the

National Standard was just as lively. Unfortunately, the Stoll Theatre, his greatest work, was demolished in 1958.

In 1889 The Standard passed into the hands of Andrew Melville and later, in 1904, to his sons Walter and Frederick Melville. An elaborate publicity leaflet, carrying the AM monogram, announced the reopening at Easter, 1889 and the fact that the house would be open 'all the year round'. Melodrama was now the big draw, with Walter Melville himself writing many of the successful pieces – a valuable preparation for the long Melville reign at the Lyceum.

In 1911, The Standard passed into the hands of Walter Gibbons, who changed its name to The Olympia and its policy to Variety and Revue. The Melville brothers must have been made a good offer for the old theatre, as out of the proceeds they were then able to build the Prince's on Shaftesbury Avenue, which they ran alongside the Lyceum as another melodrama house.

The 'new' Olympia soon got into its stride and, as part of The London Theatres of Varieties, booked strong Revue attractions, interspersed with straight Variety bills. The illustration below gives a very good idea of a typical offering just before The Great War – a sketch, classical music, recitation, comedy, juggling and other specialities: in all, something for everyone. It will be seen that Charles Gulliver has quickly replaced Gibbons as boss of the LTV circuit. One of the featured acts on the above bill was Rebla, on whose 'eccentric juggling' the well-known Rob Murray later based his act. Another act, Ronald George, was a 'cellist working his way round the Variety circuit, while Fred Dyer was possibly the first of the Welsh boxers to tour the halls as a singer as well as a boxer. Special bills advertised his challenge to local Shoreditch hopefuls, of whom there would have been plenty.

Many of the Revues that scored at the Olympia were Lew Lake's productions, among them *They Didn't Want To Do It* in October, 1916. He also did well here with *Sons of the Sea* and, in October, 1921, with *Jack of All Trades*.

Among other Revues staged at the Olympia were Harry Day's *Come Inside* and *Business As Usual*, (both in August, 1915), the former with Sam Mayo and S.W. Wyndham, the latter with Ella Shields and Ida Long. 'Colonel' Harry Day was a prolific producer of Revues, with many on the road at the same time. He had started as a bill-sticker in Bristol, and later became Labour MP for Southwark Central in London. *Splinters of 1921* paid a visit in April of that year and of course Fred Karno's Companies were also hugely successful here on their regular visits.

East Enders enjoyed just about every popular name in the Variety world during the LTV years, including Violet Lorraine, Arthur Roberts, Billy Merson, Dora Lyric, Leo Stormont, Foreman & Fannan, Joe O'Gorman and – very often here – Sammy Shields. Among the more unusual attractions were Astley's Circus and Burns' *Le Petit Cabaret*, both on the same bill in August, 1914 and two quartets and a set of twins supporting Signor Arvi in the September of the following year. During the Gulliver years the manager was Bertie Adams, who later managed the Holborn Empire and – later still – Birmingham Hippodrome. He stood no nonsense from rowdy audiences, his down-to-earth directions to the exit being legendary.

Changing tastes and fashions in the capital led to the collapse of the LTV circuit in the middle 1920s and, as a result, the Olympia became a cinema. From December, 1926 it was licensed to Arthur Gilbert as The New Olympia Picturedrome, although it did continue to hold a stage licence until 1939.

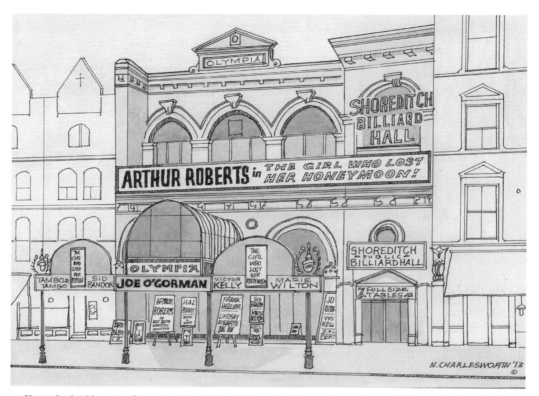

Shoreditch, Olympia (formerly The National Standard Theatre): exterior with Arthur Roberts billed

In January, 1940 the theatre was demolished for the erection of a super cinema, the owners obviously encouraged with box office results enough to invest further; but the war brought the project to an end and only a few low walls had been completed when the plan was abandoned. Colin Sorensen explored the site after the war and discovered scenery hooks remaining in place on one of the surviving walls backstage of the old building. And so ended one hundred years of drama, pantomime, circus, Variety, Revue and films on this site.

Part of an old poster from The Royal Standard Theatre, dated 1835

Shoreditch: Royal Cambridge Music Hall

136, Commercial Street, Shoreditch

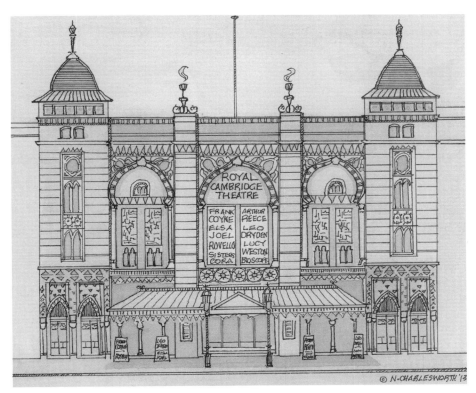

Shoreditch, Royal Cambridge Theatre of Varieties: exterior with Frank Coyne, Leo Dryden billed

I can just remember passing the Cambridge a few years after moving to London in 1926; it was running films at the time, closing for good not long after. It did seem quite an old-fashioned building, even to my inexperienced eye, compared to the new Odeons, Gaumont Palaces and Regals then sprouting up all over town. Unbeknown to me at the time, the hall had a long history, dating back to 1864, when a 2,000-capacity building opened under George William Nugent. The architect was William Finch Hill, whose firm designed several theatres in Hoxton, Islington and Holborn. Improvements and remodellings were, as usual, carried out over the years – principally by Jethro T. Robinson and Edward Clark. There is scope for further research into the very early days at the Cambridge.

For safety reasons, the hall's capacity was reduced in 1892 to 1,488 persons: perhaps this was just as well, because the place was destroyed by fire in 1896, necessitating a complete rebuilding under D. Harry Percival in the Moorish manner. This period is quite well documented and we learn that the 926-capacity, three-level hall had its foundation stone laid in April, 1897 and that the new building opened in January, 1898. Among the improvements was the provision of a saloon at Commercial Street level – the stalls floor being 10ft below street level. Learning the lessons of the earlier fire, Percival provided ample exits from the pit and gallery into both the main street and into nearby Vine Court.

Sam Sibbitt's sketch, in the colour section, is a valuable record of a typical show at the Cambridge in the palmy days of the 1890s, proving that some top acts were working the hall at that time – a situation that was to change as the years went by. The famous names of Kate Carney (always popular in Shoreditch), Harry Pleon and Marie Kendall are to the fore; The Zanettos were among the specialities that week, one of their number managing to catch a ball, thrown from the gallery, on a fork. They graduated to the West End, appearing on a bill at the Victoria Palace in 1919. Their descendants live today in Somerset.

It is of interest that E.V. Page, a City accountant who wrote comic songs, managed the Cambridge for a time; also that on its reopening in 1898 the bill included Alexandre & Vasco, who were in fact the future manager of the Metropolitan and his mother!

Good acts also appearing at the start can be seen on the programme below – Leo Dryden, Frank Coyne and Arthur Reece perhaps being the best known. An enthusiastic reviewer in *The Encore* in July, 1900 welcomed Tom Fancourt to the music hall stage, following his success in musical comedy – he had appeared as Flipper in *A Runaway Girl* at the original Gaiety Theatre in 1898. Of his three songs at the Cambridge, *Come and Have a Tiddley Round the Corner* went down well and could have been the basis of *Let's Have a Tiddley at the Milk Bar*, sung by a very young Ernie Wise in the 1930s. Others on the bill at the Cambridge that week, under the managership of C. Smith-Wilkes, included Tennyson & O'Gorman, Les Voces, Lillie Simmons, Tom Craven, Ida Heath and The Great Russian Troupe. First and second houses (at 6.45 and 9.10p.m.) varied slightly, but both included newsreel film of the funeral of Queen Victoria. Admission prices varied from 3d in the gallery to 15s in the best box. The curtain fell at 11.15pm at the second house.

About 1910, when Bud Flanagan as a 13-year old worked there as a call-boy, the Cambridge, together with the London Music Hall and Collins' Music Hall, was under one management known as LCC; a leading light was T.G. Richards, long-serving manager of the Cambridge from 1909 until 1923.

Interior with part of the proscenium arch as in 1898

On Saturdays the hall had extra-turn matinees, where Bud Flanagan made his disastrous debut as Fargo, The Boy Wizard and received a stiff clip round the ear from his father for daring to appear at a theatre on the 'shabbath'. Happily, he went on to win a singing competition run by Dora Lyric, wife of agent Walter Bentley. His entertaining story is told in his book, *My Crazy Life*.

The quality of entertainment offered gradually fell off and the hall did not feature often in the Calls published in the theatre trade press. It will be seen from the map that competition in the area was intense, with the Cambridge having rivals in the London and the big Olympia on the LTV circuit; tastes were changing and of course numerous other local halls had already left the fold. There was a brief change of management in 1923, but after only a year the Cambridge had succumbed to films. By the early 1930s it was extremely outmoded and closed for demolition in 1936; the site was used for the extension of a tobacco factory. Incredibly enough by the outbreak of WW2 there were no live theatres left in this densely-populated part of London; those seeking a night at the varieties had to take a bus to Poplar, Islington, Finsbury Park or, until it was bombed, to Stratford.

W. Knowles, one-time Chairman at The Royal Cambridge

Bud Flanagan who made his disastrous debut here

St Pancras: Euston Theatre of Varieties

Euston Road and Tonbridge Street, King's Cross

Euston Theatre of Varieties: exterior

The Euston Palace, designed by Wylson & Long with Bertie Crewe and with charming auditorium paintings by J.M. Boekbinder, opened in June, 1900. 'The Theatre is a thing of Beauty and ought to be a Joy throughout the next century and even longer', it was said at the time of its opening. Sadly, in just over sixty years the theatre had been destroyed and is now largely forgotten. But it was then a fine theatre, holding over 1,300.

With other places of entertainment some distance away (the nearest being The Grand in Islington), the new music hall had a ready-made audience provided by the three teeming railway stations nearby. The Euston Palace came under the management of George Adney Payne, followed by his son Walter Payne and eventually became one of The Syndicate Halls under the chairmanship of Henry Gros.

With a stage of fifty-six feet wide and forty-six feet deep, the hall was capable of presenting a large-sized spectacular show, as well as the usual music hall bills. Initially these ran to at least ten acts per house, as the illustration below shows. Revue of course became popular soon after the house opened and there was a scenic artist resident, T.E. Ryan, who could produce the necessary backdrops almost instantaneously. The first manager was Fred A. McAvoy, but later Pierre Cohen took over.

Despite high-quality bills, the Euston Palace lasted as a Variety Theatre only until August, 1922, when it was taken over by Sir Nigel Playfair and renamed The Regent Theatre. From then on it became a legitimate theatre, where much interesting work was done. The opening production was Arnold Bennett's play *Body and Soul*, but after a very short run the theatre was let to Sir Barry Jackson, whose production of Rutland Boughton's opera *The Immortal Hour* had an extraordinarily decent run of 216 performances.

Live entertainment ceased in about 1932, nobody having any lasting success, and The Regent became a cinema. Control passed from Variety Theatres Consolidated Ltd. to King's Cross Cinemas Ltd. The theatre settled down to a steady career as a film house through the 1930s and 1940s, apparently one of the hundreds of lost live theatres.

Surprisingly, The Regent reverted to Variety after WW2, when in 1950 the management passed to Park Theatrical Productions, also associated with New Cross Empire Theatre in south London. Some good bills were presented, the first being topped by Max Miller, but in subsequent weeks business declined and the venture failed after a few months, but not before a pantomime was presented. *Cinderella*, with Tommy Godfrey as Buttons was billed as 'a West End Show at popular prices' (these were from 2s 6d to 7s 6d). The full production, with ponies and a coach, had Phyllis Holden as Fairy Godmother and Jane Martin as Cinderella. The Ugly Sisters were played by Dawkes & Rose.

Interior looking towards the stage

Live shows finally ceased after this false dawn, films taking over again for the remaining life of the theatre. The attractive proscenium arch was modified and raised, to improve sightlines for film-use, although the boxes remained. The building had a prominent position, right opposite St. Pancras Station. Latterly it was known as The Century Cinema, part of The Granada Group and the exterior became very shabby.

A typical double-feature film programme that could be seen was Stewart Granger in *Secret Partner*, with *Ring of Fire* in support. I attended a similar programme, mainly to appreciate the interior of the old hall, and was pleased to note that the small gallery still survived above the dress circle and upper circle. Outside, an alcove accommodated coin-operated machines selling ice-cream, chocolate and cigarettes. Eventually the cinema closed, the building being demolished in about 1971. The site was used as an extension for Camden Town Hall.

The position of The Euston Theatre of Varieties, seen from the air in 1957

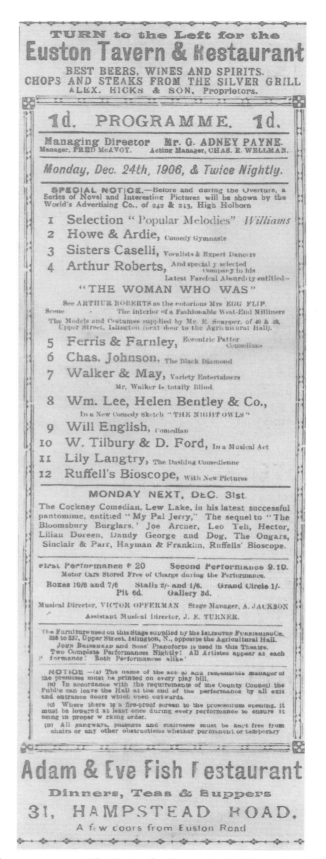

TURN to the Left for the
Euston Tavern & Restaurant
BEST BEERS, WINES AND SPIRITS.
CHOPS AND STEAKS FROM THE SILVER GRILL
ALEX. HICKS & SON, Proprietors.

1d. PROGRAMME. 1d.

Managing Director   Mr. G. ADNEY PAYNE.
Manager, FRED McAVOY.   Acting Manager, CHAS. E. WELLMAN.

Monday, Dec. 24th, 1906, & Twice Nightly.

SPECIAL NOTICE.—Before and during the Overture, a
Series of Novel and Interesting Pictures will be shown by the
World's Advertising Co., of 242 & 243, High Holborn

1 Selection "Popular Melodies" *Williams*

2 Howe & Ardie, Comedy Gymnasts

3 Sisters Caselli, Vocalists & Expert Dancers

4 Arthur Roberts, And specially selected
Company in his
Latest Farcical Absurdity entitled—
"THE WOMAN WHO WAS"

See ARTHUR ROBERTS as the notorious Mrs EGG FLIP.
Scene   The interior of a Fashionable West-End Milliners
The Models and Costumes supplied by Mr. E. Soapper, of 40 & 49,
Upper Street, Islington (next door to the Agricultural Hall).

5 Ferris & Farnley, Eccentric Patter
Comedians

6 Chas. Johnson, The Black Diamond

7 Walker & May, Variety Entertainers
Mr. Walker is totally Blind.

8 Wm. Lee, Helen Bentley & Co.,
In a New Comedy Sketch "THE NIGHT OWLS"

9 Will English, Comedian

10 W. Tilbury & D. Ford, In a Musical Act

11 Lily Langtry, The Dashing Comedienne

12 Ruffell's Bioscope, With New Pictures

MONDAY NEXT, DEC. 31st.

The Cockney Comedian, Lew Lake, in his latest successful
pantomime, entitled "My Pal Jerry," The sequel to "The
Bloomsbury Burglars," Joe Archer, Leo Teli, Hector,
Lilian Doreen, Dandy George and Dog, The Ongars,
Sinclair & Parr, Hayman & Franklin, Ruffells' Bioscope.

First Performance 6 20   Second Performance 9.10.
Motor Cars Stored Free of Charge during the Performance.
Boxes 10/6 and 7/6   Stalls 2/- and 1/6   Grand Circle 1/-
Pit 6d.   Gallery 3d.

Musical Director, VICTOR OFFERMAN   Stage Manager, A. JACKSON

Assistant Musical Director, J. E. TURNER.

The Furniture used on this Stage supplied by the ISLINGTON FURNISHING Co.,
325 to 337, Upper Street, Islington, N., opposite the Agricultural Hall.
JOHN BRINSMEAD and Sons' Pianoforte is used in this Theatre.
Two Complete Performances Nightly! All Artistes appear at each
performance! Both Performances alike'

NOTICE.—(a) The name of the actual and responsible manager of
the premises must be printed on every play bill.
(b) In accordance with the requirements of the County Council the
Public can leave the Hall at the end of the performance by all exit
and entrance doors which open outwards.
(c) Where there is a fire-proof screen to the proscenium opening, it
must be lowered at least once during every performance to ensure it
being in proper working order.
(D) All gangways, passages and staircases must be kept free from
chairs or any other obstructions whether permanent or temporary

Adam & Eve Fish Restaurant

Dinners, Teas & Suppers

31, HAMPSTEAD ROAD.

A few doors from Euston Road

The programme at The Euston for the week of 24 December, 1906

Stoke Newington: Alexandra Theatre

67–69, Stoke Newington Road

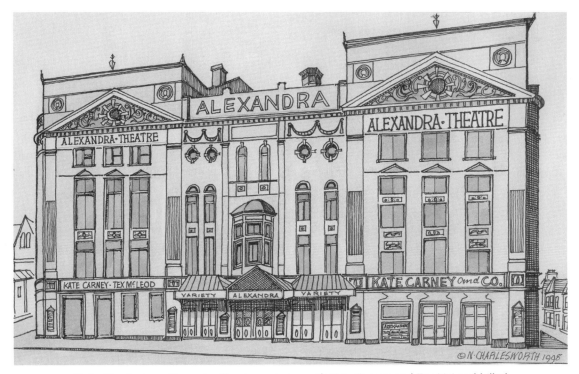

Stoke Newington, Alexandra Theatre: exterior with Kate Carney and Tex McLeod billed

Occupying a very broad main street frontage at 67–69 Stoke Newington Road, The Alexandra Theatre was opened on 27 December, 1897 by F.W. Purcell, whose family ran other theatres in the North. Designed by Frank Matcham, The Alexandra had its upper circle immediately to the rear of the dress circle. The three-tier house had seating for over 2,000 and the interior decoration in the Elizabethan manner was by de Jong.

Support in those early years must have been good, encouraging Purcell to open another house in North London, The Marlborough Theatre in Holloway Road – also by Matcham – in 1903. But in 1905 The Alexandra passed into the hands of H.G.D. Bennett and a long succession of owners followed – the longest-serving being George Barclay, the Variety agent and husband of Kate Carney, who was in charge between 1934 and 1939. The Alexandra was a nice theatre, but nobody made any money there! In fact at this period I often saw good acts playing only to the 'wood family'.

In its early years first-class plays and pantomimes were presented, but the theatre later went over to Stock at lower prices. The first pantomime was *Dick Whittington*, with a cast including Miss Billie Barlow (Dick), E.J. Lonner (Idle Jack), W.E. Richardson (Eliza the Cook) and G. Delaforce (Fitzwarren).

Exterior, while known as The Palace

Between the years 1906 and 1909 the theatre was renamed The Palace, Stoke Newington and presented Variety regularly. For ten years from 1909 it became part of – firstly – Moss' Empires Ltd. and – later – Hackney & Shepherds Bush Empire Palaces Ltd. which, of course, was controlled by Sir Oswald Stoll. So the Alexandra was part of The Big Time for a period.

During the 1920s and 30s Variety was still the regular fare, but probably as the result of the proximity of Hackney and Finsbury Park Empires, strong attractions were rare. I saw quite a few of the typical bills of the period, for example Kate Carney, supported by Tex McLeod (1935) and the Mannie Jay and Sydney Myers' revue. *Round About Big Ben* (1937), with Dave Morris, who began as one of Park's Eton Boys. I had previously seen this North Country comic in *Splendour*, another touring revue. Supporting Morris at The Alexandra were Olive & Victor Carlton and The Sensational Carsons.

Auditorium towards the stage

The theatre opened only spasmodically during the Second World War, but I managed to see Issy Bonn there and Phyllis Dixey in *Peek-a-Boo*. Performances were twice nightly, at 6.00pm and 8.00pm., to enable audiences to reach home safely in good time. The theatre was often closed during the blitz, but during one raid the audience left the auditorium for the safety of the Stalls bar, where the show continued until 4.00am! Another typical 'Alex' bill during the late 1930s, while George Barclay was still in charge, had Peter Fannan ('Great Stuff this Ass') sharing top with The Marileners and Harry Taft ('All-Baloney'); Lea-Sonia was retained for another week, following enormous success, while other well-known names appearing during the week of Monday, 20 June included Marjorie Ristori and Sherry & Kiel. The ten-act bill was presented twice nightly at 6.40pm and 9.00pm. Carnival Night was on a Friday, while Sunday Pictures were offered from 5.30pm. Despite being billed as The Family Theatre of Varieties, The 'Alex' had a tough time and George Barclay eventually pulled out. Cyril Fletcher took the theatre occasionally at Christmas, putting in a traditional panto. Marlene McAndrew remembers Nellie Wallace vividly in an endless undressing episode during the cabin scene in *Aladdin* one year.

Auditorium from a Stage Box

After the war various attempts were made to keep the place going, sometimes as a stage school, as a Yiddish playhouse (under P.W. Spellman), which did quite well for a time, and as a venue for boxing and wrestling, but luckily it was too early for the bingo boom and so it was spared that. By 1950 the handsome building had been shorn of its attractive canopy and was standing derelict. It was demolished in 1955 and today the site is occupied by a block of flats.

Ted Ray who always stayed at lodgings in Winston Road, Stoke Newington

Len Sharp, of 'Sharp's Tromboneers', another regular lodger

Stratford Empire

Stratford Broadway

Stratford Empire: exterior with Tommy Trinder, Larry Adler, Max Wall billed

Occupying a prominent position in The Broadway, the Empire opened on Monday, 10th April, 1899. It was designed by W.G.R. Sprague for The London District Empire Palaces (which was incorporated the following year as Moss' Empires Ltd.) The Stratford Empire was one of three live theatres in the borough and the most successful; it was run by Moss for the next forty years.

The theatre, built on the site of Rokeby House, seated around 1,500 in stalls, grand circle and balcony; there was a gallery set up above the balcony, making it virtually a three-tier house. A feature was the provision of boxes at the rear of the grand circle, giving it a sense of intimacy; there was also a sliding roof. Sprague provided a well-balanced neo-classical exterior, with an auditorium in the Moresque style, the prevailing colours being terracotta, gold and blue.

From the start the American Biograph featured in the Variety programme, some fourteen short films being shown (including The Boat Race) in the opening show. The films were mentioned in advance newspaper publicity even before the stage attractions – among them Lily Lena and Harry Anderson. Prices of admission ranged from 3d in the balcony to 2s in the fauteuils; boxes were 10s 6d and 7s 6d.

The management promised to present all the top Variety artistes. Prospective engagements included: Cissie Loftus, Marie Lloyd, Harriet Vernon, Lottie Collins, Dan Leno, Eugene Stratton, R.G. Knowles, George Robey, T.E. Dunville, G.H. Chirgwin, Gus Elen, Paul Cinquevalli and Little Tich – a veritable cornucopia of delights! That was not all, as it was proposed to offer 'leading specialities from Continental Cirques and Hippodromes, the stage being spacious and well-equipped'. It was an excellent start for the house. Moss also opened Empires at much the same time at Holloway and New Cross, while Stoll opened his at Hackney two years later.

Among the artistes supporting the Poluski Brothers on the programme shown above, few mean much to us today, as there was at this time a constant search for novel material in both the acts and their names; for example, Niagara & Falls – what did they do? Other acts booked in the years before WW1 were Fred Emney (the father of the large actor popular on stage, in films and television in the 'forties and 'fifties), Fred Kitchen and Harry Claff.

Only fourteen years after opening, the Stratford Empire underwent internal reconstruction and redecoration: already the cinema was making inroads into live theatres, so it was necessary to keep right up to date. On Monday, 27th October, 1913 the theatre reopened with The Ragtime Six and Walter Passmore topping a ten-act bill, which included Ina Lorimer, Johnny Danvers & Co. and Harry Jolson, the brother of Al Jolson. The Bioscope showed *Battle at Elder Bush Gulch*.

Revues which took in Stratford on their Moss tour were legion – among them *Business As Usual, All Fit, Beauties, Bran Pie* and the topical *Rations*, which was staged in July, 1918. The early 1920s saw George Mozart, the ventriloquist Coram with 'Jerry', M'Lita Dolores and Lucille Benstead, while animal acts numbered Silbon's Cats and Velanche's Football Dogs. The great Rebla juggled, while Scott & Whaley often returned – in such pieces as *The Bogus Prince* and *Business Is Business*.

It has to be said that programmes were not particularly inspired, considering the increasing threat of the cinema in larger and more comfortable venues, until the early 1930s. Then Val Parnell and George Black became highly influential in restoring the fortunes of Variety. Their success at The London Palladium and at The Holborn Empire soon rubbed off on the GTC and Moss' suburban and provincial theatres – Stratford included. Programmes became slicker, with better production values and bigger names going on tour. Suddenly we had the likes of Jimmy James, Will Fyffe, Vic Oliver and Anona Winn, names from the radio that the public wanted to see in person; and lots of big stage bands – too many, it was often felt.

Alexander & Mose, a black-faced act comprising Billy Bennett and American actor James Carew (the great Ellen Terry's third husband) – later replaced by Albert Whelan, did colossal business here, being booked-out for the entire week. It was the first Variety appearance for this popular radio act. A new act, Flanagan & Allen, closed the first half, but – due to Bud's inspired ad-libbing – over-ran by thirty minutes before leaving the stage to tumultuous applause. The headliners, Alexander & Mose, were supposed to fill the second half, but at Monday's first house they just could not match the newcomers. Not surprisingly, Alexander & Mose were switched with Flanagan & Allen for the rest of the week. The boys were on their way. Bud Flanagan in his autobiography remembers Stratford Empire as 'a beautifully constructed theatre in the east end of London'.

The entertainment offered continued to be attractive through the 1930s, a 1934 bill being topped by Elsie Carlisle & Sam Browne ('Star of A Thousand Broadcasts'), with Brookins & Van, Lucan & McShane, Murray & Mooney, Claude Lester, Howard Rogers ('The Popular Padre'), Maggie Clifton and company.

Interior from the circle

A sign of the times came in 1936, when the Stratford Empire, along with no fewer than thirteen other Moss' Empires closed for a 'Summer Vacation'. In September, 1937 Larry Adler brought his Road Show, *In Town Tonight*, with Max Wall, Tommy Trinder and Syd & Max Harrison providing a triple dose of hilarity. Four months later Charles Tucker presented *Variety Showboat*, which had Billy Bennett, probably relieved to be once again on his own, Teddy Brown, (the mountainous xylophonist with the incredibly nimble fingers), Owen McGiveney, and – in a very quick return – Syd & Max Harrison; they had obviously scored well on their last visit. Other names enjoying a good Stratford reception in the years running up to, and including the early part of WW2 were Harry Roy and his Band, Sandy Powell, Hutch, Vic Oliver and Nat Gonella. A really quite remarkable roster of big names.

In October, 1940 the revue *Shoot The Works*, reached the Stratford Empire, having played various dates around the suburbs of London. It starred Forsythe, Seamon & Farrell, Joey Porter, The Rockets and Barbara 'Red' Stetson. During its week the theatre received a direct hit in an air-raid and blazed furiously. Barbara Stetson remembers frantically trying to save costumes from her dressing room, before struggling home through streets piled with bricks and broken glass.

The Empire, like many other blitzed Variety theatres, was never rebuilt. Its remains were demolished in 1958.

MOSS TOUR.

Cranbourn Mansions, Cranbourn Street, W.C.2. 'Phone: Gerrard 2274. Tel. Add.: Depict, London.

BIRMINGHAM, Empire (R. 11) (low pitch).—Cecil G. Buckingham presents " Is Everybody Happy? " (cast includes Len Jackson.

BIRMINGHAM, Theatre Royal (R. 11) (low pitch).— The Royal Carl Rosa Opera Company (Mat. Sat., at 2.30. Second week.)

BRADFORD, Alhambra (R. 12.15) (low pitch).—Tom Arnold, Ltd., presents " Switzerland " (twice nightly. at 6.20 and 8.40. Mat. Sat., at 2.30.)

CROYDON, Empire (R. 12) (low pitch).—Syd Seymour and his Band, Lucan and McShane, O'Gorman Brothers, Martyn and Maye, Carvey and Mac, Four Aces, Wright and Marion, Constance Evans.

EDINBURGH, Empire (R. 11) (low pitch). — Carroll Levis and his B.B.C. Discoveries, Racsos Troupe, Six Glamourettes, Wensley and Dale, Lepomme and Sister, Sam Rayne.

FINSBURY PARK, Empire (R. 11.30). (low pitch).— Ambrose and his Orchestra, with Evelyn Dall, Max Bacon, Denny Dennis Vera Lynn, Les Carew, Les Terrianos, Jenks and Williams, Sirdani, Jack and Sylvia, Kellaway with Leslie.

GLASGOW, Empire (R. 11) (low pitch).—Unit Productions, Ltd., presents " Hawaiian Paradise " (cast includes Three Peters Sisters, Turner Layton, etc.).

GLASGOW, Alhambra (R. 11) (low pitch). — " Crazy Days " (Mat. Wed. and Sat. at 2.)

HULL, Palace (R. 11) (low pitch).—Jackquello's present " Time Marches on " (cast includes Stanford and McNaughton).

ILFORD, Hippodrome (R. 12) (low pitch).—Ambrose and his Orchestra, with Evelyn Dall, Max Bacon, Denny, Dennis and Vera Lynn, Les Carew, Cresso Brothers, Elray and Lady, Len and Kiki, Bob Lloyd and Betty, Marion Pola, Trixie and Jean, Eddy Bankey.

KILBURN, Empire (R. 11) (low pitch).—Charles L. Tucker presents " Tops Everything," with Hutch (Leslie A. Hutchinson), Maurice Colleano, Max Wall, Bonar and George, Toria and Rubye, Six Blonde Tops, Oxford Five, Jewel and Warriss, Olive White.

LEEDS, Empire (R. 11) (low pitch).—Florence Desmond and Company in " Taking Off."

LEEDS, Theatre Royal (R. 11) (low pitch).—The Arthur Brough Players.

LIVERPOOL, Empire (R. 11) (low pitch).—Henry Hall and his Orchestra, Freddy Zay, Hatton and Manners, Dehl Trio, Peter Sinclare, The Jardys, Three Merry Widows.

LONDON, Hippodrome (R. 11) (low pitch).—Moss' Empires, Ltd., presents George Black's Musical Frolic, " The Fleet's Lit Up " (cast includes Frances Day, Stanley Lupino, Adele Dixon, Ralph Reader, Geraldo and his Band). (Mats. Thurs. and Sat. at 2.30.)

MANCHESTER, Palace (R. 11) (low pitch).—" Balalaika " (cast includes Clifford Mollison, Clarice Hardwicke, Charles Fletcher, Muriel Barron). (Once ...

NEWCASTLE, Empire (R. 11) (low pitch).—Duncan Sisters, Les Allen and his Pianists, Hughie Green, Freda Wyn, Rome and Leonard, Robinson and Martin, Fogel, George Doonan, The Vanstrattans.

NEW CROSS, Empire (R. 11.30) (low pitch).—William Henshall, Ltd., presents " Red Hot and Blue Moments."

NOTTINGHAM, Empire (R. 12) (low pitch).—Tom Mix, Jack Edge, Ivor Vintor and Co., Nicol and Martin, Conrad's Pigeons, Arlene and Bobette, Lily Moore, Kiraku Brothers, Bud Cariell and Rosa.

NOTTINGHAM, Theatre Royal (R. 12) (low pitch). – Harry Hanson presents The Court Players.

SHEFFIELD, Empire (R. 11) (low pitch).—Two Leslies (Leslie Sarony and Leslie Holmes), G. H. Elliott, Marie Burke, Mackay and Lavalle, Anita Martell, Miller and Deane, Mito Trio, Bud Cordell, Three Stooges.

SOUTHSEA, King's (R. 1.30) (low pitch).—" Time and the Conways " (Mats. Thurs., at 2.30.)

STRATFORD, Empire (R. 11.30) (low pitch).—Charles L. Tucker presents his " Variety Show Boat," including Billy Bennett, Teddy Brown, Owen McGiveney, Sid and Max Harrison, Dorothy Stoner, Millie Jackson's Sailor Girls, Nick and Maria, Billy Kaye and Partners.

SUNDERLAND, Empire (R. 11) (low pitch).—" Going Greek."

SWANSEA, Empire (R. 12) (low pitch).—Kenneth Hyde presents The Charter Players.

The Moss' Empires line-up for the week of 3 October, 1938

Stratford Theatre Royal

Angel Lane, Stratford (now Gerry Raffles Square)

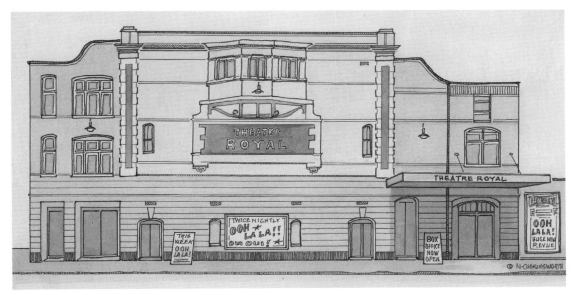

Stratford Theatre Royal: exterior with 'Ooh La La!' Revue billed

Although devoted to drama for most of its existence, the Theatre Royal has presented Variety for short periods over the years. Of the scores of theatres in suburban London at the turn of the 20th Century, the 471-seater playhouse on Angel Lane near Stratford Market is one of the few survivors.

The theatre was founded by an actor, Charles Dillon and opened on 17 December, 1884 with Bulwer Lytton's play, *Richelieu*. A local critic noted the management's determination of avoid 'the dreary pieces in which the uninstructed delight to witness a murder every twenty minutes'. Unfortunately, future managements were often obliged to resort to such 'dreary piece' – melodrama being a mainstay of the theatre.

The theatre was designed by J.G. Buckle and is believed to be his only surviving work; it was built in twelve weeks by Messrs. David G. Laing, using the frame of a former wheelwright's shop as its basis. With its two circles supported on columns, the auditorium has the feeling of a country theatre.

Charles Dillon, for all his ability as an actor, was not a businessman and in 1886 decided to sell the theatre. While he had been away on tour the Royal had been run by the old actor Fred Thomas, whose most notable production had been *Uncle Tom's Cabin*. This had offered 'Real Negroes', Banjoist, Acrobats, Bloodhounds and a Trick Donkey – almost a Variety show in itself! Please see p 320 for an illustration.

The new owner was Albert Fredericks, who extended the stage and built offices and two bars. These additions are clearly seen today in the unusual ground plan of the building; the stalls bar, in particular, has enormous character and is home to local drinkers who have no interest in entering the auditorium itself. Fredericks later built the Borough Theatre in the High Street. He put the Theatre Royal on a firm financial footing by combining the best local talent and bigger names from the West End, before devoting more of his time to establishing the Borough Theatre.

The new theatre having failed to attract the expected audience from further west, Albert Fredericks reopened the Theatre Royal as 'The Theatre Royal and Palace of Varieties' in April, 1897, but the new name lasted only two months. On Albert Fredericks' death his successor, Caroline Fredericks Ellis, took over and introduced further Variety acts, including Dr. Walford Bodie. She installed electric lighting and generally overhauled the building. The Royal became popular with local people – although over the years the local audience has been a fickle one.

Following an uncertain period after WW1, when the management lost its way slightly in the choice of plays, the Theatre Royal got by on old melodramas, just avoiding being turned into a cinema; there was also a stage fire. The newer Borough Theatre did succumb to films.

The Theatre Royal ran twice-nightly Variety from 1927 at price from 4d to 1s 6d, during which time it became a regular production date for revues, passing out of the hands of the Fredericks family in 1932.

Auditorium toward the circles, following restoration

A further season of number-three standard Variety was staged that same year, but closed after five weeks through lack of support. The neighbouring Stratford Empire was, of course, in direct competition with far better fare on offer. The Theatre Royal was closed until 1935, when John Williams re-introduced melodrama with several changes of play each week, but even this failed to attract. Closure occurred again, as it did under the following three managements. The theatre was dark from the onset of the Blitz, which hit the area hard. It did not reopen until 1943.

The well-known and experienced J. Rowland Sales then took over and gave Stratford about two years of Variety and Revue, although his time there was not particularly successful – despite the loss of the Empire, which was bombed out. Revues included such gems as *Hi-Diddle-Diddle*, with Jane of The Daily Mirror, *Bareskins and Blushes* and *Blaze Away*. A week of *Miss Camouflage* reflected current conditions in London. Prices ranged from 1s to 3s, with a typical bill shown in the colour section. Suggestions were invited from audiences for a first Christmas Pantomime. J. Rowland Sales had started as an actor and later became a theatre and cinema Estate Agent and Valuer; on his departure from Stratford the theatre faced demolition, remaining closed until the winter of 1946. This was still not the end of Variety here, however.

David Horne and Geoffrey Hastings tried more literate plays in the later 1940s with some success, but custom fell away again – attracted this time by television. Even a season of plays with guest stars, such as Derek Bond, failed to build a consistent audience. Following two more managements, one of whose plays was televised from the theatre, yet another attempt was made to introduce Variety and Revue, including the return of Jane in *Jane Comes to Town*.

The arrival of Theatre Workshop for a six-week season in 1953 changed Stratford Theatre Royal for ever. The company was at the time resident in Manchester, but also appeared in Europe. A permanent home at the Royal, even after months of touring to run-down venues in Britain, was hotly debated. The remarkable and energetic director, Joan Littlewood, aided by Gerry Raffles, developed political theatre with completely new and unconventional production methods. Improvisation was something quite unknown to experienced repertory actors, as was the ability to sing and dance in productions. The whole company was expected to be completely versatile – even to painting and cleaning the building. Scripts were often re-written during rehearsal.

Theatre Workshop later took a lease on the Theatre Royal and by 1955 had made a real breakthrough with the production of *Arden of Faversham*. Actors who appeared early on included Harry H. Corbett, Maxwell Shaw, Howard Goorney, Avis Bunnage and Gerard Dynevor; while later ones who came to prominence were Roy Kinnear, Victor Spinetti, Diana Coupland and Brian Murphy. Many productions transferred to the West End, *The Good Soldier Schweik* being the first. I saw *The Hostage* twice in a fortnight in 1958, with Murray Melvin in the title role, which made a huge impression on me.

Joan Littlewood's punch-happy musicals, whose West End transfers brought badly-needed income to the Theatre Royal, included *Fings Ain't What They Used T'be*, *Sparrers Can't Sing* and *Make Me An Offer*, the latter with Daniel Massey, Dilys Laye, Wally Patch and Sheila Hancock. Their success was a mixed blessing to Littlewood, as was the presentation by a West End management of a new chandelier for the Theatre Royal! It was even referred to in a song rendered by Roy Kinnear during the next musical there.

Music Hall evenings, or weeks, enlivened the stage between productions and some posters are shown here. Joan Littlewood returned to produce *Oh, What A Lovely War* in 1963, later made into a successful film. Sadly, she never fully succeeded in making the 'People's Theatre' a reality.

With thanks to Michael Coren, whose book 'Theatre Royal' tells the story of one hundred years of the Stratford Theatre Royal. (Quartet Books, 1984).

THEATRE ROYAL
STRATFORD

Proprietor - (Luther Villa, Cann Hall Road) - Mr. ALBERT FREDERICKS.
Manager - (to whom address all communications) Mr. W. H. FREDERICKS.
Performance guaranteed to be over at 10.48, to enable Persons to avail themselves of Trains & Trams

SATURDAY, AUGUST 18th, LAST NIGHT OF

HALF-MAST HIGH.

GREAT ATTRACTION,
ON MONDAY, AUGUST 20th,
FIRST TIME AT THIS THEATRE, SPECIAL ENGAGEMENT OF

MR. CHARLES HARRINGTON'S
GREAT AMERICAN COMBINATION.
The Largest Troupe of Real Negroes and Freed Slaves that has ever Travelled this Country.

MORNING PERFORMANCE
WEDNESDAY, AUG. 22nd., AT 1.30.
(CHILDREN HALF-PRICE TO ALL PARTS.)

MONDAY, AUGUST 20th, 1894, & DURING THE WEEK,
Grand Production of the Great Musical Drama of Slave Life in America, adapted from Mrs. BEECHER STOWE'S Beautiful Work—

UNCLE TOM'S
CABIN

As produced Throughout America and Canada. Magnificent New Scenery specially painted by C. EGERTON.

Uncle Tom	a face whose truly African features were characterised by an expression of grave good sense	Mr. CHARLES HARRINGTON
Phineas Fletcher	who has for a pair of blue eyes turned a Quaker	Mr. GEORGE VILLIERS
Mr. St. Clair	a wealthy Planter	Mr. O. H. PHELPS
George Harris	a Slave who seeks freedom	Mr. A. S. GRAHAM
Mr. Wilson	a Factory Owner	Mr. H. DOWNHAM
Legree	a Slave Owner	Mr. J. H. ROGERT
Loker	a Slave Driver	Mr. J. H. RENNY
Marks	a Lawyer	Mr. REGINALD BULLER
Adolphe		Mr. E LONARD
Sambo	a Slave	Mr. T. DAVIES
Quimbo	a Slave	Mr. J POLLARD
Andy		Mr. J. WILLIAMS
Skiggs	an Auctioneer	Mr. A. MARTIN
Waiter		Mr. G. COOKE
Eliza Harris	with a peculiar air of refinement, softness of voice and manner	Miss CHRISTINE KEMBLE
Mrs. St. Clair		Miss ETHEL VERNON
Aunt Ophelia	in her habits she was a model of order	Miss AMY TEMPEST
Topsy	an odd mixture of shrewdness and cunning	Miss AMY HALL
Aunt Chloe	Uncle Tom's better half	Miss JESSIE GREEN
Dinah		Mrs. S. BROWN
Little Eva	always in white, she seems to move like a shadow through all sorts of places without contracting spot or stain	Little SYLVIA STELLA
Cassy	a Creole Slave on Legree's Plantation	Madame ZERLINA ZERBINI

Planters, Salesmen, Negroes, Slaves, Quadroons, Octoroons, Mulattos, etc.

Act 1. — UNCLE TOM'S CABIN
Scene 2.—A Tavern by the River Side. Scene 3.—A Landscape in Winter.
Scene 4.—The great Ice Scene.—The Ohio Frozen.

Act 2. HOME OF ST. CLAIR ON LAKE PONCHATRAIN
Act 3. TAVERN ON THE OHIO RIVER
Scene 2.—A Landscape. Scene 3.—A Rocky Pass in the Hills. Rock of Freedom.

Act 4. GARDEN AT THE ST. CLAIR HOUSE
IN THE EVENING BY MOONLIGHT.
Scene 2.—A Chamber. Scene 3.—Death Bed of Eva.

Act 5. THE AUCTION MART. THE SLAVE SALE
Scene 2.—A Room in Legree's House. Scene 3.—The Cotton Plantation.

GRAND PLANTATION FESTIVAL
BY REAL NEGROES AND FREED SLAVES.
The Coons in their Songs, Shouts, Choruses, Banjo Tambourine, Bone, Mandoline and Violin Solos
COUNT PAOLA, The Musical Marvel
A Real Impersonation of Negro Life in the Cotton Fields of South America.

Act 6. A WRETCHED CABIN
DEATH OF UNCLE TOM.
GRAND TABLEAUX—Eva in the Clouds Imploring Benediction to Uncle Tom.

Stage Manager, Acting Manager, For Mr. CHARLES HARRINGTON M. C. O. H. PHELPS, Count PAOLA.

MONDAY, AUGUST 27th,

OUR ELDORADO

ADMISSION—
Dress Circle 2s. Orchestra Stalls 1s. 6d. Stalls and
(Numbered and Reserved) (Numbered and Reserved)
Balcony 1s. Pit 9d. Gallery 6d.
PRIVATE BOXES 21s.
Early Doors open at 6.45, 3d. Extra to all parts of the House to avoid Crowling.
DOORS OPEN AT 7.15. COMMENCE AT 7.30.
PRINCIPAL ENTRANCES—GREAT EASTERN ROAD AND ANGEL LANE
Seats can be Booked at ROCKLEY'S Musical Warehouses, 150 the Grove, Stratford, & 26 Woodgrange Road, Forest Gate, without extra charge.
CHILDREN IN ARMS NOT ADMITTED.

WILLIAMS & STRAHAN, Printers, 74 Bow Cut, Limehill.

Theatre Royal poster of 20 August, 1894

Tottenham Palace

Tottenham High Road North

Tottenham Palace: exterior with Harry Champion billed

Still standing, this handsome Edwardian building was one of the dozen theatres which comprised the London Syndicate Halls. This consortium included, in the first decade of the twentieth century, the Tivoli, the Oxford and the London Pavilion. Replacing the People's Palace, a much smaller hall which stood a few hundred yards away, the Ionic architecture of Tottenham Palace (designed by Wylson & Long) was greatly admired at its opening on 31 August, 1908 – quite late for a Variety house. It is now the only complete theatre by this firm still to be seen in London.

It had an impressive central pediment (now removed), pierced by an oval window, with advanced pavilions at each end, each crowned with a rounded pediment. The theatre seated just under 1,800 in stalls, dress circle and gallery with two boxes on either side at circle level. In place of stage boxes there are gilded figures in niches on either side of the proscenium arch.

Wall bracket lamp in the gallery

During its short life as a theatre, spanning only sixteen years, the Palace presented nearly all the stars of the period. As we have representative selections of artistes from every year of its life, we have decided to feature them all – showing what a wealth of talent could be enjoyed by the ordinary Londoner at a local hall:

From the Opening up to the Great War

1908   Fred Karno's Company, *The Casuals*; Victoria Monks; Dutch Daly; Chirgwin; Sam Mayo; Joe Elvin; Gertie Gitana; Little Tich; Kate Carney

1909   La Milo; Joe Peterman; Fred Ginnett's *Dick Turpin*; Florrie Forde; Whit Cunliffe; Daisy Wood; Charles Austin; Eight Lancashire Lads

1910   George Formby; *Garden of Girls*; Marie Lloyd, Ernie Mayne; Wilkie Bard; *Ghost of Jerry Bundler*; Clarice Mayne; Harry Bedford, Maidie Scott; Fred Barnes; *Jimmy The Fearless* with Charlie Chaplin; Craggs Troupe; Billy Merson; Harry Lauder; Joe Elvin; Mark Sheridan; Harry Tate; George Carney; The McNaughtons; Tom Clare

1911   Gertie Gitana; Lil Hawthorne; Victoria Monks; Harry Champion; The Two Bobs; *Hester's Mystery* by Pinero; Jen Latona; *The Yellow Fang*, Sam Stern

1912   *The Fighting Parson*; Six Brothers Luck; Fred Karno's *Mumming Birds*; Charles Whittle; Ernie Lotinga as Jimmy Josser; G.S. Melvin; Harry Randall; Julian Rose; Sam Mayo; Fred Kitchen; Alfred Lester; Harry Tate in *Motoring*; Clarice Mayne; Dusty Rhodes; Edie Greene, Marie Kendall; Hedges Bros. & Jacobson; Marie Lloyd; Dan Crawley; Dick Tubb; Horace Goldin; Reg Bolton; Robb Wilton; Harry Bedford; Nellie Wallace; Tom Leamore; Daisy Dormer; Jay Laurier & Company of 40; Jen Latona; Chirgwin; Will Evans; T.E. Dunville

1913   Alexander's Ragtime Band; King & Benson; Alexandre & Hughes; Percy Honri's *Bohemia*; Tom Foy; Harry Weldon; Marie Lloyd; The Two Bobs; G.H. Carlisle & H.M. Wellman; Four Royal Scots; Chirgwin; Ernest Shand

Interior towards the stage

The War Years

1914   Ernie Lotinga; Scott & Whaley; Lottie Lennox; *Hello, Ragtime*; Albert Chevalier; Carl Hertz; Jack Pleasants; Ernest C. Rolls' *Step This Way*

1915   *Keep Smiling* from the Alhambra with Beatrice Lillie, Gilbert Childs; Joe Boganny's Bakers; Randolph Sutton; Percy Honri's *1915 Revue*; De Biere; Charles Whittle; Talbot O'Farrell

1916   *The Million Dollar Girl*; Tubby Edlin; *Hello, Everybody*! with George Clarke; Fred Karno's *Parlez-Vous Francais?* Syd Walker; Percy Honri's *1916 Revue* (for which the free list was suspended)

1917   Marie Lloyd; Tom Leamore; C. Hayden Coffin; Haley's Juveniles; Sam Barton; John Lawson & Co. in *The Dowry*; Daimler & Eadie; three extra matinees were arranged for *The Lads of the Village*

1918   Jack Pleasants; The Mongadors; Naughton & Gold; *Zig Zag* (free list was suspended again); *The Silver King*; Bransby Williams; Joe Elvin; Torino; Ida Barr

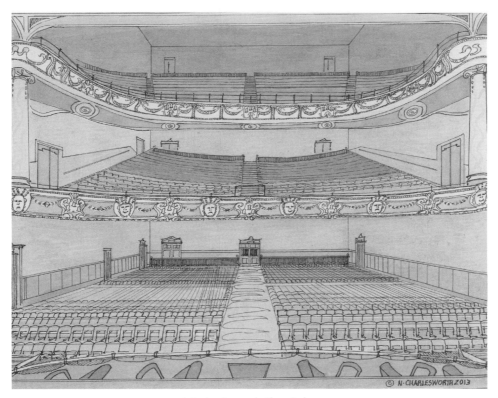

Interior towards the circles

From the Peace until films took over

1919   *Bobo* with Ida Chrispie; Charlie Bell; Will Fyffe; Terence Byron & Co.; Franco Piper; the return of *The Lads of the Village*; Cora Youngblood; Bex & Bex; Clarkson Rose & Olive Fox; Winifred Ward; Tucker, the singing violinist; Violet Essex; Carl Hertz mystifying again; Brooklyn Comedy Four; J.H. & B. Lester; The Miles Stavordale Quartette; Fred Kerr in Seymour Hicks' *Peace, Perfect Peace*; Victoria Monks, *The Girl in the Taxi*

1920   Dan Rolyat; Dalvaine's Marionettes; Kamakura Family; Phil Ascot Four; Dick Henderson; Ten Loonies; Hart & O'Brien in a sketch; L. Wright Ensemble; Queenie Leighton; Finlay Dunn; Cecilia Loftus; Nervo & Knox

1921   Joe Young in *The Far East*; Mary Redfern & Co. in *Devil's Tinder*; Lily Morris; H. Slingsby's *Oh, Laugh!* Caryll & Mundy; The Egbert Bros.; Jack Stocks

1922   Charles Cochran's £30,000 production of *The League of Notions* from The Oxford Theatre; *Jack of All Trades* with Bob Stevens; Noni & Horace; Florrie Forde; Carlton; Pierce & Roslyn; James Fawn; Max Derewski; Fred Maitland; Harry Champion; Florence Yamen; Auntie on her bike; Gertie Gitana; Charles Stevens; G.H. Carlisle

1923   Albert de Courville's *Joy-Bells*; Joe Peterman in *The Auctioneer*; Haines English Ballet; Jock McKay; Harold Walden; Vera Wootton; *Old Time Singers of Old Time Songs* with Lily Burnand & Co.; *My Pal Jerry*; *Quality Street*

1924   Kate Carney; Dolly Elsworthy; Syd Walker in *Lights Up*; Harry Day's *Spangles* (for which large crowds were expected); *Plum Blossom*; Macdonald & Young's *Maid of The Mountains*; Randolph Sutton in *Spare Parts*; Tom Gamble in *Creations*; there were crowded houses for *There You Are, Then*, which included a Fox Trot Competition

The Farewell Week of 22 September, 1924 brought *Pins & Needles*

It seemed that the changes from straight Variety to Revue to general theatrical fare could not hold back the public's infatuation with film, despite the increasing sophistication of the offerings of various managements. So Tottenham Palace became The Canadian Cinema on 21 November, 1924. On 8 January, 1926 it became the Palace again, by which name it was known thereafter.

Exterior whilst in use as a cinema

Latterly Tottenham Palace came under the Gaumont banner, although retaining its original name. It closed on 28 June, 1969 with the final film programme being *File of The Golden Goose* and *Sam Whiskey*. Thereafter it became a bingo hall under the Mecca and Jasmine names.

More recently the Tottenham Palace has been converted to a church. As it is well looked after, with the plasterwork well worth seeing, conversion back to theatre use could be a possibility. Maybe the central pediment could one day be reinstated. It is one of only a handful of large suburban Variety houses still standing.

Talbot O'Farrell

The Rexanos, well-known balancing act

Walham Green: Granville Theatre of Varieties

Fulham Broadway

Walham Green, Granville Theatre of Varieties: exterior with 'This Is The Show' billed

The Granville was one of Frank Matcham's smaller gems, opening on 19th Septtember, 1898. Various capacities have been quoted for the house – 1,122 or 737 – but my understanding is that it held 779 in stalls, dress circle and gallery. The site, bounded by Vanston Place, Jervan Place and Fulham Broadway, was so small that there was no room for boxes in the auditorium, the sides of the tiled circles extending almost to the proscenium arch. The stage itself was only about 10ft deep when built, although it was extended in 1926 to 30ft, when two shops and offices at the rear, belonging to Bastings Ltd., were acquired for conversion.

The Granville was developed by Dan Leno and Herbert Campbell and operated in conjunction with the Clapham Grand. Other directors were Harry Randall, Henry Joyner, Fred Williams and G.E.S. Venner; the General Manager of both theatres being Jesse Sparrow. Several of these names are also linked to Camberwell Palace and Croydon Empire.

The opening weekly bill was topped by Dan Leno, who then very generously held himself over for the following two weeks! Other well-known artistes to appear there in later years included Gus Elen,

George Robey, Marie Lloyd, Arthur Roberts, Tom Costello and Harry Champion. After the initial Campbell-Leno-Randall management, which ended with the deaths of the two former in 1904, the Granville passed through many hands and, because it was such a small theatre, found it difficult to compete with the much larger surrounding theatres – Fulham, Chelsea, Putney and the three theatres in Hammersmith. As a result it was, for most of its time, a number-two hall. Nevertheless, entertaining Variety bills and revues were presented each week. Many of the bigger names seen on the Granville's stage were past their prime – although there were exceptions, such as Gracie Fields, Naughton & Gold and Marie Loftus.

In January, 1905, under the managership of A.J. Barclay, a crowded and rather foreign-sounding bill was presented. Topping was Percy Murray's company in *An Affair of Honour*, supported by the popular Lottie Lennox. The other acts were: Three Faues, Zanfretti & Napio, Willie Benn, Jessie Albini, Booker & Narbis, George Mackney, Mezzetti & Mora, Lawrence Barclay, The McConnell Family, not forgetting Harry Edson and his dog, Doc.

A bill of August, 1914 included the names of Fred Russell and The Atlas Vulcana Troupe, while another bill of 1915, under the managership of George Clare, included the name of Archie Pitt – later to be married to Gracie Fields. Artistes appearing during WW1 included Sam Stern, Fred Stone, Coverdale, Maxwell Carew, Winnie Wayne, Five Bombays, Wee Mat Dance and Raglus, the 'Champion Ball Bouncer' – well, it was a number two!

Things did not improve much once hostilities ended; for example, Will Collinson & Co. topped a bill in April, 1921 which also had Clark Sisters & Jenkins, Hugh Ogilvie, Lily Flexmore, Gaston Morel, Harvey & Courtney, Aggie Nolan and Billy Fry in the company. As elsewhere, revues became the rage through the 1920s and 30s, titles including *Hot and Bothered* (what a name for a summer show), *Ladies & Laughter* and *All You Wish Yourself*. A strong Variety bill with Larry Kemble, Tom Leamore, Claire Ruane, Sam Linfield and Charlie Higgins ('A Fool if only he knew it') broke the pattern in May, 1929.

Interior towards the circles

The deepening of the stage in 1926 allowed bigger and more extravagant shows to visit, especially as larger dressing rooms were built. Most of the work was done while the theatre was actually operating, the old back wall being taken down during a single week's closure. The circle was also re-seated and some re-carpeting carried out. While the stalls seats at the Granville were tip-ups, those in the dress circle were fixed and gallery patrons had to make do with carpet-covered steps. An orchestra of six was normally in the pit, conducted by Scarsfield O'Dwyer. Audiences may not have had a chance to see the great personalities in their prime, but often welcomed them as "old-timers", as shown on the 1935 bill in the colour section.

A notable show was toured by the actor and director Peter Cotes, appearing at the Walham Green house for the week of 14th April, 1939. Nora Ford, 'The Max Miller Girl', made a firm impression – Miller then being at the height of his powers. Veteran artistes appearing on another Revival show in 1940 included Wilkie Bard, Billy Merson, Rosie Lloyd and Vivian Foster, the 'Vicar of Mirth'. Variety continued during the early part of WW2, with J. Rowland Sales and Bernard Delfont among others who briefly guided the Granville's fortunes. The latter presented Flanagan & Allen, then very big names, on a bill in 1942.

Al Podesta and his Playboys and the number-manipulator, N'gai, were strong draws around this time, but the theatre was unusual in losing ground during the normally busy war years. In fact it had become a straight playhouse before peace was declared.

A.A. Shenburn, of Regis Theatres, took over the running in 1942. A repertory policy was introduced for a time, before a season of *Grand Guignol* was presented in 1945. The short, horrific dramas drew in curious audiences from the West End for a few months, before straight plays returned. These were normally put on for a run, usually three weeks. In 1946 I saw Renee Ray in *Patricia's Seven Houses*, part of a memorable season at the Granville. The Irish-born actor Richard Leach had his first London parts there that year, appearing in *Marrowbone* as a house surgeon: ironically, he had given up medicine to go on the boards!

Plays gave way to Variety again in about 1948, although there were odd weeks when other attractions took the stage – The Ballet Negres playing a week in 1949. The autumn of the following year saw two well-known producers trying their luck: the first was Terry Cantor, who presented and appeared as comic in *Venus Goes Gay*, with Dorothy Black, the dancers Morgan & Gray, The Flying Renoes and, of course, the girl currently playing Miss Venus herself. The second producer was Hylda Baker, who presented *Red Hot & Saucy* with Gus Morris, Ricky Morecambe, Jackie Wilson and Ronnie Coyles, who later made quite a name for himself in Summer Show and Pantomime.

The Granville was now (like Collins' Music Hall), a number-three house, notorious for shows such as *Don't Point – It's Nude*, *The Jane Show* and *This Is The Show*. How on earth did they get that one past the local Watch Committee? The death of the theatre's owner led to its closure in 1956, the final show being *Kiss Us Goodbye*. In its last years the theatre was billed as 'A Little Corner of Paris' – the corner in question being Montmartre, of course.

Tearful regrets were expressed from the stage at the end of the final Saturday night, interrupted by a member of the audience, who shouted: "What about the cinemas closing?" The theatre was turned into a commercial television studio, where equipment was demonstrated. A floor was constructed out over the stalls, with control rooms in the circle, but apparently the stage rake remained. The studio was not a great success.

Interior showing tiles

While the exterior of the building decayed badly, patched with brick where decorative details had fallen to pieces, the wonderful interior of the theatre somehow survived. The entire auditorium was faced in Royal Doulton coloured faience tiling, enabling it to be washed down easily and leading to Dan Leno's description of 'these Sanitary Varieties' at its official opening back in 1898.

All of this was suddenly destroyed over the weekend of 30th September, 1971, when developers ordered a demolition ball to be dropped through the roof, fearing opposition to their plans. The site stood empty for some years, before an office block was built there. However, the sad loss of the Granville led to a thorough reappraisal of remaining old theatres, with many more becoming listed buildings as a result. Some pieces of the coloured tiling were rescued from the wreckage.

Thanks to Norman Fenner, John Bradbury and John Earl for their additional reminiscences.

Walthamstow Palace

High Street, Walthamstow

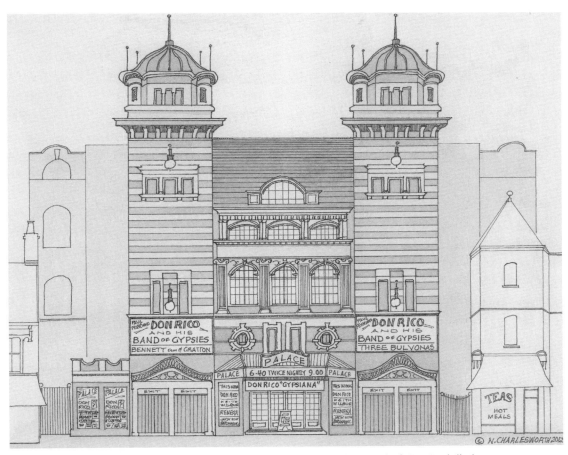

Walthamstow Palace: exterior with Don Rico and his Band of Gypsies billed

One of the Syndicate Halls, the Walthamstow Palace was developed and opened in 1903 by Walthamstow Palace Ltd. The following year Variety Theatres Consolidated Ltd. (VTC) was formed to gather all the constituent parts of The Syndicate Halls.

Although there was already The King's Theatre in Hoe Street and regular concerts at the Baths, the local population of over 100,000 provided great potential for another popular theatre. The Palace seated 1,625 in stalls, dress circle, gallery and boxes. The directors included George Adney Payne, Henri Gros and Henry Tozer – names familiar from The Metropolitan and a string of some twelve London halls at that time.

The features remembered from the brick-and-stone exterior were two prominent towers crowned with stone and metal turrets, which sported flag poles at the centre and spikes at the corners. We do not have a picture of the interior of the theatre, so that I regret that I cannot provide an illustration. But we know that the decoration was quite lavish, with a colour scheme in red, white and gold, with crimson velvet hangings. There were two private boxes on either side of the proscenium. The proscenium arch was 30ft 4ins wide and 24ft high, the stage was 25ft deep; there were eight single dressing rooms and 35 sets of hemp lines. In 1946 it maintained a resident orchestra of nine: piano, bass, clarinet, trombone, trumpet, drum, two violins plus a conductor – pretty typical of its time. The architects were Wylson & Long, who designed the majority of halls for this circuit.

The general manager, Arthur J. Barclay, a former actor, had managed The Granville in Walham Green, for five years prior to his appointment to Walthamstow. On the opening programme for the week of 27 December, 1903 were Fred Karno's Company, Harriet Fawn, Harry Bancroft, Silent Tait, Frank Seeley, Esmé Gordon, Arden & Abel, Lambert & Glover, The Lavender Troupe and The Allisons.

The total artistes' bill for the week came to £133 0s 0d, nearly half of which went to Karno's Company, who were retained for the second week; they returned in November. By the third week of the Palace's life Raymond's Pictures appeared on the bill. Big names welcomed during that first year included Fred Russell, J.W. Rickaby, Lily Flexmore, Capt. Slingsby, Wilson Hallett, Jack Pleasants, My Fancy and The Lancashire Lads.

Not considered by those in the profession as prestigious as some Syndicate Halls, Walthamstow Palace nonetheless did offer over the years Marie Lloyd, Harry Lauder, Eugene Stratton, Vesta Victoria, Gus Elen and many others. *National Sunday League Concerts* were presented here regularly and at the first one, in 1904, the chief performers were The Band of The Coldstream Guards.

Although the rise of the cinema in the 1920s and 30s caused many Variety theatres to be 'wired for sound', the Walthamstow Palace managed to hold its own, albeit by staging revues, musical comedies and even plays some weeks. Among these were Grossmith & Laurilard's *Potash and Perlmutter*, *The Silver King*, the popular *Love On the Dole*, *Lady Luck* and a run of Edgar Wallace thrillers.

A true Variety bill for the week of 10 January, 1930 was topped by Gertie Gitana, with seven supporting acts: Hayden, Nevard & Wheldon; Bob Fisher; Jean Kennedy; The Rodney Hudson Troupe; Cyril & May; Phil & Phlora; and Barry Ono.

The same decade brought Macari and his Dutch Serenaders and Don Rico and his Band of Gypsies, each heading a full Variety bill; other headliners included Horace Goldin and Linga Singh & Company. Productions staged were *Beauties of Paris*, *Lights Out at Eleven* and *This Way Please*. The years of WW2 brought the real decline of the Palace, although there were still good shows among the lesser offerings. The manager for many years was Harry Loss, brother of bandleader Joe Loss – who, of course, headlined a number of times at Walthamstow. Other musicians who entertained here included Carl Barriteau, Harry Parry and – the longest-running bandshow of the halls – Billy Cotton's.

Re-opening after a period of closure, the Walthamstow Palace staged the revue *United Notions* with principal comedian Mark Rivers for the week of 10 April, 1944. Variety fan Dick Playle lived locally and attended the Palace regularly, until he went away to the army for two years in 1948. In his absence the decline continued. Many of the bills were headed in press advertisements by just one big name – Issy Bonn & Co., Suzette Tarri & Co., or 'Hutch' and supporting Variety bill. A successful week was that of 21 April, 1948 when Robbie Vincent, Harry Korris and Cecil Frederick appeared in the big radio feature, *Happidrome*. Another big draw was Don Ross' *Thanks For The Memory* in 1949, which gave local audiences a chance to appreciate the polished talents of real stars – G.H. Elliott, Gertie Gitana, Ella Shields, Lily Morris, Randolph Sutton, Talbot O'Farrell and Billy Danvers. The momentum lasted through to the following week, when Elsie & Doris Waters pulled them in.

Circuses were certainly popular at the Palace; they had taken to theatre stages during WW2 when touring a tented show became difficult. Don Ross' Royal Imperial Circus was billed to appear for the week of 2 April, 1948. However, the show was lost in a big fire on its way to Walthamstow and *Naughty Girls of 1948* was hastily substituted. Erskine Road, near the Palace, had access to the lane at the side of the theatre; animal cages and stables were set up here when a circus played at the theatre, or when ponies had to be kept for productions of *Cinderella*.

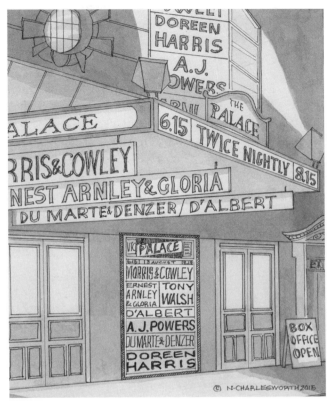

Exterior under canopy (second house just gone in), 13.8.1948

Plays had replaced Variety shortly before the end of the war and in the week the war ended the theatre was presenting *A Soldier for Christmas*. The Countess de la Marr had taken an interest in the Palace at this time. After a period in which shows had become poorly-attended and – in the words of one local couple – even sleazy, an attempt to establish repertory was made, with well-known pieces like *Jane Eyre* and *Tobacco Road*, but the response was very disappointing with only a handful of people in the large auditorium.

The Walthamstow Palace then had one final shot at Variety; one of the last stars appearing was the one and only Max Miller, but even he could not turn the tide. The theatre closed in 1954 and remained boarded up with greengrocers' boxes heaped against its doors. In 1957 the VTC circuit was then bought by the Granada Group and demolition followed in 1960 – dashing local hope of its reopening as a municipal theatre. A parade of modern shops then took its place.

Walthamstow Palace had its own artesian well for water supply, as did one or two other local business, including a large dairy; but careful readings had to be taken and consumption accounted for or there would be arguments with its other users. There was a Carnival Night each week, in common with most London Variety theatres after WW2. Regulars recall prizes being thrown to the audience from an oval wicker basket; especially remembered are the jars of green Brilliantine. The Spot Prize was another regular favourite, but tended to be won by the same girl each week; her boyfriend worked the follow-spot and was advised before the show where the girl would be sitting. The spot somehow seemed to fall on her each time!

ARTISTE.	Contract No.	No. of P'forms.	Salary.			AGENT.	Agent's Commission 7½ per cent.		Palace Commission 2½ per cent.		Total Commission.		Remarks
Harriet Fawn			4	10		Fortune & Granville	6	9	2	3	9		
Harry Bancroft			4	10		Fortune & Granville	6	9	2	3	9		
Silent Tait			8			George Barclay	12		4		16		
Frank Seeley			10			George Barclay	15		5		1		
Esmé Gordon			5			T. Shaw	7	6	2	6	10		
Arden & Abel			10			Direct	(nett)		–	–	–		
Lambert & Glover			10			T. Higham	15		5		1		
Lavender Troupe			11			T. Higham	16	6	5	6	1	2	
F. Karno's Co.			60			Direct	(nett)		–	–	–		
The Allisons			10			T. Shaw	15		5		1		
			£133				4	14 6	1	11 6	6	6	

Walthamstow Palace: The Commission Sheet for the opening week of 2 January, 1904

Dewert, cycling gymnast

Wilton's Music Hall (The Old Mahogany Bar)

Grace's Alley, Wellclose Square, near Tower Hill

Whitechapel, Wilton's Music Hall: exterior in the 1930s

The first occasion in modern times when Wilton's Music Hall came to the public consciousness was in 1964, when two members of The British Music Hall Society discovered that it was still standing. By that time it was in use as a rag warehouse and an L.C.C. planning scheme for the area threatened its continued existence; this was opposed by the Society at a public enquiry, resulting in a preservation order and the later purchase of the premises by the G.L.C., as the L.C.C. had by then become. Members Ray Mackender, John Earl, Ellis Ashton and John Betjeman all exerted pressure for a stay of execution.

The Prince of Denmark public house had opened in 1830 and its first proprietor added a concert room which later became the Albion Saloon, a minor theatre where Jack-a-shore could enjoy the bloodthirsty melodramas popular at the time. (A glance at a street map will show how close to the Thames the theatre is.) According to John Earl of The Theatres Trust, The Prince of Denmark tavern was reputedly the first in London to have mahogany counters and fittings, hence its alternative name, which stuck to it for well over a century, of Old Mahogany Bar. But John Wilton and his wife Ellen, who took over in 1850, followed the example of Charles Morton at the Canterbury and converted the saloon into a music hall. Its success justified his adding a balcony in 1853. In 1858 Ellen laid the foundation stone of Wilton's Music Hall, running at right angles to the old saloon, and in essence this is the hall as it stands today. The architect is thought to have been Jacob Maggs.

Main entrance doors

Programmes at Wilton's did not change weekly, as at later music halls and Variety theatres: many artistes were engaged for weeks, or even months, but with sufficiently frequent changes to maintain interest. The vocal department was of the highest importance in those early days, and most bills consisted of a soprano, a mezzo, a tenor, two baritones and a bass, augmented by comic singers and specialities.

The first stars were Sam Cowell, W.G. Ross and Charles Sloman, who owed their fame to the Song & Supper Rooms, but soon the proliferating music halls were producing their own stars. There was E.W. Mackney, the first coon delineator; Sam Collins, the Irish ex-chimney sweep who built Collins' Music Hall and J.H. Stead (of 'The Cure'). On the distaff side were the serio-comics – Annie Adams, Jenny Hill, Nellie Power, and one who was a great Wilton's favourite although neglected by most historians, Georgina Smithson.

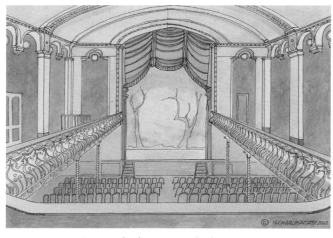

Interior looking towards the stage

Then came the Lions Comiques – handsome Harry Clifton, Arthur Lloyd, G.H. Macdermott, The Great Vance and, most famous of all, George Leybourne. And in support there were Ethiopian entertainers, dancers like the ubiquitous D'Aubans, and speciality acts of all categories. Variety was already becoming international, for Wilton in his diary gives a detailed account of the performance of a Portuguese wire-walker, Don José Manuel.

All the great names of the first three decades of music hall made their entrances. Dan Leno, as a boy clog dancer, and Herbert Campbell both appeared at Wilton's long before their triumphs at Theatre Royal, Drury Lane. At the age of nineteen Harry Rickards did a trial turn 'with some success': he was later to become Australia's leading Variety impresario, opening Tivoli Theatres everywhere. There are revealing facts among Wilton's writing – Leybourne was the first to break the £100 barrier, working turns – and on disputes about rights to songs. And there are sad records of the early deaths of so many. The first ever performance of the Can-Can in London was reputedly staged here – and was promptly banned.

In December, 1872 John Wilton, having opened a West End restaurant, sold the lease and the hall fell into other hands, although he remained proprietor and never lost interest in its fortunes. By 1874 the property was operating as Frederick's Royal Palace of Varieties. After a disastrous fire in 1877 it was restored, but too late even for William Holland, who had succeeded Charles Morton at the Canterbury, to restore its fortunes. It closed in 1880. The Old Mahogany Bar was considered to be a public house bar with the usual licensing hours. Other bars in the building were restricted to the theatre or restaurant patrons at the hall.

The hall was a Mission from 1888 to 1956, after which it became the rag warehouse which the B.H.M.S. members first entered in 1964. That same year saw the loss of another early hall, The Star in Abbey Street, Bermondsey. Wilton's own future looked distinctly uncertain, as this extract from an L.C.C. Architect's Department shows:

> "I agree that Wilton's Music Hall is of some historic interest, but it is in an area where redevelopment is likely to take place in the near future. It is unlikely that the council would feel justified in preserving Wilton's if this would prejudice the proper redevelopment of the area. In the event of the building being demolished, full records would be made for publication in The Survey of London".

Interior from the stalls

In the event, all the surrounding old buildings were cleared, but Wilton's survived. In 1985 Peter Honri's fine book 'John Wilton's Music Hall' was published after a labour of love lasting two decades. He was responsible for the plans for the rehabilitation of the building, not only as a working Variety theatre but also as a school for the teaching of the Variety arts.

On 15 December, 1972 a non-profit-distributing trust was set up to acquire a lease on the hall; sadly, a shortage of funds hampered a full restoration of Wilton's (including the Danish Embassy and a marvellous row of Essex clap-board cottages), but it was hoped that one day this would be taken seriously. Together with McDonald's in Hoxton High Street, this is an exceptional survivor of the early days of music hall in London. In the meantime, despite its fragile condition, the hall has occasionally been open to the public for live entertainments and tours. It has also been used for filming from time to time.

Rear of the building in the 1970s

In the 1990s Fiona Shaw appeared in her acclaimed reading of T.S. Eliot's *The Waste Land* when stalls and balcony were once again filled with appreciative audiences. A memorable talk was given by Colin Sorensen, entitled *Seeking Miss Beesley*. She had been a student teacher who appeared at his primary school with a model theatre: for Sorensen this was the beginning of a lifelong passion for theatres. Sorensen was a graphic designer devoted to Victorian London and old theatres. He was the first Keeper of the Modern Collection at the Museum of London. His great-grandfather had come to England from Denmark in the 1860s; Sorensen died in 2001, much missed.

Finally, a tenant was found in the form of Broomhill Opera, who took a long lease in 1999. Under its proprietor and General Director, Mark Dornford-May, regular performances were at last being given at Wilton's Music Hall; the theatre is very handy for the City of London now that the Mermaid Theatre is out of use as a playhouse. Broomhill Opera opened on 29 March, 1999 with *Silverlake* in a new translation by the German-speaking satirist, Rory Bremner.

The British Music Hall Society held a three-day Festival of Music Hall and Variety at Wilton's in September, 2013, to celebrate its Golden Jubilee. There were exhibitions, stalls and twenty-seven hours of entertainment, with artistes as diverse as Ken Dodd, Wyn Calvin, Roy Hudd, Vincent Hayes, June Whitfield, Peter John, Victoria Wood, Freddie Davies, Jools Holland, Jan Hunt, Andy Eastwood, Michael Pearse and Ruth Madoc on stage. There were fascinating talks, including one by Sir John Major about his father – Tom Major-Ball – who was a music hall performer, as well as a steady stream of music from dawn to dusk.

With its 'barley sugar' cast-iron columns, bombé-fronted balcony, tall proscenium arch and high stage, now well restored, the hall merits its epithet, 'The Handsomest Room in Town'. A bar previously opened from the pub into the hall at stage left, but this has long gone. As we go to press, a wonderful restoration has been completed on the other houses to the front of the hall. Do not miss an opportunity to be part of an audience at this amazing theatre!

It must be noted that 'John Wilton's Diary' included in *John Wilton's Music Hall* was an invention of the author Peter Honri.

Willesden Hippodrome

High Street, Harlesden

Willesden Hippodrome: exterior with Scott & Whaley billed, 7.11.1938

Originally planned as Willesden Empire, the Matcham-designed Hippodrome which opened on Monday, 16 September, 1907 was actually in Harlesden! The large theatre initially seated over 3,000, but in 1927, when its policy changed temporarily to Ciné-variety, this was reduced to 2,400. The lofty building, with its pitched roof and towering lantern, could easily be seen from the dome of St. Paul's Cathedral; it had a passing family likeness to the Empires at Wood Green and Chiswick, both opened five years later. The theatre backed onto Rocklidge Avenue.

There had been an earlier proposal to build a Willesden Theatre & Assembly Rooms, with an architect's drawing by Robert F. Hodges, A.R.I.B.A., being published in *The Willesden Chronicle* on 24 July, 1903. However, the projected 1,600-seater building was never started and the people of the expanding districts of Willesden, Harlesden and Kensal Rise had to wait a further four years for their much-needed theatre and music hall.

Under the managership of Percy H. Gallagher, later at The New Theatre & Hippodrome, Northampton, the Willesden Hippodrome's opening bill was topped by the rising star George Robey, with vocalist Annie Laurie, comedian Chris Richards and comedienne Katie Marsh among the extensive company; George Robey returned later with *The Bing Boys*.

Nearly every notable star of the Variety world appeared on the well-equipped Hippodrome stage over the following few years, including the young Noel Coward in a playlet on a suburban tour as part of a Variety bill. It was only a few years before the theatre was absorbed by the fast-growing London Theatres of Varieties circuit (LTV), under whom it prospered for some seventeen years – first under Walter Gibbons and, later, Charles Gulliver. Gibbons of course considered that a lot of London suburban Variety houses were poorly run and maintained; managing to acquire many of them at attractive prices and building up a powerful circuit centred on the newly-built London Palladium and rebuilt Holborn Empire.

The LTV management had to book a mixture of attractions to feed the hungry circuit, so Variety was not the only entertainment presented; when it was, artistes often doubled with a nearby circuit hall, such as Putney Hippodrome. The great Charles Coborn wowed the Willesden audiences for a week in August, 1914, as did Violet Lorraine, Harry Lauder and Harry Tate in subsequent weeks. Among Harry Day's many revues was *Made In England*, with a supporting bill including Victor Travers, Eddie Gray and The Moray & Bobby Trio. Other presenters of revue were Bleriot with *The Man In The Moon* and Fred Wardin and Karl Hooper with *Five Nights*. The theatre was later used for orchestral concerts.

West End actor Seymour Hicks was not averse to appearing at a London suburban hall: he and Isobel Elsom appeared for a week in July, 1918 in *The Bridal Suite*. Old-timers Marie Kendall and Austin Rudd delighted crowded houses on the same bill, together with David Poole, Norman Field, Betancourt, Mollie Butler and Doc Campbell. Perhaps a typical Willesden bill was a 1921 offering which was topped by Betty Barclay & George Glover, with Sam Mayo, The New McNaughtons, Ristori & Partner, George Gilbey, Oswald Bemand, Ted Marcelle and Daisy Stratton providing great entertainment value.

Following the crash of the LTV circuit in 1924, Willesden Hippodrome was bought and renovated by Sidney Bernstein and run as a cinema for just over ten years. There was an Opening Ceremony on 16 September, 1927, after which the theatre was known as Harlesden New Hippodrome: this was to avoid confusion with Bernstein's existing Willesden Empire cinema. The Hippodrome offered one or two acts between the films. In July, 1928, for example, there was a typical split-week with The U.S.A. Three, followed by The Ten O'Shea Girls and Terry. Later that year there was another split week, when Stanelli & Edgar appeared for three days, followed by Blondie Hartley for the rest of the December week.

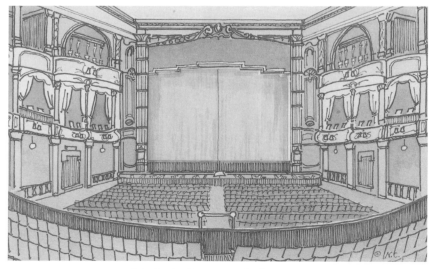

Interior looking towards the stage

Bernstein Theatres reduced the number of cinemas offering live acts from 1929, although the houses booking them did increase the number of acts booked. Nevertheless, the crash of LTV (and the wiring for sound of countless other halls) drastically reduced the good dates available to Variety artistes. Bernstein's more modern Willesden Empire was the one chosen in the district to stage live acts.

Unexpectedly, Variety returned to the Hippodrome in 1938, when it joined the expanding circuit of B. & J. Theatres; this was managed by Harry Joseph and J. Idris Lewis, who also operated Lewisham Hippodrome. Harry Joseph also ran Leeds City Varieties, later concentrating his theatrical activities there.

Willesden Hippodrome reopened with a great flourish on Monday, 31 October, 1938 with an Overture written by Eric Coates (The Knightsbridge March from *In Town Tonight*), a Fanfare and an Opening Ceremony by the Mayor and Mayoress of Willesden. Following the National Anthem, the packed audience enjoyed a first-rate nine-act bill. As shown on the programme kindly loaned by Terry Lomas, the tops were Troise and his Mandoliers and Elsie & Doris Waters, then enjoying huge popularity on the wireless. Comedy clearly dominated the programme; leaving audiences in no doubt that hilarity would dispel the threatening war clouds in the area. Nixon & Morrison from Canada, Cliff Cook and Murray & Mooney provided the laughs, while young dancers, a miniature Circus, a "Phantasy in Smoke" and Swan & Leigh's "thrills without spills" backed the two big bill-toppers.

Quality shows followed that opening week, with Scott & Whaley, Phyllis Robins and The Two Leslies appearing the next week. Fred Bentham, the lighting artist and engineer, clearly remembered being taken by his father to the Willesden Hippodrome whenever a play was presented. There he saw productions such as *Alf's Button*, *The Flag Lieutenant* and Edgar Wallace's *The Ringer*. His family tended to see any Variety acts at the Shepherds Bush Pavilion. In his book, *Sixty Years of Light Work*, he remembered entering the theatre underground, emerging into the stalls from the centre vomitory and seeing all the people massed up behind. Equally awe-inspiring was the change over between houses with crowds getting in and out at the same time.

Sadly, the theatre's renewed success was brought to an abrupt close when it received a direct hit; on 2 October, 1940 – a German bomb destroying the stage end of the theatre, putting paid to any possible revival until hostilities ended. The Willesden Hippodrome enjoyed a sort of twilight existence, still retaining its entertainment licence, for a decade. Then, in November, 1950 it was announced in *The Performer* that the Middlesex authorities had decided not to renew the licence, as no attempt had yet been made at reconstruction. After standing derelict for several more years, the rotting structure was demolished in 1957.

I suppose that, without the bombing, live shows could have continued into the early 1950s, with a possible return to films for a few more years until the television threat appeared. This is what happened at Lewisham Hippodrome, but both theatres were really unsuitable as cinemas, with their overhanging boxes and vast galleries; projection from distant spot-boxes led to distortion on steeply-angled screens. In the event, Willesden Hippodrome gave way to government offices, which opened in 1958, and the area lost a valued asset.

Fatima Zohra, novel contortionist

Wood Green Empire

High Road, Wood Green, N22

Wood Green Empire: exterior in the High Road with Harry Tate billed

Whilst living in Finchley, my 'local' hall was Wood Green Empire and I went there more than to any other Variety theatre. It was a much friendlier theatre than Finsbury Park Empire, which I felt took itself rather too seriously. To me the Wood Green Empire represented the last word in luxury – the red upholstered seats, the eight boxes which, especially when occupied, gave the large auditorium the intimacy which more modern theatres lack, the huge dome, the gorgeous curves of Frank Matcham's circles, the clusters of electric lights, the cream-and-gold decor and Shakespeare's words above the arch: 'All the world's a stage'.

The Empire opened on 9 September, 1912 with Tottenham Palace, Finsbury Park Empire and Edmonton Empire already well-established. The opening bill set the pattern to be followed throughout the theatre's history – two good tops and seven other acts plus the Bioscope. The stars were Guy Standing in *The Blackmailer* and The Great Rameses. The magician was born as Albert Machinski in Russia in 1876, of Jewish parentage; through marriage he was related to Maurice Fogel. Another early bill-topper, this time from musical comedy, was Marie Studholme. In fact, Wood Green Empire was never purely a music hall, much of its time being devoted to plays and musical comedies. Among the Variety stars who headed bills during that first season were Albert Chevalier, Whit Cunliffe, G.H. Elliott, Joe Elvin, Will Evans and many other 'greats' Even in those early days there was no room for complacency, for within fifteen months of the Empire's opening three cinemas also opened in the immediate vicinity.

Early in 1914 the main entrance on Wood Green High Road was opened, leading to greatly increased patronage. The 'firework display' of coloured lights over the canopy provided entertainment for patrons waiting for their trams home. The arrival of revue made for fuller use of the large 37ft. deep stage. In *Splash Me!* for instance, 20,000 gallons of water and thirty girls were employed. The early revues were dressed-up versions of the comedy sketch, which continued to flourish with Fred Emney in *A Sister to Assist 'Er*, Charles Austin in the *Parker PC* sketches, Harry Tate in *Fishing* and *Motoring* and Alfred Lester in *The Village Fire Brigade*.

The outbreak of WW1 saw no deterioration in the quality of programmes. Patriotic spectacles were no novelty on the halls, but now gained added significance. Charles Austin had a sketch, *Parker Captures the K....r* (no prizes for supplying the missing letters) and Hetty King sang 'When Women do the Work of Men'. But apart from *Kiss Me Sergeant*, the revues of 1915 kept to such non-military titles as *The Red Heads* and *Don't Tempt Me*. The stars of Variety continued to headline bills. On one great bill there were four comics: Will Evans, Jack Lane, Alfred Lester and Ernie Mayne.

Auditorium from the rear stalls

The year 1916 saw the imposition of Entertainments Tax – truly an example of the thin edge of the wedge. At first this 'temporary' measure exacted only 1d from gallery and pit patrons and 2d from stalls and circle ones. It increased with time and remained a crushing burden for over forty years. Another event was the strike of Stoll musicians. Top-liners of 1916 included Betty Barclay, Chirgwin,

May Moore Duprez, Olga, Elgar & Eli Hudson and Charles R. Whittle with his topical song 'Let's have the Lights up in London'. Revues, now occupying the full bill, included Ralph Lynn in *Peaches*, Stanley Lupino in *Girl Wanted* and Jimmy Learmouth in *Look Who's Here*. The following year, 1917, brought Whit Cunliffe singing 'Good Old Salisbury Plain'. Revues included de Courville's *Good Bye-ee* and the most famous ever, *The Bing Boys are Here*. New names at the top were Datas the Memory Man, May Henderson and Lorna & Toots Pounds. In 1918 the management brought the war-weary audiences sketches like Fred Karno's *Mumming Birds* and the topical military musical *The Lads of the Village*, which played two separate weeks. A cloud was cast over the theatre by the death on the stage of Chung Ling Soo.

It is a remarkable fact that pre-war prices remained unchanged, apart from tax, until September, 1919, when the circle became 1s, the balcony 6d and gallery 4d. Wilkie Bard, Du Calion, Queenie Leighton and Wish Wynne were some of the attractions that year. A revue with a war-time flavour was Lew Lake's *Sons of the Sea*. Indeed the early 1920s saw revues grow steadily more spectacular. *The Circus Queen*, for instance, included a horse-race and a complete circus on the stage. These revues brought a crop of new comedians, notably George Clarke, Bert Coote and Gracie Fields. Some also made names in the West End, including Syd Howard, Arthur Riscoe, Gene Gerrard and Gertrude Lawrence. A somewhat ominous sign was a revue whose title was *Listening In*. The folk singers Muriel George and Ernest Butcher made several appearances, but the novelty of Pattman and his Mammoth Organ was soon lost by duplication in scores of super cinemas.

Marie Lloyd, a regular at Wood Green Empire, died in 1922. However, others in the great tradition, like Fred Barnes, Will Fyffe and Talbot O'Farrell were now established stars. War-time humour lived on in Tommy Handley's *The Disorderly Room*. Song writer Leslie Stuart made appearances in the flesh in 1923, a year which closed with Lily Morris playing in a lavish once nightly pantomime, which included a traditional Harlequinade. In the mid 1920s performances were at 6.20 and 8.35pm (while Finsbury Park's were at 6.50 and 9.00pm). Plays and musical comedies became more frequent, Macdonald and Young being responsible for many of the latter, but revues were beginning to run out of ideas – an exception being Albert Burdon in *On the Dole*. Successful West End plays included Matheson Lang in *The Bad Man* and several Aldwych farces.

Auditorium seen from a stage box

Bands were now firmly established. One of the first to go into Variety was The London Sonora Band, but now the names of Jack Hylton, Debroy Somers and Alfredo were to the fore. Old and newer names to appear at Wood Green Empire were Kate Carney, Florence Smithson, Dorothy Ward, Billy Bennett, The Houston Sisters and George Formby, as well at Jack Gallagher, Nor Kiddie and, most popular of all in the suburbs, Ernie Lotinga. The worst was feared when, in the summer of 1929, the theatre was wired for sound. Projectors were installed in a new box on the top tier, which was re-seated. The theatre re-opened in August with the epoch-making Jolson movie, *The Singing Fool*. But after three separate fortnights of films, live shows returned. Twice-nightly plays appeared more frequently, those of Edgar Wallace being especially popular. Musical comedies like *Sunny* and *No, No, Nanette* still drew, but if straight Variety bills were fewer, there was no decline in quality. Typical was a bill that I saw headed by José Collins (who sang the Jewel Song from *Faust*). She was supported by Sam Barton, Harry Champion and Ernest Shannon.

On 26 March, 1930 a man committed suicide in the theatre. Then in January, 1931 films reappeared, firstly as part of Ciné-Variety presentations (in one of which Lew Grade danced), but by August double-featured film programmes had driven the live performer from the stage – in many such cases theatres were lost for all time. Fortunately, Wood Green Empire remained under Sir Oswald Stoll, whose roots were in the music hall. When it became clear that the talkies had not killed Variety, he lost little time in converting his theatres back to their original use. Live shows returned on 30 August, 1937 with Joe Loss and his Band, with Nellie Arnaud & Brothers, Olsen's Sea Lions, Morris & Cowley and The Three Jokers. However, Ernie Lotinga's topical revue, *Sanctions*, indicated that storm clouds were on the horizon. A hit of The Royal Variety Show that year, Revnell & West, did great business, sharing top with Leon Cortez and his Coster Pals.

Popular radio stars were Florence Desmond, Cyril Fletcher, Hutch, Charlie Kunz and Vic Oliver, while bill-topping bands included those of George Elrick, Ken 'Snakehips' Johnson and Lou Praeger. Revues had become less lavish, although Wm. C. Doorlay's *Tropical Express*, with seventy-one artistes and one-hundred-and-one scenes, was retained for a second week! Variety's international character was maintained by The Australian Air Aces, Dante the magician, The Duncan Sisters, Eddie Peabody and The Quintette du Hot Club de France. Strangely, Wood Green Empire continued to be unlucky for magicians, apart from Chung Ling Soo. In 1937 the American illusionist Russell Swann was unable to complete his week after officials called to see his permit; while in 1939 Horace Goldin died after opening at the Empire the previous night.

Exterior of the Lymington Avenue frontage, while used as a TV studio

The difficulty of securing sufficient good tops – and the lack of a drinking licence – led to a two-month repertory season in the summer of 1939, but all places of entertainment closed on the outbreak of WW2. The theatre reopened in February, 1941, and we began to see pseudo-French revues with titles like *Scandals of 19-Naughty-2* , with bill matter such as 'It's new – it's saucy – ooo-la-la!' A star brought in to strengthen a show would only unbalance it. Road shows had tended to replace revues and stars who found it convenient to tour their own combinations (and give good value for money) included Big Bill Campbell, Gaston & Andrée, Lucan & McShane, Murray and Vic Oliver. Managements whose war-time offerings I remember with particular pleasure are Tom Arnold (Revnell & West in *Looking Ahead*) and Bertram Montague (Caryll & Mundy in *One for the Road*). Bands were still in favour and the managements of Harry Benet, Emile Littler and James Shirvell were responsible for some good musical comedies, mostly revivals. Distinguished bill-toppers not normally seen in Variety included Richard Tauber.

Sid Field had toured for years before he gained stardom, while radio helped Issy Bonn, Michael Howard, Vera Lynn, Hal Monty, Suzette Tarri and Jack Train to the top. War-time affluence helped Variety to boom and Jack Hylton and Prince Littler put big twice daily pantomimes into Wood Green Empire. Theatres quickly raised their standards to their pre-war level, presenting some first-class bills. American acts welcomed back included Borrah Minnevitch, The Deep River Boys and The Three Peters Sisters. Stars like Max Miller, Norman Evans, Harry Lester's Hayseeds and Nat Mills & Bobbie were seen more often than revues. The late 1940s saw the return of first-class productions of shows like *The Dancing Years* and *Song of Norway*. In 1948 the Empire's new amplification system was used to sensational effect by George & Bert Bernard, but the Variety event of the year was Don Ross's *Thanks for the Memory*, for which I was unable to obtain a ticket for any performance.

The word 'television' was now creeping into artistes' bill matter, but the Empire did not despair of Variety, weathering the storm as it had done after the talkies. In 1950 the theatre closed for one week for re-seating, re-carpeting and re-decoration. Strong attractions that year included Prince Littler's *White Horse Inn* with a company of one hundred, Ted Heath and his Music, Charlie Chester's *Stand Easy*, The Carl Rosa Opera Co., The Piddingtons, Allan Jones and Tom Arnold's *Ice Revue*. At Christmas the Empire presented C.B. Cochran's *Bless the Bride* for a three-week season – followed by a fortnight of pantomime; then early the following year a BBC broadcast from Wood Green Empire featured Ethel Revnell and Arthur English. The American film comedian Buster Keaton, since recognised as one of the all-time greats, was an interesting visitor that year.

Attractions of 1952 included *King's Rhapsody*, which played once nightly for a fortnight, and the veterans' show *Do You Remember?* which brought back Turner Layton, Georgie Wood, Albert Whelan, Dick Henderson and Marie Lloyd jnr. A wonderful week's business resulted from Winifred Atwell's heading a bill with strong support from Jack Jackson, Fayne & Evans, The Three Monarchs and Jimmy Wheeler. The following year G.H. Elliott made his farewell tour in *Chocolate and Cream*, while other bill-toppers that year were The Beverley Sisters, Richard Hearne, David Hughes and – still pulling them in on his umpteenth visit – Max Miller.

The year of 1954 was not a vintage one. Once nightly presentations were few, but new names in the Variety firmament included Shirley Bassey, Billy Dainty, Alma Cogan and Frankie Vaughan. Sadly audiences were not there to give them the success they later earned elsewhere, although ticket prices still remained at 1s to 3s 6d. Business had been bad during the autumn of 1954, and unless improvements were made backstage, the Middlesex County Council were unwilling to renew the licence. The local paper blamed falling attendances on the preponderance of radio and recording stars, but discounted the importance of changing social habits. In fact, of course, Wood Green Empire had to the end, offered the best available in all forms of entertainment.

With the balcony closed, it struggled on through Christmas, the last attraction being an excellent once-nightly pantomime, *Cinderella*, with a star cast and a chorus of twenty girls and sixteen juveniles. The theatre finally closed on 31 January, 1955. The theatre never became the resort of seven men watching nudes trying (not very hard) not to move. In its latter years Wood Green Empire was impeccably conducted by George Hoare, son of music hall comedian George Willenor, and later manager and archivist at The Theatre Royal, Drury Lane.

Remaining High Road frontage as it looked in the 1990s

ATV took over the theatre as a television studio, using its large stage for presenting 'spectaculars'. The main street entrance was sold for a dress shop, but the auditorium was well-maintained and was, in fact, re-decorated shortly before ATV unaccountably gave up the tenancy. The auditorium of the Empire, after some years of disuse, was finally demolished in 1970, leaving most of the facade but with its lantern removed. It is, nevertheless, completely recognisable as the old Wood Green Empire entrance. The two adjoining wings, with their small towers, ogée roofs and finials, are still intact. The whole parade, believed to by Frank Matcham, was restored in the early 1990s, encouraged by Haringey Council.

STOLL TOUR.

ALHAMBRA (re., 10).—Delfont Boys, Lupino and Mott, Victoria Girls, Dorrie Dene, Hal Swain's Band, Stanley Holloway, Van Horn and Inez, Three Kiewnings, Reso and Reto.

ARDWICK EMP. (re., 12.30).—"On Parade."

BRISTOL HIPPO. (re., 12.30).—"Young Bloods of Variety."

CHATHAM EMP. (re., 2).—"Mercenary Mary."

CHISWICK EMP. (re., 12).—Sidney Firman and company, Clarkson Rose, Joe Boganny, Moran Sisters and Mammy, Les Storks, Bransby Williams, Kuhn Bros., Rego Twins.

HACKNEY EMP. (re., 12).—"League of Neighbours."

LEICESTER PAL. (re., 12).—Houston Sisters, Leo Sax Trio, Conrad's Pigeons, Shishtl's Wonderettes, Three Pirates, Zellini, Stan Stafford, Christo and Strand.

LONDON COLISEUM (re., 10).—G. H. Elliott, Jim the Bear, Cromwell Knox, Rich and Adair, Ann Penn, Will Morris, Pauline and Diana, Short and Long, Chinese Syncopators, Heather Thatcher and company.

MANCHESTER HIPPO. (re., 10; mats. Monday and Tuesday).—"Clowns in Clover."

SHEPHERD'S BUSH EMP. (re., 12).—"The Bull's Eye."

WOOD GREEN EMP. (re., 12).—"Paris, 1929."

The Stoll Tour as in the week of 24 May, 1929

HALLS SOUTH OF THE THAMES

Balham Hippodrome

Balham Hill, Corner of Yukon Road

Balham Hippodrome: exterior with Jenny Howard and Terry Wilson billed, 1935

Built with enormous confidence on a prime site where Balham Hill House – a red-brick Tudor building – had once stood, the Balham Hippodrome was one of a number of former legitimate playhouses that pursued careers as Variety Theatres after a few years as drama houses. Opening in 1899 as The Royal Duchess Theatre at a cost of £35,000, the theatre was designed by W.G.R. Sprague, who was responsible for many of the delightful small playhouses still open in London's West End.

The opening ceremony was conducted by Charles Wyndham and Miss Mary Moore. The new theatre had a capacity of 1,268 on four levels, although the inflated figure of 2,500 was quoted at its opening: this was quite normal, as it probably included standing room and a benched gallery. The theatre was built by a local man, Walter Wallis of Ramsden Road; the Musical Director at the time was Henry Sprake, while bookings were handled by H.G. Dudley Bennett, of The Shakespeare Theatre, Clapham Junction. A beautiful Act Drop, portraying 'Venus Afloat', was painted by Arthur J. Black, a copy of which was reproduced in Cassell's *The Magazine of Art* in 1900. An illustration of the interior of the theatre is most elusive.

Unusually, the architect himself was licensed to run the theatre until 1903, while another member of the Sprague family – Isabel Katherine – resumed responsibility for two years from 1921. In the early years the Duchess showed mainly Musical Comedy and the first production was *The Geisha* by Messrs. Morell & Mouillet's London Company. This was followed by *The Belle of New York*, *The Circus Girl*, *La Poupée*, *Runaway Girl* and *White Heather*. In June, 1902 Leah Marlborough was said to have broken house records when she starred in *The Sorrows of Satan*.

In 1903, now renamed The Duchess Palace, the theatre was controlled directly by Walter Gibbons, whose growing circuit, London Theatres of Varieties Ltd. at its height consisted of seventeen Variety Theatres in the capital – including The Holborn Empire and The London Palladium. After three years as The Duchess Palace, it became The Balham Hippodrome and was run as a Variety Theatre. A bill for Christmas week of 1909 is preserved in The Mander & Mitchenson Theatre Collection. It is topped by Vesta Victoria ('The People's Idol'), supported by Adele Moraw and Three Laurels, with five other acts, a comedy sketch and The Bioscope. Performances were twice nightly, at 6.45 and 9.10pm; Saturdays tended to over-run, so the first house started fifteen minutes earlier. Prices were from 3d to 1s 6d, with boxes up to 10s 6d. On Boxing Day, instead of a Pantomime, there was a Grand Bioscope Performance, starting at 7.30pm – a sign of things to come in later years; being a Sunday, the performance was held in aid of charity. For the week commencing Monday, 17 August, 1914 the Balham Hippodrome offered Courtice Pounds' *Swankers by the Sea*, supported by Three Laurels, Victoria Campbell, Goodfellow & Gregson (who were doubling LTV's Rotherhithe Hippodrome), Four Powers, George D'Albert, Gordon Murray and company. After the crash of LTV Ltd. the theatre had a chequered career.

The cinema took over the Hippodrome for a period from 1932, a difficult time for the living theatre. Managements around this time included London and Counties Theatres Ltd. (1925–32) and W.G. Arrowsmith (1935–37). During the tenure of the latter, there was a successful return to Variety and Revue around 1935 – presumably because so many purpose-built cinemas had opened locally. The first bill was headed by Leon Cortez and his Coster Pals. That same year Jenny Howard and Percy King headed a strong bill which included Terry Wilson, The Four Aces, Barton & Yorke, Young & Younger, Jeanette Adie, Russell, Marconi & Vernon, Freddy Zay, Matzsuko & Chana, and The Eight Black Streaks. The Hippodrome's manager was F.J. Walsh, while the M.D. was Fred Conquer. At that time *The Stage* reported: 'Variety is becoming firmly established in Balham, where audiences are amongst the most receptive in the suburbs'. Jenny Howard was doubling Balham with Croydon Grand that week. Another bill, shortly after, included Leslie Strange, Leslie Sarony & Leslie Holmes, Mamie Soutter, Gaillard Trio, Douglas Four, Billy & Idylle Shaw, Kimberley & Page, Sandford & Austin, Stanley, Tonie & Mae Four. Audiences certainly seemed to be getting full rations at this time, but it was not to last.

A sketch of the exterior

Sadly, The Balham Hippodrome was put out of use by enemy action in WW2, last being licensed by the LCC in 1939; at the time of its bombing it was operated by Robert Lear Productions Ltd. We are still seeking an interior view of the theatre with its fourteen boxes. The fine exterior is widely known and stood for some years after the war, but the theatre was never restored and Council flats now occupy the site.

Battersea Palace
(The Washington)

32, York Road, Battersea

Battersea Palace (formerly The Washington): exterior

The old Battersea Palace in York Road was a familiar sight as a deserted cinema, but with two different working public houses embedded in its frontage – in true music hall style. One, the Washington, was named after its American founder, George Washington, late of The Moore & Burgess Minstrels; the other was known as The Royal Standard. In 1876 the Surrey justices granted it a music licence on condition it was not used as a music hall. However, ten years later Moore successfully submitted plans to either convert part of his pub or add The Royal Standard Music Hall at its rear. Confusingly, it was referred to either by this 'official' name (sometimes contracted to The Standard) or colloquially as 'Washington's Music Hall' even in printed publicity. The foundation stone was laid by Miss Victoria Moore and the actual opening took place in 1886 using – it is said – the dancing platform brought from the closed Cremorne Pleasure Gardens.

After only three years its success had necessitated a reconstruction to plan by H.J. Newton, giving a capacity in 'area' (stalls) and balcony of 600 plus about 60 standing. The enterprise was a family affair, with Moore's son, George, as proprietor and manager and Mrs. George Moore in charge of the bars of The Washington. Despite its official capacity, an 1889 account states that as many as 1,500 people could be seated. It is reassuring to be told that they could leave the building in under one and a half minutes!

The hall was known locally as 'Shangri-la', after a Chinese performer who had on one notorious occasion been pelted with large quantities of vegetables by several local men who had visited both ale-houses adjoining the theatre. Another favourite name was 'Bramall's Crystal Palace' on account of the elaborate system of myriad small bulbs.

The hall was crowded each night with local working men and tradesmen including many costermongers together with their wives and daughters. The names of Tom Bass and The Brothers Passmore are recalled today. For some reason, the Screaming Sketch entitled *On The Sands* was not performed – maybe it did not find favour with the Battersea crowd. The audience was, however, promised the appearance of Gertrilla (the Female Athlete) the following week. Seat prices ranged from 6d to 1s 6d, private boxes being one guinea (£1.05) and half-a-guinea (£0.53); half-price applied from 9.45pm.

Two clearly-printed programmes of consecutive weeks in June, 1902 give an excellent idea of the entertainment in one of the lesser halls at the start of the Edwardian era. The great Charles Coborn appeared for the week of 2nd June (his name in bigger type), with the hall's manager, Theodore Gordon, displaying his baritone voice.

Battersea Palace, interior looking towards the stage

During the second week Pongo the Human Monkey made his promised appearance; Wal Pink, later a well-known sketch writer, deputised for Wal Curtis; while Theodore Gordon once again regaled the crowd following the overture. On the Saturday night the Extra turns included, according to a member of the audience, Ellis & Mayne Boys' Quartet, as well as 'a dead rotten sketch'.

Reference books show that George W. Moore was licensee from 1886 to November, 1908, although not continuously. The hall went to auction on 28 February, 1906 through Messrs. Douglas Young & Co. at The Mart, Tokenhouse Yard, London, E.C. At that time the freehold property was described as Battersea Empire and Royal Standard P.H., a plan from the prospectus giving a valuable view of a pub-music hall of the period. The re-drawn plan is shown on the page opposite.

The names of Rhodes, Kirk, Leach and McGuinness appear in records of The Washington as one-time licensees. Joseph Nolan filled the position for a year, before the hall suddenly became part of a nationwide circuit, albeit only for three years or so.

In February, 1908 Frank Macnaghten added what had by then become Battersea Empire to his growing theatre group. This was administered from Sheffield and was mainly in the north of England, but also reached as far as Bath and Southampton. It was said Macnaghten was too busy building up his circuit to find time to marry! At its height the bachelor impresario's group encompassed some sixteen theatres, three of them in London. The majority were called "Palace", the Battersea property soon being thus renamed. A strong bill for 1908, in the standard Macnaghten style, is show below.

The headliners on the August, 1908 bill, The Bouncing Dillons, still have family descendents working in the entertainment business today; also billed is Harry Tomps ('and his Funny Dog'), who is related to the performers Percy, Mary and Peter Honri. Macnaghten installed his old henchman, Fred Baugh, at the Palace. Although Battersea was no longer part of the circuit after 1912, Baugh managed the theatre himself until 1924 with a fair measure of success. The Macnaghten Circuit was finally wound up in 1959, by then reduced to theatres in Huddersfield and Halifax.

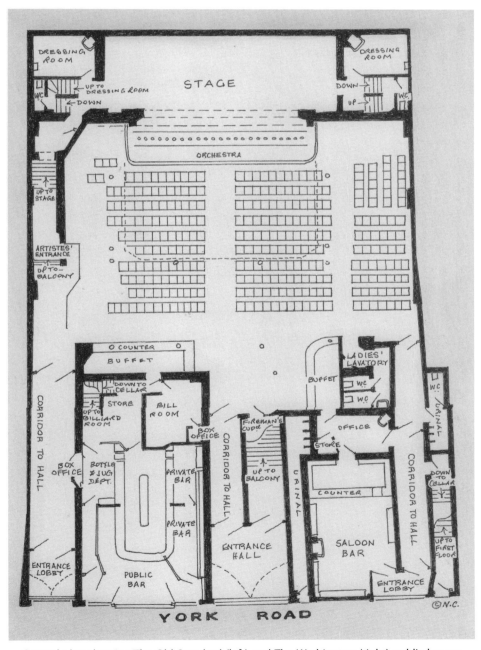

Ground plan showing The Old Standard (left) and The Washington (right) public houses

There was clearly severe competition from the nearby at Clapham Grand, as well as the Shakespeare Theatre in Lavender Hill. The Battersea Palace became a full-time cinema in 1924. The auditorium was completely modernised, with Greek motifs running round the walls, and the entrance being remodelled for its new role. In 1929 it was given the name Super Palace, despite its quite lowly position among south London's cinemas. For a time it was managed by the Summers Brown Circuit during the 1930s.

A programme for October, 1951 advertises the film *Pool of London* which, strangely enough, included scenes filmed in a number of London Variety theatres, among them The Camberwell Palace and The Poplar Queen's.

Films ceased in 1958 and the building remained empty until in 1963 it was demolished by Battersea Council (except for the two pubs) to build a housing scheme.

Theodore Gordon, Chairman at The Washington in the early 1900s

With thanks to Claire Jones and Gerald Smith for their contributions.

Bermondsey: Star Music Hall

Abbey Street, Bermondsey (sometime Neckinger Road)

Bermondsey, Star Music Hall: close-up of exterior with Miss Florrie Forde billed

Formerly The Star & Garter public house, at 189 Abbey Street (near the railway bridge), this hall was licensed from 1867 until 1919. Sometimes known locally as 'The Rats', it had a capacity of 1,395 with seats for 821. The name of the original architect has not yet been discovered, but alterations were carried out in 1883 by Snook & Stock. It had quite a high proscenium arch with a diaper pattern and two balconies, whose fronts were formed of individual cast iron railings, curving in a bombé pattern. The stage was relatively shallow, with very little headroom, resulting in upstage cloths having to be tumbled; wing space was restricted.

The exterior of The Star was most unusual, being carefully built entirely in brick – even to the pediments, arches and the curly brackets supporting the first-floor window; white brick was used as contrast. The columns at the entrance had what Geoffrey Fletcher described as "Byzantine" basket capitals. The adjoining public house matched it perfectly.

In August, 1885, when she was fifteen years old, Marie Lloyd worked The Star. And in 1891, when he was working The Oxford, George Robey made the mistake of doubling with the Bermondsey hall for a salary of £3 for the week. It was a Bank Holiday Monday and the audience was more lively than usual. No respecters of persons, they gave The Prime Minister of Mirth the bird; Robey took his ten shillings and never went into the place again. Charlie Chaplin appeared as an unknown at The Star in a Fred Karno sketch, but The Star was chiefly associated with Leo Dryden, well-known for his rendering of *The Miner's Dream of Home* and other songs of the Empire.

Exterior to Abbey Street, after closure

Among the managers of The Star was the quaint little Harry Hart, who had also run The Raglan and The Salmon. The story is told of how he met Sir Henry Irving in the Strand. Although a somewhat imperious gentleman, Sir Henry had a great fellow feeling for other managers, however humble their scale of operations. Slapping Harry on the shoulder, he hoped that all was well at The Star. Harry

Interior looking towards the stage, 1964

replied that 'bithneth was blooming bad'. 'Well, my boy, we managers have our ups and downs', Irving consoled him. 'We at The Lyceum have felt the draught for a bit, for you see just now a good many of our patrons are going to the opera'. 'Yeth', answered Harry, "and all my blinkin' customers are going 'opping'.

John Barber recalls that his grandmother always went to the pantomimes as guest of the Harts. Upon their visits to the London Palladium they were always met by Dick Hart after the show and went off to Pinoli's Restaurant in Wardour Street for a four-course supper with Chianti for 3s 6d per head! The Harts tended to frequent this restaurant as the whitebait was the best in London.

Our illustration of a typical programme at The Star comes from this period and included three sketches on the near-three hour show, which was still once nightly, as well as ten other acts. The chairman at this time was the well-known Mr. Rodney Polglaze.

Interior looking towards the circles

At the end of The Great War, The Star was feeling the competition of the cinema and in 1919 it went over to films itself. Silent films were accompanied by a 'full orchestra'. However, it retained its annual pantomime until 1939, when the whole place closed down. The Star then faded from public consciousness, becoming yet another rag store – like Wilton's in the East End. In this state, with crude internal timberwork and steps from the stalls to the stage to fit it for its new role, the hall remained as a store until the early 1960s. In this state, it was 'discovered' in 1963 by Geoffrey Fletcher, who wrote a short piece for *The Daily Telegraph*, illustrated by one of his wonderful line drawings.

Exterior of the stage house and flank wall just before demolition, 1964

There were calls for The Bermondsey Star to be saved, but its interior was in a poor state, with parts of the balconies collapsing and demolition was threatened. Sadly, its moment had passed and the preservation movement had not yet gained momentum in the capital. Just before its demolition in 1964 it was drawn by BHMS member, Brian Davis. Cast iron balcony fronts were saved by another member of the Society, which was founded the year before, and for some time were understood to be stored over a shop in The Old Kent Road. One day perhaps we shall see their re-use.

The Hart family's connection with entertainment continued, as Harry Hart's eldest son, Dick, was understood to have been stage manager at The London Palladium: no doubt Sir Henry Irving would have been impressed.

Rodney Polglaze, once the Chairman at The Star

Blackfriars: Surrey Music Hall

124, Blackfriars Road, St. George's Cross

Blackfriars, Surrey Music Hall (while The Surrey Theatre): exterior in 1805

A large and very old theatre, which served as a circus, drama house, music hall and cinema, the Royal Circus and Equestrian Philharmonic Academy first opened in 1782. Although Variety extended its life towards the end of its existence, it did not lead to future greatness – as happened at Sadler's Wells Theatre, for instance. The Royal Circus was founded by song-writer Charles Dibdin in partnership with trick rider Charles Hughes, at a cost of about £15,000.

The circus was a great success for some months, but as it did not have a licence, the local magistrates decided it must close. When the police arrived to carry out their orders they found a large audience unwilling to leave, fighting broke out and the Riot Act had to be read. Hughes spent some time in gaol as a debtor subsequently. Stardom came in 1788 to two dogs, Gelert and Victor, who worried the villain to death nightly in one of the gruesome dramas staged. The manager at the time, the buffo Delphini, in fact produced a number of wonderful spectacles, including a 'real stag hunt', which brought prosperity to the house for a time.

Following a fire in 1803, the theatre was rebuilt to the designs of Rudolphe Cabanel jnr., its exterior showing a clear family likeness to the same architect's Waterloo Road elevation of the Old Vic. It reopened in less then a year, with the eccentric actor-manager Robert Elliston becoming proprietor in 1809. The circus amphitheatre and stables were removed the following year.

The building was renamed The Surrey Theatre in 1816 and as such enjoyed quite a long period of success after the ups and downs of its recent past. One particular triumph was Douglas Jerrold's *Black Eyed Susan*, which created a run on the box office for over 400 nights. Another very popular production under Elliston's successor, Osbaldiston, was the murder thriller *Jonathan Bradford*.

In November, 1838 a dramatised version of Charles Dickens' *Oliver Twist* was staged; it is said that the author attended one of the unauthorised performances, but left unimpressed, having spent the last act hiding on the floor of his box. Alfred Bunn, who took over the Surrey in 1847, made a brave attempt to introduce opera with established performers; sadly, his excellently-staged offerings failed to draw and his pioneering venture lasted only a year.

The new building of 1865, with Leo Dryden billed

Fires were very common in Victorian theatres, with the Surrey being no exception: it was burned-out again in 1865. This time its replacement was designed by John Ellis and built by C.M. Foster of New Wharf, Whitefriars at a cost of £25,000. Its classical portico dominated Blackfriars Road for the next 70 years, although its superb interior was altered when the theatre became a permanent music hall. The new house was said to have seated 2,160, plus a considerable number of standees, on four levels. But however grand the rebuilt theatre, its fortunes sagged – until the advent of George Conquest in August, 1881.

For the next 20 years under Conquest the Surrey Theatre enjoyed its greatest period as a truly popular theatre. Well over 250 productions, including revivals and several works written by Conquest himself, were staged during this heyday.

The opening production, for a fortnight's run, was *The Danites*, a drama of the American backwoods. It was followed by the spectacular melodrama *The New Babylon*, which had enjoyed a big success at the Holborn Theatre before its fire. Here at the Surrey it ran for two months, preparing the ground for the fantastic success of *Mankind*, with George Conquest as the old miser Daniel Groodge and of the aptly-named *Forever*, which originally ran for nearly five hours! Happily for Surrey patrons, it was later cut back to three and a half hours – they built 'em tough in those days.

Pantomimes had been staged at the Surrey before his regime, but under Conquest, with his amazing acrobatic ability, they reached new heights, often running well into the spring. Each year they were followed by a season of melodrama. While the resident stock company went out on tour, other travelling companies came in for a week or more. In the autumn there was a season of plays from the permanent company, including revivals of popular pieces from the West End such as *The Harbour Lights* or *The Silver King*, together with an important new production. Locals also packed the house for Conquest's own offerings, among them such crowd-pullers as *The Stranglers of Paris* (he was well-versed in French plays), or *Saved from the Streets*.

Interior of 1865 looking towards the stage

The annual pantomime was one of the most eagerly-awaited events at the Surrey, produced by George Conquest and full of novel effects, with beautiful scenery and transformations. He himself had to cut back on his acrobatics by the mid-1880s, but his younger sons Fred and Arthur took over, George jnr. being too large for this work. There were several other family members who took part, supported by the strong Surrey company.

Dan Leno made his first London pantomime appearance here in *Jack & The Beanstalk* in 1886 and was booked again for *Sinbad* the following year – an outstanding show by all accounts and the only one in which George Conquest, snr. actually appeared. He took semi-retirement after his wife was killed in a coach accident, dying in 1901 and leaving over £64,000 in his Will. With his death and that of Queen Victoria just before him, the Surrey's greatest era drew to its close.

A period of decline had set in for theatres presenting the old blood-and-thunder melodramas, so Fred and Arthur Conquest worked with the well-known George Belmont, who booked Variety at cheap prices (2d to 9d), so keeping the theatre open. Performances were twice nightly at 6.30 and 9.15p.m.

However, the following year George jnr. gave up his job as a publican to try his hand again at the theatre where his father had triumphed for so long. He put on lurid fare, with such plays as *Tempted to Sin* and *Vultures of London* appearing on local billboards again. Pantomime also returned, with *Aladdin*, *Cinderella* and finally, in 1903, *The Forty Thieves*.

Problems with the L.C.C., who insisted on expensive alterations to the venerable theatre, and a general change in tastes, caused George jnr. to bring the Conquest reign to an end – although family members did continue to appear on the Surrey's stage from time to time under other managements. Music halls were booming all over London, so it was as a music hall that the theatre was able to carry on for a few more years.

In October, 1902 plans for improvements were submitted by Frank Matcham. These mainly concerned fire-resisting materials and the necessary separation of the stage from the dressing rooms, but no action appears to have been taken at that time – presumably because of the expense involved in pouring money into a failing theatre. An auction of the building was announced in April, 1904, but it did not take place. Instead, further plans were put forward in the November by Kirk & Kirk, for new boxes, improvements in sanitary arrangements and other matters. After a complete renovation, the Surrey reopened on Monday 28 November, 1904 as a music hall to be operated by Frank Macnaghten, of the Macnaghten Vaudeville Circuit.

The Stage reported that no expense seemed to have been spared, with lavish lighting, a re-laid stage and redecoration in cream, pink and gold; two houses per night, with a Monday matinee for women and children, would be the pattern for the future. It was also announced, somewhat controversially, that two bars had been abolished, as Mr. Macnaghten 'felt sure that success could be obtained without the stimulus of alcohol'. He was another in the Oswald Stoll mould who, as *The Stage* reported, '*has done as much as any man to raise the tone of the music halls*'. It has to be said that none of Macnaghten's London ventures lasted very long, perhaps for this very reason!

Nevertheless, the new Surrey Theatre of Varieties got off to a good start, under the managership of Frederick Baugh, with prices ranging from 2d to 1s and a well-filled house at the opening performance. After the singing of a verse of the National Anthem by Sybil Montague, 'accompanied by a strong orchestra', the house was entertained by Vivani, in a good display of national dancing; others on the opening bill included Johnny Danvers, George Brendon (vocalist), Brothers Kroney, the comedians Foreman & Farman, Russell & Roper, Fred Brooke, Gipsy Woolf and further offerings from Sybil Montague.

In April of the following year, 1905, *The Stage* announced that: '*We have been asked to state that there is no truth in the rumour circulated that the Surrey is about to close, or that Mr. Frank Macnaghten is about to sever his connection with the south side hall*'. The hall continued to present Variety until around 1909, although after that it was interspersed with other fare. Stars like Marie Lloyd, George Formby (snr.) and Charles Austin did appear, but a lot of the bills were filled with lesser lights. In August, 1914 Leo Dryden topped, with support from Ike & Will Scott, Ted Waite, Eddie Gray & Boys, Rennie & Roxborough, Pim & Popay, with a sketch, *A White Mother*, to complete. The year 1915 saw items like *Get over There*, *Cheer Up* and *We'll Learn 'Em*, (all reflecting the Great War then raging) and the appearance on a Variety bill of Fred Conquest. In fact, an air raid closed the Surrey Theatre of Varieties for a year, adding to its difficulties in retaining local audiences. It was often said that the theatre never really recovered after the war closure.

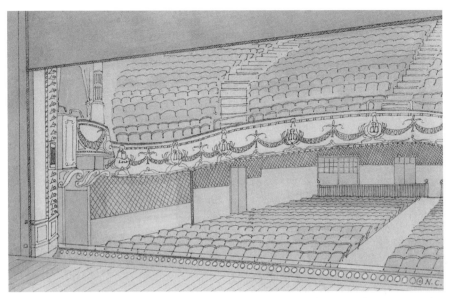

Interior of 1904, converted for use as a Variety Theatre (before demolition in 1934)

For the rest of the time, when Variety was not being presented, the theatre offered a hotchpotch of farces, comedies, musicals and such plays as *Denbigh's Divorce*. There was a slight revival, when in 1920 the Fairbairn-Milne Opera Company and the Ben Greet Players appeared. The final pantomime – and the last live show of all at the Surrey – was *Mother Goose* for the 1921–22 Season: appropriately, the goose was played by a young member of the Conquest family.

As a final fling the old theatre became a cinema for a year from 1923, under the managements of H.S. Chambers and David Roth, closing down for about a decade before its demolition. There were the usual rumours of a revival as a melodrama house to be run in the old style, but they came to nothing. The site was bought for the building of an extension to The Royal Eye Hospital and today is covered by McLaren House, part of South Bank University.

> **London Granville** (rehearsal, 2).—
> Friend and Downing, Edmund Edmunds and
> company, Amber Stone, Fred Stone, Five
> Bombays, Winnie Wayne, Coverdale, Fyne and
> Hurley.
> **London Palace** (rehearsal, 11.30).—
> *The Passing Show*, Albert Whelan, Samaroff
> and Sonia.
> **London Queen's Poplar** (rehearsal,
> 12).—Scott and Whaley, Jack Lorimer, Ack-
> royd Trio, Bert Terrell, Joe Geerts, Katie
> Marsh, Albert Voyce, Lily Maxwell, Ethel
> Parsons.
> **London Surrey** (rehearsal, 12).—Frank
> Armstrong, Friend and Downing, Five Bom-
> bays, Fred Douglas, *We'll Learn 'Em*.
> **London Victoria Palace** (rehearsal,
> 11.30).—Fred Farren and Ida Crispi and com-
> pany, T. E. Dunville, May Moore Duprez,
> Millie Payne, Harry Webber, De Wynne Duo,
> The McNaughtons, Hugh Hughes.

The Surrey takes its place in the Calls for w.c. 11.1.1915

THE GRIFFITHS BROTHERS

ATHLETIC DROLLS

THEATRE ROYAL DRURY LANE, GRAND PANTOMIME, 1888-89.
THE PRINCIPAL LONDON HALLS TO FOLLOW.

The Brothers Griffiths

The Brixton Empress

Brighton Terrace

Brixton Empress: exterior of the old building with The Six Brothers Luck billed

Although the Brixton Empress did not face the main road, its striking façade attracted attention. The light and airy auditorium initially held 1,260 people, its domed ceiling richly ornamented with Du Barry-style paintings above the four boxes. It was designed by Wylson & Long, responsible for most of the Syndicate Halls.

The proprietors, Burney & Grimes, opened on Boxing Day, 1898 with a gala Variety show of twenty acts, including local favourites Kate Carney and Tom Leamore, with prices ranging from 3d in the gallery to 7s 6d for a box for four. There were regular all-night trams to the West End. Brixton being home to scores of Variety artistes, the Empress always attracted a knowledgeable and appreciative audience.

The usual suburban fare was presented: John Lawson in *The Monkey's Paw*, Arthur Lennard in *Skylark* and Bransby Williams in adaptations of Dickens. E.A. Maskelyne and David Devant were among magicians who mystified everyone and Barclay Gammon was renowned for his piano interludes. Gertie Gitana topped at the Empress in 1907 and was appearing there again nearly half a century later. Other stars of the Edwardian era included Sam Mayo and Victoria Monks. During the week commencing 17 October, 1910 when Variety was at its peak, three great stars shared top-billing: Harry Lauder, Marie Lloyd and Joe Elvin. Later Fred Karno, whose Fun Factory was a near-neighbour, presented his daring sketch *The Yap Yaps*, supported by Dutch Daly, the wise-cracking concertina player.

Original interior showing the stage boxes

Public tastes changed during WW1, with fast-moving revues now occupying most weeks, but individual acts were still popular. There was one outstanding show of the mid-twenties, *Us*, in which Florrie Forde introduced Flanagan & Allen to the public. Norah Blaney & Gwen Farrar also scored at this popular hall which, in spite of depression elsewhere, was optimistic enough to embark on extensive alterations and refurbishment in 1931. The architect for the adapted building was Andrew Mather.

There was little of architectural interest, apart from the hard Art Deco-style corner tower, in The New Empress. Boxes were removed and the horseshoe-shaped circle and gallery replaced by a longer and wider circle and upper circle, spotlight towers being placed between these two circles. A screen and sound system were installed, with the larger theatre, now accommodating 2,000 people, assuming the character of a cinema.

A crowded house at the reopening night on 19 October, 1931 was played-in by Sydney Hampton's Orchestra and heard a fine speech by George Robey. The bill included Billy Caryll & Hilda Mundy, Lily Morris, Jenny Howard & Percy King, The Five Sherry Brothers, Rupert Hazell & Elsie Day, Collinson & Dean, The Ando Family of Japanese equilibrists and Ten Gordon Ray Girls.

Popular stars of the 1930s included Ernie Lotinga, George Clarke, Charles Austin, Talbot O'Farrell and, on 24 January, 1938, Gracie Fields. In the same year Walter Payne became Managing Director of the Syndicate Halls and attractions included the Don Ross show *George, Gertie & Ted Personality Parade* and Oscar Rabin & his Band. It was business as usual during WW2, with Max Miller an oft-repeated draw.

Exterior following the remodelling of 1931 with Les Allen billed

Like most halls, the Brixton Empress flourished during the immediate post-war era. In 1948 Don Ross chose it for the production date of *Thanks for the Memory* with Gertie Gitana, G.H. Elliott, Nellie Wallace, Ella Shields, Talbot O'Farrell, Randolph Sutton and Billy Danvers, which ran for two weeks. The show returned to the Empress a number of times, usually billed as 'Final Appearance on Any Stage'. In 1949 Walter Payne died and the renowned agent Gerard Heath replaced him. That year Empress Theatre of Varieties Ltd. made a trading profit of £18,417, down from over £20,000 the previous year. The long-serving W.W. Matthew was also made a Director. In 1952 the Empress celebrated the 21st Anniversary of its rebuilding and for the week of 20 October the bill was topped by The Beverley Sisters and Dr. Crock and his Crackpots; also to be seen were Morecambe & Wise and the unsupported ladder act of George & Lydia.

New interior towards the stage, 1931

During the 1950s Variety began to decline, although the Empress continued to present good bills headed by such stars as Charlie Chester, Billy Russell, Moreton & Kaye, Nat Gonella, Jimmy Wheeler and Billy Dainty; there were slick shows like *Rhythm is their Business*, with Lita Rosa. New stars in the firmament included Arthur Haynes, Johnny Silver, The Southlanders, Micki & Griff and Bertice Reading, but before these newcomers had time to establish themselves Variety was on its last legs.

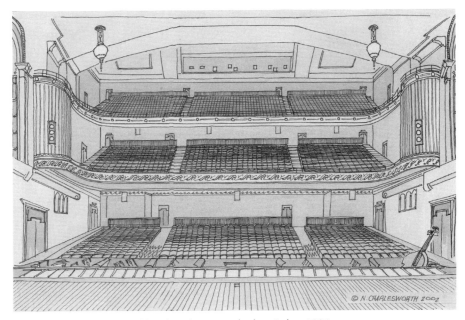

New interior towards the circles, 1931

The three remaining Syndicate Halls, which included the Empress, were taken over by Granada Theatres, who promised to continue with good-quality Variety bills. However, in January, 1957, following a season of *Aladdin* with Bill Maynard and Alma Cogan, the curtain fell on *The Max Miller Show*, with Dawn White's Glamazons among the supporting acts. The closure of the theatre was met with little comment or regret in the local press.

Exterior side view of the old stage house and new frontage of 1931

The Brixton Empress functioned for several years as a Granada Cinema, where I saw Diana Dors in *Tread Softly, Stranger*. There was a wonderful fortnight in March, 1964 when Variety briefly returned with Don Ross' *Thanks for the Memory* (prices from 3s 6d to 8s 6d), with members of The British Music Hall Society attending in force. Hetty King, Sandy Powell and Cavan O'Connor topped for the first week, with Randolph Sutton, Kitty Masters ('Little Man, You've Had a Busy Day') and Terry Wilson for the second. The season provided a rare opportunity to see other artistes, such as Billy Danvers, Marie Lloyd jnr., Kitty Gillow ('Following in Father's Footsteps') and Ellis Jackson (an elderly but vivacious, coloured trombonist), who made a big hit during the second week. Jackson had previously featured with Billy Cotton and his Band on stage and on television. Leon Cortez, in mortar board and gown, 'heducated the higgorant' with his usual rasping tones. Al Freid directed the full pit orchestra, giving a real Variety atmosphere, appreciated by crowded houses for the fortnight.

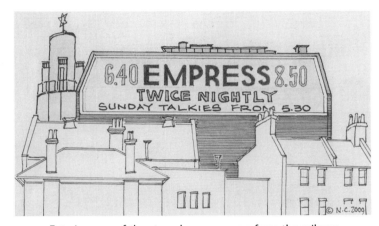

Exterior, rear of the stage house as seen from the railway

There was *A Hoottenanny Night*, with Robin Hall, Jimmie MacGregor, Long John Baldry and Steve Benbow in the cast; then in January, 1965 a season of *Puss in Boots*, before films took over again. The following year the Empress became a bingo hall, but that operation eventually folded and the building became derelict for many years.

Demolition work started on 31 October, 1992 and it was discovered that more of the original building had survived that the experts had previously supposed. The Victorian red-brick stage house had been retained, but the masses of the main building were also clearly detectable. On the rear wall could be seen the lettering EMPRESS – TWICE NIGHTLY, brave to the end. By Christmas the Empress had gone, its place later taken by flats, which for some unexplained reason were called 'Pavilion Mansions'! The star surmounting the Brixton Empress tower was rescued for further use on the top of The Ritzy Cinema, Brixton.

THE SYNDICATE HALLS

Brixton Empress (rehearsal, 12).— Marie Lloyd, Harry Grattan and Herbert Clayton's *On Duty*, Harry Weldon, The Melody Makers, Janette Denarber, Alfred Doring, Arthur D'Orville, Nathan Rickter and company.

Chelsea Palace (rehearsal. 12)— Ernie Lotinga and company, Jack Norworth, Tom Edwards, The Corinthians, Jock Whiteford, The Eleven Romps, Halma, Gwennie Hasto, The Camerons, Walter Emerson.

East Ham Palace (rehearsal. 12).— Alec Flood and Pierre De Reeder's *Robinson Crusoe*.

Euston (rehearsal, 12.)—*Keep Smiling*, Edna Payne, David Poole, Wynn Mentone.

Metropolitan (rehearsal, 12.15).—Two Bobs, Beatie and Babs, Henri De Vries's *On Secret Service*, Beth Tate, Haydn Wood and Dorothy Court, Sydney James's Strolling Players, Grahame and Wheeler, The Camerons.

South London (rehearsal, 12).—Company as booked.

Tottenham Palace (rehearsal, 2).— Arthur Rigby's *Little Red Riding Hood*.

Walthamstow Palace (rehearsal, 1).— Grossmith and Laurilard's *Potash and Perlmutter*.

Watford Palace (rehearsal, 1).—Leonard Willoughby's *The Lady Slavey*.

The Syndicate Halls open in January, 1915

Brixton Hippodrome

Coldharbour Lane, Brixton (backing onto Rushcroft Road)

Brixton Hippodrome: exterior while The Brixton Theatre. Built behind The Tate Library, showing stage house on right

The Brixton Hippodrome enjoyed a career as a Variety theatre for a very short time, having opened as a drama house on 21 September, 1896 after a two-year delay. The foundation stone had been laid by Henry Irving on 3 May, 1894, the opening production being *The Sign of The Cross* with Wilson Barrett and Murray Herriot. The Frank Matcham-designed Brixton Theatre was owned by T.Phipps Dorman and presented mainly touring West End successes for a week's residency.

This theatre was unusual as, like a shrinking violet, it showed only its entrance face – the remainder of the building being wedged behind the Tate Central Free Public Library. Matcham made a bold statement with the entrance tower, but the theatre did not make a huge impression on the Coldharbour Lane townscape; until its destruction, it backed onto Rushcroft Road. Incredibly the original capacity was 2,500 but this was soon reduced to 1,500.

Under the managership of Charles Rider Noble, the licensee from the opening until 1899, the Brixton Theatre staged touring plays, musical comedies and opera. The theatre provided a south London home for an annual Christmas pantomime, *Cinderella* being the one staged in 1906. Unfortunately like its myriad neighbours south of the river, it enjoyed only a modest success. But when one realises that there were also the Camberwell Metropole, the Shakespeare Theatre in Clapham, the Duchess Theatre in Balham, the Crown Theatre in Peckham and others in Kennington, Deptford and The Elephant, it is clear that competition for a drama audience was intense.

Later, most of these competing houses became either Variety theatres or cinemas, sometimes each in turn. The Brixton Theatre was thus able to survive as a drama house long after the others had succumbed. However, this was not before it slipped into the Variety net itself, albeit for only a year or so, from October, 1906. The theatre had had a succession of managements since its opening – including those of E.G. Saunders; Lockwood, Mouillot and Calvert in 1902; and, for a year, that of E. Stevens. The house was clearly vulnerable to a takeover.

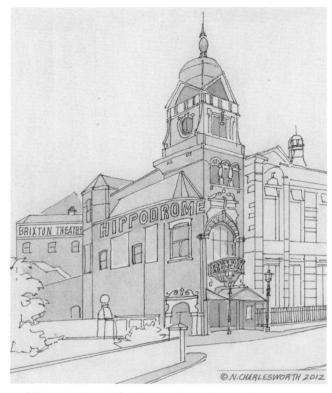

Exterior, while operating as The Brixton Hippodrome, showing main entrance

The neighbouring Brixton Empress had its opening in 1898 under Burney & Grimes two years before that of the Brixton Theatre, but successfully outstripped its competitor with its first-class Variety programmes. In October, 1902 The Empress Theatre of Varieties (Manager: W.E.V. Page) actually became the proprietors of the Brixton Theatre, which they renamed The Brixton Hippodrome, to show that it was now pursuing a Variety policy. But, it soon became evident that the Empress was too well-established and had the edge over the newcomer in the field. Even allowing for a Variety theatre in every London high street at that heady time (and Brixton was the home district of hundreds of variety artistes), two houses within striking distance of one another could not be sustained. Camden Town (Bedford/Hippodrome), Poplar (Queen's/Hippodrome) and Islington (Collins'/Empire) were other districts where duplicate Variety houses lost out to stronger rivals or favourite local haunts. Most of these excess houses became cinemas.

In October, 1907 the Brixton Theatre reverted to its old name and came under the control of Frederick Melville for the next 30 years; the policy changed back to straight plays – and a hugely popular Christmas pantomime, often specially written for this house.

In the 1933 production of *Beauty and The Beast*, the Variety artistes included Mary Honri, Bream & Bream and Dick Tubb, jnr. It is worth noting that this production, scaled-up for the bigger stage, also had Lyceum Theatre showings in 1928/29 and 1937/38. Other successful Brixton pantomimes were *Cinderella*, *Babes in the Wood* and the rarely-seen *Hop o' My Thumb*, which appeared in 1925/26. Between pantomimes The Brixton Repertory Company, under Frederick's daughter June Melville, kept the drama flag flying, largely producing plays currently running in the West End, at popular prices.

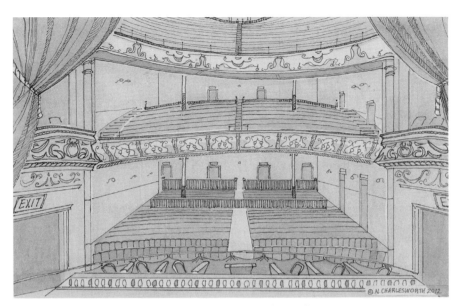

Interior looking towards the circles

The brothers Walter and Frederick Melville had earlier been associated with the old Standard Theatre in Shoreditch, and had controlled the Prince's Theatre on Shaftesbury Avenue for most of the time since its opening as a melodrama house in 1911. They are best remembered, however, for running the Lyceum Theatre off The Strand, establishing themselves there soon after that theatre's unsuccessful period as Variety house. Their famous Lyceum pantomimes, with elaborate transformation scenes, were great annual events here; many of these found their way to Brixton Theatre but, of course, these transfers ceased when the Lyceum was closed in 1939.

Following the death of Frederick Melville, in April of 1938, management of Brixton Theatre (now renamed Melville Theatre) passed to Bert Ernest Hammond. His was only a short regime, however, as the Brixton house was blitzed on 8 November, 1940 and was never rebuilt. The present Public Hall now occupies the site, while the old foundation stone survives at Brixton Oval.

Mr. Walter Munroe

Camberwell Empire

The Triangle, at the corner of Denmark Hill and Coldharbour Lane

Camberwell Empire (formerly The Metropole Theatre): exterior

Apart from the Camberwell Palace, the borough had another lesser, Variety theatre for a few years. This was the Camberwell Empire, a beautiful and ornate theatre which had opened as The Metropole Theatre on Monday, 29 October, 1894. The capacity at opening was just over 2,000, although reduced later; the architects were Bertie Crewe and W.G.R. Sprague, both of whom had worked at the Frank Matcham office. The proprietor was J.B. Mulholland, whose name is also associated with The Wimbledon Theatre and the Hammersmith King's Theatre.

The Metropole was opened for plays and opera – one of some thirty such playhouses built in the London suburbs. The first production was *The Sign of The Cross*, prices ranging from sixpence to forty-two shillings, with the management presenting a different programme each week.

In 1895 D'Oyly Carte's Savoy Theatre company appeared here in *Cox and Box* and *The Chieftain*. In the same year Miss Kate Santley was seen in Thackeray's *Vanity Fair*, while other notable productions included *The Three Musketeers* and Pinero's *The Second Mrs. Tanqueray*. A first-class pantomime was staged at Christmas time. It is of interest that at The Grand Theatre, Nottingham (another Mulholland enterprise) one of the scenes in their 1895 pantomime, *Little Dick Whittington*, was entitled 'The House That Jack Built', being the exterior of The Metropole Theatre in London. This was just a year after the Metropole's opening.

There were other similar playhouses not far away in Kennington, Brixton, Peckham, Balham and New Cross, so The Theatre Metropole, as it had become known, found the competition quite fierce, despite the quality of its offerings. Even visits by Lewis Waller and Ben Greet's Company were insufficient to balance the books.

Interior looking towards the stage

In 1906 the Metropole changed its name to Camberwell Empire, becoming a Variety theatre for around twelve years, firstly under Percy Ford, followed by the managements of Cissie Lawson and Oscar Berry. Competing directly with Camberwell Palace almost opposite, the Empire offered a mixed programme of sketches, Variety acts, ballet and a newsreel. Prices were 'popular' ranging from tuppence to one shilling, with a slight increase for the second house on Saturday nights. Shows were twice nightly at 6.15 and 9.05pm. A Grand Concert was presented every Sunday at 7pm.

Shows were not publicised widely outside the Camberwell area, the Empire rarely featuring in the theatrical trade papers. Two famous names are, however, connected with the house. One is John Lawson, the actor famous for the sketch *Humanity*, who controlled the fortunes of the Empire between 1915 and 1918. The second is Val Parnell, who later rose to great heights at The London Palladium and as Managing Director of Moss' Empires Ltd., but who gained much of his early experience in the box office of Camberwell Empire.

Motion pictures were, of course, part of the Empire's programme while it ran as a Variety house, but from 1918 films took over largely from live shows, although they did not completely finish there until 1924. Charles Gulliver ran both the Empire and Camberwell Palace for two years; while under his control the Empire became Camberwell Theatre and Picture Palace. One wonders whether, by taking control of the Empire and introducing films there, Gulliver was trying to limit the competition to his live shows at the Palace.

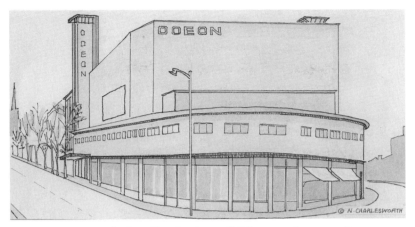

Exterior, rebuilt as The Camberwell Odeon on the same site

Films continued at the converted theatre until it was announced in the local press, in August 1937, that the building was to be demolished to make way for a new Camberwell Odeon. The ultra-modern cinema opened on 20 March, 1939 with the film *Men with Wings*. It had a capacity of 2,470, which was around one thousand more than the old theatre, and was designed by Andrew Mather. Films ran until 5 July, 1975, the last one being *The Night Porter*.

After closure, Camberwell Odeon became Dickie Dirts, a clothing warehouse, until it was demolished. At the time of writing the site is occupied by Nando's Restaurant.

Charles Gulliver

Val Parnell

Wie-Waa, Trick Xylophonist

Camberwell Palace

Corner of Denmark Hill and Orpheus Street

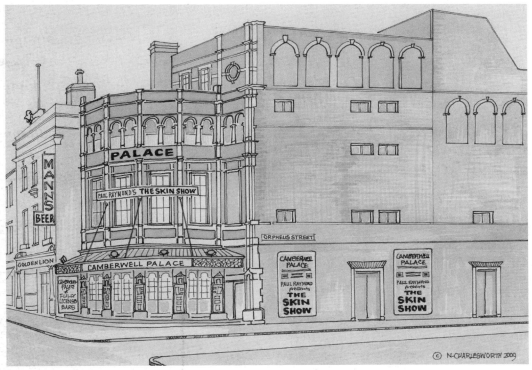

Camberwell Palace: exterior with 'The Skin Show' billed

The Oriental Palace of Varieties was opened in 1896, but soon proved inadequate and three years later was rebuilt as The Camberwell Palace, to the designs of E.A.E. Woodrow. Among those interested in the new enterprise were four well-known music hall artistes – Dan Leno, Harry Randall, Herbert Campbell and (not so well remembered today) Fred Williams. The substantial building held 1,553 in stalls, balcony and gallery; it was constructed by Mr. C. Gray Hill, of Coventry. Changes were made in 1908 by Lewen Sharp.

The bright colours employed in the auditorium were unusual, as was the liberal use of coloured leaded glass, both in the bars and in the spaces under the private boxes. The original colour of the ceiling was blue, relieved with a strong red.

The new house was at first managed by Fred Reeves, late of the Empires at Leicester and Bristol. The Palace orchestra under the baton of A.F. Greco, launched the Palace on 20 November, 1899. Strong bills were booked by J. Sparrow, who was also responsible for engagements at The Clapham Grand, The Granville at Walham Green and The Croydon Palace (later Croydon Empire). Sparrow later became actual and responsible manager at Camberwell.

At the first night there were the usual problems of double-booking of seats, which the acting manager, E. Giles, had to sort out diplomatically. Once launched, Camberwell Palace maintained a fairly consistent policy and was a successful Variety and Revue house for over thirty years. The experienced Charles Gulliver controlled its fortunes for twelve years while it was part of his London Theatres of Varieties circuit, astutely disposing of his interest just before its sudden decline.

Interior towards the proscenium

By the time of the Fourth Anniversary Celebration on Friday 20 November, 1903, the Directors were shown as Arthur W. Bray, H. Comfort, E.A. Golding, H. Joyner and W. Howard Smith. The programme listed the incredible number of fifty-four items, although it was stressed that only "as many turns as time will permit will be given". Among those artistes best remembered today were Harry Champion, Fred Russell, The Karno Trio, Lily Burnand, Herbert Campbell and Vesta Victoria.

Young Fred Wescott, a plumber and glazier, teamed-up with two other gymnasts and performed a few dates around London. On one occasion they were asked to deputise for The Three Karnoes, which could well have been on the 1903 Camberwell Celebration bill. So successful was the trio that they were thought to be the original act. They stuck with the name, Fred changing his surname to Karno. Later he ran his Fun Factory in Southwell Road, just behind King's College Hospital, sending out innumerable shows on tour. The building still stands today and in good condition, being used by various artistic businesses. Therefore only about half a mile from Camberwell Palace a link still exists to the great days of Fred Karno, Charles Chaplin and Stan Laurel.

For this special evening Fred Reeves, late manager of Hammersmith Palace and formerly at Camberwell, was stage director. The orchestra was under the direction of Leon A. Bassett, who was later at the Oxford.

During WW1 the Camberwell Palace hosted a strong variety of acts such as Chirgwin, Ernie Lotinga, May Moore Duprez, Sam Mayo, Tom Clare, The O'Gorman Bros. and – on a number of occasions – Phil Ray. In August, 1915 a Charlie Chaplin Competition was held; revues often took the place of straight Variety bills by this time – the Frank Rubens production of *Mind the Step*, with The Five Jovers, was one of these. Similar shows were *Search Me*, with T.E. Dunville, George Barclay's *Don't Crush*, with Ella Retford and Harry Freeman, and *Jollities*, a Harry Day production which toured all over the LTV circuit.

On the collapse of LTV in the late 1920s three other managements did their best to keep live entertainment going at Camberwell, but it eventually went over to films full-time in 1933 under the ABC banner.

In July, 1928 the Camberwell Palace, in common with six other halls, was under the Summers Brown banner, with Martin Henry's production of *Alf's Button* as the attraction; the play was by W.A. Darlington, later the long-serving theatre critic of *The Daily Telegraph*. Over the next three years, still under Summers Brown control, there were showings of *Abie's Irish Rose*, Tommy Mostol Productions' *They're Off* and – in January, 1930 – *Two Little Vagabonds*, with Tod Slaughter. A good old stand-by, *Maria Martin*, or *The Murder at The Red Barn* was also staged at this period, giving a fair idea of what was being offered to tempt Camberwell audiences away from the cinema.

Interior from the circle

By December, 1932 the Summers Brown Circuit was no longer running its seven halls. Greater London Theatres & Cinemas Ltd. were now in control, although live bookings for just four of the old Summers Brown halls were handled by de Frece's Agency. Camberwell was not among them, as it was about to enter its phase as a cinema. Again, although ABC Cinemas staged a live segment in its film programmes at many suburban houses, the Palace did not seem to be chosen and it was not until the early part of WW2 that Variety made a come-back. Two other Cinema managements, including that of the Hyams Brothers, ran it for short periods from 1940 to 1943.

Sensing that morale-boosting live shows should do well while Londoners were experiencing worrying times, A.A. Shenburn of Regis Entertainments took over Camberwell Palace and ran it from 26 April, 1943 for a number of years. His circuit included halls at Walham Green, Rotherhithe, Stockport, Ipswich and Southend. Some quite attractive bills were presented during the war and just after. One in 1945 was topped by the magician Sirdani ('Don't Be Fright'), with Roy Walker and Jack Warman among the supporting company; another in the following year was topped by Nan Kenway and Douglas Young – then at the peak of their fame on the wireless.

The Palace orchestra was conducted during this era by Conrad Leonard, the MD of the Lyceum Theatre in The Strand between 1936 and 1938; when the Palace presented drama he played on one of the two pianos in the pit. At the time of his death, aged 104, in April, 2003 he was Britain's oldest professional musician.

Camberwell Palace is fondly remembered by John Pope, the journalist and editor of *Sid Phillips News*. As the number and range of radio programmes swelled after war-time limitations, it was necessary for the BBC to look at other outside premises as possible extra studio space. The Camberwell Palace was one of a number of London houses used, in this case on Sunday evenings.

While visiting venues for BBC radio shows, John Pope became friendly with, among others, Leslie, father of singer Petula Clark, who at that time was a frequent broadcaster; they used to meet at Camberwell around 1949, when Pet was performing for *Variety Bandbox*, a weekly Sunday evening entertainment on the Light Programme. Such up-and-coming comedians as 'Cheerful' Charlie Chester, Reg Dixon ('Confidentially'), Arthur English ('Prince of the Wide Boys'), Derek Roy and Frankie Howerd were regularly featured in the shows. The music was provided by an orchestra conducted by Billy Ternent, later at The London Palladium. No changes were made for the 'studio', the front tabs and half-runners being the only settings. John Pope and Les Clark used to watch events from the dress circle, as there was no room at stage level.

Exterior of the stage house and flank wall in Orpheus Street

Unfortunately, such great comedians were not normally seen at Camberwell Palace during week-days, while Variety shows continued. A typical show at this period was a production of *This Was The Army*, with Jack Lewis, Sonny Dawkes and Tommy Rose, Arthur Knotto, Peter Taylor, Ralph Humber, The Melody Six and supporting company, which was presented for the week of 27 November, 1950.

I attended Camberwell Palace on two occasions and latterly it was becoming quite tatty and run-down. By the early 1950s the theatre alternated between seasons by Harry Hanson's Court Players (when budding playwright John Osborne appeared) and strip-tease shows with titles like *The Skin Show*, *Nudes in the News* and *Guys and Gals* (mostly Gals!).

When John Cliff attended the Palace and went for a drink in the interval he was served by a lady whom they called 'Auntie', who had come from New Cross Empire. She advised them in a hushed voice: 'Don't have the Guinness – it's been here for years!'

The straight plays provided an opportunity for numerous actors and actresses. For the week of 13 September, 1948 Noel Coward's Blithe Spirit was presented, the cast including Newsome McCormack as Madam Arcati. Later the same month Daphne Du Maurier's successful play, *The Years Between*, came to Camberwell from Wyndham's Theatre. The artist Alexander Cameron Simm often drew the interior of the Palace at this time, while studying at Goldsmith's College.

Revue was again the attraction for the week of 21 July, 1952, when Foursome Enterprises staged *Let's Go* with Eltham & Sharpe, Gena Mae, The Merry Three, George Chicane and Dorian Claire among the company.

The raciness of the strip-tease revues seen in the last years of the Palace has been somewhat overstated. John Benstead of Rotherhithe used to look in for the show on the way to his TA drill hall nearby. He remembers *Nudes of The World*, and in his opinion most of the girls probably came from Bolton, while the closest most of those in *Slightly French* had been to France was likely to have been Margate Hippodrome!

The Camberwell Palace's manager in its last years, Gilbert Oscroft, considered that the Camberwell shows had to be fairly mild in order to get a showing at all, owing to the attentions of the local licensing authority. The shows were, therefore, cleaner and more closely watched by the management than at any other Variety house in the country. In fact it was said that some revue companies carried an alternative script – purely for running at Camberwell.

Ted Bottle once met Dennis Castle who used to produce pantomimes and he put one on at Camberwell in the early 1950s. The penultimate act was the song scene, complete with sheet and a number of children from the audience. Castle told of one small girl who refused to leave the stage. She was, she insisted, in Fairyland and wanted to be with the magic. What could they do? They took her off at the end of the scene, reassuring her mother in the audience, then brought her on in the walk-down at the end of the show. What a pity other Camberwell children cannot indulge in a spot of magic now.

Side wall towards Camberwell Green, when derelict

Although there were often such Christmas pantomime seasons, it was the strip-tease shows that kept the theatre going. Variety as such was unfortunately no longer a draw. Managements presenting the shows included Paul Raymond, who kept many a shaky Variety Theatre open, Terry Cantor and Barry Piddock, whose *The Naughtiest Nights of Your Life* was one of the final shows seen here. The Camberwell Palace eventually closed in 1956, but not before Pauline Penny got into trouble by moving during a nude pose – a mouse on stage was said to have been the cause of the outcry. Boarded-up for over ten years and often vandalised, the Camberwell Palace was demolished in around 1968. A bank now stands on the site.

LONDON THEATRES OF VARIETIES.

Balham Hippodrome (rehearsal, 1).—Rameses, Bellman and Poluski, the Poluskis, Ella Shields, Bessie Knight, Chris Baker, Esmond.

Camberwell Palace (rehearsal, 12).—*Search Me*, T. E. Dunville, S. W. Wyndham, Cromo and Hamilton, Lecardos.

Clapham (rehearsal, 1).—The Poluskis, Daisy James, Mayne and Tate, the Finneys, Herbert Rule, Phil Parsons, Rex Fox, Two St. Johns, Decars.

Croydon Empire (rehearsal, 12).—Geo. Robey, May Moore Duprez, Lulu Leigh, Delafo, Two McKays, Fred Russell, Pompindens, Bertini.

Hammersmith Palace (rehearsal, 1).—Chung Ling Soo, Maidie Scott, Solo, Edna Lyall, Walter Emerson, Gwennie Hasto.

Holborn Empire (rehearsal, 12).—Lew Lake's *Daylight Robbery*, Ella Shields, Jock Whiteford, Cole and Rags, Florence and Lilian, Minnie Mace.

Ilford Hippodrome (rehearsal, 12).—F. Rubens' *Mind the Step*, Nora Delany, Joe Elvin and company, J. H. Wakefield.

Islington Empire (rehearsal, 1).—Wish Wynne, Joe Elvin and company, Zigeuner Quartet, O'Gorman Brothers, H. O. Wills, Phil Parsons, Ray Wallace, Frank Maura, May Denva.

Kilburn Empire (rehearsal, 1).—James Welch, Haley's Juveniles, Jock Whiteford, Soho Trio, Elsie Bower, Daisy James.

Lewisham Hippodrome (rehearsal, 12).—Harry Day's *Hullo, Everybody!* May Moore Duprez, James Stewart, Lecardo Brothers, Carina Sisters.

Palladium (rehearsal, 11.30).—Geo. Robey, Mayne and Tate, Four Holloways, T. E. Dunville, Billy Merson, Wish Wynne, Ernest Hastings, Beti Tate, Marie Lloyd, Weedon Grossmith and company.

Poplar Hippodrome (rehearsal, 1).—E. C. Roils's *Good Evening*, Sammy Shields, Sisters Jerome, Ferguson and Mac.

Putney Hippodrome (rehearsal, 12.30).—H. Grover's *Follow the Frill*, Phil Ray, Doody and Wright, Edie Veno.

Rotherhithe Hippodrome (rehearsal, 1).—Sisters Jerome, J. Peterman's *Colonel Cobb* and *The Hairdresser*, etc.

Shoreditch Olympia (rehearsal, 12.30).—Signor Arvi, Billy Merson, Sammy Shields, Z'geuner Quartet, Terry Twins, Society Quartet, Halma, Lily Long, Doreen O'Connor.

Willesden Hippodrome (rehearsal, 12.30).—Harry Day's *Made in England*, Victor Travers, Edie Gray, Moray and Bebby Trio.

Woolwich Hippodrome (rehearsal, 12).—Fred Karno's *Parlez Vous Francais*, H. O. Wills, Lily Langtry, Pasqualis, Real McKays.

The London Theatres of Varieties, w.c. 27.9.1915

The Grand Theatre, Clapham

St. John's Hill, Clapham Junction

Clapham Grand: exterior in 1938 with Vic Oliver billed

Perhaps the first thing to say about the Clapham Grand is that it is *still standing* and being used for entertainment – although not of the type that it was built for! The theatre has excellent sightlines from every level and is full of atmosphere.

Following a trial run at the flat-floored Munt's Hall nearby, Dan Leno and Herbert Campbell were sufficiently pleased with the public's response to commission a brand-new Variety theatre. The New Grand Palace was designed by E.A. Woodrow who had already built the Camberwell Palace for the promoters, and opened on 26 November, 1900. It is this architect's only completely surviving theatre.

The exterior, of red machine-made brick and crowned by two slightly "Indian" towers, rears above Clapham Junction station; its delightful interior is – by contrast – in the Chinese manner: dragons' heads with illuminated eyes adorn the dress circle. The pagoda canopies over the boxes have also survived, although their draperies have now vanished, together with most of the rich decoration around the proscenium. When opened, the theatre's capacity was given as 3,000, but by 1912 this figure had been reduced to 2,500. It passed through many hands, including those of Fred Williams (for Leno and Campbell), Charles Gulliver, George Barclay, Nat Tennens and W.J. Chegwidden.

For the first ten years the promoters battled to secure the best acts for their new hall, but the pressure from the big syndicates proved too much for them so that by 1910 the Grand became part of Gulliver's London Theatres of Varieties Ltd.

Interior towards the stage

For a week in January, 1901, not long after its opening, the bill included Selkirk's New Juvenile Spectacle *The Gallant Gordons*, performed by one hundred Clapham Junction children! The eleven supporting acts included Arthur Lennard, Tom Bass, Elsa Joel, Charles Deane, Maggie Carr and Welsh Miller. August, 1914 saw Fred Zola, Martin Camp, Helen Charles, Dolly Lee, Eadie & Ramsden, The Dreadnoughts and Pelton's sketch, *Now We Know*. In the summer and autumn of the following year Clapham was entertained by some better-known names – Joe Elvin, Dale & O'Malley, Scotch Kelly, The Poluskis, Clarice Mayne & 'That', Austin Rudd and – probably given a cheer by the locals – The Two St. Johns. Scotch Kelly was back in 1916, together with R.A. Roberts, Lily Langtry (the Variety star not the actress) and Rameses.

By 1928 the LTV circuit had crashed, the Clapham Grand becoming part of the seven-strong Summers Brown circuit for a few years. That year the theatre presented Harry Bentley's revue, *Contrasts*, one of innumerable revues on the road. Tod Slaughter was a regular visitor, in *It's Never Too Late To Mend* and, a few months later, in *Nell Gwynne*.

Films took over the Grand during the early 1930s, with back-projection to start with, from a specially-built extension. Full front-projection was installed in 1935. The theatre came under a number of different managements at this period, including Greater London Theatres & Cinemas Ltd.

I attended the Grand in the mid 1930s, when it returned to Variety, with a bill headed by Syd Seymour and his Mad Hatters, supported by Harry Claff, Stanford & McNaughton, Verek & Moir and Max Hoffman. Shortly after this the theatre experimented with three-hour shows, once nightly. These were clearly not to the liking of Clapham audiences, as it soon reverted to twice-nightly presentations. There was a noticeable improvement in the quality of bills in the years up to WW2, but it was only a short flowering. In October, 1935, under Montague Lyon Direction, the ciné-variety programme offered Don & Honey Ray Company, Benny Leven, The Juvelys and Two Guys and a Dame.

Exterior from Clapham Junction Station

Leon Cortez and his Coster Band were at the Grand in July, 1936 with Joyce & Shields, Jack Warman and Eight Corona Kids in the company. Tommy Handley & Co. could be seen in September of the following year: the others on the bill included Martyn & Maye, Five Cyclonics, Barlow & Griffiths and – to make his name later – Arthur Haynes. The expanding Granada Cinema circuit provided tremendous local competition when its spectacular Clapham Granada opened in November, 1937 on the bridge above the Junction station. For example, during the week of 24 January, 1938 the Grand presented Vic Oliver, Murray & Mooney, Harry Angers and Oswald Waller, Rubio Sisters, Vine, More & Nevard, Barrie Andre & Brett, Rome & Leonard and the Three Milsom Sisters. At the Clapham Granada, in support of the full film programme, audiences were offered Leslie Strange, Cingalee and The Four Urbanis for the full week.

In that same year control of the Grand passed for two years to London & District Cinemas Ltd., before transferring to Loughborough Playhouse Ltd., the holding company for so many London Variety houses. Good bills sometimes still appeared, though, with Bebe Daniels & Ben Lyon for the week of 14 April, 1939, with Tessie O'Shea, Stone & Dell, Len Jackson, Len Childs & Co. in support. Jan Tors 'The Fiddling Fool', appeared the following year, described in the press as "Still one of the Funniest Front-Cloths".

In 1942 the agent George Barclay assumed control of the Clapham Grand, followed three years later by his wife, Mrs. Katherine Mary Shea (Kate Carney). Twice nightly shows were at 6.30 and 8.45pm, with prices very reasonable at 1s to 2s.

Now booked by The National Vaudeville Corporation, Gordon Norval and Millie Jackson presented at the Grand their show, *Young Ideas* in April, 1944. The company included Dan Young, Douglas Francis, Frank Taylor, Eric Watt, Rita Bond, Constance Field, James Scott Douglas and The Millie Jackson Girls. It was in another, similar, Gordon Norval show that Morecambe & Wise took Clapham by storm: this was *Fig Leaves & Apple Sauce*, when they were engaged for £10 for the week, shared between them. This was increased to £12 before opening, on condition that they did *two* ten-minute spots. The second spot had to be hurriedly written at their digs, but they went well and were booked straight away into Kilburn Empire the following week. A return to the Grand was followed by another week at Kilburn, where they topped the bill!

I went to the Clapham Grand again in 1948 when, under the direction of Nat Tennens, the attraction was *The Stars We Remember*. Really a number-two version of *Thanks For The Memory*, it was a good show and was playing to full houses on the Saturday when I attended. The stars were impersonated by Marie Lloyd jnr., Frank Formby, Kitty Gillow, Theo Lambert, Harry Tate jnr. and Chris Wortman: the latter's impersonation of Eugene Stratton earned him an encomium in The News-Chronicle.

Clapham Grand became part of the expanding Essoldo cinema circuit, operating many old live theatres shortly after this. However, live shows alternated with films for a time and in 1949 it staged *No, No Nanette* for a week.

Eventually films dominated Essoldo theatres, with the exception of the odd week of Variety or Pantomime. As late as November, 1950 Mannie Jay's Variety Agency still advertised in The Performer that it represented a number of Essoldo theatres, including Clapham Grand which had by now become the London show-date for new Variety acts seeking bookings, replacing The Victoria Palace, fully occupied by The Crazy Gang. Cinema use ended on 31 August, 1963 but almost immediately on 11 October, it re-opened as The Vogue Bingo Club, a false ceiling having been inserted, to cut off the balcony.

Exterior while Essoldo Cinema

This operation ended eventually, the theatre going dark for a time, but somehow the building survived. In early 1992, still in good condition, but with its balcony revealed but closed, it was refurbished to become a music venue.

There were a number of management changes and an attempt by actor Corin Redgrave to make it into a working theatre and stage school. The Clapham Grand also narrowly avoided becoming a J.D. Wetherspoon theme pub. Eventually, in December, 2003, the local press announced the theatre's re-opening with a New York-inspired look as The Grand, a lavish nightclub. It retains its two circles and 28ft deep stage.

The Croydon Empire

North End, Croydon

Exterior while the under management of Moss' Empires, 1938 with Hutch billed

In a career spanning some sixty-four years, the Croydon Empire (as it is best known) was a Circus, a Variety theatre with occasional films in its programmes, a Cinema with occasional Variety acts, a Variety theatre again and finally a Cinema once more for its last six years. Not a trace of it exists today, although some of the greatest entertainers bestrode its stage and it is immortalised in a poem about the Afghan War.

The era began on 25 March, 1895 when the new National Hall & Grand Circus opened: weekly advertisements showed that it normally presented Circus-type programmes. Its first year saw a frequent number of name changes and a gradual move towards Variety entertainment; there were numerous improvements to the decorations and even a 're-arrangement' of the interior – presumably to accommodate normal theatre seating.

An early programme of 1899 shows that performances were once-nightly at 8.00pm and that among the ten artistes was Harry Bawn, 'versatile comedian', who was later to run The Edmonton Empire; while Croydon was London's most southerly hall, Edmonton was its northernmost one. Others on that programme included Gipsy Woolf, 'comedienne and dancer', and Rumbo Austin and his Four Comical Nippers.

The Directors of The National Hall were Herbert Campbell (Chairman), Dan Leno, Fred Williams, J. Sparrow, H. Joyner, Harry Randall and G.E.S. Venner. So it can be seen that this was largely the same team responsible for launching The Camberwell Palace, The Clapham Grand and The Granville at Walham Green. Acts could be booked for this miniature circuit, giving it greater power than an independent theatre. The Resident Manager at Croydon was Eustace H. Jay.

By the May of 1901 T. Gardiner Hales had joined the Directors and he clearly moved the enterprise forward, as will be seen. Outstanding among the eleven acts seen on the programme for the week of 6 May were Leo Stormont and Percy Honri, with his famous *Concert-in-a-Turn*. It was stated that 'in future, a greatly augmented programme will be given'. Other notable artistes to appear that year were Foreman & Fannan in *The Millionaires*; Gladys Mavius and Tom Fancourt. The following year the building changed its name to Croydon Palace of Varieties. On 22 December, 1904 Marie Lloyd headed the bill for an Anniversary Celebration, for which a silk souvenir programme was printed.

Business must have prospered, as T. Gardiner Hales engaged W.G.R. Sprague to re-design the theatre. The old building was demolished and a completely new one costing £30,000 was built and opened in 1906. The Empire Palace, as it was now called, seated around 1,250 in stalls, circle and gallery. There were six boxes, a 30ft deep stage and an orchestra pit for fourteen players.

Croydon Empire: interior when The National Palace of Varieties

A major change came about in around 1910, when The Croydon Empire became one of the seventeen London Theatres of Varieties (LTV), controlled at first by Walter Gibbons and later by Charles Gulliver, the renowned pioneer of Variety management, who became a Director of Moss' Empires Ltd. Thus began a period of prosperity that was to last for nearly twenty years, bringing top names in Variety to Croydon, as well as numerous Revues and the occasional play, such as *The Creaking*

Chair. A brief review of the years gives an impression of the era, bearing in mind that the town had two other theatres operating for much of the time.

In August, 1914 the house was presenting Herbert Shelley, Phil Ray, Edie de Lisle and The Three Laurels. A year later we could enjoy Ernie Lotinga, May Moore Duprez and Gwennie Hasto, supported by Fred Ginnett, Emerson, Fyne & Hurley, Victor & Valma, The Carina Sisters and we could have participated in a currently very popular Charlie Chaplin Competition. Shortly after this Marie Lloyd came back to the Croydon Empire, topping a bill that included Sam Mayo and Belmon & Poluskis.

Towards the end of September, 1915 May Moore Duprez made a rapid return 'by popular demand', with George Robey, Lulu Leigh, Delafo, Two McKays, Fred Russell, Pompindens and the musician Bertini (later famous for his Blackpool Band). *Irish and Proud of It* included Croydon in its tour for the week of 30 October, with Leo Bliss, Lily Iris and W.L. Payne among the company.

Not every week brought artistes who would be remembered today, however. This could be show by the line-up for 8 July, 1918 when the bill comprised Oswald Williams, Yvonne Granville, Billy Simpson, Hetty Hartley, Nora Moore, Will & Smith, Lilian Rickard and Josie Leyton – hardly names that trip off the tongue today!

With the more relaxed years after WW1, 1921s offerings included the Revue *Sons of The Sea* in April; the ever-popular Ernie Lotinga with George Mozart, Eric Randolph, The O'Gorman Bros. and company in October; with Little Tich, Jack Pleasants, Fred Curran, Jack & Betty Riskit (The Dental Riskits) and Marie Lawton in November.

Interior – an impression of the auditorium looking towards the stage

On the collapse of LTV in 1928, Croydon Empire became for a few years part of the seven-strong Summers Brown Circuit. Loughborough Playhouse Ltd. were the proprietors and the lessees were The Greater London Theatres and Cinemas Ltd. Prices at this period ran from 6d to 3s, with a slight increase in the cheaper seats on Saturdays and Bank Holidays.

For the week of 20 July, 1928 the Empire presented Hough & Clayton's *Barbed Wire*, while in December of that year Maurice Cowan's *Will o' the Whispers* was one of the attractions offered. Summers Brown control lasted until November, 1930, when the Empire became a cinema, opening with *What Price Melody?* with *Near the Rainbow's End* and *Movietone News* in support.

Films continued until 1938, although Variety acts were soon added to spice-up the programmes. For example, in March, 1933 live acts included Maxwell Carew, Three Sherina Sisters and the Bavers Trio. With rather too many cinemas in the central Croydon area, the Empire's operators, Twentieth Century Cinemas, arranged with Moss' Empires to present Variety again from 5 September, 1938. Films continued on Sundays, together with a concert – as at a number of halls.

View from the tower when operating as Eros Cinema, 1959

Moss' Empires put in some strong bills, such as that for the week commencing 12 September, 1938 which offered a mouth-watering array of entertainment: not just Charlie Kunz, Beryl Orde and Jewel & Warriss, but Max Wall and Hutch as well! Betty Hobbs' Globe Girls (in three spots), Lalage the aerialist and The Oxford Five completed the line-up. Again, for the week of 28 October a sparkling bill offered Syd Seymour and his Band, Lucan & McShane, Wright & Marion and The O'Gorman Bros. Typical Sunday pictures were Robert Young in *Married Before Breakfast* and Max Miller in *Take It From Me*.

Among other big names who followed were Bebe Daniels & Ben Lyon, Billy Bennett, Tommy Trinder (from just up the road in Streatham), Dick Henderson, Afrique, Clapham & Dwyer, Les Allen and Sid Millward and his Nitwits. After the short Moss tenure, the shows were presented by Metropolitan & Provincial Cinematograph Theatres Ltd. and, latterly, by Metropolitan Music Halls (Croydon) Ltd.; behind the company were the Hyams brothers, who eventually bought the Empire in 1946.

Some good Variety bills and pantomime seasons were still presented: *Little Red Riding Hood* and *Babes in the Wood* were two of the post-war pantomime subjects staged. Among magicians who baffled Croydon audiences were Jasper Maskelyne, 'The Royal Command Magician', and Murray, the Australian escapologist – the latter supported by Roy Walker, Murray & Hinton and Eugene and his Serenaders.

Exterior of the stage house from the playing fields, 1959

Orchestras and Bands included those of Henry Hall, Billy Cotton and Harry Roy, whose engagement was rudely interrupted, as recalled by Bryan Prosper. Cables holding the safety curtain snapped during the interval of the first house on VJ evening, sending the iron crashing to the stage and slightly injuring two stage-hands. The show was unable to continue and crowds waiting for the second house, including Bryan's relations, had to be turned away.

After WW2 Variety and pantomimes continued, the quality of the bills provided by The Lew & Leslie Grade Agency remaining the best available; inevitably, Revues revolved round the girls. For the week commencing 27 November, 1950, for instance, Deen Moray presented *Bon Soir, Mesdames* which gave top billing to Billy Rhodes & Chika Lane and included Nudes International as well as Scotty Bayes' Parisienne Peaches! S.H. Newsome was responsible for an excellent Variety presentation, entitled *Let's Step Out* which starred The Five Smith Brothers, George Doonan and a strong bill. Bob & Alf Pearson topped on another attractive show that included Harry Worth, then appearing as a ventriloquist before he became a big name on television.

But with audiences steadily falling away, the Hyams brothers announced in 1953 that Croydon Empire had lost over £10,000 during the previous two years and that live entertainment would have to cease. The final show was *Soldiers in Skirts*, which played for the week commencing 4 May, 1953.

A hectic couple of weeks' work then changed the Empire into the Eros Cinema, a sister to the former Lewisham Hippodrome at Rushey Green. It reopened on 18 May with the entrance altered to give direct access to the stalls and the boxes removed as they blocked the view of the wide screen, which had to be placed at quite an acute angle for better projection from the lofty spot box. "X" certificate films provided the mainstay, with conventional re-issue programmes on Sundays. At holiday periods "U" films for family audiences were presented.

By the beginning of 1959 there were rumours of closure ahead and these proved to be correct, as the Eros Cinema closed on Saturday, 30 May, 1959. The last programme was the drama *Compulsion* with Orson Welles, supported by *Streets of Loredo* with William Holden and Mona Freeman. The Croydon Empire was acquired by a Mitcham development company and the cleared site was offered for sale in the national papers.

Cranleigh Property Investments Ltd. of Manchester then built the present Whitgift Shopping Centre, the entrance to which stands on the site of the Empire's narrow entrance hall. This entrance was very unusual in that one ascended stairs to the stalls; more stairs then led one towards the circle, but it was then necessary to descend more stairs to reach it. How on earth did such an arrangement pass the licensing authorities? Incidentally, one wonders what became of the fine statue of Eros on the tower. Probably in a country garden somewhere.

Murray mystifies at Croydon Empire in 1946

Exterior while Eros Cinema

Croydon Grand Theatre

High Street

Croydon Grand Theatre: original exterior with 'The Crooked Billet' billed

The Grand Theatre & Opera House had a fairly chequered career. It was designed by an architect named Brough and opened in 1896, a boom time for new theatres. The foundation stone was laid by Sir Herbert Beerbohm Tree, praise being lavished by none other than George Bernard Shaw on the 'comfortable' building. The Croydon Grand had an attractive auditorium, despite its being described in the 1950s as 'a great draughty barn', and seated 1,240 in stalls and three circles. Had it been built in a better part of the High Street, its history might have been more successful.

The Grand was conceived as a legitimate house and there was considerable concern in 1904 when it was suggested that it might become a music hall. In the event, the Croydon Empire monopolised this trade after it was rebuilt in 1906 and re-launched as a number-one hall. When the Empire embraced films in 1930 full-time, the Grand soon filled the hole. A typical Variety bill in October, 1935 was topped by Tommy Handley, with Joe Young, Kimberley & Page, Max Hoffman, Plant & Rosslyn, Pat Hyde and Clown Argo in support. As the theatre had a seating capacity and stage depth identical to the Empire's, it was an attractive alternative to Variety bookers.

Incidentally, it was in the early 1930s that Nick Charlesworth's uncle, Harry Davis, made his stage debut here in a straight play. He later went to Hollywood to make appearances, as Tyrrell Davis, in some seventeen minor films, alongside Googie Withers, David Niven and a host of lesser names.

Interior looking towards the stage

In 1936 the Croydon Grand underwent some rebuilding work – possibly in the hope that it was going to remain the town's home of Variety – but the good times did not last long. Variety bookings were made by National Vaudeville Corporation (NVC), including that of a bill topped by Scott & Whaley in September, 1937. Sadly for the theatre, the Croydon Empire reverted to its traditional fare the following September, so – after a week with The Great Carmo and company – the Grand's stage was occupied by The Malvern Players, presented by Roy Limbert. NVC then gave up booking the Croydon house.

F.J. Butterworth ran the Grand for a short time as part of his extensive circuit; it was operated by Will Hammer for a considerable period after WW2, much of the time as the home of The Croydon Repertory Company. Hammer had theatres mainly in seaside towns, such as Weymouth, Clacton and Bournemouth (the New Royal): the Grands at Croydon and Basingstoke were the exceptions.

Pantomime was the saviour at Christmas time, particularly after the Empire's closure in 1953, but it was a struggle for the rest of the year. Cyril Fletcher and his wife, Betty Astell, took the theatre one Christmas and put in a charming production of *Mother Goose*. There were many changes of management. In 1957 the Grand suddenly mounted a season of Variety – the Empire was now showing horror and continental films. Mark Newell saw the opening bill, which was topped by Billy Cotton & his Band and Arthur English; subsequent shows offered Jimmy Wheeler, Fred Emney with Terry, Norman Evans and Max Miller. He was delighted when his idol, Max Wall, was booked for a week. As Newell recalls in an issue of *Wall Paper*: "On a very rowdy Saturday night Max Wall, in his guitar spot, dealt with some personal insults and booing in traditional fashion ('I wouldn't like to enquire into your parentage'). Then, looking wistfully up into the boxes, reflected on his marriage troubles ('They remind me of my responsibilities'). The piano act later was better received". Newell added: "It is probably true that Max's skills were seen to better advantage as the top of the bill in Variety than in the one-man show".

The 'modernised' exterior with Variety billed on hoarding

In 1958 over 100,000 people signed a petition, asking the Council to buy the Croydon Grand, but in April, 1959 the theatre manager disappeared before the Monday night performance. There were one or two Rock 'n' Roll shows staged, before the theatre closed for good. The Grand was demolished in 1960. All three of the town's theatres – the Empire, the Davis and the Grand – were standing closed when I visited Croydon in the previous year. The Ashcroft Theatre was subsequently built in the town centre to cater for drama, adjacent to the Fairfield Halls.

T.E. Dunville Illustrated. T.E. Dunville in many guises in 1899. Drawn by Sam Sibbitt

Croydon Hippodrome

Crown Hill, Croydon

Croydon Hippodrome (formerly Theatre Royal): full exterior with Lamberti billed

Always something of a mystery theatre, the 'live' life of The Croydon Hippodrome is said to have begun as far back as 1800, when it was known as The Theatre Royal, Croydon. It was reconstructed in 1867/68, but the name of the architect is unknown.

Many distinguished actors and actresses performed there in the Victorian era, until its popularity for straight plays started to fade; for a while it became a music hall, The Empire Theatre of Varieties – not be confused with The Croydon Empire at North End! The theatre then reverted to drama and even showed some of the very early moving pictures.

The Theatre Royal, Croydon was acquired by Moss' Empires in 1909 and immediately demolished. A brand new 1,500-seater Variety theatre, Croydon Hippodrome, designed in his recognisable style by Frank Matcham, and built at the usual speed for the day, opened in August, 1910.

At that time Oswald Stoll was still connected with Moss' Empires, although soon to concentrate on his own circuit with its headquarters at The London Coliseum. Details of Variety bills of this era are scarce but it is known that performances were twice nightly at 6.30 and 8.45pm. Strangely, there were also matinees daily at 2.30pm! It is known that films occupied part of the programme from the beginning, so this might explain the unusual timings. London Theatres of Varieties Ltd. (LTV) was founded in 1910 with the amalgamation by Walter Gibbons of many London suburban Variety theatres, the construction of three new theatres and the rebuilding of The Holborn Empire.

The inside of the musical comedy programme below shows that touring shows, including West End successes, had already started to displace Variety at the Croydon Hippodrome by 1912. The neighbouring Empire had been rebuilt only six years before and was already part of the LTV circuit. Clearly, there was not room for two large Variety houses in the town: hence the need to diversify. Interestingly, this programme shows Oswald Stoll as chairman of LTV and Walter Gibbons as managing director. Prices of admission ranged from 6d to 2s 6d, with boxes at 15s and 21s (one guinea). *The Waltz Dream* started at 7.45pm with a Saturday matinee at 2.30pm.

Interior looking towards the stage

By 1914 the Croydon Hippodrome was no longer a part of LTV, nor was listed with the other live theatres in the trade papers; and in fact in 1918 it went over to films completely, the seating capacity being reduced to 1,250. However, the stage was often used in prologues to films in the full three-hour programmes, complete with orchestra. Film prices ranged from 3d to 1s 3d; the boxes were still occupied for film shows, these being charged at 8s 6d for four persons.

The Croydon Hippodrome ran as a cinema for the rest of its life, a highlight coming in May, 1929 when for six months it offered the only talking picture in the town – *The Jazz Singer*. Earlier that year the theatre had become the first London cinema outside the West End to install the sound-on-disc system.

Associated British Cinemas took over the theatre's lease in 1931, with Odeon acquiring it in 1942. They bought the freehold four years later, but kept the 'Hippodrome' name. Films continued until 3 November, 1956, the final attraction being *Run for the Sun*. It was one of nearly sixty cinemas closed by Rank at that time. British Home Stores Ltd. added the demolished Hippodrome to their existing store in Crown Hill, although the altered frontage remained.

Exterior showing the tower

Later, on 26 August, 1972, three small cinemas were opened on the site for the Classic Circuit, together with other leisure facilities. After various name changes, these closed on 14 August, 1982. A tenuous link with entertainment remains, as the premises were converted into a snooker club and fitness centre.

With acknowledgements to Allen Eyles and Keith Skone, The Cinemas of Croydon, Keytone Publications, 1989.

The Urbanis in action

Elephant & Castle: The South London Palace

92 London Road, Lambeth

Elephant & Castle, South London Palace: exterior soon after opening in 1860s

In the days of the stage coach the locality of The Elephant & Castle was well-known to travellers going south of London and the tavern of that name was equally celebrated a stop for rest, refreshment and entertainment. In the latter part of the nineteenth century The South London Music Hall (as it was called) was another famous rendezvous.

Opened on the 30 December, 1860 at 92, London Road and known to the locals as 'The Sarf' the first building was said to have been the converted Roman Catholic chapel of St. George, having a capacity of 1,200. The management was J.F. Tindall and R.E. Villiers. After nine years the theatre was destroyed by fire (like many others), but was rebuilt to the designs of William Paice and reopened on 19 December, 1869. It now held 4,000, if the published figures can be believed! Actually, 1,303 people could be seated, on three levels. The theatre was widely believed to be haunted by nuns, who resented the music hall on the site of the former chapel.

The Palace interior looking towards the stage, 1869

The South London Palace was a very popular theatre during the earlier part of its eighty years' history and presented such favourites as George Leybourne, of 'Champagne Charlie' fame; The Great Mackney and his fiddle; and the colourfully-dressed Great Vance. Blondin, who had just crossed the Niagara Falls on a tight-rope, was here in 1870 and 'Jolly' John Nash, one of the most popular comics of the early days, also appeared, his infectious chuckle earning him the nickname of 'The Laughing Comic'. J.H. Stead also went 'Sarf' at this time under R.E. Villiers' management, bringing his famous song, *The Perfect Cure*, which he accompanied by a jumping dance. He jumped so many times that bets were taken on how many jumps he would achieve during his turn.

Exterior during Gertie Gitana film week

Villiers was succeeded in management by Henry Speedy and John Poole in 1873 and various members of the Poole family retained control until 1896. In 1893 the interior was completely rebuilt by the architects Wylson & Long, but sadly an illustration of this interior has not yet been discovered. I remember it as being fairly long and narrow. The old W. Paice building had by the 1890s begun to look out of fashion. Other managements followed, until eventually the theatre came under the control of Syndicate Halls (later known as Variety Theatres Consolidated Ltd.). Syndicate Halls had been formed in 1904 to take over Chelsea Palace and Walthamstow Palace, as well as the new South London Palace.

Exterior just before bombing of 1941 with 'Shoot the Works' billed

Vesta Victoria, who American successes were even greater than her British ones, first sang her famous song, *Daddy Wouldn't Buy Me a Bow-Wow* at The Sarf, it was written by Joseph Tabrar. Up to the 1920s The South London Palace still presented first-class shows, such as Albert de Courville's revue, *Smile*, but by the mid-30s, possibly as a result of the competition of the neighbouring Trocadero, one of London's most prestigious ciné-variety theatres, it had deteriorated and was regarded as a No. 2, comparable with Collins' Music Hall in North London. To combat local opposition, the house was modernised in the early 1930s and a board advertising 'Quick Fire Variety' was displayed on the front of the theatre.

During the period when I attended The South London Palace from 1935 it was said to pay only £150 per week for its bills. Typical attractions were *The House Scream* with Val Butler and The Jerry Builders, Frank A. Terry's *Pleasure on Parade* and such individual acts as The Four Roadsters, just beginning their career, and Fred Barnes, nearing the end of his. Among others making their London debuts at The Sarf was the ventriloquist, Arthur Worsley, who appeared there in 1935, aged fourteen. He was soon working principal theatres around the country.

Interior after being bombed

The working life of this well-established Hall was cut short by the blitz in 1941. Although the damage was tidied-up, the Hall was never rebuilt and the auditorium was demolished in 1955. The street frontage lingered on into the 1960s, the front windows covered in billboards carrying posters for the current London Palladium show and 'Soldiers of The 60s' army recruitment; eventually this, too, disappeared and shops were built on the site.

An impression of London Road, Elephant & Castle, showing The South London Palace on the horizon after the Blitz

Greenwich Hippodrome

Stockwell Street, Greenwich

Greenwich Hippodrome: main entrance while a Variety theatre and cinema with Mark Melford billed

There has been a place of entertainment on this site for some 150 years, since a music hall was built above or in the large garden at the back of The Rose & Crown in 1855: this had the advantage of being on a corner site. The public house still stands, although now separated from the new Greenwich Theatre. It was re-built in 1888 – some say by Frank Matcham.

In 1871 C.S. Crowder opened a reconstructed music hall under his own name, following building work by W.R. Hough. Like the Canterbury it boasted a Picture Gallery. Crowder ran the hall for seven years, handing over to A.A. Hurley in 1878. Greenwich had the advantage of attracting not only local people to patronise its ten theatres and music halls, but was (then as now) a popular tourist destination as well. Not far from the river landing stages were a number of pubs and halls, among them the Gloucester, the North Pole and the Good Duke Humphrey. One should not overlook the presence of naval and military establishments in the locality – providing another eager audience. A few drinks, something to eat and lively entertainment at a local hall provided a good end to a day out on the river for many Londoners.

Extant side wall while The Parthenon Palace

The 1878 Act of Parliament led to improvements in safety and comfort in the music halls, and Crowder's was accordingly rebuilt by the architect J.G. Buckle in 1885. It was by now run by Hurley, whose son Alec Hurley was a great music-hall star and one of Marie Lloyd's husbands. There were further changes of name to Greenwich Palace of Varieties and The Parthenon Palace, before a further reconstruction (to plans by W. Hancock) in 1895. This included the front entrance so familiar until the 1960s when The Parthenon name could still be made out on a plaster panel on the side wall of the building.

Derelict auditorium before conversion for the new Greenwich Theatre

A name long linked with the music hall in Greenwich was that of David Barnard, who ran the hall from 1903 to 1912 and it was known as 'Barnard's' for years after his departure. The family also ran halls in Woolwich, Chatham, The Elephant & Castle Theatre and Portsmouth. By this time, of course, bars had been separated from the auditorium, with the audience seated in rows of tip-up seats.

Due to poor communications, South East London did not attract many of the stars, nor the powerful theatre chains, to the area. Small local halls could not afford the fees that the big names attracted. By 1924 the Greenwich Hippodrome, as it was by then known, became a cinema – although there were some stage turns. After a period as a repertory theatre, still remembered by local people, the Hippodrome closed down in 1949, becoming a store.

In 1964 newspapers announced plans to reconstruct the old theatre as a playhouse, to be known as the Greenwich Theatre, where a local audience could dine, see a show, have a drink and visit the picture gallery – shades of the old hall! The local council approved the project and a £60,000 restoration fund was launched, with the actor and director Ewan Hooper appointed as the director-designate. At a fund-raising meeting at Greenwich Town Hall the main speaker was Dame Sybil Thorndike.

Main entrance when rebuilt as The Greenwich Theatre

Longer-term and enthusiastic fund-raising got under way, with popular music hall nights at The Green Man, Blackheath swelling the coffers. In 1965 the old Greenwich Hippodrome frontage was demolished and rebuilt, with the main building being gutted. Inside the old shell of the Parthenon arose a modern single-rake auditorium with an open-thrust stage, designed by Brian Meeking. The building opened on 21 October, 1969 and the new playhouse has generally been a great success, despite occasional closures due to funding problems. Strangely, the old Hippodrome/Parthenon has attracted back music hall performers over the years, almost as if the site could not give up its long associations.

The well-known theatre historian and dealer in ephemera, David Drummond, has been behind several Music Hall Nights while *Only a Verse and Chorus*, based on the songs of Weston & Lee, featuring Roy Hudd and Billy Dainty premiered there in the 1980s. The theatre closed in 1997, following cuts to The Arts Council's budget caused its funding to be axed. But, it eventually re-opened in 1999 after a protest march attended by Juliette Stephenson, Miriam Karlin, Prunella Scales, Janet Suzman and others. Extensive renovations were made to lighting, carpets and decorations. In 2001 Ian Liston's Hiss & Boo Company appeared, with The Greenwich Theatre securing a £60,000 annual grant from London Arts the following year. Director Hilary Strong worked hard to make the house into a home for musical theatre. Celebrations were held in 2004 after restoration of the remaining Victorian side wall of the old Parthenon Palace.

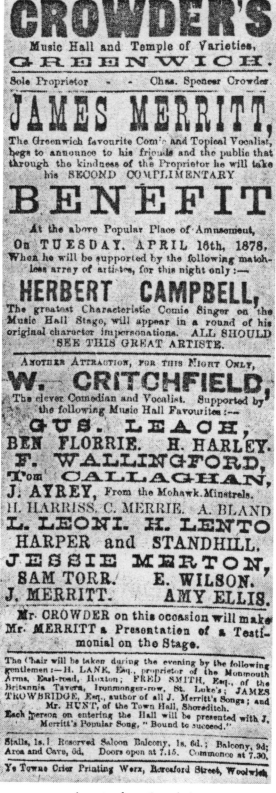

A poster from Crowder's
Music Hall, dated 16.4.1878

The Lewisham Hippodrome

Rushey Green, Catford (south corner of Brownhill Road)

Lewisham Hippodrome: exterior with Troise & his Mandoliers billed, 1939

Reputedly the largest Variety theatre in London and not far from open country when built, The Lewisham Hippodrome was designed by Frank Matcham and opened on 13 February, 1911 – at a time when London already boasted sixty Variety theatres. It was one of four theatres ordered simultaneously by Walter Gibbons of The Capital Syndicate, the others being The London Palladium, Ilford Hippodrome and a rebuilt Holborn Empire. Gibbons was also a director of London Theatres of Varieties Ltd. (LTV), formed eight months earlier to create a circuit of fourteen London suburban halls; further theatres were added later. LTV took over the running of Lewisham Hippodrome until 1928, Charles Gulliver soon taking over from Gibbons.

The capacity of The Lewisham Hippodrome is variously quoted as 2,448, 3,222 and 3,500, but it was certainly a giant. The somewhat curious exterior of the theatre was brick-built with stone facings in the neo-Georgian manner fashionable at the time; it had a two-storey domed box office and outer vestibule, which was linked to the main block by a communicating building, presumably because of the shape of the site. Inside, the architect and his contractors, H.M. Nowell of Stockon-on-Tees, again excelled themselves, although the details of the plasterwork were perhaps coarser than usual. As usual, Matcham managed to give the theatre a sense of intimacy despite its great size.

An early bill included Ernie Lotinga & Co., Violet Essex, Cruikshank, Ivy & Dorice Lee, Jack Lane, The O'Gorman Bros., The Gladiators and Zaleski. Whit Cunliffe headed another bill, with support from Ristori & Partner, J.P. Ling, George Pickett & Dorothy Wilmer and Penrose & Whitlock, nine

413

acts in all. Whit Cunliffe was a great favourite at Lewisham, as was Marie Lloyd, who built herself a tiny theatre at Tanners Hill, SE13. The Lloyd family still live in Lewisham, but the theatre is now a factory.

Other stars seen during WW1 included Charles Whittle, Fred Barnes, George Robey, Little Tich, Mark Sheridan, George Formby, Hilda Glyder, Harry Weldon and Billy Russell. The Lewisham Hippodrome also took tours of pre- and post-West End productions. One such was the London Hippodrome production of *That's A Good Girl*. This played a week from Monday 22 April, 1929, presented jointly by Moss' Empires Ltd. and Jack Buchanan, the show's star. Prices ranged from 1s to 5s 9d for this attraction, rather higher than for straight Variety. Soon after, the Great Musical Success, *The Desert Song* was presented.

Interior looking towards the stage

The Lewisham Hippodrome was acquired from the failed LTV in 1928 by Empire Kinema (Lewisham), run by Sidney L. Bernstein, and opened for films on 4 April, 1931. Live shows had faltered in the late 1920s, but the celluloid era was short-lived, with new super cinemas soon taking film audiences away from such converted halls as the Hippodrome. Full live Variety returned to Lewisham from 16 October, 1933, but two feature films continued to be offered – with a stage show – on Sundays from some years. There were various managements through the years, but Harry Joseph (B & J Theatres) controlled the theatre from 1936 until 1947, for some of that time also running The City Varieties at Leeds. Later he disposed of Lewisham to devote his time to the Leeds theatre, which he made world-famous.

Bills in the period prior to the war were topped by stars such as Troise and his Mandoliers, Roy Fox and his Band, Florrie Forde, Devito & Denny, with G.H. Elliott and Tommy Handley sharing top one week. Musical directors included Horace Sheldon, who had earlier wielded the baton at The London Palladium and had acted as a stooge to comics there, and Harold Collins, later at The London Casino. At this period the MD's name appeared on the posters among the other artistes. After the bombing of The Holborn Empire, Sydney Kaplan was appointed MD at Lewisham, later going to Finsbury Park Empire when the Hippodrome closed. After that he went to America.

Interior looking towards the circles

Two months before the outbreak of war, Tommy Trinder headed a Variety bill that included A.J. Powers, The Ovaltineys, Murphy & Mac, Billy & Idylle Shaw, A.J. Powell's Banjo Octette and Delvaine's Royal Marionettes. Prices were 6d to 2s 4d at this period. Trinder was followed in by Nat Mills & Bobbie in *Nice People* ('the Muffins and Crumpets'), with Syd Seymour and his Mad Hatters the following week.

The London Borough of Lewisham has in its archives a bill for the week of 22 July, 1940 which shows a typical wartime revue, *We're In The Army Now*, starring the Lancashire comic Tom Moss and a cast of forty. Other wartime shows, under British Union Varieties management, were *Home Service Scandals* with Low & Webster and the veteran Harry Champion; and *Runnin' Wild* with Archie Glen ('Still Blotto'), Bennett and Williams, The Three Jokers and Bettina Richman in 'The Dance of The Veils'. But the blitz was soon to start and the theatre was not licensed during 1941–42; however, it escaped bomb damage.

During the later war years and the immediate post-war period the Lewisham Hippodrome enjoyed a measure of prosperity. With the right show the theatre's huge capacity could prove a money-spinner, but the market was gradually falling away with the change in social habits. Early in 1947 Laurel & Hardy paid a visit during their first extensive UK tour, with special matinees on three days to complement the normal performances at 6.15 and 8.30pm. Good bills were headed by such attractions as Henry Hall and his Orchestra, Big Bill Campbell's Rocky Mountain Rhythm and Ralph Reader's *Gang Show*. This last came direct from its successful season at The Stoll Theatre and included Reg Dixon, Dick Emery, Douglas (Cardew) Robinson and Johnny Groves.

After Harry Joseph gave up the theatre, it came under the management of L. Morley-Clarke. A mixed programme was offered, including plays before and after their West End runs – rather as at Golders Green Hippodrome and Streatham Hill Theatre. Such a play was Ted Willis' *No Trees in the Street*, played twice nightly and described thus: 'It's Naked! Raw!! Gripping!!!' There was a visit by The Daniel Mayer Company in *Peter Pan*, starring Margaret Lockwood and with prices set as 2s, 3s and 4s. A big attraction in its last year as a live theatre was *Radio Headliners of 1952*, when the stars of *The Goon Show*, Harry Secombe, Spike Milligan and Max Geldray, topped a Variety bill.

Exterior (Brownhill Road looking towards Rushey Green, Catford)

In spite of its accessibility – the Lewisham Hippodrome was served by trains from Charing Cross and London Bridge, as well as six bus and three tram routes – counter-attractions were proving too strong. Television was stopping people from going out so much at night. In a last bid to win audiences, it became a cinema again from 12 May, 1952, as did its sister theatre The Croydon Empire – both theatres changing their name to The Eros Cinema. A typical programme offered when I was looking at the building in 1959 was *The Hangman*, supported by Dean Martin and Jerry Lewis in *Artists and Models*. With its dome festooned with neon tubes, Lewisham Hippodrome held its last audience on 15 November, 1959 with *The Demons of the Swamp* and *Tank Commando*. The sale of the site was announced in the evening papers and demolition took place in July, 1960 with some decorative plasterwork from the dress circle being rescued by a future member of The British Music Hall Society. A lorry loaded with the blue stall tip-up seats was seen making its way through north-west London. Later Eros House arose on the site. Live entertainment still flourishes at the nearby Lewisham Theatre, recently refurbished and renamed The Broadway Theatre. Her Majesty The Queen attended a Gala Show in 2002 with Max Bygraves and The Beverley Sisters among the artistes appearing. As we go to press, it has been announced that further improvements are to be carried out at The Broadway.

New Cross Empire

New Cross Road and Watson Street

New Cross Empire: exterior with Johnny Lockwood billed, 1947

Originally to have been named the Deptford Empire, this magnificent theatre was designed by Frank Matcham and opened on 31st July, 1899 by Moss and Stoll. The managing company was officially London District Empire Palaces Ltd., also controlling Holloway Empire and Stratford Empire at this time. Seating 1,734 in stalls, dress circle, upper circle and gallery, and with a twelve-piece resident orchestra, the New Cross Empire opened with a mixture of films and Variety. New Cross Empire remained under the control of Moss' Empires from its opening until April, 1946, after which a series of other managements attempted to run it as a Variety theatre, with decreasing levels of success. But for nearly fifty years it was rated as one of London's top Variety houses, on a par with Finsbury Park Empire. Prices ranged from 3d in the gallery to 2s in the Fauteuils. At its opening the management boasted that all seats were upholstered, except, of course, the gallery.

The first programme opened with The National Anthem, sung by Miss Katie Cohen and ended with John Lawson's famous sketch, *Humanity*. A survey of the years will show how well this densely-populated part of London was catered for by its music hall, bearing in mind that New Cross had The Broadway Theatre, a drama house, nearby. This was also operated by Moss' Empires for a few years, although largely a cinema by that time. From 1914 onwards the revue craze can be detected in the Empire's programmes, with musical comedies being added as the years went by. In August, 1914 the Empire's bill comprised The Sisters Reeve, Freddie Hackin, Walter Aubrey, Vernon Watson (who, as Nosmo King, later made a name for himself), Francis Dooley (who toured Australia's Tivoli Circuit the following year), Rowlands & Ford, Smarte Bros., and George Leyton & Company. The year 1915 offered revues entitled *Parlez-Vous Francais* and *Pick-Me-Up*, as well as Variety bills such as the one topped by Little Tich and Lily Morris during August Bank Holiday week.

Moss' Empires, with its booking power, was able to give its audiences the pick of available entertainment – not surprising, as the company at that time ran or presented shows in no fewer than thirty-eight theatres. For example, two touring shows to visit the Empire in 1928 were Firth Shepherd's *Whispering Wires* and The Daniel Mayer Company in *Aloma*. The following year Macdonald & Young presented *Rose Marie*, the big West End success. For the week commencing 10th January, 1930 there was a particularly strong Variety company at New Cross Empire – Lily Morris, Gladdy Sewell, Albert Whelan, Harry Gunn, Miss Ida & Co., The Detelfanos, Johnson Clarke and Bennett & Williams. Stage bands were becoming a huge attraction, none less than Jack Payne and his Band. They topped the bill for the week of 16th December, 1932, with support from Ara & Zetta, Cal & Nona Kay, Edwin Lawrence, Leslie Strange, Fred Brezin and the popular double act, Payne & Hilliard. Non-Variety attractions during the 1930s included *The Show of Shows*; Prince Littler's production of *Tulip Time*, one of the last shows staged at The Alhambra, which played New Cross Empire in September, 1937; and *Tropical Express of 1938*, a very spectacular show which was on a World Tour. However, by the April of 1939 Harry Hanson's Court Players were in residence, staging such plays as *The Greeks Had a Word for It*.

With WW2 now raging, Variety returned to the Empire. The bill for the week of 13th May, 1940 was topped by the BBC feature, *Youth Takes a Bow*, compered by Bryan Mitchie and including two unknowns, Eric Morecambe and Ernie Wise. The supporting acts that week included Tessie O'Shea, Iizuka Bros., Deveen and his Blondes, Jenks & Williams and Pointer, Gray & Dawn. The show was presented by Jack Hylton. In April, 1944 Lew & Leslie Grade's show *Mr. Brown Comes to Town*, topped by Teddy Brown, came to New Cross; others on the bill were Connor & Drake, Jackie Hunter, Will & Marie Vine, Audrey Marshall, Jimmy Lyons, Hilda Gregory and The West End Glamour Girls. Moss' Empires could never be accused of stinting on quality, as that same year saw bills topped by stars of the calibre of Vic Oliver; Billy Thorburn with Betty Driver; George Robey with Tex McLeod; Georgie Wood with Tommy Fields; Anne Shelton; and Geraldo with Wilson, Keppel & Betty. Other bands appearing that year included those of Maurice Winnick, Joe Loss, Billy Cotton and Oscar Rabin.

Interior looking towards the stage

There were two Pantomimes during the 1945/46 season: *Puss in Boots*, with Roy Lester, Winsor & Wilton and Violet Field; and *Cinderella*, with Archie Glen, Elsie Winsor, Audrey Hewitt and The Moxham Bros. Not long into the year the news broke that Moss' Empires would no longer be presenting shows at New Cross Empire, the closing night being on 13th April, 1946. At the same time the company disposed of some of their provincial theatres, such as Hull Palace and Gateshead Empire, which were no longer proving profitable. There was a seamless transition, as The Peoples' Entertainment Society/Park Theatrical Productions opened the Empire for business on the Monday night, 15 April, 1946. This company also had connections with The Devonshire Park Theatre at Eastbourne, The Swindon Empire and The Regent, Kings Cross in London. They had a run of over five years at New Cross, but in the end had to admit defeat, finishing on Saturday, 25 August, 1951.

Colling Productions were the next to take up the challenge, presenting good bills from Monday 27 August, 1951 – again taking straight over from the previous management. The Joint Managing Directors were R. Colling Pyper and J. Grant Anderson. The Musical Director was Sam Bray, 'late R.N.' The pantomime that opened the 1951/52 season was *Dick Whittington*, starring Dorothy Squires and Joyce Golding; it ran for three weeks, breaking all house records at the Empire, being produced by the extraordinarily popular Dorothy Squires herself. Boosted by its enormous success, Colling Productions extended the following year's pantomime – Deen Moray's lavish *Aladdin*, to a five week season, twice nightly from 24 December, 1952. The production starred Wally Wood, Eva Kane and Jennie Hayes, but this wonderful show attracted very poor business, nearly bankrupting J. Grant Anderson. His partner in New Cross Empire, Colling Pyper, had numerous hotel interests in addition to his theatrical ones, so was more able to withstand the heavy losses. Sadly, in consequence, Colling Productions were forced to withdraw from New Cross on Saturday, 31 January, 1953.

The Coronation Year saw a very short tenure by Medway Enterprises, who strove to keep the New Cross Empire open from Monday, 2 February until Saturday, 5 April, 1953. When they failed, the theatre remained closed for over three months.

Another plucky management, Regent Variety Enterprises opened on Monday, 27 July, 1953 with great plans; their optimism showed with their first programme featuring Jimmy Wheeler, Suzette Tarri, Scott Sanders and Robin Richmond on his Hammond organ – a fine array by any standard. In support were Bill & Babs Adams, The Micheles, Taro Naito the foot juggler, with The Max Sisters opening each half of the programme. Charles Tovey and The Empire Orchestra were in the pit. The following week saw Gladys Hay, Harold Behrens, Herschel Henlere and Mooney & King heading a sparkling bill.

During Dorothy Squires' week in June, 1954 John Cliff, a member of the theatre staff, was asked to fetch Rock and Chips from the shop in Watson Street and deliver them to her dressing room. On entering he was a bit taken aback to find the star in a state of undress but, as usual, she packed the place out at virtually every performance.

The high standards set in the opening weeks were maintained throughout the rest of 1953, up to Christmas Pantomime. *Cinderella* with Leon Cortez, Doreen Harris, Janet Brown and Ford & Sheen was staged with prices from 2s to 5s. Variety stars seen during that year of celebration were legion: Afrique and Sirdani; Stanelli with Leslie Sarony; Alfred Marks; Sam Browne with Jill Manners; Peter Sellers; Archie Lewis with Chan Canasta; Radio Revellers; Billy Russell with Turner Layton; Dr Crock & His Crackpots; Charlie Chester; Dorothy Squires with The Western Bros.; Hutch; Arthur English with Eddie Gray in *Open the Cage*; Phyllis Dixey; and finally Tommy Fields with Kitty Bluett and Randolph Sutton. It was a superb meal for fans of Variety; but, as John Cliff recalls, the public were not supporting the enterprising new management in great enough numbers. In an attempt to make the theatre pay, outgoings on shows were reduced and from 6 March, 1954 the quality of entertainment can clearly be seen to decline.

Shows like *Call Us Mister, Stop, Look and View* and *We Couldn't Wear Less* were no match for top stars available on television in the comfort of one's own home. True, there were occasional returns to good Variety bills; Billy Cotton & his Band came in 1954 and The Great Levante mystified for a week in June of that year. For the rest of the time it was a diet of *Taking off To-night*! and *Paris After Dark*. 'The Glamour Spectacle of The 20th Century' – *Folies Parisienne* – starred Jimmy Mac, for so long the mainstay of pantomime at Bath Theatre Royal. It was a case of reduced investment leading to reducing audiences, with the result that the management pulled out of New Cross Empire on Saturday, 10 July, 1954. The theatre faced a long closure of two and a half years.

Diana Dors was one of the stars appearing during the last weeks before closure and she certainly attracted local attention on the opening Monday. Her big streamlined American car was mobbed by a crowd of nearly a thousand, who managed to lift it onto two wheels. Considerable damage was done, while later in the week between houses Miss Dors had an unexpected visitor. A teenage boy, who had scaled the ten foot wall at the back of the theatre, forced open her dressing room window and started to climb inside. The redoubtable Miss Dors stopped him in his tracks by dowsing him with a pot of cold water and slamming the window shut. A few seconds later a dustbin hurtled through, shattering the window but very luckily not hitting the star, who must by then have wished she had stayed in the safety of the film studios.

The New Cross Empire was in fact occasionally now being used a film studio, for example, in Herbert Wilcox's 1955 production of *King's Rhapsody*. The producer said they wanted a 'rather tired' building to represent L'Opéra, Paris, with the Empire rather unfortunately by now fitting the bill perfectly. The film starred Anna Neagle, an equally 'rather tired' looking Errol Flynn and Patrice Wymore.

Two short seasons of pantomime were the only occasions when live entertainment was seen again on the Empire stage. After the performance of *Dick Whittington* on 29 December, 1956 'The Showplace of South London' was no more. Unfortunately, this final pantomime season was even shorter than planned, as Sarah the Cook suddenly disappeared with the box office takings! Thereafter, the cast manned the counter, dividing the meagre income amongst themselves. It was not a happy conclusion to nearly sixty years of live entertainment in New Cross.

Interior from the stage

The New Cross area certainly had its share of tough characters and curious events. Performers in a play at the Empire were once fascinated by a razor fight which took place in the Dress Circle one night between two members of the audience. The artistes tried to follow the progress of the fight without missing their lines. I later got to know one of John Cliff's colleagues, John Barber, who remembered many details of the theatre. His first job was as a follow-spot operator, up aloft in the disused gallery slips, both sides of which housed the limes; later he progressed to the stage lighting board. The bio-box was located at the rear of the upper circle, from which he used to project the interval advertising slides. Occasionally John had to visit the roof void to lower chandeliers for cleaning. He was horrified to visit the Empire for a *Marathon Piano Presentation*. Admission was 2s, to see and hear the poor pianist playing day and night to win a World Record Cup, but no more was heard of the result. After closure, New Cross Empire was also used in several long sequences of the film *Charlie Moon*, featuring Max Bygraves. This film had its West End season at another former music hall – The London Pavilion. The Empire building was eventually bought from the People's Entertainment Society by Oliver Cutts, who had plans to turn it into a Sports Arena, but it was pulled down in 1958 and a car wash now occupies the site.

MOSS EMPIRES, LTD.

ABERDEEN H.M. (re., 12).—William Daunt, in " Collusion."

BIRMINGHAM EMP. (re., 12.30).—T. F. Convery's " Formby's Night Out," including George Formby.

BIRMINGHAM GRAND (re., 1).—" Simba " film.

BIRMINGHAM ROYAL (re., 11).—" The Desert Song."

BLACKPOOL GRAND (re., 11).—" The Patsy."

BLACKPOOL OPERA HOUSE (re., 11).—Tallulah Bankhead, in " Her Cardboard Lover."

BRADFORD ALHAM. (re., 12.15).—Archie Pitt's " The Show's the Thing," including Gracie Fields

CARDIFF EMP. (re., 1).—Frank Lawton, in " Young Woodley."

EDINBURGH EMP. (re., 12).—Tom Arnold's " One Dam Thing After Another."

FINSBURY PARK EMP. (re., 1).—Jane Ayr and Billy Childs with their Embassy Six Band, Hatch and Carpenter, Burr and Hope, Linga-Singh, The Junetros, the Two Van de Peears, Johnson Clark, Harold Walden.

GATESHEAD EMP. (re., 1).—" The Terror."

GLASGOW ALHAM. (re., 11).—Jack Hylton and his Band.

GLASGOW EMP. (re., 11).—Burns and Allen, Mark Griver and his Scottish Revellers, Nellie Forbes, Ricoro Brothers, George Betton, George and Fay Staples, the Two Stavanys, May Henderson.

HANLEY GRAND (re., 12.30).—" Crazy Rhythm," including Bobbie Hind and his Band, Chick Farr, Mello and Nello, Trixie Maison, Cyril Lamb, Fynch and Payne, Lilian Francis, Oswald Waller, Peel and Curtis.

HULL PAL. (re., 1).—Frank E. Franks's " The Seafarers."

LEEDS EMP. (re., 1).—Debroy Somers and his Band, Jack Lee, Cissie Hughes, Garret, Alda and Doret, Ada and Eddie Daros.

LEEDS ROYAL (re., 11).—Nelson Keys, in " Burlesque."

LIVERPOOL EMP. (re., 1).—B. A. Meyer's " Lucky Girl."

LONDON HIPPO. (re., 11).—" The Five O'Clock Girl."

MANCHESTER PAL. (re., 11).—" The Truth Game," including Lily Elsie, Ivor Novello, Lilian Braithwaite, Viola Tree.

NEWCASTLE EMP. (re., 1).—" The League of Stars," including the Two Rascals, Payne and Hilliard, Dmitri and Lorina Neil McKay, Mitchell and Peru, Betty Mack, Spencer's Wonder Girls, the Rascals Band.

NEW CROSS EMP. (re., 1).—Macdonald and Young's " Rose Marie."

NEWPORT EMP. (re., 12).—Joe Morrison, in " Harmony Hall."

NOTTINGHAM EMP. (re., 1).—Tom Arnold's " All Fit," including Nellie Wallace.

NOTTINGHAM ROYAL (re., 12).—" The Yellow Mask," including Norman Griffin and Margery Conyers.

PORTSMOUTH ROYAL (re., 11).—" Many Happy Returns."

PRESTON EMP. (re., 11).—Denville Stock Company.

SALFORD PAL. (re., 11).—" Abie's Irish Rose."

SHEFFIELD EMP. (re., 11).—Will Garland's " Swanee River."

SOUTHAMPTON EMP. (re., 1).—Clayton and Waller's " Virginia."

SOUTHSEA KING'S (re., 1.30).—M. Barry O'Brien's " Broadway."

SOUTH SHIELDS EMP. (re., 1).—" Pontoon."

SOUTH SHIELDS ROYAL (re., 1).—Denville Stock Company.

STRATFORD EMP. (re., 1).—Scott and Whaley, in " Business is Business."

SUNDERLAND EMP. (re., 11).—" Change Over."

SWANSEA EMP. (re., 2).—Francis Laidler's " Billy Blue," including Tom D. Newell.

VICTORIA PAL. (re., 11.30).—Babe Egan and her Hollywood Redheads, the Gresham Singers, Charles Hayes, Les Athena, Arthur Astill, Jack Grieve, two Hiawathas, the Fanjacks.

WEST HARTLEPOOL EMP. (re., 12).—" The Police Force."

The thirty-eight halls owned or run by Moss' Empires Ltd. in May, 1929

Peckham Hippodrome

Peckham High Street, Peckham

Peckham Hippodrome: exterior (formerly The Crown Theatre) with Jake Friedman billed, 1910

Built on an old fairground which had possibly been the site of a former playhouse, the Crown Theatre was one of a myriad drama theatres in the London suburbs. It was designed by Ernest Runtz, built like a battleship, and opened on 31 October, 1898. The Cardiff New Theatre is Runtz's only theatre remaining in operation, although his Middlesbrough Empire is still there – as a pub – and the shell of his Hastings Hippodrome contains amusement machines.

The Crown, like many of the other suburban houses, staged plays, musical comedies and operetta straight from their West End runs. It was built for Isaac Cohen, who had run the Pavilion, Whitechapel until 1894. Interestingly, Ernest Runtz made radical alterations to that theatre in the same year. The Crown's first production was *The Sign of the Cross*, given by The Wilson Barrett Company. Peckham audiences enjoyed numerous musical comedies like *Floradora*, *The Belle of New York* and *The Geisha* when they went on tour. Courtice Pounds starred in *Chilperic* and Marie Lloyd was a regular favourite there in the annual pantomime. Indeed, for two years in the 1890s Marie Lloyd lived locally, at 196 Lewisham Way, with her husband of the time, Percy Courtney. Their Sunday evening parties became famous!

Local people loved Marie in her usual role of principal boy, which she played in the first Peckham pantomime, *Dick Whittington*, in 1898. She was in *Cinderella* the following year and both shows ran for two months. Supporting casts often included the talents of Dan Crawley, The McNaughtons and two of Marie's sisters, Alice Lloyd and Daisy Wood. There was great competition among Peckham and

Camberwell's girls to be members of the chorus. Almost resident at the Crown's pantomime was Arthur Lawrence, a bass singer who always played the Demon. Never a big star himself, his daughter – Gertrude Lawrence – certainly was.

Interior looking towards the circles

Church services were also held at the theatre and on one occasion it is said that the congregation exceeded 3,700. But a successful pantomime season, or even packed church services, proved to be insufficient to keep the big, plush Crown Theatre afloat for the whole year. Strong competition from the New Cross Broadway Theatre and the even closer Camberwell Metropole resulted in falling attendances at the Crown. Even membership of Robert Arthur Theatres, who ran a number of the London suburban houses and who controlled the Crown for a time, failed to stop the rot. Drama gave way to Variety at the end of 1908, including the inevitable Bioscope. The theatre became Peckham Hippodrome around this time, although the proprietors were still given in the programme as 'Crown Theatre Ltd.' The house was briefly controlled by Walter Gibbons – always on the look-out for failing drama houses to turn into music halls – but was not part of his London Theatres of Varieties for long. It would of course have been in direct competition with LTV's nearby Camberwell Palace and Balham Hippodrome. Shown below is a typical Variety bill of the period, for the week of 31 October, 1910 with ten acts on offer twice nightly at 6.40 and 9.00pm. The manager Cecil Paget was here for several years from 1901, later managing Daly's Theatre in Leicester Square until the latter's closure in September, 1937.

Only a year later the Peckham Hippodrome succumbed to full-time films as part of the Biocolor Picture Theatres circuit. Biocolor was taken over by the original Gaumont company in 1926. Clearly the old theatre was outmoded, so the new owners closed and pulled it down just two years later.

It was four years before its replacement, the 2,300-seater Gaumont Palace, opened on 8 February, 1932 with *The Calendar* and *Almost a Divorce*. The new building was said to have incorporated the façade of the old Hippodrome. But if this was so, then it must have been radically remodelled in the process. The new cinema was designed by Verity and Beverley, but had very limited stage space compared with the original theatre. There was, however, a Compton theatre organ. There was no fly tower and the stage was only 18ft deep. Ciné-variety was presented some weeks – for example, the live acts for the week of 19 July, 1936 were Flack & Lucas (tap dancers); Louis Almaer; and Bemand's Pigeons. During a sample week in the summer of 1938 the Peckham house was not offering any Variety, although nine other Gaumont-British cinemas in London were. A month or two later the number was down to six and with the outbreak of WW2 live acts disappeared completely.

Exterior showing 1932 replacement as Gaumont Palace Cinema

The Peckham Gaumont was bombed twice, in 1941 and 1944, but was patched-up and continued showing films until 14 January, 1961 when *The Bulldog Breed* brought the curtain down for the last time. Seats were then removed and the organ broken up. Only four months later, in May, it reopened as Britain's first Top Rank Bingo Club – a trial run to gauge the public's reaction. In fact, the 'trial' continued for thirty-seven years – longer even than the time spent on films. Eventually, falling admissions led to the hall's closure in December, 1998. It was demolished four years later.

MARIE LE BLANC,

DESCRIPTIVE AND COMIC VOCALIST.

CHRISTMAS ARRANGEMENTS—

CANTERBURY.   PARAGON.   ROYAL ALBERT.

MARIE LE BLANC'S *repertoire* for '89 will include, amongst others, "*Before the Beak,*" by Oswald Allan; "*Wayside Inn,*" "*etcetera, etcetera.*" "*The Little Drummer Boy,*" by Harrington and Le Brunn; "*Lay These Flowers on My Comrade's Grave,*" by Frank Egerton; and "*The Boat Race,*" by F. V. St. Clair.

Sole Agent, EDWARD COLLEY.

THE CRAGGS,

GENTLEMEN ACROBATS.

LONDON PAVILION and ROYAL CAMBRIDGE till Easter.

CANTERBURY, PARAGON, EMPIRE, ROYAL, and COLLINS'S, to follow.

J. W. CRAGG, Sole Proprietor, Theatre Royal, Leigh, Lancashire.

PERMANENT ADDRESS—

68 KENNINGTON ROAD, LONDON, S.E.

Agent, WARNER & CO.

THE CELEBRATED

ALBERT AND EDMUNDS

GREAT ECCENTRIC COMIC TROUPE,

FROM

THEATRE ROYAL, DRURY LANE, AND ALHAMBRA THEATRE, LONDON:

PROSPECTIVE ARRANGEMENTS for 1889.

SURREY THEATRE, LONDON, FOR PANTOMIME, 1888-89.   Fifth Season.
Grand Stadt Theatre, Vienna—April and May.
Canterbury, Paragon, Metropolitan, Alhambra, Middlesex, & Foresters—June, July, August, and September.
Manchester, Liverpool, Newcastle, Edinburgh, and Glasgow—October, November, and December.

Address—H. M. EDMUNDS, en route; or Agent, FRANK ALBERT, 165, Stamford St., London.

MISS NELLIE RICHARDS.

AMERICA'S PRIDE.

PRINCIPAL LONDON MUSIC HALLS NIGHTLY

Agent - - - Mr EDWARD COLLEY.

Calling cards for some of the Variety artistes

Penge Empire

High Street, Penge

Penge Empire: exterior with Tommy Handley billed

The Penge Empire was designed by W.G.R. Sprague for Clarence Sounes in the 'correct', but slightly cold, Roman style then in vogue; it opened in 1915 when Music Hall had passed its zenith and seated 1,501 in stalls, dress circle and gallery. Sounes was connected with a number of theatres in the London area, notably at Poplar, Woolwich and Kingston.

After a period as an independent hall, it eventually came under the Abrahams Group, before becoming part of George Black's General Theatre Corporation; this was the company that also controlled two major West End houses (The London Palladium and The Holborn Empire), as well as a string of Hippodromes in Birmingham, Brighton, Wolverhampton, Boscombe and other centres.

The company's attitude to Penge is exemplified by a story about Flanagan & Allen. Then making their first success, they were given a severe wigging by Val Parnell for 'misbehaving'. He warned them that if they persisted in accepting Stoll dates, they would not play The Holborn Empire ever again and all their existing dates would be transferred to The Penge Empire! "We made you and we can break you", the great man said. But in spite of that, Penge did enjoy the 'big time' for quite a few years. Amongst those performing were Jimmy James (in *The Spare Room*), G.T. Pattman, *Splinters*, Layton & Johnstone, Clarkson Rose, Houston Sisters, Billy Bennett, Albert Whelan and Jack Straw. Who said politicians had nothing in common with comedians!

Interior looking towards the stage

A spin-off *Crazy Show* was presented at Penge in March, 1933 to capitalise on the success of the real thing at The London Palladium. The principal fun-makers were Dave & Joe O'Gorman, aided and abetted by Joe Young (The Hot Dog of Vaudeville). Strong support came from Michael & Arnova, Allen & Lavoie, The Carson Sisters, Toni Raglan (on his jam jars) and The Nifty Nineties. When I was there bedlam erupted at the company's antics during the *Arkiddy* sketch. It only subsided when the popular manager, Jimmy Molloy, appeared in the stalls to bellow: 'The bar is open!'

The following week saw Jack Payne and his Band, supported by Lewis & Lawn, Haig & Escoe, Earle & Eddie Franklyn, Peter Fannan 'The Erector of Laughs', Tom Davies and Bud Ritchie 'Where the Laughs Come From'. That week Jack Payne was doubling with The Holborn Empire, twice nightly – no mean feat considering the distance between them. The Empire's conductor at this time was Jack Frere, directing a band of twelve.

The week of 20 September, 1937 saw Lew Lake's *Blackberries*, with The Cole Brothers and 'Pep' Graham in the company. Variety was already ceasing to attract such large audiences at Penge, while Southend, Leeds, Sheffield, Liverpool and Newcastle Hippodromes had already been disposed of; but at least Penge remained open. George Black then changed tack by instituting a Repertory policy at The Penge Empire. Harry Hanson's Court Players, having had a brilliant summer season at Nottingham Theatre Royal – with which George Black had connections – were in 1937 offered the South London house. The Hanson magic was equally effective here: the company had an unbroken run at Penge Empire for seven years, a run only brought to a sudden end in 1944 by a bomb which closed the theatre.

Among regular members of The Court Players were Noele Gordon, Brian Reece (later television's 'PC49'), Mona Washbourne, Basil Dignam and Dorothy Reynolds (a co-author of *Salad Days* in the late 1950s). Plays were produced twice nightly at The Empire.

After the Second World War the theatre was repaired, following which Bernard Delfont attempted to reinstate Variety, but without great success. Moss' Empires Ltd., who had acquired all the remaining live theatres of the G.T.C. group at the end of 1947, soon decided to dispose of Penge Empire as being 'unsuitable'.

Interior looking across the auditorium

The new management, the well-known Derek and Reginald Salberg, presented The Globe Players in weekly repertory for about eighteen months. Plays included *Pygmalion*, *Trespass* by Emlyn Williams and *Lottie Dundas* by Edith Bagnold. The last was the attraction for the week of Monday 4 October, 1948 and included Anthony Howard in the cast. The pit orchestra had given way to two pianos. The house was advertised daily in the national press entertainment columns.

However, the days of live shows ended (with very occasional exceptions) in September, 1949 when Penge Empire was bought by the Essoldo circuit. After some remodelling, it opened on 31 October, 1949 as a cinema, enjoying a run of about ten years. Using rear projection (from behind the screen), the theatre was limited to a 16ft by 12ft screen by poor sightlines. The Penge Essoldo became the first London suburban cinema to launch CinemaScope, with a much larger screen – in June, 1954. Closure came on 9 April, 1960 with a double programme – *Jazzboat* and *12 to The Moon*.

Exterior when remodelled as The Essoldo Cinema

London lost another well-equipped theatre, with a 29ft deep stage and twelve dressing rooms; there were 40 hemp lines in the grid. The building was later demolished and the pub opposite, where artistes had refreshed themselves between houses, also vanished.

Cruikshank

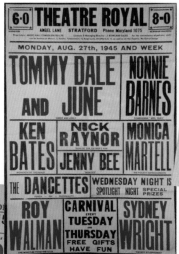

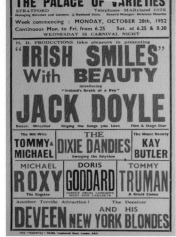

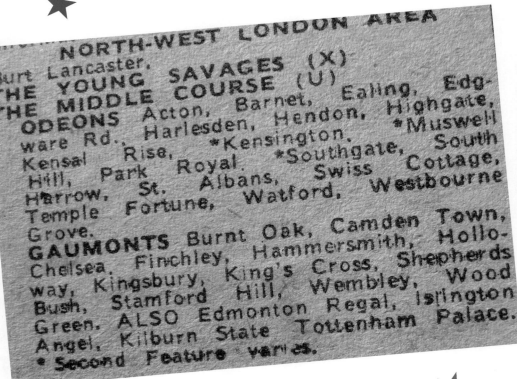

Wilton's Grand Music Hall in Wellclose Square E.1 is the only remaining hall of its colourful era & is the only entertainment hall of this importance. Restoring Wilton's to be part of the entertainment industry demands the cost of living theatre. Please help & all...

WILTON'S GRAND MUSIC HALL

Grace's Wellclose Square

NEEDS FR...

and £££'s...

WILTONS MUSIC HALL
1 GRACE'S ALLEY, LONDON E1 8JB
Box Office: 020 7702 2789   www.wiltons.org.uk

THE BRITISH MUSIC HALL SOCIETY
President: Roy Hudd OBE   Chairman: Doreen Hermitage

Proudly celebrates its 50th anniversary

WITH A THREE DAY
NATIONAL FESTIVAL OF
MUSIC HALL
AND
VARIETY

From FRIDAY to SUNDAY
20-22 SEPTEMBER 2013
Open each day 11.00 a.m. - 8.00 p.m.
27 HOURS OF ENTERTAINMENT **27**

CHARLESWORTH, STRAY PRINTER, WESTLEFF, WILTONS

A SPECIAL OFFER to The Theatres Trust to come to
Wilton's Music Hall
'For ONE NIGHT ONLY at London's Oldest Victorian Music Hall'

AN EVENING OF MUSIC & COMEDY
TUESDAY, JUNE 30TH 6.30 to 10.30pm
Graces Alley, off Ensign St., London E1 (Tube: Tower Hill)
Starring Artistes who have been praised EVERYWHERE with SHOUTS OF APPLAUSE and ENTHUSIASTIC DELIGHT BY VAST CONCOURSES OF PEOPLE, including

James 'BIDDIE' Biddlecombe
singing a selection of favourite Music Hall songs for your pleasure

'DOCKYARD DORIS' & 'SOPHIE TUCKER'
re-created by Mr. Colin Devereaux, Guardian Pantomime Dame of the Year

Opera della Luna
performing enchanting excerpts from English Operas

...MMER & FRAME
...act of TIM HOLMES & 'Bristow's Frank Dickens
...YRNE   BRIAN DAUBNEY
...onist & Comic   Presents Music Hall Memories
...clude a Delicious Victorian Buffet Dinner,
..., Magic Tricks and An Exhibition of THEATRICAL CARTOONS

Tickets @ £27.50 or £50 a Pair   =£_____
...Tickets @ £25 or £45 a Pair for Theatres Trust =£_____
...l cheque to The Cartoon Art Trust for the total £_____
                    Address_____

...cheque & SAE to arrive BY FRIDAY JUNE 26th to: The Cartoon Art Trust,
...EC1N 8JY. For Credit Card & Late Bookings, Please Ring: 0171 405 4717
...to change. In aid of The Cartoon Art Trust, Registered Charity No. 32797

'A RUMBUSTIOUS PRODUCTION' SUNDAY TIMES   **'ACTED WITH REAL FLOURISH'** THE GUARDIAN

THE
TAMING of the
SHREW

ONLY UNTIL 28 APR

WILTON'S MUSIC HALL   020 7702 2789 020 7434 7592 24 HRS   www.wiltons.org.uk

BMHS 50th Anniversary
Sat 21 Sep 13 - 10:00AM   £20.00
Stalls - H20

Nicholas Charlesworth Order No. 13-ED-0OMA

WILTON'S
THE CITY'S HIDDEN STAGE

Wilton's Music Hall, Graces Alley, London E1 8JB.
Box Office 020 7702 2789 - wiltons.org.uk
Registered Charity No. 1003041. VAT No. 583681407

Willesd...
HIPPODR...

Opening Programme

Week commencing Monday, October 31st, 1938

1 **OVERTURE—**
The Knightsbridge March from '' In Town To-night ''   *Eric Coates*

2 **FANFARE**

3 **OPENING CEREMONY**
by His Worship the MAYOR OF WILLESDEN
Alderman H. W. PROTHERO, J.P. and THE MAYORESS
MISS DILYS PROTHERO

4 **THE NATIONAL ANTHEM**

5 **THE THREE DYNAMITES**
Britain's Most Popular Young Dancers

6 **NIXON & MORRISON**
The Canadian C...

7 **PEPINOS CIRCUS**
The Funniest of All Miniature...

8 **CLIFF COOK** ... ... The Eccentric...

9 **ELSIE & DORIS WATERS**
Radio's '' Gert '' and...

10 **INTERMISSION—**
Memoirs of Famous Musical Shows ... *arr. by...*

PROGRAMME CONTINU...

PROGRAMME CONTINUED

11 **RALPHONO & PAGE**   A Phantasy in Smoke

12 **TROISE and his MANDOLIERS**
The Popular Broadcasting Band
With DON CARLOS

13 **MURRAY & MOONEY**
The Famous Comedians

14 **SWAN & LEIGH** ...   Thrills Without Spills

Stage Furnitur...

Next Week commencing Monday, Nov...

A TERRIFIC VARIETY SHOW...
SCOTT & WHALEY
THE TWO LESLIES
PHYLLIS ROBINS
CHARLES DUDLEY and his FAMOUS
LEON & KIKI
EDDIE BAYES
MR. THOMAS, ESQ.
READING & GRANT
and Supporting Company

COMING—Monday, June 5th
Another Great
CRAZY SHOW
with
SYD SEYMOUR
AND HIS MAD HATTERS
SUPPORTED BY THE CRAZIEST OF
ALL CRAZY ACTS

WE ADVISE YOU TO RESERVE YOUR
SEATS BEFORE IT'S TOO LATE

Hippodrome
WILLESDEN

THIS IS A THEATRE

PROGRAMME
TWOPENCE

NEXT WEEK
MONDAY, MAY 29th, 1939
6.40 — TWICE NIGHTLY — 8.50

GRAND 'WHIT WEEK' ATTRACTION!
E. B. SEENER
presents his
CONTINENTAL REVUE SENSATION
"GOING GAY"
IN 20 GAY, GLAMOROUS AND GORGEOUS
GLIMPSES OF UNPARALLELED SPLENDOUR
Featuring
THE SENSATION OF THE AGE
MDLLE. YVONNE
Direct from Paris
The famous Fan Dancer,
presenting
'' THE DANCE OF THE
SEVEN VEILS ''
and
'' THE DANCE OF THE
FANS ''

JACK CLIFFORD
and
NAT JACKLEY
The Inimitable Pair

THE GOING GAY GIRLS
GLORIA KAYE
MICHAEL O'NEIL
MARGARET TURNER
AUDREY & ERIC
LES BORISOFFS
THREE CHORDS
BEREL & OSTRAN

LAUGH AND BE GAY—AN ENTERTAINMENT
YOU WILL TALK ABOUT FOR WEEKS!

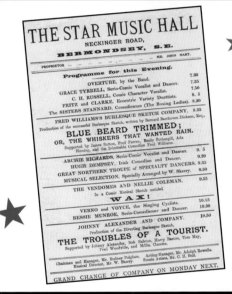

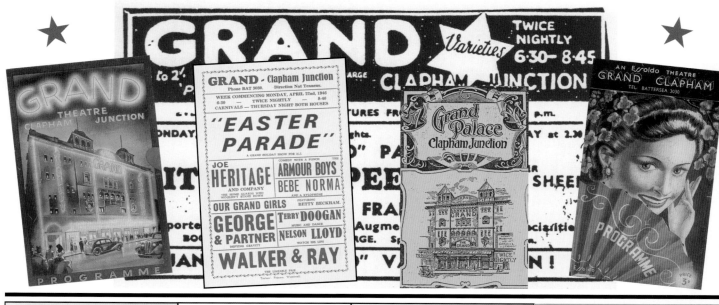

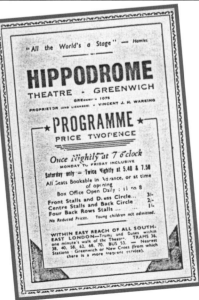

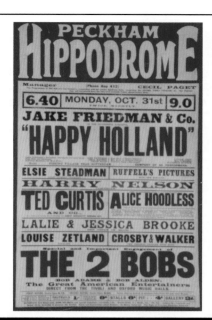

CANTERBURY

THEATRE OF VARIETIES, WESTMINSTER BRIDGE ROAD.
Proprietors - - - - Messrs. CROWDER & PAYNE
And of the Paragon Theatre of Varieties, Mile End Road.

EASTER HOLIDAYS!
BANK HOLIDAY, MONDAY, APRIL 11th, and
Every Evening until further notice.

The Greatest Combination & Variety Entertainment in London

PAUL MARTINETTI
And his American Pantomime Company in an Eccentric Sketch, entitled,

THE MAGIC FLUTE
In which the following Artistes will appear:—
Mr. ALFRED MARTINETTI
Mdlle. Josephine MARTINETTI
Mr. JOHN HEARD,
Mr. W. CRAIG,
Mr. J. DE CONRA,
And the Inimitable
PAUL MARTINETTI
Bonnie Kate Harvey
Frazer & Allen.

Important Engagement and First Appearance of Mdlle.

ALCIDE CAPITAINE
QUEEN OF THE AIR!
The most Astounding Lady Gymnast in the World.

Prof. MACCANN, KITTY WREN.
SPECIAL ENGAGEMENT of LIEUT.

WALTER COLE
King of Ventriloquists.

Kennedy & Allen,
JOCKEY WATSON
Re-production of the Laughable Musical Sketch, entitled

THE DEVIL BIRD
INTRODUCING
MISS MILLIE HOWES,
MISS LOUIE GILBERT,
MR. LEO STORMONT,
And the Laughter-provoking
FRED WILLIAMS.
SCENERY BY N. HINCHEY.

Agnes VERBECK
HARRY LEANDER.
Re-appearance of the Celebrated Acrobatic and Risley Troupe,

THE CRAGGS
Premier Acrobats of the World.

TWO MIKES,
TOM COSTELLO
George BELVERE

Doors Open Bank Holiday and Tuesday at 6, Commence at 6-30.

PRICES:— 3d. to £2.2s.
General Manager - - - - Mr. A. THIODON.
JAMES UPTON, Baskerville Printing Works, Birmingham.

CANTERBURY
Theatre of Varieties, Westminster Bridge Rd.
Manager - - - - ERNEST LEPARD.
Week Commencing July 24th.
One Performance Nightly.
Half-Time 9-30 p.m. See Special Bills.

CHAS. AUSTIN | CLARICE MAYNE
PARKER'S PROGRESS | ELSIE ELLIS
CHAS. F. BEST | MILNER & STOREY
FELIX & FISHER | VIVIAN FOSTER
FLO DUDLEY | DAISY WOOD
BARRY LUPINO | DAN WHITLEY
MOZETTO | Ruffell's Bioscope
CONWAY & LELAND | GARDEN OF GIRLS

CANTERBURY
Theatre of Varieties,
WESTMINSTER BRIDGE ROAD
(And Paragon, Limited).

Christmas & New Year's Holidays!
BOXING NIGHT, DEC. 26th, 1887
And Every Evening.

PINAUDS
In Original Grotesque Act.
Miss Nelly L'ESTRANGE
HENRI CLARK.
MISS BESSIE BELLWOOD
MISS JENNY JOY.
The ROLMAZ TRIO
FOX & FOX,
T. W. BARRETT
THE HANLON VOLTAS
HARRY ANDERSON
SEGOMAR,
THE TWO MIKES.
Mdlle. ESKE AND FRANK VOLIER
A. P. BOSWELL.
FLORENCE HAYES
NAUGHTY JACK
ALICE MAYDUE, and SAM SAUNDERS, WALTER GROVES, The HIBBS QUARTETTE
OPEN AT 6 O'CLOCK, COMMENCE AT 6-45.
Prices:— 6d. to £2.2s.

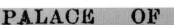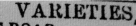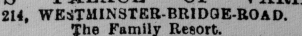

C. GATTI'S
ADMISSION FREE
NEW AND MAGNIFICENT HALL,
76, WESTMINSTER ROAD,
NEAR THE BRIDGE,
IS NOW OPEN!

GATTI'S PALACE OF VARIETIES,
214, WESTMINSTER-BRIDGE-ROAD.
The Family Resort.
Proprietors, Messrs G. and L. CORAZZA-GATTI.

GATTI'S PALACE OF VARIETIES,
WESTMINSTER BRIDGE ROAD.

445

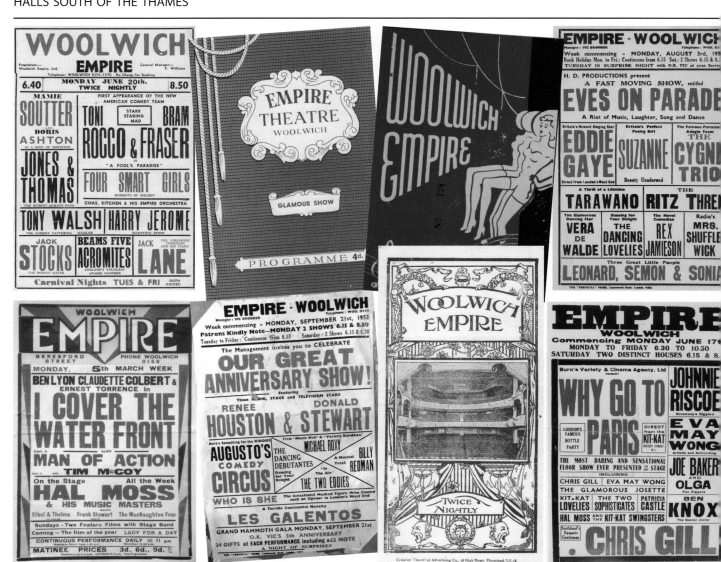

Putney Hippodrome

Felsham Road (formerly Gardener's Lane), off High Street, Putney

Putney Hippodrome: exterior from the High Street

A large theatre seating nearly 2,000, the Putney Hippodrome was built on corporate ground in a side road just off the main High Street, but drew attention to itself with its lofty tower. This was crowned by a revolving illuminated ball, not unlike that atop The London Coliseum, which could be seen all over Putney.

The foundation stone for the huge building was to have been laid by Sir Henry Kimber on 3 March, 1906 with current copies of *The Daily Telegraph* and *Entre'act* being buried under it. The architect was Frederick Hingston and the theatre opened on 5 November, 1906. Although Kimber's name was on the stone, in fact, as he was ill on the great day his son did the honours. A typical Variety bill of those early years was topped by Marie Dainton and Sam Mayo, with Harry Hemsley (the child impersonator) later so popular on the wireless, George Gilbey, The Michaeloff Trio, McRae & La Port, Guilly & Jeanny and Kitty Dale in support.

The Putney Hippodrome was a popular theatre before WW1, although there were two management changes quite early on. It was one of a bunch of halls rounded up by Sir Walter Gibbons in 1913. Thereafter, the Hippodrome was run for eleven years by The London Theatres of Varieties Ltd. under Charles Gulliver. It was generally agreed that the auditorium was comfortable, but somehow lacked warmth.

In August, 1914 Putney enjoyed opera with The Dillon Shallard Company topping the bill; also booked that week were Joe Elvin in a sketch, Fred Earle, Nora & Sydney Kellog, Frank Maura and Phyllis Venney, while Vikram Mysteries baffled the crowded houses.

Interior from the gallery

The years of WW1 heralded the Revue era, with many productions touring the LTV circuit: the Hippodrome presenting *S'Nice*, *Follow the Frill* and *High Explosives* among a host of similar shows. In 1915 Cyril Gilbert presented *Burning Forest*, with New Macs and Charles Cory in support. Individual bills offered a chance to see The Poluskis, Phil Ray, Connie Howard, Laddie Cliff, Ina Hill and George Jackley, with a great many other acts not so well remembered today.

On the crash of LTV in 1924 the Putney Hippodrome was acquired by United Picture Theatres Ltd. (UPT), which ran a fairly ramshackle group of old theatres and music halls as cinemas. The market for Variety acts did not completely disappear, however, as two or three were booked on split weeks to appear between films. In July, 1928, for example, Fred Brezin and Willy Gardner were at Putney for the first half of the week, with Sammy Shields and Patti Loftus booked to follow them. To give some idea of the reduced demand for live acts, the nine UPT halls in 1928 employed only two dozen acts between them during a typical week, compared to, perhaps, eighty acts (some doubling) for a typical week's Variety.

UPT was formed by a South African, I.W. Schlesinger and very quickly expanded to sixteen properties – but equally rapidly went downhill, never making a profit after 1929. Their theatre buildings were old and they had paid over the odds for them; there was a high cost in wiring them for sound; and the rental terms for the new sound films were prohibitive. Six of the halls, including Putney Hippodrome, were losing money so were sold off in 1934, the Hippodrome going to the ABC circuit for a time.

Theatre name over the main entrance

Up to this time the ciné-variety policy had continued and many well-known artistes were booked to appear on the Putney stage. In 1928: Philip Shapiro, Claire Ruane, The Spyras, Collinson & Dean, Anton & Flo and Lee David & Partner; in 1929: Valliere & Assistant, Godwin & Roy, Tommy Sandilands, Masu & Yuri, Peter Fannan and Keith Gerrard; and in 1930: Morris & Cowley, Beryl Orde, Michell & Peru, Bob Barlow, Mahala and Olga Zita.

Live bookings at Putney ceased when ABC took over, although the circuit did have live acts at other of their halls. An exception was in October, 1935, just after the takeover, when Eddie Sharp and The Three Zarovs were booked – the latter doubling at Fulham Forum, one of ten ABC London halls with live acts that week.

Exterior in Felsham Road

Once their own Regal had opened in the town, ABC sold off Putney Hippodrome to the Odeon circuit, but it retained its old name to the end. It continued showing films until 14 January, 1961 when it was considered to be 'surplus to requirements' and was closed. Hippodrome billboards could be seen in outlying areas for some time afterwards. In 1972 the theatre was used for the filming of *Theatre of Blood* with Vincent Price, which I saw for old time's sake: a body crashed through the dome into the stalls and the building set alight at the end. In fact this was just a special effect and the building was undamaged. The building was re-boarded up until most of it was demolished in 1973. Six years later the remainder was demolished and the site redeveloped for housing and shops.

London :: :: :: ::

ALHAMBRA.—" The Bing Boys on Broadway."

BALHAM, Hippodrome, (R.) 4—Amateur Carnival Beauty Competition, Phil Parsons, Alice Lakin, R. and R. Walters, Syd Sydney, Vivian Foster, Belvoir Trio, Fred Land.

BRIXTON, Empress, (R.) 12.—Henshall presents " Introduce Me," Ethel and May, Lowell Bros.

CAMBERWELL, Palace, (R) 4.—O'Gorman Bros., Tom Clare, Gomez Trio, Edna Payne, Fisher and Lea, Woodward and Page, Marcelle Molray, Syd Cotterill and Co., Joe Archer.

CANNING TOWN, Imperial Theatre.—Leonard Mortimer and Co., in " Deliver the Goods."

CHELSEA, Palace, (R.) 12.—S. Bransgrove's Co., " The Prince and the Beggar Maid," Mart and Pep.

CHISWICK, Empire, (R.) 12.—Pynkie Whyte, Yelson Trio, Jen Latona, Mazuz and Mazette, Mlle. Doria, Barleycorn Players.

CLAPHAM, Grand Palace, (R.) 4.—Syd. Bransgrove, presents " Two Little Vagobonds."

COLISEUM, (R.) 10.—Alfred Lester and Co., in " Simpson's Stores," G. P. Huntley and Co., in " A Change or Tactics," George Mozart, Broughton and Creedon, Zellini, Sara Melita.

CROYDON, Empire, (R.) 4.—Oswald Williams, Yvonne Granville, Billy Simpson, Hetty Hartley, Eddy Reed, Maisie Ayling, Nora Moore, Will and Smith, Lilian Rickard, Josie Leyton.

EAST HAM, Palace, (R.) 12.—Joseph Millane's Co., in " The Confessions of a Wife."

EUSTON, Palace, (R.) 12.—Frank Van Hoven, The Melodious Scots, Dusty Rhodes, Alfred Woods and Maude Williamson and Co., in " The Home Wreckers," Jean and Josie, Emeric and Ainslie, Fasano, Lily Eyton.

FINSBURY PARK, Empire, (R.) 1.—" Jack in the Box," Edgar Curtis, Harry Herbert, Maisie Danvers.

HACKNEY, Empire, (R.) 12.— The Lads of the Village."

HAMMERSMITH, Palace, (R.) 4.—Wilkie Bard, Dick Tubb, Bessie Clifford, Gus Harris, Sisters, Sprightly, Bruce Green, Hand and Sinclair, Rae Duo, Hilda Nelson

HOLBORN, Empire, (R.) 4.— Jack and Evelyn, Vera Wooton, Tom D. Newell, Duncan and Godfrey, Mary Law, Winston Players, Denton's Sunrays, Alice Hollander.

ILFORD, Hippodrome, (R.) 4.—A. P. De Courville, presents " The 13th Chair."

ISLINGTON, Empire, (R.) 4.—Robert Arthur, presents " A Soldier's Bride."

KILBURN, Empire, (R.) 4.—Daisy Dormer, Hector and Lolette, Radford and Russell, Shirley and Ransome, Louie Tinsley and Co., The Link, Fay Black, Margaret Kay, Borneo Gardner, Manny and Roberts, Helen Charles.

KINGSTON, Empire, (R.) 12.30.—George Ali, Femina Quartette, Will Lacey, May Erne and Erne Chester, Mdme. Renee, Maidie and Gent, Les Marbas, Tom E. Hood, Two Lillies.

LEWISHAM, Hippodrome, (R.) 4.—Andrew Melville, presents " O.H.M.S."

LONDON Hippodrome, (R.) 11.—" Box o' Tricks."

LONDON, Palace Theatre.—" Hearts of the World."

METROPOLITAN, (R.) 12-15.—Louie Pounds and Co., in " The Absent Minded Husband," Frank Van Hoven, Red, White and Blue Trio, Ray and Bunnie Kingston, Mart and Pep, Alice Craven, Sinclair's Three Diamonds, Ian McLean.

NEW CROSS, Empire, (R.) 1.—" Smile."

NEW MIDDLESEX, (R.) 12.—" Revue and Vanities."

OXFORD, Music-hall, (R.) 12.—C. B. Cochran's production " The Better 'Ole."

PALLADIUM, (R.) 11.30—Daisy Jerome, Harry Weldon, Max Darewski, Fred Russell, Jay Whidden, Gresham Singers, Dorothy Ward, Dainty Doris, Jean Aylwyn and Co., Herbert Cave, Peter Bernard and Pianist, 5 Whartons.

PENGE, Empire, (R) 12.—G. T. Pattman, The Altos, Wee Georgie Harris, Topsy Johnson, Halma, Alexandre, Jack Straw, Ray Compton.

POPLAR, Hippodrome, (R.) 4.—John Lawson and Co., " Bully of Berlin," Amy Evans, Rene Ralph, The Grumblers, Phil Bransby, Stephanie Anderson, Fred Hawtree.

PUTNEY, Hippodrome, (R.) 4.—Nella Webb, Harry Brown, Daisy James, Wyn Bulm, May Hopkins and Taffles.

ROTHERHITHE, Hippodrome, (R.) 12.—" All Black " Revue, and company as booked.

SHEPHERD'S BUSH, Empire, (R.) 12.—Loie Conn, Wells and Mayban, Ernie Mayne, May Sherrard, Scotch Kelly, Takio.

SHOREDITCH, Empire.—Ragard and Madge Brownie, Phil Ascot Four, Walter O'Brien, Harry Marvello, Maudie Ford, Amourgis Duo.

SHOREDITCH, Olympia, (R.), 4.—Selkirk's Spectacle, Lee Stormont and Co., Herbert Reilley, Dora Lyric, Fatty Roma, Kitty Gray, Rose Cambry, Harry Moore.

SOUTH LONDON, (R.) 12.—Marie Loftus, Tom Costello, Cavendish Four, Glenroy Troupe, Gwen Thomas, May and Francis, Arthur Maynard, Two Casinos.

STRATFORD, Empire, (R.) 1.—" Rations," Mengadors, Kirkby and Hudson, Bell and Betty.

TOTTENHAM, Palace, (R.) 12.—S. Bransgrove's Co. in " Under Two Flags."

VICTORIA, Palace.—Neil Kenyon, Tucker, Beth Tate, Cicely Courtneidge, Gt. Wieland, Chas. Rich, The Picquays, Hall Wright, Hawaiians and Miss Leilani.

WALHAM GREEN, Granville Theatre, (R.) 12.—Daisy Griff, Sam Hilton, Manuel Vega, Paul Rocy, Gertrude Orchard, Alfred Wellesley and Co., Madge Clifton, Raglus.

WALTHAMSTOW, Palace, (R.) 1.—C. W. Somerset and Co., in " The Silver King."

WATFORD, Palace, (R.) 1.—The Burlesque Productions present " High Pressure," Skinner and Hill, Harriett Vernon.

WILLESDEN, Hippodrome, (R.) 4.—Fred Wardin and Karl Hooper, presents " Five Nights."

WOOD GREEN. Empire, (R.)—Marcelle de Vere, Elven Hedges, Sutcliffe Family, Julien Henry, Orpheus.

Some of the forty-four London halls open in July, 1918

Rotherhithe Hippodrome

34 & 36, Lower Road, Rotherhithe

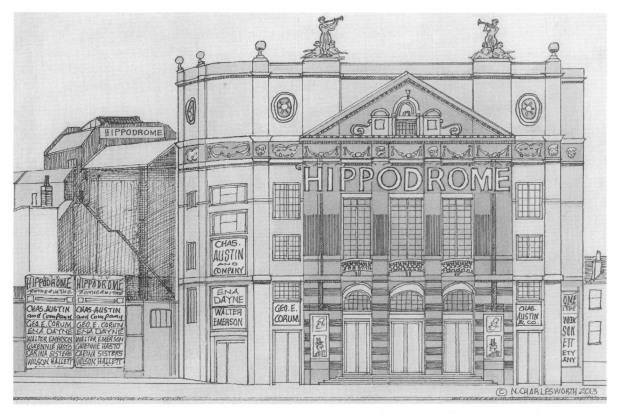

Rotherhithe Hippodrome (formerly Terriss Theatre): exterior in 1915 with Chas. Austin billed

A magnificent new playhouse, Terriss' Theatre, opened on Monday, 16 October, 1899 under E.G. Saunders, who also managed Brixton Theatre and the Notting Hill Coronet. An audience of some 2,000 in the two-decker theatre saw *The White Heather*, a recent drama from The Theatre Royal, Drury Lane, with Susie Vaughan, Marion Hume, Julian Boyce and Wilfred Taylor among the cast. The theatre was named after the actor William Terriss, who had been brutally murdered two years earlier near the stage door of the Adelphi Theatre.

The fine brick-and-stone building was designed by W.G.R. Sprague and among the promoters was Sydney Marler, who was later one of the board of London Theatres of Varieties (LTV). The spacious auditorium was in the Louis XV style, 'providing a standard of comfort quite unknown' in this quarter of S.E. London. The theatre was built by Walter Wallis & Co. at a cost of £25,000.

Plays in the following weeks included *A Life of Pleasure*, *East Lynne*, *Alone in London* and *Cheer, Boys, Cheer*. The first pantomime, *Dick Whittington*, came 'direct from Drury Lane', with Julie Mackay, Ernest Heathcote, Florence Trevelio and J.A. Cave. There was quickly a change of management, with George Conquest, jnr. taking over in October, 1900, but lasting only ten months. While there, he excelled in the pantomime *Sinbad*, with Maud Nelson. Various companies brought *Why Woman Sins*, *The Sign of the Cross* and *Secrets of the Harem*. Sunday concerts were introduced, including one by the Grenadier Guards Band.

Walter & Frederick Melville continued to present plays at the Terriss during their six-year reign there, beginning in 1901 – many from their own pens. Works with titles like *The Female Swindler*, *A Disgrace to her Sex* and *The Ugliest Woman on Earth* give a flavour of the fare on offer. Such pieces appealed to audiences in the suburbs long after they lost ground in the West End. Pantomimes written and staged by the Melvilles appeared at Christmas time, among them *Cinderella* and *St. George and the Dragon* at prices from 4d to 2s.

Our interest in this really begins late in 1907, when it became the Rotherhithe Hippodrome under Walter Gibbons and soon came under the umbrella of LTV Ltd. Variety became the mainstay from this point, although sketches and playlets – such as *The Feast of the Wolves* – were often included in the bills. The opening one included the strong man, Hackenschmidt, as well as the Bioscope.

In August, 1914 the attraction was Roland Carr's *While You Wait*, with supporting Variety company including Goodfellow & Gregson. In August, 1915 Charles Austin headed a bill with George E. Corum, Ena Dayne, Walter Emerson, Gwennie Hasto, Wilson Hallett and The Carina Sisters. The Rotherhithe Hippodrome was now sharing in the varied diet of shows and bills booked over the powerful LTV circuit – although the Rotherhithe audience retained affection for lurid drama longer than some houses elsewhere. During WW1 visitors included The Sisters Jerome, Joe Elvin and Mary Mayfran: while among the productions offered were J. Peterman's *Colonel Cobb*, *The Hairdresser* and Walter Bentley's *All Stop Here*.

From 1918 to 1921 Wally Rice held the theatre's lease, introducing Revue as well as Variety. In July, 1918 the *All Black Revue* formed part of the bill, but gradually such productions made up the entire bill after the Overture. Good touring companies filled in vacant weeks, with *Seven Days' Leave*, *The Belle of New York* and similar attractively-staged shows.

Revue held the fort after Rice's departure until the crash of the LTV circuit, following which most of its properties were gobbled up by cinema chains. The Rotherhithe Hippodrome was closed from July to December, 1923 when Charles Gulliver took over and installed the Dorothy Mullord Company which re-established melodrama here for several years. By 1927 this type of play was thoroughly old-fashioned, and Ciné-Variety took over the theatre, managed from 1930 by Associated British Cinemas.

There was a grand re-opening of Rotherhithe Hippodrome in June, 1931 to celebrate the first showing of 'Talkies' at the theatre; it was attended by Councillor G.S. Tingle, Mrs. Tingle and other worthies. Films at the time included *The Lone Rider* (Buck Jones), described as 'Thrills from start to finish'.

Films could easily have seen out the life of the theatre, but live theatre returned to complete the tale. Due to wartime conditions, the cinema operation closed in June, 1943. A.A. Shenburn, of Suburban Century Cinemas Ltd. took on the lease, with Rotherhithe Hippodrome joining Camberwell Palace, The Granville and various provincial halls as a Regis Theatre. By September, 1943 Shenburn was staging eight-act Variety bills twice nightly at 6.15 and 8.15pm. The show for the week of 20 September offered Billy Reid and Dorothy Squires, Joe Young & Co. in *Buying A Theatre*, Claude Lester & Doreen and Arthur Knott (The Little Twister).

He followed up with a Revue entitled *Spangles from Broadway* with Vic Montague, Nora Craven and The Four Hermans. Shenburn deserved an award for his efforts in bringing entertainment to this heavily-bombed part of London's docklands. He also staged *Shoot the Works*, with Bennett & Moreny, Marie Lloyd, jnr., Haig & Escoe and The Diacoffs in the company. This show was one of the last to play at The South London Palace and *the last* at Stratford Empire, both of which received direct hits in the Blitz.

Another direct hit during the run of a twice-nightly play, *Rebecca* by Daphne du Maurier in February, 1944 put Rotherhithe Hippodrome out of action. The play was presented by Benson Repertory Co., with Harley Walter, Marie Hast, Bernard J. Benson, Leon Reeves and Edwina Howell among the cast. The following week's production was to have been *While Parents Sleep*, billed on the programme as 'London's Naughtiest Comedy'.

Sadly, the Rotherhithe Hippodrome was not repaired. The teenaged John Cliff and John Barber, of the future British Music Hall Society, explored the ruined building, which they found in a highly dangerous state; among the exposed girders the advertisement-covered fire curtain still hung from what remained of the grid. The shell of the building was demolished in 1955.

Willy Pantzer & Company

Miss Ida's Troupe

Waterloo: The Canterbury Hall

143, Westminster Bridge Road, Lambeth

The Canterbury Hall: exterior

The great days at the Canterbury had long been over when I arrived in London as a small boy in 1930, but I remember it as a slightly dilapidated cinema which sported two or three Variety acts between the films. It was quite old-fashioned, retaining the look and feel of a theatre, but it vanished from the scene during the Blitz in 1942.

Charles Morton, born in Hackney in 1819, who later became a far-sighted businessman, decided early in life that he wanted to become an entertainment provider. He had already been the licensee of taverns in Pimlico and elsewhere in London before taking The Canterbury Arms in Westminster Bridge Road (then known as Upper Marsh) in 1849.

Two years later he started what was at first a series of twice-weekly concerts for men only, but was soon prevailed upon to lay on a weekly Ladies' Night, so that wives and girlfriends could come along and enjoy an evening with their menfolk. The success of his early venture encouraged Morton to construct a small concert room over the skittle ground behind The Canterbury Arms. The hall held only about seven hundred, with a platform at one end and music supplied by a piano and harmonium. The entertainment was paid for by the purchase of a sixpenny refreshment ticket, which gave you one drink and all the entertainment you wanted to see.

Such was the popularity of his enterprise that Morton decided to build a larger hall which opened in December, 1856. The architect was Samuel Field who cleverly built the 1,500-seater hall in two halves – avoiding a single night's closure. Better accommodation was provided, with the audience being able to follow the evening's programme from a printed book, which also contained the words of the songs and glees being performed. Four years later Morton added a separate supper room and picture gallery which became known as 'The Royal Academy over the Water' and was open day and night.

Charles Morton paid his artistes very well – up to forty pounds a week, which was far more than they had earned at similar establishments like Evans' in Covent Garden. As a result, he was able to attract the top names such as George Leybourne. He also staged dramatic sketches, which got him into trouble with the Lord Chamberlain. But, having built up an enormously profitable business, he sold up in 1868 and William Holland took over. Morton moved to The Oxford, which he had already built and was operating, while Holland covered the floor of The Canterbury with a huge Axminster carpet – advising London, 'Come to the Canterbury and spit on Bill Holland's thousand guinea carpet!' Morton himself became known as 'the Father of the Halls' after his pioneering work at The Canterbury, The Oxford and The Palace Theatre of Varieties. He died in 1904.

Interior looking towards the stage

On a further change of ownership to Frederick Villiers, the old-fashioned Canterbury Hall was pulled down and in 1876 a huge new theatre-style auditorium built, with a proscenium arch, proper stage and a patented sliding roof. It is worth noting that Morton never called his hall a 'music hall', but The Canterbury Hall. Now called The Canterbury Music Hall it moved right away from its humble origins, taking on a more formal atmosphere. With the patronage of The Prince of Wales (later King Edward VII) it even called itself The Royal Canterbury Theatre of Varieties. Amazingly, the original public house survived all the changes and was discovered by Archibald Haddon in 1935, with its doorway in a narrow roadway carrying the inscription:

Erected 1852

Canterbury Hall

Licensed pursuant to the Act of the 25th year of King George II

By this time the old doorway had become the gallery entrance – probably the oldest detail of any music hall in London at that time.

The architect of the latest theatre was Albert Bridgman and the builders were W.H. Bracher & Son. Audiences clearly remember the circuitous entrance to the auditorium by way of a series of tunnels and passageways under the railway line coming out of Waterloo Station. The latest reopening was on 23 September, 1876 and the work was said to have cost £40,000. In time the Canterbury came under the management of The Canterbury and Paragon Ltd., controlled by George Adney Payne, and its reputation grew with its dramatic sketches running for several weeks in the changing Variety programmes.

With its huge popularity, the new hall attracted Royalty, including the Duke of Cambridge and the Duke and Duchess of Teck, as well as becoming a rendezvous for music hall performers. At the entrance stood their array of cabs, barouches, broughams, growlers and carriages as they met for their 'Late Night Final'. As music hall began to decline, prices of admission were reduced, which stemmed the desertion for a time, but G.A. Payne relinquished the theatre in 1909, the control passing through a number of hands, with the final night of Variety being held in 1912. Thereafter, the hall ran Ciné-Variety under H.T. Brickwell and others. As the hall ran at a loss, only poor acts and amateurs were engaged.

Phil and Sid Hyams took over in 1921 and found the theatre full of fleas and generally run-down. They put it to rights, gradually improving the acts, building up audiences and introducing afternoon shows as well as increasing evening charges. They sold the Canterbury to Gaumont-British in 1927, as the company was looking for suitable venues to wire for sound. After this the hall was not licensed as a theatre or music hall, although keeping its Lord Chamberlain's licence, as it continued to present Ciné-Variety. For example, during the week commencing 14 October, 1935 the Variety acts were Blum & Blum, Robert Reilly and Mary Ann, with The Omega Trio and Jean Kennedy billed for the following week. On my only visit to the Canterbury to see films, the Variety segment of the bill was The Radio Revellers ('Four Men – One song').

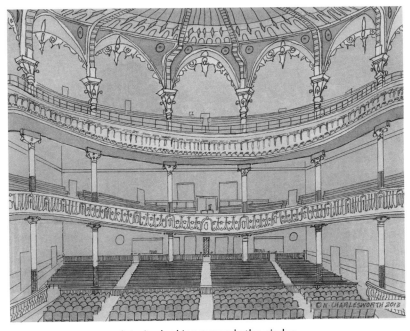

Interior looking towards the circles

Gaumont-British at that time also ran Ciné-Variety at the Marlborough Theatre in Holloway, at Tottenham Palace and at twelve other halls. Rehearsals were often held at The Blue Hall in Islington. Sometimes the orchestra, conducted by Firmin Shackleton, accompanied community singing, when a little of the old atmosphere returned with the well-remembered songs.

In 1942 Phil Hyams negotiated with Gaumont to buy back the old theatre at a knock-down price. He had even signed the contract, but another appointment prevented his looking the place over that day. He and Sid had planned to reopen it as a music hall again, having enjoyed their time there in the 1920s. But overnight German bombers hit the theatre and the next day they called in to find just a heap of rubble. Gaumont had been paying The Southern Railway £3,000 per year for access to the hall under their tracks.

The bombed Canterbury Hall was never repaired, the remains being cleared away in 1955. However, the final traces (including glass melted by the air raid fire) were not removed until the early 1990s, when work was carried out on the site in connection with the building of the Channel Tunnel Rail Terminal at Waterloo Station. Even today decorative tiles can be seen at the old theatre entrance, situated behind hoardings immediately east of the railway bridge in Westminster Bridge Road.

The Canterbury was once part of a group of entertainment venues – Gatti's-in-the-Road, The Surrey, The Bower Saloon and Astley's Amphitheatre among them, but today only The Old Vic remains from that era.

GAUMONT-BRITISH PICTURE CORPORATION, LTD.

BALHAM PAV. (re., 12).—Jack Wynne and Co.; May 23, Rosie Lloyd.

BYKER GRAND (re., 1).—Miller Phlora; May 23, Fred Decuna.

THE CANTERBURY (re., 10.30).—Kay and Jay, Norman Clare, the Cycling Brocks; May 23, the Young Stars, the Gladiators, George Jackley.

DALSTON PICTURE HOUSE (re., 11).—Pauline Grey and Her Playmates; May 23, Howard Rogers.

EDGWARE ROAD GRAND KINEMA (re., 11.45).—Gertie Gitana; May 23, Les Jardys.

HOLLOWAY EMP. (re., 11).—Gandy's Comedy Circus, Juliette Vedey and Ileene Evelyn.

HOXTON BRITANNIA (re., 1).—Barclay and Schofield, Virginia Clay; May 23, Salter and Hanlon, Vernon Harvey.

LAVENDER HILL PAV. (re., 11).—Claude Dampier.

NEW CROSS SUPER KINEMA (re., 11).—Taro Naito, Stradella Boys, Louisoff and the Dancing Revels; May 23, Ringle Bros., Haywood, Hay, and Dorina, Norman Clare.

NORTH SHIELDS BOROUGH (re., 1).—Fred Decuna; May 23, Miller and Phlora.

PALMERS GREEN PALMADIUM (re., 11).—The Young Stars; May 23, June Dancers.

ROTHERHITHE LION KINEMA (re., 1).—Salter and Hanlon; May 23, the Stradella Boys.

SHEPHERD'S BUSH PAV. (re., 11).—U.S.A. Four.

STRATFORD BROADWAY SUPER KINEMA (re., 11). — Barlow and Griffiths, June Dancers, etc.; May 23, the Cycling Brocks, Harrington and Oliviere, etc.

Ciné-Variety at The Canterbury, while part of The Gaumont-British circuit in May, 1929. Holloway Empire and Hoxton Britannia are also shown

Waterloo: Gatti's Palace of Varieties ('Gatti's-in-the-Road')

214–6, Westminster Bridge Road, Lambeth

Gatti's-in-the-Road: exterior with Six Brothers Luck billed

For the history of the Gatti family in London up to this point, the reader is referred to the chapter on Gatti's Charing Cross Music Hall, otherwise known as 'Gatti's-under-the-Arches', near to the site of the later Players' Theatre Club (page 21).

It will be seen that, on the sale of the Hungerford Market to The South Eastern Railway, Carlo Gatti had to close his music hall; but he relocated to south of the river and in May, 1863 opened a Refreshment Hall at 76, Bridge Road, as it was then called. The venture was really a large café, rather in the continental manner, with musical entertainment comprising an orchestra and singers. Carlo Gatti gave his name on the posters advertising the new venture, although it was the talented and cultivated Giovanni Gatti who displayed the qualities of an impresario and who was probably behind the formal change into a licensed music hall. The area was quite a local centre of entertainment at that time, not only with the famous Canterbury Hall, but with Astley's Amphitheatre, The Victoria Hall (Old Vic) and the Surrey Theatre nearby. Not far away were Vauxhall Gardens and Apollo Gardens. The new hall was almost opposite the family shop, where Agostino and Gaspero Gatti were selling artificial flowers during the 1850s.

Concerts, as they were called, started on 11 November, 1865 and began at 7.45pm. Admission to Balcony and Area (Stalls) was by refreshment ticket at 6d. Among the dozen or so 'Talented Artistes' on the opening bill were The Great Lingard, Albert Steele, Smith & Williamson ('Delineators of Negro Life'), Parelli & Costello ('Astounding Gymnasts'), Lydia Lattimer and Fanny Webster. The manager and conductor was G. Hart, who may well have been the same G. Hart who was advertised as 'Baritone' on the bill. It was quite common for the management to fill in if an artiste was late or indisposed. A little later the Chairman, Ben Baker, often stepped into the breach and gave a turn himself.

From its opening Gatti's-in-the-Road was a success, despite the much larger Canterbury Hall opposite. Even so, Gatti's was described as a 'humble little affair, with a tiny stage and only two dressing rooms'. By 1870 the starting time for the evening show was 8pm, but there was 'No advance in the prices'. By Whit Monday of that year the stage had been extended to accommodate a 'Grand Ballet with Magnificent Scenery and Superb Dresses'. Following redecoration by Messrs. Macintosh and Homann Jnr. in 1872, a reopening bill in the April disclosed that the programme of artistes changed each evening. Better known names were being engaged, among them Jenny Hill – The Dashing; Fred Coyne – The Sterling; and W.H. Barry, who was held over due to his great popularity. By this time, Rosa (Carlo's daughter) had become one of the proprietors. Carlo Gatti himself died in 1878.

Interior when a cinema

With continued success, the proprietors rebuilt the premises in 1883, some thirty years after its first opening. The architect was 'a Mr. Bolton of Lincoln's Inn Fields', the contractor being G. Gaisford. The hall now seated 454 in the Stalls and 236 in the Balcony. Tom Tinsley was in the chair during the 1890s, when Vesta Victoria, James Fawn ('If You Want to Know the Time, Ask a Policeman') and Tom Costello were stars in the firmament. The decade also saw Eugene Stratton, the long-lasting

Duncan's Collies and Bessie Bonehill on the bills; but one of the biggest names was T.E. Dunville making his debut in 1889 at Gatti's (*trebling* with the Middlesex and the Foresters'). An artiste who turned out to be an even bigger name in the future was Harry Lauder, whom London saw for the first time in 1900, singing an *Irish* comic song. He performed continually on stage until 1935, then going into semi-retirement but still making the occasional film before eventually dying in 1950.

Gatti's remained in the family until 1911, when films began to throw their moving shadows over the halls. Three others tried their luck here in management, but it became clear that the game was up and the little hall became a popular full-time cinema in 1924. The Canterbury Hall opposite had similar problems, but there at least a few live artistes could still be seen between the films.

At Gatti's local children packed the place at 4d in the Balcony and 6d in the Stalls. They would run up the stairs on the side of the building and sit on wooden forms bolted to the floor. A refreshment counter had by then replaced the bar at the back of the stalls. Gatti's-in-the-Road kept the projectors running until it was bombed in WW2. The wrecked building was eventually demolished for the widening and re-alignment of Westminster Bridge Road in 1950.

Ben Baker, sometime Chairman at Gatti's-in-the-Road

F. RIDDLE,

MUSICAL DIRECTOR,

ROYAL CAMBRIDGE MUSIC HALL.

ADDRESS—76, NICHOLS SQUARE,

HACKNEY ROAD.

W. G. EATON.

PROFESSOR OF MUSIC.

MUSICAL DIRECTOR

PARAGON THEATRE OF VARIETIES.

Address as above, or

CROWN AND SCEPTRE,

CUMBERLAND MARKET, REGENT'S PARK.

CHAS. A. WAREHAM,

MUSICAL DIRECTOR,

COLLINS'S MUSIC HALL, ISLINGTON, N.

Violin, Organ, and Harmony Lessons.

Private Address—

59 Brighton Road, Stoke Newington, N.

A. L. MORA,

MUSICAL DIRECTOR,

SOUTH LONDON PALACE,

Composer and Professor of Music.

W. T. WILKINSON,

MUSICAL DIRECTOR,

GATTIS' PALACE OF VARIETIES,

WESTMINSTER BRIDGE ROAD.

W. J. TUBBS,

Late Musical Director,

SOUTH LONDON PALACE.

"THE YORK MINSTER,"

DEAN STREET, SOHO.

PETER CONROY,

Chef D'Orchestre,

BELMONT'S NEW SEBRIGHT,

HACKNEY ROAD.

Manager and arranger to the *élite* of the Profession.

EDMUND BOSANQUET,

Musical Director,

CANTERBURY THEATRE OF VARIETIES.

PROFESSOR OF THE VIOLIN.

Pupils receive every attention, Music arranged, Lessons also given on the Pianoforte. Seiler's Pianos used. Professionals before buying a Piano are invited to try this splendid Instrument.

WALTER LOOSLEY,

MUSICAL DIRECTOR,

QUEEN'S PALACE, POPLAR, E.

Violin and Pianoforte Taught.

Private Address—

4 Crowbar Cottage,

Beford Street, Poplar.

FRED. KNAPP,

MUSICAL DIRECTOR,

ROYAL ALBERT MUSIC HALL,

CANNING TOWN, ESSEX.

283 WICK ROAD, SOUTH HACKNEY.

ALFRED LEGGETT,

M.B.A.M. AND F.O.S.,

Musical Director,

THEATRE OF VARIETIES, HAMMERSMITH.

Author and Composer of over 500 SUCCESSFUL SONGS. Melodies taken from the voice and efficiently arranged. Songs written to order and music covers supplied. A. L. has received **Two Awards of Merit** and a Handsome **Medal** for his Compositions, and is the Composer and Arranger to *The élite of the Profession.*

HARRY SPRATT,

PROFESSOR on the BANJO.

TEN LESSONS FOR ONE GUINEA.

10, DUKE STREET, ADELPHI, W.C.

Musical Directors at some of the London halls

Woolwich Empire

Beresford Street (Ropeyard Rails ran to the rear of the theatre)

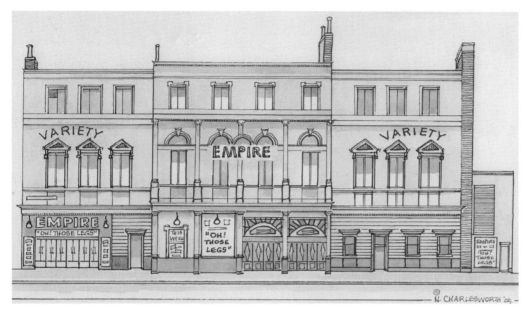

Woolwich Empire: exterior with 'Oh! Those Legs' billed

In January, 1835 the New Portable Theatre opened in Beresford Street, Woolwich, when Woolwich Ropeyard fell into decay. The portable theatre, held together with iron bolts, is thought to have come from Creek Road (formerly Bridge Street), where it had opened the previous year. The site of the Rope Walk was purchased by a Mr. George Smith of Woolwich.

Funds were sought and the Portable Theatre was replaced by a permanent building, The West Kent Theatre, in 1836; it was re-named The Duchess of Kent's Theatre in the following year. The tragedy of *Othello* was performed 'under the express sanction of Her Royal Highness', the evening concluding with *The Irishman in London*. Later the theatre's name was changed again to the Woolwich Theatre Royal, although its name varied a great deal through the years.

Reconstructions were undertaken in the 1880s by – it is thought – J.O. Cook, and in 1892 by Edward Clark; the latter is believed to have been responsible for the domestic-looking exterior with which we were familiar in later years. During the 1890s the theatre became known as Barnard's, being managed by Samuel Barnard for many years. The name lingered on after his ownership ceased, the Barnard family also running theatres in Chatham and Greenwich; in addition they controlled The Elephant & Castle Theatre for twenty years until it became a cinema.

At Woolwich Empire the presentations tended to be lurid and sensational, but as Mr. Barnard apparently did not believe in spending money to advertise his shows in the local press (comparatively as expensive then as now), details are sparse. It is notable that among the items in a show in 1901 were short films, including one of Queen Victoria's funeral. Her Majesty had travelled by train to Woolwich the previous year to visit soldiers wounded in the Boer War. Barnard's had been full that night and, at Mr. Barnard's request, one of the artistes sang *God Save the Queen*. He was followed by the leader of the orchestra, who gave a rendering of Rudyard Kipling's popular patriotic piece entitled *The Absent-minded Beggar*.

Interior looking towards the stage

The theatre had been rebuilt internally by Frank Matcham between 1899 and 1900 and, although a comfortable and attractive auditorium arose, it was clearly a modest job done on a tight budget, as Barnard himself admitted. Further improvements were made in the late 1920s.

David Barnard took over the family business in 1930 and struggled on against the strong tide of the talkie craze until he went bankrupt in 1932. A new company, Woolwich Empire Ltd., was formed, but it is not known whether David Barnard had any interest in it. Nevertheless, as Woolwich Empire, the theatre took its place among the regular London Variety houses, presenting some good bills.

Dance Bands were all the rage here, as elsewhere, before WW2 and one of these was Eric Day and his Band, who topped for the week of 14 October, 1935 supported by The Three Jacks, Edwin Lawrence and Iris Day. The Band was re-booked for the following year, with The Hokums, Al Marshall and Don Philippe & Loretta among the company.

Many other famous stars appeared, among them The Western Brothers (Kenneth and George) and Max Miller, who reopened the theatre after a closure – a gesture he made more than once. The opening of the lavish Woolwich Granada, with its ciné-Variety policy, clearly hit Woolwich Empire, particularly when the Granada's opening show featured Reginald Dixon, the famous organist. In September, 1937 while the older Beresford Street house had The Great Levante presenting *How's Tricks?*, the Granada had Bobby Howell and his Band, Drury & Raymond and Murray Stewart in support of its full film programme – no doubt at competitive prices and in greater comfort than at the Woolwich Empire.

Locals remember pre-war visits of circuses to the Empire, which caused great excitement and annoyance. Wild animals were confined back-stage and kept many locals awake at night. Horses and elephants were more popular as they were a lot quieter and stabled in the open at a builder's yard down by Woolwich Ferry. At this time Woolwich Empire had a barring clause against the Poplar Queen's Theatre for two weeks before a Woolwich appearance, even though it was on the other side of the river and only accessible by the famous ferry.

As at other London Variety houses, business was brisk at the Woolwich Empire during and just after WW2, although strippers were regularly taking their place on the bill. A lady I know well remembers being taken to the Empire for a Variety show as a fourteenth birthday treat by a neighbour, only to be advised to close her eyes when an undraped female came on stage. Another friend recalls a lady coming on stage in crinoline and bonnet, then shedding all except two stars and a triangle "where it mattered". Koringa, a strong woman and snake charmer, was a bright act in more ways than one. She lay on the stage while an enormous man placed a paving slab on her. He then hammered the slab with a mallet until it broke into pieces. Koringa brushed them aside, swiftly leapt to her feet, smiled graciously and took her bow as if nothing unusual had happened.

A typical wartime show, with the inevitable visits to The Cookhouse, The M.O.'s Office and The Dormitory, was Elkan Simon's latest laughter revue, *Frills & Drills*, which starred Harry Orchid, Dave Jackley, Nan Kennedy and Renee Stirling. This was a sort of slightly more elaborate than usual E.N.S.A. show for which we servicemen had to pay, even though it was of a No. 3 standard. After the war was over, sometimes there were some quite strong bills. A typical revue of the type described above came during the week of 2 November, 1952: *A Mighty Fine Double Programme* contrived to present both *Radio Fanfare* with Alfred Thripp, the blind pianist, Jimmy Hill (no, not the racing driver) and Shek Ben Ali, together with *Golden Prairie* with Wally Brenan, Peggy Bailey, Vic Merry and The Harmony Hillbillies. An attractive theatre inside, the Woolwich Empire in 1946 had an orchestra of nine and could stage a show with eighteen lines. Surprisingly, counterweight gear was also installed. The popular manager at this time was Vic Brooker (known to all as 'O.K. Vic'), later succeeded by Frank Tomsett. Conductors included Charles Kitchen and, in its declining years, Sammy Ross.

However, the theatre soon descended to No. 3 status, not even appearing in the entertainments columns of the London evening papers. There were week after week of Girlie shows, audiences and the size of the orchestra ever shrinking. *All Fluff and Nonsense*, *Stars Without Bras* and *Bareway to Stardom* were titles of typical offerings in the 1950s. John and Val Earl booked in advance to make sure of seats to see the veteran Nat Travers, only to find that they were the only ones in the stalls; while John Cliff remembers the same two backdrops that appeared at every show – a sudden draught causing them to flap and reveal the artistes' Exit board on the back wall of the stage. Cinema-style roll tickets were dispensed at the box office, enabling the audience to sit where, and for however long, it pleased. After a lick of paint, the place was re-launched at one stage as The New Woolwich Empire, but no one cared any longer.

Interior, close-up of proscenium arch

Woolwich Empire was remarkably long-lived, closing in 1958 just a few months before Collins' Music Hall in Islington. By the time that Ted Bottle saw the final show, *Exstasy*, in March of that year, even the house tabs were no longer in use, each half opening and closing with the No. 1 runners; the orchestra was down to little more than piano and drums. Although the show was continuous, Ted could not bear to see it through a second time, so dreadful was the standard. Had he stayed on he would have heard the valedictory speech in which the closing of the theatre regretted. A voice from the stalls caused consternation when it loudly interrupted: 'Do you call this a *Theatre*?' No matter, the Woolwich Empire did feature in the national press, when *The Daily Mail* ran a piece entitled 'I Was There When A Music Hall Died', revealing that the current star stripper's agent was hopeful of presenting her in the West End. The sadly familiar smells of a dying theatre (stale dust, cats and disinfectant) were also mentioned.

So ended some one hundred and twenty-six years of popular entertainment on this site. In 1960 the Woolwich Empire came down, to be replaced by an auto-stacker car park which jammed on its first day – never to be used again. A petrol station occupies the area today, but one of the Exit signs lives on in a Somerset cottage.

Capt. Ringman Mack in a sensational, but clearly painful, act

Woolwich Hippodrome

Wellington Street, Woolwich

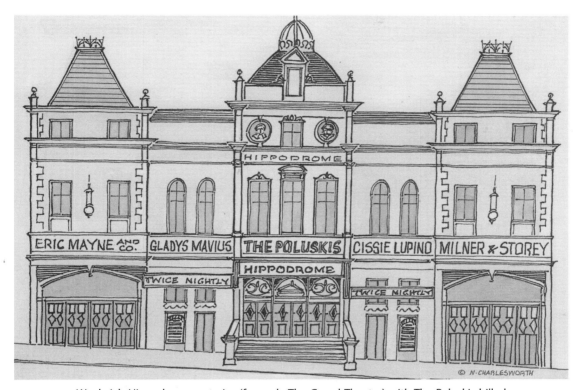

Woolwich Hippodrome: exterior (formerly The Grand Theatre) with The Poluskis billed

One of many drama houses that quite quickly became Variety theatres, this one opened on 18 October, 1900 as The Grand Theatre and Opera House. It was designed by Bertie Crewe and built by W. Johnson & Co. of Wandsworth Common. After the opening by Sir Henry Irving, the Grand was the home in South-East London for West End principal provincial touring companies, with a weekly change of production.

The proprietor and manager was Clarence Sounes, whom we also find connected with the Empires at Penge and Kingston, as well as with the New Prince's at Poplar, later the Hippodrome. In addition, Sounes ran drama houses in Birmingham, Aldershot and Newport, Monmouthshire.

The Woolwich Grand seated 1,680 in well-raked stalls, dress circle/balcony and gallery; there were six boxes seating 32. At the time of opening the stage was stated as being 42ft deep and 80ft wide. Externally the theatre was built in red brick with Bath stone pilasters and dressings.

Unable to hold a regular audience with the fare for which it had been designed, the theatre was taken over in 1908 by Walter Gibbons as part of his growing London Theatres of Varieties chain. After the early disappointments at the flagship theatre, The London Palladium, Gibbons stepped down, to be replaced in 1913 by Charles Gulliver. The Grand had been renamed the Woolwich Hippodrome on its acquisition by LTV, enjoying sixteen years of relative prosperity as a Variety house, bearing in mind that Woolwich supported, amazingly, three live theatres at this time.

As Britain entered WW1, The Two Bobs, Harry Ford and Doring's Pigeons were part of a bill wowing 'em at the Woolwich Hippodrome, with its nearby military establishment. From then on a cavalcade of entertainment followed, with straight Variety mixed with revues and occasional musical shows. Among numerous managements touring was Fred Karno with his 1915 production of *Parlez Vous Francais?* with H.O. Wills (what became of W.D.?), Lily Langtry (the variety artiste not the actress), Pasqualis and The Real McKays. The following year Lew Lake brought his war-inspired *Lights Out London*, featuring Fred Keeton, Griff and Dolly Elsworthy. Towards the end of WW1, in July, 1918, the Darnleys presented *Mr. Mayfair.*

Interior looking towards the stage

Fred Keeton returned to the Woolwich boards in April, 1921 on a bill headed by Daisy Dormer, Jack Lane, the young Sandy Powell, The Bartle Quartette, Marjory Fulton, The Brandons, The Eldons and Arthur Ferris. Jack Lane scored heavily, returning later that year topping a bill which included Tom R. Finglass and Queenie Leighton.

With the crash of LTV in 1924, Woolwich Hippodrome became a cinema under the ill-fated United Picture Theatres (UPT), once described as 'the company that should never have seen the light of day'. However three live acts were engaged to appear during the film programmes, keeping the tradition going. Artistes were changed mid-week to maintain the public's interest. The UPT circuit, increasingly supported by Gaumont-British, controlled a lot of quite old ex-theatre properties throughout the capital. Some were eventually re-built, but the company was always short of funds. In consequence, the Woolwich Hippodrome ran as a cinema in its 1900 form until it was demolished in 1939.

A typical week's ciné-Variety in December, 1928 offered for the first half of the week Collinson & Dean, Anton & Flo and Jack Allen; with The Three Elysees, Robbie Vincent and Deen & Ross engaged for the second half. Deen & Ross were dancers, Don Ross later marrying Gertie Gitana and becoming a noted agent and impresario.

Exterior when the ABC Regal Cinema, 17.7.1961

In 1929 a similar split-week offered Varney & Butt, Keith & Joan Dingley and The Two Sharpes; changing to Derry & Sloan, Tommy Sandilands and De Marr & James for the Thursday–Saturday slots. However, when ABC took an interest in the Woolwich Hippodrome from about 1930, live artistes were no longer engaged and as the building had become so out-moded it was decided to build a proper cinema. However, WW2 intervened and the site remained empty. After the war steel and other building materials were in short supply – a licence was required to obtain them but quite remarkably a new cinema was eventually built on the site. Designed originally by W.R. Glen its construction was supervised by C.J. Foster. It opened as the Woolwich Regal on 19 September, 1955 with *The Dambusters*. It became the Woolwich ABC on 19 December, 1971, finally closing with *Who Dares Wins* on 20 November, 1982. After lying derelict for many years, it ran as the Flamingo Nightclub, so live entertainment continued one hundred years after the old Grand first opened its doors. At the time of writing its demolition has been announced.

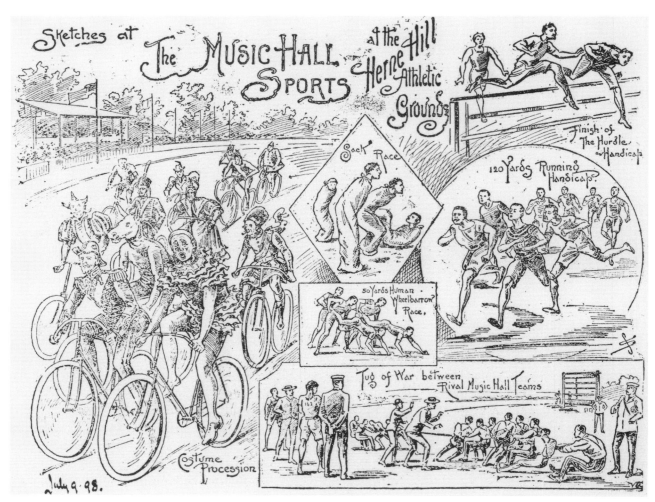

The Music Hall Sports in 1898. Drawn by Sam Sibbitt

Epitaph

New Cross Empire: exterior during demolition in January, 1958

The sad scene on 31 January, 1958, as New Cross Empire met its end. The Frank Matcham theatre was built like a battleship and did not give up easily. Several managements had tried hard to make it pay after Moss' Empires Ltd. had declared it superfluous in 1946 – but in the end none succeeded. Scenes like this were repeated all over Greater London, as beautiful Variety theatres, no longer commercially viable, were reduced to rubble. Some could well have become straight theatres, if only the will had been there.

South London has suffered badly, as really only two Variety theatres remain from those covered: the 'Chinese' Clapham Grand Palace, which is now a music venue, and Greenwich Parthenon/Palace/Hippodrome, the outer walls of which enclose a completely modern auditorium – The Greenwich Theatre. Although the Brixton Empress and Brixton Hippodrome have both left the scene, The Ritzy Cinema stands very close to the site of the latter. The Streatham Hill Theatre, formerly a playhouse, remains as a bingo hall, although it did present Variety bills during WW2.

The West End of London has fared better, as one would expect of an area recognised as 'Theatreland'. Still pulling in audiences is the restored Adelphi, having long given up Variety-Revue; the Leicester Square Odeon remains on the site of the old Alhambra, with a fully-equipped stage which sees occasional use; The Leicester Square Empire is also still on the Square, but has an interior reconstructed in 1962 from the entirely rebuilt 1928 cinema. But do not miss the remaining part of the old Empire Theatre around the corner in Leicester Street dating from 1893; the building that for a short, but lively time, housed Fielding's Music Hall still remains, but became a cinema when live shows finished; Leicester Square Theatre, minus its original interior, is being demolished as we go to press. The London Casino, once home to Bernard Delfont's Variety bills, has reverted to its original name of The Prince Edward Theatre; The London Coliseum came back from being a Cinerama house in 1968 and is now the home of English National Opera; The London Hippodrome looks terrific after its long-awaited restoration and is now a casino and cabaret venue right in the centre of Theatreland and The London Palladium is a successful home of musicals, occasionally hosting star artistes on Sundays. However, pantomimes are now rarely seen here, as long-running musicals cannot be taken off for a six or eight-week season.

The London Pavilion, used as a cinema since the 1930s, is merely a shell and serves as a shopping centre. However, The Lyceum Theatre arose from the dead in 1996 and its large capacity as a musical house is a great asset to the West End; The New London Theatre occupies a site in Drury Lane devoted to entertainment (the Mogul, The Middlesex and The Winter Garden) for some 300 years, while the Palace, Prince of Wales and Victoria Palace have all found thriving futures as homes of musical shows. The latter is still redolent of The Crazy Gang. Part of the site of the vast Stoll Theatre is occupied by The Peacock Theatre, first opened as The Royalty in 1962 and The Windmill Theatre, which in 1964 lost its role as the home of 'Revuedeville' and the first step for many an aspiring comedian, is now a gentleman's club.

North of the Thames much has been lost, including Matcham's Granville and Metropolitan Theatres and it is a mixed story for what remains. The frontage of Collins' Music Hall facing Islington Green still stands, although the building now houses a bookshop. Sprague's Camden Hippodrome, lacking its open lantern, is a popular nightclub, still welcoming an audience. Golders Green Hippodrome, for some time a BBC concert studio, is now a church, although it is available for live performances if required. Fragments of walls at Crouch End Hippodrome are all that remain of that theatre. The Stratford Theatre Royal still presents shows, as does Matcham's magnificent and regenerated Hackney Empire. Its sister theatre, Shepherds Bush Empire, is a successful music venue and was used at first for 'Strictly Come Dancing'. Further to the southwest, one of Matcham's most complete theatres, Richmond Theatre, is a Number One touring house, famous for its pantomimes; while Kingston Empire, not far away, is now a public house. In the East End the Coronet Cinema stands of the site of the old Paragon Theatre of Varieties.

We are lucky that two of London's oldest music halls, McDonald's in Hoxton and Wilton's in Stepney, are both safe and in regular use. The former is an educational centre owned by the Quakers and run as an extremely active Youth Arts Centre, while the latter is well worth a visit for its imaginative programme – or even for a drink in its lively bar. A revitalised Sadler's Wells Theatre in Islington (rebuilt in 1998) thrives as London's dance theatre. Finally, Tottenham Palace, the last theatre in the capital by Wylson & Long, is now a church; and the frontage is all that remains of Wood Green Empire, but the stage where Chung Ling Soo was fatally shot is now occupied by a supermarket.

All the rest, from Chiswick to Croydon, Balham to Bow and Walthamstow to Woolwich, have vanished.

How blind we were.

Nicholas Charlesworth

A fragment of the Granville lives on in London SE9

Bibliography

Agate, James (1945), *Immoment Toys – Light Entertainment*, Jonathan Cape, London

Anderson, Jean (editor) (1943), *The Players' Theatre, Late Joys*, T.V. Boardman & Co., London

Bailey, Peter (editor) (1986), *Music Hall: The Business of Pleasure*, Open University Press, Milton Keynes; Philadelphia

Baker, Richard Anthony (2005), *British Music Hall – An Illustrated History*, Sutton Publishing, Stroud

Baker, Richard Anthony (2011), *Old Time Variety*, Remember When (Pen & Sword Books), Barnsley

Barker, Felix (1957), *The House that Stoll Built*, Frederick Muller, London

Bentham, Fred (1992), *Sixty Years of Light Work*, Lights! (Strand Lighting), Isleworth

Bevan, Ian (1952), *Top of the Bill*, Frederick Muller, London

Bergan, Ronald (1987), *The Great Theatres of London*, Prion (Multimedia Books), London

Blake, J.O. (1995), *No Sails on Huttoft Mill*, The Badger Press, Westbury

Burke, Thomas (1941), *English Night-Life from Norman Curfew to present Black-Out* , Batsford, London

Coren, Michael (1984), *Theatre Royal: 100 Years of Stratford East*, Quartet Books, London

Disher, Maurice Wilson (1938), *Winkles and Champagne*, Batsford, London

Earl, John (2005), *British Theatres and Music Halls*, Shire Publications/The Theatres Trust, Princes Risborough

Earl, John and Sell, Michael (2010), *The Theatres Trust Guide to British Theatres*, A. & C. Black, London

Ellacott, Vivyan (2010), *An Encyclopaedia of London Theatres & Music Halls*, Ellacott, Ilford

Eyles, Allen (1996/99), *Gaumont British Cinemas*, Cinema Theatre Association, London

Eyles, Allen (2005), *Old Cinemas*, Shire Books, Princes Risborough

Eyles, Allen and Skone, Keith (1991), *London's West End Cinemas*, Keytone Publications, Sutton

Federation of Theatre Unions (1953). *Theatre Ownership in Great Britain*, The Federation, London

Flanagan, Bud (1961), *My Crazy Life*, Frederick Muller, London

Fleetwood, Frances (1953), *Conquest: The Story of a Theatre Family*, W.H. Allen, London

Gammond, Peter (1971), *Your Own, Your Very Own!* Ian Allen, London

Glasstone, Victor (1975), *Victorian & Edwardian Theatres*, Thames and Hudson, London

Green, Benny (editor) (1986), *The Last Empires, A Music Hall Companion*, Pavilion/Michael Joseph, London

Honri, Peter (1973), *Working the Halls*, Saxon House, Farnborough

Howard, Diana (1970), *Lost Theatres and Music Halls, 1850–1950*, The Library Association, London

Hudd, Roy (1993), *Roy Hudd's Book of Music Hall, Variety and Showbusiness Anecdotes*, Robson Books, London

Hudd, Roy and Hindon, Philip (1997), *Roy Hudd's Cavalcade of Variety Acts*, Robson Books, London

Hurren, Kenneth (1977), *Theatre Inside Out*, W.H. Allen, London

Kilburn, Mike (2002), *London's Theatres: Photographs by Alberto Arzoz*, New Holland Publishers, London

Macqueen-Pope, W. (1947), *An Indiscreet Guide to Theatreland*, Muse Arts Ltd., London

Macqueen-Pope, W. (1959), *Theatregoer's London*, London Transport, London

Mander, Raymond and Mitchenson, Joe (1965), *British Music Hall*, Studio Vista, London

Mander, Raymond and Mitchenson, Joe (1968, 1976), *The Lost Theatres of London*, Rupert Hart-Davis, London

Mellor, G.J. (1970), *The Northern Music Hall*, Frank Graham, Newcastle-upon-Tyne

Napier, Valantyne (1986), *Act as Known*, Globe Press Pty. Ltd., Brunswick, Victoria

Napier, Valantyne (1996), *Glossary of Terms used in Variety*, The Badger Press, Westbury

O'Gorman, Brian (2013), *Roundabout Paramount*, The Badger Press, Westbury

Owen, Maureen (1986), *The Crazy Gang*, Wiedenfeld & Nicolson, London

Pulling, Christopher (1952), *They Were Singing: And what they sang about*, Harrap, London

Read, Jack (1985), *Empires, Hippodrome & Palaces*, The Alderman Press, London

Rowell, George (1979), *The Victorian Theatre, 1792–1914*, Cambridge University Press, Cambridge

Sachs, Edwin and Woodrow, Ernest A.E. (1896–98), *Modern Opera Houses and Theatres*, Batsford, London

Scott, Harold (1946), *The Early Doors: Origins of the Music Hall*, Nicholson & Watson, London

Sherson, Erroll (1925), *London's Lost Theatres of the XIX Century*, John Lane, London

Short, Ernest (1946), *Fifty Years of Vaudeville*, Eyre and Spottiswoode, London

Stamp, Gavin (2010), *Lost Victorian Britain*, Aurum Press, London

Summerson, John (1964), *The Classical Language of Architecture*, Thames & Hudson Ltd., London

Walker, Brian (editor) (1980), *Frank Matcham – Theatre Architect*, Blackstaff Press, Dundonald

Weightman, Gavin (1992), *Bright Lights, Big City*, Collins & Brown, London

Weinreb, Matthew (1993), *London Architecture – Features and Facades*, Phaidon Press, London

Wilmore, David (editor), (1998), *Edwin O. Sachs: Architect, Stagehand, Engineer and Fireman*, Theatresearch, Summerbridge

Wilmore, David (editor) (2008) *Frank Matcham & Co.*, Theatreshire Books Ltd., Dacre

Wilmut, Roger (1985), *Kindly Leave the Stage*, Methuen, London

Wilson, Albert Edward (1954), *East End Entertainment*, Arthur Barker, London

Index of Artistes

Index of Theatres

Index of Architects

Index of Productions

Index of Managements

Guide to the colour sections

Personalities in pictures shown in the colour sections
(left to right, head to foot)

The West End Halls

Page Nos.	Name of Theatre	Names of Artistes
pp 111–122	Adelphi	Jimmy Edwards, Tony Hancock
	Alhambra	Rebla with George Robey
	Holborn Empire	George Mozart, Flanagan & Allen, Balliol & Merton, Max Miller
	London Casino	Dick & Dot Remy
	London Coliseum	Sir Oswald Stoll
	London Hippodrome	Sir Edward Moss, Channing Pollock
	London Palladium	Harry Roy, Joséphine Baker, Harris Twins & Loretta, Jack Warner, Danny Kaye, Max Bygraves, Wilson, Keppel & Betty, Ralph Olsen and Jean
	Lyceum	Albert Burdon, Clarkson Rose, Jill Esmond, Dave & Joe O'Gorman
	Palace	Shani Wallis, Robertson Hare, Reg Dixon, Laurence Olivier, Benny Hill, Rene Strange
	Prince of Wales	Tommy Cooper, Sid Field, Bob Hope
	Stoll	Howard de Courcy, Richard Hearne, Ted Ray
	Victoria Palace	Lewis Davenport & Winifred Wynne, Danny Lipton Three, The Tiller Girls, Kazbek & Zari

Halls North of the Thames

Page Nos.	Name of Theatre	Names of Artistes
pp 122–126	Foresters'	Brigitte Bardot in 'Babette Goes to War' shown at The Foresters'
	Imperial	Walter Leaver, London's last Chairman
	Chelsea Palace	George French, Hackford & Doyle, The Four Morrellys
	Chiswick Empire	Arthur Askey, Johnny Lamonte, Laurel & Hardy
pp 271–286	Finsbury Park Empire	Jimmy Wheeler; Wilson, Keppel & Betty; Max Wall
	Golders Green Hippodrome	Alec Pleon, Harry Bailey, Jimmy James with Dick Carlton
	Harrow Coliseum	Stanelli
	McDonald's Music Hall	Trevor Morton, Splinters & Danny

Page Nos.	Name of Theatre	Names of Artistes
	Ilford Hippodrome	George Formby jnr, a young Syd Kaplan (Conductor)
	Collins' Music Hall	Terry & Adele Cantor
	Sadler's Wells	Roy Hudd
	Kilburn Empire	The Four Franks
	Kingston Empire	Frankie Vaughan, Lord Delfont
	Paragon	Joe Elvin
	Metropolitan	Max Miller, Patsy Silva; Seven Irish Comics: Jimmy Harvey, Harry O'Donovan, Jack Harrington, Cecil Sheridan, Jim Jonson, Jimmy O'Dea, Mike Nolan; Nosmo King, Ivan Dozin (at back, with Roy Castle and a King Brother)
	Poplar Queen's	Ted Rogers
	Shepherds Bush Empire	Robb Wilton, Lily Morris, 'Jane' of The Daily Mirror', The Two Condons practising
	Shoreditch London	Ted Ray, Gertie Gitana, George Mozart
	Shoreditch Olympic	Joe O'Gorman snr, Rebla
	Stoke Newington Alexandra	Carlton Sisters, Chris Gill
	Stratford Empire	The Fredyanis
pp 431–434	Walthamstow Palace	The Reid Twins
	Wilton's Music Hall	Some of the BMHS Founder Members (David Drummond, Nick Charlesworth, Gerald Glover, John Cliff and Maurice Friedman) with Chairman Doreen Hermitage in September, 2013
	Wood Green Empire	Diana Decker, The Nordics, The Ben Abdrahman Wazzan Troupe

Halls South of the Thames

Page Nos.	Name of Theatre	Names of Artistes
pp 435–446	Brixton Empress	Elsie & Doris Waters, Manley & Austin, Rosemary Andrée
	Croydon Grand	Harry Davis, Max Wall, Cyril Fletcher, The Dehl Trio
	South London Palace	Charles Chaplin jnr
	Lewisham Hippodrome	Charlie Kunz, Clarkson Rose, Laurel & Hardy
	Penge Empire	Herschel Henlere, Jenny Howard with Johnny Lockwood and Tessie O'Shea
	Rotherhithe Hippodrome	Marie Lloyd jnr
	Canterbury Hall	Charles Morton

Other Theatre Books published by The Badger Press, Westbury, Wiltshire:

Bristol's Forgotten Empire by Terry Hallett	£10.00
The Lost Theatres of Dublin by Philip B. Ryan	£10.00
Glossary of Terms used in Variety by Valantyne Napier	£7.00
Tivoli King by Gae Anderson (distribution)	£12.00
Roundabout Paramount by Brian O'Gorman (distribution)	£10.00
Coventry's Forgotten Theatre by Ted Bottle (distribution)	£10.00

Post paid in the U.K.

Pantomime-themed Christmas Cards and a large range of postcards can be viewed and ordered on our website:

www.vaudeville-postcards.com

We regret that our terms do not cover sale or return on either cards or books.